Negro Heritage Library

NEGRO HERITAGE LIBRARY

The Winding Road to Freedom

A DOCUMENTARY SURVEY OF NEGRO EXPERIENCES IN AMERICA

Edited by ALFRED E. CAIN

Drawings: Horace Varela

M. W. LADS

New York – Philadelphia

 FIRST EDITION

Designed by Harold Franklin

PRINTED IN THE UNITED STATES OF AMERICA BY
GOODWAY, INC., PHILADELPHIA, PA.

DEDICATION

TO MY MOTHER, who taught me that freedom is a precious, though elusive, thing and urged me on in its pursuit.

I do not know how long 'twill be,
Nor what the future holds for me;
But this I know, as my God leads me,
I shall be free—someday.

M. W. LADS — OFFICERS

Chairman

MILTON WOLK

President

DONALD WOLK

Vice President

BERYL WOLK

Secretary

PAUL R. ROSEN, Esq.

Treasurer

JOHN J. GALLAGHER, JR.

A NOTE FROM THE PUBLISHERS

THE NEGRO HERITAGE LIBRARY is M. W. Lads' response to a major historical, social and psychological necessity of our times. There is little question that the Negro has emerged as the dominant figure on the American scene today, and yet he remains a stranger to most white Americans and often to himself as well.

Too many Americans, Negro and white, have scant knowledge of the fact that the Negro has a proud heritage of notable achievement. This ignorance—and euphemisms serve no valid purpose here—is easily explained. The standard texts on the history of America and the Western world, the very sources from which we have drawn our knowledge of Man and Society, have consistently excluded the Negro's contribution. I submit that this omission has been a significant factor in the perpetuation of white prejudice and the distortion of Negro self-esteem. An honest reckoning of the Negro's contribution to the building of our society is long overdue.

Accordingly, we have set ourselves the combined tasks of:

strengthening the Negro's confidence and assurance
that he *has* historical roots deep
within the soil of Western civilization, and

restoring to History those missing pages whose absence
has crippled America's ability to understand the Negro,
hence retarding fulfillment of the American ideal of equal justice
to all men, regardless of race, creed, color or national origin.

This can only be done by a truthful and accurate recounting of the Negro's remarkable story. It is our hope that the content of these volumes will serve this high purpose.

Table of Contents

WE SHALL OVERCOME   11
PREFACE   14

Section I — The House of Bondage   22

Philip Corven of Virginia Petitions for Freedom   26
The Germantown Quakers' Anti-Slavery Resolution   28
"Felix" of Massachusetts Protests Enslavement   30
Jefferson's Early Draft of the Declaration of Independence   32
Jefferson's Dilemma: The Immorality of Slavery—Inferiority of Negroes   36
The Quock Walker Case   41
Falconbridge Relates the Horrors Aboard Slave Ships   42
George Washington's Plan for Manumission   54
Benjamin Banneker's Letter to Thomas Jefferson   56
Jefferson's Reply to Banneker   59
Richard Allen and Absalom Jones Denounce Philadelphia Ingratitude   60
Richard Allen and Absalom Jones Speak Out Against Slavery   64
The Importation of Slaves Prohibited   66

Section II — Let My People Go   68

William Hamilton Refutes Alleged Negro Inferiority   74
James Forten of Philadelphia Protests Negro "Registration"   76
Resolutions Against Proposed Colonization in Africa   80
The Missouri Compromise   82
Reverend Nathaniel Paul, Albany (N.Y.) Baptist Preacher,
    Hails Emancipation in New York   86
Freedom's Journal, First Negro Newspaper Appears March 16, 1827   88
Freedom's Journal Reports a Lynching   91
Minutes of the First Negro Convention   92
The Liberator, *First Edition*   95
Philadelphia Negroes Petition the Pennsylvania Legislature   96
Rev. Nathaniel Paul Protests Mistreatment of Lady Educator   100
Constitution of the American Anti-Slavery Society and
    Its Declaration of Sentiments   102
David Ruggles, New York Bookseller, Refutes an Anti-Abolitionist   106
South Carolina Resolutions on Abolitionist Propaganda   108
Resolutions of African Methodist Episcopal Church Annual Conference   110
Announcement of New York Teachers' Meeting   111
Charles Lenox Remond Addresses Massachusetts Legislative Committee
    Against Segregation in Travel   112
Prigg *v.* Commonwealth of Pennsylvania   116
Henry Highland Garnet Urges Slave "Resistance"   120
Editorial in the Inaugural Edition of the North Star   124
Clay's Resolutions on Slavery in the Territories and District of Columbia   126
Fugitive Slave Act   127
The Georgia Platform on the Extension of Slavery Question   130
Resolutions of the Nashville Convention Opposing Congressional Control of Slavery   131
"What to the Slave Is the Fourth of July?"   133
Robert Purvis Protests Segregated Education   137
The Sentencing of Mrs. Douglass for Teaching Negro Children to Read   138

Appeal of the Independent Democrats Against the Nebraska Slavery Bill   140
The Kansas-Nebraska Act   143
Massachusetts Personal Liberty Act   144
Dred Scott *v.* Sandford   146

Section III — The Walls Came Tumblin' Down   152

John Brown's Speech After Being Adjudged Guilty of Treason   156
The Correspondence of a Slave-owner and Her Former Slave   158
Lincoln's Proposals for Compensated Emancipation   160
William Wells Brown Presses for Negro Participation in the Civil War   164
Greeley and Lincoln Exchange Views on Slavery   166
The Emancipation Proclamation   169

Section IV — The Wilderness of Emancipation   170

Resolution of the Illinois State Legislature in Opposition to the Emancipation Proclamation   175
A Negro Eyewitness Describes Anti-Negro Violence in Detroit   176
Sgt. Carney (CMH) Tells About Himself   178
Sentiments of the Colored People of Memphis on the First Anniversary
    of the Emancipation Proclamation   179
Congress Establishes the Freedmen's Bureau   180
The "Black Code" of Mississippi   182
The Thirteenth Amendment   184
The First Reconstruction Act   185
The Fourteenth Amendment   187
KKK Rules of Order   188
First Negro Senator Makes His First Speech to the Senate   190
The Fifteenth Amendment   194
"Ku Klux Klan" Act   195
Heroism of Negro Troops   198
The Civil Rights Act   199
Grant's Proclamation to Deter Terrorism   200
Mrs. Selina Wallis Tells the Senate How Her Husband was Murdered   202
Booker T. Washington's Address at the Opening of the Cotton States' Exposition   205
Plessy *v.* Ferguson   208
The Last Negro in Congress Says "Goodbye"   212

Section V — Bound For the Promised Land   216

Dr. DuBois' Affirmation of Faith   222
The Niagara Movement Sets Forth Its Principles   224
The Birth of the NAACP   227
The Urban League Emerges   229
Founders Launch Journal of Negro History   231
World War I (*Pictorial*)   232
Marcus Garvey Outlines Program of U.N.I.A.   234
Congressman DePriest on Equal Justice   240
The Lynching of Claude Neal   244
Executive Order 8802   257
World War II (*Pictorial*)   258
President Truman Ends Segregation in the Armed Services   260
Brown *v.* Board of Education   262
Ninety-Six Southern Congressmen Denounce the Supreme Court   265

President Eisenhower's Little Rock Intervention 267
President Kennedy Authorizes Troops to End Segregation at University
   of Mississippi 269
Governor Wallace Defies the Supreme Court 271
President Kennedy Calls for Action to End Segregation 272
Birmingham Manifesto 276
Episcopal Bishop's Message at Whitsuntide 278
The Cardinal's Message to New York Catholics 280
Reform Judaism's Call to Racial Justice 282
The March on Washington (*Pictorial*) 284
The Civil Rights Act 286
Digest of Civil Rights Act of 1964 324

The Summation — President Lyndon B. Johnson — July 2, 1964 326

Supplement — A Digest of Significant Supreme Court Rulings 330

An Appreciatory Note: NAACP Legal Defense Fund,
   Friend of the Court and Justice 331
Guinn *v.* United States 332
Buchanan *v.* Warley 333
Moore *v.* Dempsey 334
Nixon *v.* Herndon 335
Powell *v.* Alabama 336
Norris *v.* Alabama 337
Brown *v.* Mississippi 338
Hale *v.* Kentucky 339
Gaines *v.* Canada 340
Lane *v.* Wilson 341
Chambers *v.* Florida 342
Smith *v.* Allwright 343
Morgan *v.* Virginia 344
Patton *v.* Mississippi 345
Sipuel *v.* University of Oklahoma 346
Bob-Lo *v.* Michigan 347
Lee *v.* Mississippi 348
Hurd *v.* Hodge 349
Shelley *v.* Kraemer 350
Cassell *v.* Texas 351
McLaurin *v.* Oklahoma State Regents 352
Sweatt *v.* Painter 353
Henderson *v.* United States 354
Brown *v.* Board of Education 355
Reece *v.* Georgia 356
Fikes *v.* Alabama 357
Heart of Atlanta *v.* United States 358
Katzenbach *v.* McClung 359

Glossary of Court Terms 360

Notes 362

Bibliography 374

Acknowledgements 378

Index 378

"For the Dignity of Man and the Destiny of Democracy"

AT TIMES, HISTORY AND FATE MEET AT A SINGLE time in a single place to shape a turning point in man's unending search for freedom.

So it was at Lexington and Concord. So it was a century ago at Appomattox. So it was last week in Selma, Alabama.

There, long suffering men and women peacefully protested the denial of their rights as Americans. . . .

There is no cause for pride in what has happened in Selma. There is no cause for self-satisfaction in the long denial of equal rights of millions of Americans. But there is cause for hope and for faith in our democracy in what is happening. . . .

For the cries of pain and the hymns and protests of oppressed people have summoned into convocation all the majesty of this great Government—the Government of the greatest nation on earth.

Our mission is at once the oldest and the most basic of this country—to right wrong, to do justice, to serve man.

In our time we have come to live with the moments of great crisis. Our lives have been marked with debate about great issues, issues of war and peace, issues of prosperity and depression.

But rarely in any time does an issue lay bare the secret heart of America itself. Rarely are we met with a challenge, not to our growth or abundance, or our welfare or our security, but rather to the values and the purposes and the meaning of our beloved nation.

The issue of equal rights for American Negroes is such an issue.

And should we defeat every enemy, and should we double our wealth and conquer the stars, and still be unequal to this issue, then we will have failed as a people and as a nation.

For, with a country as with a person, "What is a man profited if he shall gain the whole world, and lose his own soul?"

There is no Negro problem. There is no Southern problem. There is no Northern problem. There is only an American problem.

. . . This was the first nation in the history of the world to be founded with a purpose. The great phrases of that purpose still sound in every American heart, North and South:

"All men are created equal." "Government by consent of the governed." "Give me liberty or give me death."

And those are not just clever words, and those are not just empty theories.

In their name Americans have fought and died for two centuries. . . .

Those words promised to every citizen that he shall share in the dignity of man. This dignity cannot be found in a man's possessions. It cannot be found in his power or in his position. It really rests on his right to be treated as a man equal in opportunity to all others.

It says that he shall share in freedom. He shall choose his leaders, educate his children, provide for his family according to his ability and his merits as a human being.

To apply any other test, to deny a man his hopes because of his color or race or his religion or the place of his birth is not only to do injustice, it is to deny America and to dishonor the dead who gave their lives for American freedom.

Our fathers believed that if this noble view of the rights of man was to flourish it must be rooted in democracy. The most basic right of all was the right to choose your own leaders.

The history of this country in large measure is the history of expansion of that right to all of our people. Many of the issues of civil rights are very complex and most difficult. But about this there can and should be no argument: every American citizen must have an equal right to vote.

There is no reason which can excuse the denial

We Shall Overcome

Excerpts from a speech by

Lyndon B. Johnson

President of the United States

To a Joint Session of the Congress

March 15, 1965

of that right. There is no duty which weighs more heavily on us than the duty we have to insure that right. Yet the harsh fact is that in many places in this country men and women are kept from voting simply because they are Negroes.

Every device of which human ingenuity is capable has been used to deny this right. The Negro citizen may go to register only to be told that the day is wrong, or the hour is late, or the official in charge is absent.

And if he persists and, if he manages to present himself to the registrar, he may be disqualified because he did not spell out his middle name, or because he abbreviated a word on the application. And if he manages to fill out an application, he is given a test.

The registrar is the sole judge of whether he passes this test. He may be asked to recite the entire Constitution, or explain the most complex provisions of state law.

And even a college degree cannot be used to prove that he can read and write. For the fact is that the only way to pass these barriers is to show a white skin.

Experience has clearly shown that the existing process of law cannot overcome systematic and ingenious discrimination. No law that we now have on the books, . . . can insure the right to vote when local officials are determined to deny it. In such a case, our duty must be clear to all of us.

The Constitution says that no person shall be kept from voting because of his race or his color. . . .

. . . I will send to Congress a law designed to eliminate illegal barriers to the right to vote. . . .

This bill will strike down restrictions to voting in all elections, Federal, state and local, which have been used to deny Negroes the right to vote.

This bill will establish a simple, uniform standard which cannot be used, however ingenious the effort, to flout our Constitution. It will provide for citizens to be registered by officials of the United States Government, if the state officials refuse to register them.

It will eliminate tedious, unnecessary lawsuits which delay the right to vote.

Finally, this legislation will insure that properly registered individuals are not prohibited from voting.

. . . experience has plainly shown that this is the only path to carry out the command of the Constitution. To those who seek to avoid action by their national Government in their home communities, who want to and who seek to maintain purely local control over elections, the answer is simple: open your polling places to all your people.

Allow men and women to register and vote whatever the color of their skin.

Extend the rights of citizenship to every citizen of this land.

There is no constitutional issue here. The command of the Constitution is plain. There is no moral issue. It is wrong—deadly wrong—to deny any of your fellow Americans the right to vote in this country.

There is no issue of states' rights or national rights. There is only the struggle for human rights.

. . . on this issue, there must be no delay, or no hesitation, or no compromise with our purpose.

We cannot, we must not, refuse to protect the right of every American to vote in every election that he may desire to participate in.

And we ought not, and we cannot, and we must not wait . . .

We have already waited 100 years and more and the time for waiting is gone.

. . . for from the window where I sit with the problems of our country I recognize that from outside this chamber is the outraged conscience of a nation, the grave concern of many nations and the harsh judgment of history on our acts.

But even if we pass this bill the battle will not be over.

. . . a far larger movement . . . reaches into every section and state of America. It is the effort of American Negroes to secure for themselves the full blessings of American life.

Their cause must be our cause too. Because it's not just Negroes, but really it's all of us who must overcome the crippling legacy of bigotry and injustice. And we shall overcome.

As a man whose roots go deeply into Southern soil, I know how agonizing racial feelings are. I know how difficult it is to reshape the attitudes and the structure of our society. But a century has passed—more than 100 years—since the Negro was freed.

And he is not fully free tonight.

It was more than 100 years ago that Abraham

Lincoln . . . signed the Emancipation Proclamation. But emancipation is a proclamation and not a fact.

A century has passed—more than 100 years—since equality was promised, and yet the Negro is not equal.

A century has passed since the day of promise, and the promise is unkept. The time of justice has now come, and I tell you that I believe sincerely that no force can hold it back. It is right in the eyes of man and God that it should come, and when it does, I think that day will brighten the lives of every American.

For Negroes are not the only victims. How many white children have gone uneducated? How many white families have lived in stark poverty? How many white lives have been scarred by fear, because we wasted energy and our substance to maintain the barriers of hatred and terror?

And so I say to all of you here and to all in the nation . . . that those who appeal to you to hold on to the past do so at the cost of denying you your future. This great, rich, restless country can offer opportunity and education and hope to all—all, black and white, all, North and South, sharecropper and city dweller.

These are the enemies: poverty, ignorance, disease. They are our enemies, not our fellow man, not our neighbor. And these enemies too—poverty, disease and ignorance—we shall overcome.

Now let none of us in any section look with prideful righteousness on the troubles in another section or the problems of our neighbors.

There is really no part of America where the promise of equality has been fully kept. In Buffalo as well as in Birmingham, in Philadelphia as well as Selma, Americans are struggling for the fruits of freedom. This is one nation. What happens in Selma and Cincinnati is a matter of legitimate concern to every American.

But let each of us look within our own hearts and our own communities and let each of us put our shoulder to the wheel to root out injustice wherever it exists.

. . . I have not the slightest doubt that good men from everywhere in this country, from the Great Lakes to the Gulf of Mexico, from the Golden Gate to the harbors along the Atlantic, will rally now together in this cause to vindicate the freedom of all Americans.

For all of us owe this duty and I believe that all of us will respond to it. . . .

The real hero of this struggle is the American Negro. His actions and protests, his courage to risk safety, and even to risk his life, have awakened the conscience of this nation. His demonstrations have been designed to call attention to injustice; designed to provoke change; designed to stir reform.

He has called upon us to make good the promise of America. And who among us can say that we would have made the same progress were it not for his persistent bravery and his faith in American democracy?

For at the real heart of battle for equality is a deep-seated belief in the democratic process. . . .

We will guard against violence, knowing it strikes from our hands the very weapons which we seek—progress, obedience to law, and belief in American values.

. . . we seek and pray for peace. We seek order, we seek unity, but we will not accept the peace of stifled rights or the order imposed by fear, or the unity that stifles protest—for peace cannot be purchased at the cost of liberty. . . .

The bill I am presenting . . . will be known as a civil rights bill.

But in a larger sense, most of the program I am recommending is a civil rights program. Its object is to open the city of hope to all people of all races, because all Americans just must have the right to vote, and we are going to give them that right.

All Americans must have the privileges of citizenship, regardless of race, and they are going to have those privileges of citizenship regardless of race.

But I would like to caution you and remind you that to exercise these privileges takes much more than just legal right. It requires a trained mind and a healthy body. It requires a decent home and the chance to find a job and the opportunity to escape from the clutches of poverty.

Of course people cannot contribute to the nation if they are never taught to read or write; if their bodies are stunted from hunger; if their sickness goes untended; if their life is spent in hopeless poverty, just drawing a welfare check.

So we want to open the gates to opportunity. But we're also going to give all our people, black and white, the help that they need to walk through those gates. . . .

We Shall Overcome   ☐   13

Preface

Men who are sincere in defending their freedom,

will always feel concern at every circumstance

which seems to make against them;

it is the natural and honest consequence

of all affectionate attachments,

and the want of it is a vice.

But the dejection lasts only for a moment;

they soon rise out of it with additional vigor;

the glow of hope, courage and fortitude, will,

in a little time, supply the place

of every inferior passion,

and kindle the whole heart into heroism.

TOM PAINE
The Crisis, Number 4

THE QUEST FOR INDIVIDUAL FULFILLMENT is as old as mankind. Highly personal, it does not readily lend itself to exact description; yet a vague expression—"the pursuit of happiness"—has been widely accepted as the near-perfect embodiment of Man's highest, though self-centered, purpose in life.

The pursuit of happiness is an idea that presupposes an environment of freedom in which the individual may realize his fullest potential for growth and development. This free environment was, and is, one of the great promises of America. Over the years this promise has lured men and women from all corners of the world to these shores. In vary-

ing degrees the promise has usually been kept. The most notable exception—and the most troublesome—has been America's failure to allow Negroes the full enjoyment of her largesse.

On August 28, 1963, in a rousing speech at the March on Washington, Dr. Martin Luther King cited this exception when he stated:

> "When the architects of our Republic wrote the magnificent words of the Constitution and the Declaration of Independence, they were signing a promissory note . . . but it is obvious today that America has defaulted on this promissory note insofar as her citizens of color are concerned."

Dr. King and other speakers on the occasion of the March on Washington were evincing neither petulance nor ill-tempered belligerence. Instead, they were reaffirming to themselves and their listeners the righteousness of the Negro cause; at the same time, they were advising the nation that payment on a note held by Negroes for more than three centuries was ridiculously long overdue.

In the summer of 1963, the opposition to the Negro's claim to first-class citizenship most often found public expression in a pious lament that the Negro was pushing too fast. What would constitute a more appropriate timetable was not explained, and proponents of gradualism returned incoherent mumblings to the Negro's question:

> "Isn't three hundred years long enough to wait for freedom in a society which has gone to wars, engaged in police actions, and even lectured the whole world—all in the name of freedom?"

When he found that he need not expect valid answers to this question, the Negro roared out what was once a plea, but now an urgent demand—FREEDOM NOW!

Some people looking for subversive influences behind the Negro's zeal for freedom in the Twentieth Century chose to ignore the fact that the chant, "Freedom Now," merely paraphrased the inspiring Declaration of July 4, 1776. The Negro's aspiration to be free is as patriotic as John Hancock's oversized signature on a defiant document or Patrick Henry's impassioned avowal that death is to be preferred to liberty withheld.

Concurrent with the arrival of the first Negroes at Jamestown in 1619, the seeds of freedom commenced to sprout in the intellectual and emotional soil of this nation. That very same year the Virginia House of Burgesses was founded. A representative assembly, it became the first such body in America to provide an effective agency for democratic self-government.

One year later, in 1620, the "Pilgrim Fathers" came seeking a place where they might enjoy "the right worship of God, according to the simplicitie of the Gospell, without the admixture of men's inventions." Before debarking onto the shores of Cape Cod, the Pilgrims drew up and adopted the celebrated "Mayflower Compact"—their covenant of self-government.

Religious liberty was the magnet for others. Their patience at an end with the "Romanish" practices of the Church of England, the Puritans established a haven for their sect in the Massachusetts Bay Colony, and, conversely, because he felt that the Church of England and other Protestant groups were unfriendly to Catholics, George Calvert, the first Lord Baltimore, when he received a royal proprietary charter for Maryland, immediately determined to provide a refuge for migrant Catholics.

The colonies of Rhode Island and Pennsylvania had broader libertarian bases. Roger Williams of Rhode Island was solidly opposed to the enforced orthodoxy of some of the religious colonies (Williams was himself religious); and laws devised by William Penn, a Quaker, who was awarded the proprietary charter for Pennsylvania, were among the earliest American laws permitting freedom of conscience to all the Colonists.

In the other colonies, altruism as a demonstrable factor is not easily documented. There, usually, greater stress has been placed on another essential benefit, economic opportunity.

As the colonies grappled with the problems of settling in a new environment, significant libertarian developments abroad nurtured the growth of the idea of freedom in America. England's "Glorious Revolution" of 1688—during which James II, holder of the proprietary charter of New York, was deposed—culminated in the Bill of Rights of 1689. Under the terms of this bill the supremacy of Parliament was affirmed, and a Constitutional Monarchy replaced the traditional rule by divine right.

John Randall, in his authoritative survey of the mainstream of intellectual thought entitled, *The Making of the Modern Mind,* gives much credit for the success of the "Glorious Revolution" to John Locke, the English philosopher and political theorist. According to Randall, Locke "summed up the ideas that had been worked out in the seventeenth-century struggles, and formulated them into a system that furnished the official apology for the English Revolution of 1689." Locke's *Treatise on Civil Government* (1689) spelled out his concept of the "state of nature," i.e., his view of human nature as it would be in the absence of civil government. He observed:

". . . we must consider what estate all men are naturally in, and that is, a state of perfect freedom to order their actions, and dispose of their persons and possessions as they think fit within the bounds of the law of nature, without asking leave or depending upon the will of any other man. A state also of equality, wherein all the power and jurisdiction is reciprocal, no one having more than another, there being nothing more evident than that creatures of the same species and rank promiscuously born to all the advantages of nature, and the use of the same faculties, should also be equal one amongst another."

(Locke, II *Treatise on Civil Government*, Chapter 2, quoted in Randall, *op. cit.*)

Locke's concept of the "social contract" avers that individual freedom might be subordinated to majority government only if thereby one could better protect his rights.

> "Men being by nature all free, equal and independent, no one can be put out of this estate and subjected to the political powers of another without his own consent, which is done by agreeing with other men, to join and unite into a community for their comfortable, safe and peaceable living, one amongst another, in a secure enjoyment of their properties, and a greater security against any that are not of it . . ."

(Ibid; Chapter 8)

When the 18th century reached the half way mark, the idea of liberty as a *natural* right was abroad in the land.

The propitious moment for the idea of freedom had come. In France, the idea was seized upon and expanded by Jean Jacques Rousseau, apologist and philosopher for the French Revolution; and, in America, Thomas Jefferson pondered the theories of Locke, later incorporating his understanding of the Lockean doctrine (though there is some question that Locke would have acknowledged paternity) into the American Declaration of Independence.

To commemorate the Golden Jubilee of its exercise of legislative and fiscal powers, the Pennsylvania Assembly, in 1751, resolved to have Europe's most famous bellmaker cast a huge "Liberty Bell." Isaac Norris, the Quaker Speaker of the Assembly, recommended that the bell carry a quotation from the Old Testament:

> "Proclaim Liberty
> Throughout All The Land
> And Unto All The Inhabitants Thereof"

(Leviticus 25:10)

Surviving a chain of well-known mishaps, the bell finally assumed its function, heralding news good and bad and summoning townsfolk to meeting. But essentially its message was "Liberty."

The Negro too, heard its vibrant voice, and thrilled to its message.

Moreover, he understood the message.

The Negro, it must be remembered, came to the New World with a heritage of individual freedom. The language may have differed; the idea had been embedded in his mind in the land of his birth. Benjamin Quarles in his valuable study delineating the part played by *The Negro in the Making of America* points out:

> ". . . the Negroes who came to the New World varied widely in physical type and ways of life, but there were many common patterns of culture. Whatever the type of state, the varied groups all operated under orderly governments, with established legal codes, and under well-organized social systems. The individual might find it necessary to submerge his will into the collective will, but he shared a deep sense of group identity, a feeling of belonging. And there was ample scope for personal expression. . . ."

The Negroes who landed in Jamestown in 1619—not free, yet not slaves—had every reason to expect liberation after a few years. As indentured servants their terms of servitude were fixed on the basis of their degree of indebtedness to their masters for the costs of the ocean voyage and other expenses incident to coming to the New World.

For a time, religion was also a barrier to enslavement. The Jamestown party of Negroes had been baptized as Christians and, under the laws of England, a convert to Christianity lost his status as an infidel and was thereby eligible for eventual freedom. Only debt bound him to a master.

This situation changed radically before the passage of many years. By 1640, Negro slavery had found a permissive home in America. Ironically, in the voluminous writings about slavery—seldom honest, frequently prejudiced and almost always mythological—Negro docility and acquiescence is sometimes coupled with slaveholder benevolence in explanation of slavery's entrenchment. The thesis is not easily supported—but then that is the state of special grace enjoyed by the creators of myths. Accounts from aboard slave ships often give a diametrically opposed view. One account, dated 1788, notes that: ". . . very few of the Negroes can so far brook the loss of their liberty. . . ." Indeed, the account continues:

> ". . . they are ever upon the watch to take advantage of the least negligence in their oppressors. Insurrections are frequently the consequence, which are seldom suppressed without much bloodshed. Sometimes they are successful, and the whole ship's company is cut off. They are likewise always ready to seize every opportunity for committing some act of desperation to free themselves. . . ."

Modern scholars like Melville Herskovits and Basil Davidson also refute the fable of acquiescence. Davidson, in his book, *The Lost Cities of Africa,* completely rejects the notion that Negroes, African or American, "entered and endured the slaving centuries with greed, docility, or dumb acceptance. . . ." In Davidson's eyes this is "a notion somewhat favored by those who have argued or still argue, the inherent inferiority of Negroes" and the "slavish nastiness of African society. . . ." Such a proposition, he concludes,

> ". . . has no foundation in the record. The weak might go to the wall; they did not therefore like it. African society had been relatively peaceful and generous and even gentle; the world these peoples were thrown into was one of death and horror. The best and strongest took the first or second chance to resist or revolt; the rest endured. But endurance did not mean acceptance."

Conditioned by his African heritage to conceive of freedom as the *natural* state of man, the African in America was sensitively attuned to receive the message of the Liberty Bell and, later, the noble hopes and promises of the "Declaration of Independence." And when Jefferson said he intended the Declaration "to be an expression of the American mind," the Negro included himself in that vast mind-body. All too soon he would be disabused of his naive optimism. He would learn that *all,* in the context of "all men are created equal," had undergone a strange contraction in its meaning and thus excluded the Negro.

This is but one of the many turns in *the winding road to freedom.* Time and time again, as the documents which comprise this book show, believing the fullness of America's gifts to her citizens to be within his reach, the Negro has seen the proffered bounty snatched away before he could claim it. Frustration of hope is therefore, an inescapable part of this book. Yet, there is also a picture of a rejected minority rising from dejection aglow with fresh hope, courage and fortitude, and heroism rekindled within their hearts.

The parallel cases of the Children of Israel in Egypt and the Negro in America have become a cliche in the literature about the Negro. Nonetheless the similarities are plain and the analogy valid. Over and over a promise was made by Egypt's Pharaoh that the Israelites would be granted their freedom. Usually Pharaoh's promises were secured during periods of crisis in Egypt. With the return of less troubled times, however, Pharaoh once more would suffer a "hardening" of his heart. Hope inspired in crisis would be crushed into the dust of Egypt as Pharaoh refused to honor his pledge to the captives. And so it has been with the Negro in America.

Hope stirred in Negro hearts when the Continental Congress on October 20, 1774 adopted a resolution, known to history as the "Association," containing the proviso: "We will neither import nor purchase any slave imported after the first day of December next; after which time we will wholly discontinue the slave trade, and we will neither be concerned in it ourselves, nor will we hire our vessels, nor sell our commodities or manufactures to those who are concerned in it."

Hope flamed higher as the Colonies resolved to resist British rule in their "Declaration of the Causes and Necessity of Taking Up Arms," July 6, 1775, and questioned that it would be possible for "men who exercise their reason to believe that the Divine Author of our own existence intended a part of the human race to hold an absolute property in, and an unbounded power over others."

Hope knew no bounds as the Declaration of Independence proclaimed the *self-evident* truths "That all men are created equal and endowed by their Creator with certain inalienable rights . . . life, liberty and the pursuit of happiness."

During the Revolutionary conflict freedom became the tantalizing jewel in the courtship of the Negro recruit by both British and American military establishments. This situation was documented in the 1963 Report to the President by the United States Commission on Civil Rights. Their report, *Freedom to the Free*, stated:

". . . it is of interest to note that the first 'emancipation proclamation' in the New World was issued on November 7, 1775, by Lord Dunmore, Governor General of the Colony and Dominion of Virginia. Lord Dunmore declared free all those in bondage who were willing and able to bear arms for the King in putting down rebellion in the Colony. It was not long before General Washington approved the enlistment of free Negroes. Slaves who served on either side in the War for Independence were often granted their freedom."

The notion that the Revolutionary War would bring freedom to the Negro was so pervasive that at the war's end many in England took it to be an accomplished fact. According to Dwight Lowell Dumond, author of *Anti-Slavery: The Crusade for Freedom in America*, "It is a singular fact that many learned men in England thought that slavery had been abolished in America by the Declaration of Independence." Dumond cites a speech before the Corporation of the City of Oxford, made in 1788 by William Agutter of St. Mary Magdalene College:

"The Western Empire is gone from us never to return; it is given to another more righteous than we;

who consecrated the sword of resistance by declaring for the universal abolition of slavery. . . ."

The Englishman, however, envisioned a righteousness that did not in fact emerge in the new nation's Constitution. Although many scholars argue that the "Fathers of the Constitution" were opposed to slavery's continuance, the Constitution contains no language that supports their claim. Rather, the language is sufficiently vague as to be susceptible to a contrary interpretation. Dumond concedes that:

> "The Convention wanted to abolish slavery, but it could not risk or thought it could not risk, losing ratification by the cotton states of Georgia and South Carolina."

(The triumph of political expediency over democratic principles is but one more recurring theme in the Negro's history in America.)

The 1963 Civil Rights Commission's Report summarizes the effect of the new Constitution as follows:

> "To the abolitionists and others with anti-slavery sentiments the new Constitution of 1787 came as a disappointment. Despite the fact that 6 of the original 13 States had previously acted to abolish slavery, the Federal Constitution contained no such provision. In fact it recognized slavery as a firmly entrenched institution by providing for the counting of three-fifths of the Negro slaves in determining the basis of taxation and representation and by the fugitive slave provision requiring that a slave escaping into a free State be 'delivered up on a claim of the party whom

. . . service or labour may be due.' Further, the Constitution precluded Congress from prohibiting the importation of slaves prior to 1808, although it authorized a tax or duty of up to $10 for each slave brought in."

Those who believed the Constitution to be an instrument for the "containment" of slavery were to find their expectations smashed to nothingness by the Dred Scott decision of 1857. The constitutionally deferred legislation prohibiting the importation of slaves—when it became operative in 1808—was only partly effective. And the three-fifths compromise reposed in the hands of the Southern slaveholders a disproportionate share of power in both the House of Representatives and the Electoral College.

Freedom once more had eluded the Negro and his principal oppressor had gained new strength.

Slavery was finally abolished by the Thirteenth Amendment, ratified on December 18, 1865 and the nation undertook a vast program of reconstruction. This program embraced not only the binding of wounds inflicted by the bitter sectionalism that had erupted into Civil War, but also "defining the status of more than three and one-half million southern Negroes, no longer slaves. . . ." With slavery dead the period promised "a new birth of freedom" for the Negro. The Fourteenth Amendment was ratified on July 28, 1868 and thereby the American-born Negro became a citizen. His rights, privileges and immunities were not subject to abridgement by the states. He could not be deprived by the States of "life, liberty, or property" without due process of law, and denial of equal protection of state laws was forbidden. And, in a reversal of the three-fifths rule, he was to be counted as a whole person in any census upon which Congressional representation was to be apportioned.

On March 30, 1870, the Fifteenth Amendment, guaranteeing the Negro that neither his race, color, nor previous status as a slave constituted grounds for his denial of the vote by the States.

Dressed in the new clothes of human dignity the Negro joined in the task of reconstruction with great enthusiasm and energy. He became active in politics and before the century closed 22 Negroes had represented Southern constituencies in the Congress in Washington. Two were Senators: Hiram R. Revels (1870–1871) and Blanche K. Bruce (1875–1881). The 20 members of the House of Representatives were:

Richard H. Cain	(1873–1879)
Henry P. Cheatham	(1889–1893)
Robert C. DeLarge	(1873–1874)
Robert B. Elliott	(1871–1874)
Jeremiah Haralson	(1875–1877)
John A. Hyman	(1875–1877)
John M. Langston	(1889–1891)
Jefferson P. Long	(1870–1871)
John R. Lynch	(1873–1883)
Thomas E. Miller	(1889–1891)
George W. Murray	(1893–1897)
Charles E. Nash	(1875–1887)
James E. O'Hara	(1883–1887)
Joseph H. Rainey	(1871–1879)
Alonzo J. Ransier	(1873–1875)
James T. Rapier	(1873–1875)
Robert Smalls	(1875–1887)
Benjamin S. Turner	(1871–1873)
Josiah T. Walls	(1871–1876)
George H. White	(1897–1901)

Their Congressional colleague, James G. Blaine's appraisal that

> "They were as a rule studious, earnest, ambitious men, whose public conduct . . . would be honorable to any race,"

has become a standard summation, notwithstanding the fact that no legislation of lasting note bears their names. Like many other members of the federal legislature, before and after them, they were good, though—considerations of race aside—unexceptional men, who dutifully went about their tasks of representing the voters in their states.

At the state level, the Negro filled a number of important political posts. Three Negroes became lieutenant governors of Louisiana. Pinckney B. S. Pinchback, the most famous of the three, was briefly the acting governor of the state following the removal of Governor Henry C. Warmoth. Many were delegates to the state constitutional conventions, others were members of state legislatures.

Three states—South Carolina, Mississippi, Louisiana—had impressive rosters of Negro officials in the highest offices. The following list, by no means complete, suggests the variety and scope of Negro officialdom in those states.

SOUTH CAROLINA
    Francis L. Cardozo,
            Secretary of State (1868–1872)
                    Treasurer (1872–1876)
    Samuel J. Lee,
        Speaker of the House (1872–1874)
    J. J. Wright,
        Justice, Supreme Court (1870–1877)

MISSISSIPPI
    James Hill, Secretary of State
    John R. Lynch, Speaker of the House
    T. W. Cardozo,
            Superintendent of Education
    Rev. J. J. Evans, County Sheriff

LOUISIANA
    Oscar J. Dunn, Lieutenant-Governor
    P. G. Deslonde, Secretary of State
    Antoine Dubuclet, State Treasurer
    W. G. Brown,
        Superintendent of Public Education

Augustin G. Jones,
Parish Chancery Clerk

The Negro politicians proved to be less interested in avenging the wrongs endured than in aiding their respective states to achieve significant socio-economic goals. Langston Hughes and Milton Meltzer have described their motivations and accomplishments in *A Pictorial History of the Negro in America:*

> "Uneducated Negro legislators wanted education themselves, so they wrote into the new state constitutions provisions for free public schools. Colored men wanted equality before the law so liberal measures upholding this concept were introduced by them and passed. The freedmen wished to maintain the federally-granted suffrage, so they saw to it that it was written into the official codes of their states. . . . Since they were poor, Negro law-makers proposed no property qualifications for voting or for holding office."

Other reforms were set in motion by the new state legislative bodies. Some states did away with their debtor prisons, and cruel and humiliating practices such as branding, public whippings, the use of the pillory and the stock as forms of punishment were discontinued. Much of the progressive legislation—for example, free public education—of the Reconstruction era has lasted until this day, and is almost inseparable from any description of the "American way of life."

The combination of emancipation and Negro good works, however, did not long survive the onslaught of Southern white reaction. The white masses and the upper classes, their ancient differences momentarily forgotten, determined to put the Negro back "in his place" and to restore white supremacy. Their cause was aided by a combination of factors:

The deaths of Thaddeus Stevens and Charles Sumner removed from Congress two of the Negro's most effective champions—

The North lost interest in the Negro—

Big business and industrial development became the paramount concerns of the Republican party—

The Amendments to the Constitution and the body of laws passed during Reconstruction to secure the rights of Negroes were given such narrow interpretation by the Supreme Court that they were virtually emasculated.

Then, under the terms of the "Hayes-Tilden Compromise," in 1877 federal troops were withdrawn leaving the faltering Reconstruction regimes powerless before the superior forces of Southern conservatism and reaction.

The death knell for Reconstruction was sounded. Once more Negro hopes were frustrated. Once more America let slip through her mighty fingers an opportunity to become in fact *the land of the free, the home of the brave.*

Today, at a crucial moment in the Negro's suit for full participation, as a man and as a brother, in American society, history offers America another chance to redeem her libertarian birthright. The Negro is encouraged by scattered evidence that the nation at last intends to give meaning to the Constitution and to the principles of the Declaration of Independence. But the Negro is no longer susceptible to the lure of noble words unsupported by effective action. He agrees with President Johnson that these are decisive times for American democracy.

THE HOUSE OF BONDAGE

And the Lord said,
I have surely seen the affliction
of my people which are in Egypt,
and have heard their cry
by reason of their taskmasters;
for I know their sorrows.

Exodus 3: 7

INTRODUCTION

Jamestown, Virginia
August, 1619

Into Chesapeake Bay sailed a vessel,
*"a dutch man of warre
that sold us twenty Negars."*

THIS WAS THE UNDRAMATIC BEGINNING of Negro history in America. It is derived from an account by John Rolfe, Virginia tobacco grower, who became the husband of Pocahontas, legendary Indian princess credited with saving the life of Captain John Smith.

The twenty "Negars" were not slaves, but indentured servants. Their welcome in the New World was assured because they filled a vital need for laborers. Except for their dark skins they were not considered different from white laborers who were also bound servants. The duration of their periods of servitude were specified, and it was customary that upon completion of the prescribed tenure the released servant was given a parcel of land and enjoyed the rights and privileges of other freed laborers in the community.

Slavery, as we know it, appeared approximately two decades later. It grew out of a need to stabilize the labor force, and the Negro, if he could be bound to *perpetual* servitude, provided the best solution to the problem. Earlier, efforts had been made to enslave the Indians but they often grew sick and sometimes died before becoming accustomed to enforced labor. White indentured servants, though most desired, frequently ran away and were easily lost track of in the rapidly growing population. Moreover, their replacement at the expiration of their terms of servitude was not always easily accomplished. Supply was not equal to the demand. On the other hand, the runaway Negro was detectable because of his color, and by the simple extension of his term of service—giving him, as it were, a "lifetime contract"—reduced the nuisance of being short-handed. After 1640 few Negroes held indentures and increasingly their freedom depended upon the disposition of their "owners."

This extension of service acquired legal sanction in Virginia in 1661. A Negro imported after that time became the property of his purchaser. He lost all control of his person, his productivity and his progeny.

The tightening of the Negro's bonds accompanied other developments destined to have a profound influence on the course of American history. The colonies had strong ties to Great Britain and participated in the mother country's efforts to establish her sovereignty in the New World. With the Colonies' financial and moral support, Britain engaged in numerous diplomatic and military skirmishes designed to negate the power of Spain and France in America. Under the terms of the 1763 Treaty of Paris, following the Seven Years' War, Britain emerged as the supreme power not only in North America but the world.

After the war, Great Britain turned to putting her Empire in order. Her coffers were depleted by war. Her administration was loose and ineffectual through neglect. Long used to a form of semi-autonomy, the Colonies soon chafed under the new restraints and obligations. The Revenue and Currency Acts of 1764 and the Stamp and Quartering Acts of 1765 were widely resented in the Colonies, touching off debate and resistance. The Stamp Act was especially resented. Merchants signed Nonintercourse Agreements which instituted a boycott against British businessmen. A newly-formed organization, the Sons of Liberty, policed the enforcement

IN THE BEGINNING: *This 19th century painting—attributed to Howard Pyle, prolific illustrator of American historical subjects—depicts the landing of a Dutch "Man of warre" at Jamestown, Virginia, during the colonial period. Negroes were highly prized cargo.*

(The Bettmann Archive)

of the Agreements and intimidated the Crown's collectors of Stamp Taxes. The Stamp Act was repealed in 1766, but Parliament at the same time adopted the Declaratory Act which asserted the absolute authority of the King and Parliament over the Colonies.

In 1767, a new Chancellor of the Exchequer, Charles Townshend, imposed new duties on tea, glass, lead, paper and paint— the Townshend Act. Intended to offset the reduction in British revenue resulting from a cut in English land taxes, this new attempt at taxation was also met by hostility in the Colonies. Boycotts were reinstated against the British and, occasionally, violence flared up, climaxed by the Boston Massacre. Crispus Attucks, a Negro seaman, was slain by British troops in this incident and has come to be known as the first martyr of the Revolution.

Peace was tentatively restored in 1770 by the repeal of the Townshend Act, but the embers of rebellion were stirred again in 1772 by the passage of the infamous Tea Act. A chain of reaction and retaliation ensued:

AMERICAN
      —The Boston "Tea Party"—1773
BRITISH
    —The Port or "Intolerable" Acts—1774
AMERICAN
    —The First Continental Congress' Declaration of Rights and Grievances—1774

BRITISH
—Siege of Concord and Lexington—1775
AMERICAN
—The Declaration of Independence—1776

War, the American Revolution, came and the Colonies gained independence through the Treaty of Paris of 1783.

Recognizing the inadequacies of the wartime Articles of Confederation, the fledgling nation tackled the many faceted problem of establishing effective government. What was to have been a revision of the Articles of Confederation was transformed into the Constitution of the United States. Among its stated purposes: "secure the Blessings of Liberty to ourselves and our Posterity."

Unstated but felt by approximately .75 million Negro slaves, was the Constitution's recognition of slavery as a "firmly entrenched institution." It provided, without using the words "Negro" or "slave," that slave importation could not be halted until 20 years later, that fugitive slaves might be returned to captivity from a free state, that a duty of $10 or less might be charged on each new slave coming into the country, and that slaves were to be counted as three-fifths of a person for purposes of representation and taxation.

The slave throughout this period troubled the consciences of the "masters" and the new national leaders. Some few achieved liberation. Vast numbers of others could only wait.

THE MANPOWER BEHIND KING COTTON'S THRONE: *After the invention of the cotton gin, the dominant factor in the South's economy became cotton production. Negro slaves constituted the essential labor force.*
(The Bettmann Archive)

Phillip Corven of

Virginia Petitions for Freedom

1675
Virginia

An appeal for
manumission
in the Colonial period

To the R^T Honble [Right Honorable] Sir William Berkeley, Knt., [Knight] Gover^r [Governor] and Capt. Genl. of Virg^a, [Virginia] with the Hon. Councell of State.

The Petition of Phillip Corven, a Negro, in all humility showeth: That yor [your] pet^r [petitioner] being a servan^t to Mrs Anny^e [Annie] Beazley, late of James Citty County, widdow, de^ed [deceased]. The said Mrs Beazley made her last will & testament in writing, under her hand & seal, bearing date, the 9th day of April, An. Dom. [Anno Domini] 1664, and, amongst other things, did order, will appoint that yor pet^r by the then name of Negro boy Phillip, should serve her cousin, Mr. Humphrey Stafford, the terme of eight yeares, then next ensueing, and then should enjoy his freedome & be paid three barrels of corne & a sute of clothes, as by the said will appears. Sonne [soon] after the makeing of which will, the said Mrs Beazley departed this life, yor pet^r did continue & . . . abide with the said Mr Stafford, (with whome he was ordered by the said will to live) some yeares, and then the said Mr. Stafford sold the remainder of yor pet^r time to one Mr. Charles Lucas, with whom y^or pet^r alsoe continued, doeing true & faithfull service; but the said Mr. Lucas, coveting yor pet^r's service longer then of right itt was due, did not att the expiracon of the said eight yeares, discharge y^or pet^r from his service, but compelled him to serve three years longer than the time set by the said Mrs. Beazley's will, and then not being willing y^or pet^r should enjoy his freedome, did, contrary to all honesty and good conscience with threats & a high hand, in the time of yor pet^r's service with him, and by his confederacy with some persons compel yor pet^r to sett his hand to a writeing, which the said Mr Lucas now saith is an Indenture for twenty yeares, and forced yor pet^r to acknowledge the same in the County Court of Warwick.

Now, for that itt please yor Hon^r, [Honor] yor pet^r, who all the time of the making the said forced writeing, in the servicee of the said Mr. Lucas, and never discharged from the same, the said Mr Lucas alwaies unjustly pretending that yor pet^r was to serve him three yeares longer, by an order of Court, w^h [which] is untrue, which pretence of the said Mr. Lucas will appeare to yor hon^s [honors] by y^e [the] testimony of persons of good creditt

Yo^r Pet^r therefore most humbly prayeth yor hon^rs [honors] to order that the said Mr Lucas make him sattisfaction for the said three yeares service above his time, and pay him corne & clothes, with costs of suite.

And yor pet^r (as in duty bound) shall ever pray, &c.

The

Germantown

Quakers'

Anti-Slavery

Resolution

THESE are the reasons why we are against the traffic of men-body, as followeth: Is there any that would be done or handled at this manner? viz., to be sold or made a slave for all the time of his life? How fearful and faint-hearted are many at sea, when they see a strange vessel, being afraid it should be a Turk, and they should be taken, and sold for slaves into Turkey. Now, what is this better done, than Turks do? Yea, rather it is worse for them, which say they are Christians: for we hear that the most part of such negers are brought hither against their will and consent, and that many are stolen. Now, though they are black, we cannot conceive there is more liberty to have them slaves, as it is to have other white ones. There is a saying, that we should do to all men like as we will be done to ourselves; making no difference of what generation, descent, or colour they are. And those who steal or rob men, and those who buy or purchase them, are they not all alike? Here is liberty of conscience, which is right and reasonable; here ought to be likewise liberty of the body, except of evildoers, which is another case. But to bring men hither, or to rob and sell them against their will, we stand against. In Europe there are many oppressed for conscience-sake; and here there are those oppressed which are of a black colour. And we know that men must not commit adultery —some do commit adultery *in* others, sepa-

February 18, 1688
Germantown,
Pennsylvania

Earliest account
of religious distaste
for slavery

rating wives from their husbands, and giving them to others: and some sell the children of these poor creatures to other men. Ah! do consider well this thing, you who do it, if you would be done at this manner—and if it is done according to Christianity! . . . This makes an ill report in all those countries of Europe, where they hear . . . that the Quakers do here handel men as they handel there the cattle. And for that reason some have no mind or inclination to come hither. And who shall maintain this your cause, or plead for it? Truly, we cannot do so, except you shall inform us better hereof, viz.: that Christians have liberty to practice these things. Pray, what thing in the world can be done worse towards us, than if men should rob or steal us away, and sell us for slaves to strange countries; separating husbands from their wives and children. . . . therefore, we contradict, and are against this traffic of men-body. And we who profess that it is not lawful to steal, must, likewise, avoid to purchase such things as are stolen, but rather help to stop this robbing and stealing, if possible. And such men ought to be delivered out of the hands of the robbers, and set free as in Europe. Then is Pennsylvania to have a good report, instead, it hath now a bad one, for this sake, in other countries; Especially whereas the Europeans are desirous to know in what manner the Quakers do rule in their province; and most of them do look upon us with an envious eye. But if this is done well, what shall we say is done evil?

If once these slaves (which they say are so wicked and stubborn men,) should join themselves—fight for their freedom, and handel their masters and mistresses, as they did handel them before; will these masters and mistresses take the sword at hand and war against these poor slaves, like, as we are able to believe, some will not refuse to do? Or, have these poor negers not as much right to fight for their freedom, as you have to keep them slaves?

Now consider well this thing, if it is good or bad. And in case you find it to be good to handel these blacks in that manner, we desire and require you hereby lovingly, that you may inform us herein, which at this time never was done, viz., that Christians have such a liberty to do so. To the end we shall be satisfied on this point, and satisfy likewise our good friends and acquaintances in our native country, to whom it is a terror, or fearful thing, that men should be handelled so in Pennsylvania.

This is from our meeting at Germantown, held ye 18th of the 2d month, 1688 . . . .

Garret Henderich,
Derick op de Graeff,
Francis Daniel Pastorious,
Abram op de Graeff.

"Felix" of Massachusetts

Province of the Massachusetts Bay To His Excellency Thomas Hutchinson, Esq; Governor; To The Honorable His Majesty's Council, and To the Honorable House of Representatives in General Court assembled at Boston, the 6th Day of *January*, 1773.

The humble PETITION of many Slaves, living in the Town of Boston, and other Towns in the Province is this, namely

That your Excellency and Honors, and the Honorable the Representatives would be pleased to take their unhappy State and Condition under your wise and just Consideration.

We desire to bless God, who loves Mankind, who sent his Son to die for their Salvation, and who is no respecter of Persons; that he hath lately put it into the Hearts of Multitudes on both Sides of the Water, to bear our Burthens, some of whom . . . Men of great Note and Influence . . . have pleaded our Cause with Arguments which we hope will have their weight with this Honorable Court.

We presume not to dictate to your Excellency and Honors, being willing to rest our Cause on your Humanity and Justice; yet would beg Leave to say a Word or two on the Subject.

A slave invokes
the principles of "liberty"
abroad in the Colonies

Protests Enslavement

Although some of the Negroes are vicious, (who doubtless may be punished and restrained by the same Laws which are in Force against other of the King's Subjects) there are many others of a quite different Character, and who, if made free, would soon be able as well as willing to bear a Part in the Public Charges; many of them of good natural Parts, are discreet, sober, honest, and industrious; and may it not be said of many, that they are virtuous and religious, although their Condition is in itself so unfriendly to Religion, and every moral Virtue except *Patience*. How many of that Number have there been, and now are in this Province, who have had every Day of their Lives imbittered with this most intollerable Reflection, That, let their Behaviour be what it will, neither they, nor their Children to all Generations, shall ever be able to do, or to possess and enjoy any Thing, no, not even *Life itself*, but in a Manner as the *Beasts that perish*.

We have no Property! We have no Wives! No Children! We have no City! No Country! But we have a Father in Heaven, and we are determined . . . as far as our degraded contemptuous Life will admit, to keep all his Commandments: Especially will we be obedient to our Masters, so long as God in his sovereign Providence shall *suffer* us to be holden in Bondage.

It would be impudent, if not presumptuous in us, to suggest to your Excellency and Honors any Law or Laws proper to be made, in relation to our unhappy State, which, although our greatest Unhappiness, is not our *Fault;* and this gives us great Encouragement to pray and hope for such Relief as is consistent with your Wisdom, Justice, and Goodness.

We think Ourselves very happy, that we may thus address the Great and General Court of this Province . . . the best Judge, under God, of what is wise, just and good.

We humbly beg Leave to add but this one Thing more: We pray for such Relief only, which by no Possibility can ever be productive of the least Wrong or Injury to our Masters; but to us will be as Life from the dead.

Signed,
FELIX

Jefferson's Early Draft of the

When in the course of human events it becomes necessary for one people to dissolve the political bonds which have connected them with another, and to assume among the powers of the earth the separate and equal station to which the laws of nature and of nature's god entitle them, a decent respect to the opinions of mankind requires that they should declare the causes which impel them to the separation.

We hold these truths to be self-evident; that all men are created equal; that they are endowed by their Creator with inherent and inalienable rights; that among these are life, liberty, and the pursuit of happiness; that to secure these rights, governments are instituted among men, deriving their just powers from the consent of the governed; that whenever any form of government becomes destructive of these ends, it is the right of the people to alter or to abolish it, and to institute new government, laying its foundation on such principles, and organizing its powers in such form as to them shall seem most likely to effect their safety and happiness. Prudence indeed will dictate that governments long established should not be changed for light and transient causes. And accordingly all experience hath shown that mankind are more disposed to suffer, while evils are sufferable, than to right themselves by abolishing the forms to which they are accustomed. But when a long train of abuses and usurpations, begun at a distinguished period and pursuing invariably the same object, evinces a design to reduce them under absolute despotism, it is their right, it is their duty, to throw off such government, and to provide new guards for their future security. Such has been the patient sufferance of these colonies, and such is now the necessity which constrains them to expunge their former systems of government. The history of the present king of Great Brit-

Declaration of Independence

ain is a history of unremitting injuries and usurpations, among which appears no solitary fact to contradict the uniform tenor of the rest, but all . . . have in direct object the establishment of an absolute tyranny over these states. To prove this let facts be submitted to a candid world, for the truth of which we pledge a faith yet unsullied by falsehood.

He has refused his assent to laws the most wholesome and necessary for the public good.

He has forbidden his governors to pass laws of immediate and pressing importance, unless suspended in their operation till his assent should be obtained; and when so suspended, he has neglected utterly to attend to them.

He has refused to pass other laws for the accommodation of large districts of people, unless those people would relinquish the right of representation in the legislature; a right inestimable to them, and formidable to tyrants only.

He has called together legislative bodies at places unusual, uncomfortable, and distant from the depository of their public records, for the sole purpose of fatiguing them into compliance with his measures.

He has dissolved Representative houses repeatedly and continually, for opposing with manly firmness his invasions on the rights of the people.

He has refused for a long time after such dissolutions to cause others to be elected whereby the legislative powers, incapable of annihilation, have returned to the people at large for their exercise, the state remaining in the meantime exposed to all the dangers of invasion from without, and convulsions within.

He has endeavored to prevent the population of these states; for that purpose obstructing the laws for naturalization of foreigners; refusing to pass others to encourage their migrations hither; and raising the conditions of new appropriations of lands.

He has suffered the administration of justice totally to cease in some of these states, refusing his assent to laws for establishing judiciary powers.

He has made our judges dependent on his will alone, for the tenure of their offices, and the amount and payment of their salaries.

He has erected a multitude of new offices by a self-assumed power, and sent hither swarms of officers to harass our people, and eat out their substance.

He has kept among us, in times of peace, standing armies and ships of war, without the consent of our legislatures.

He has affected to render the military independent of, and superior to, the civil power.

He has combined with others to subject us to a jurisdiction foreign to our constitutions and unacknowledged by our laws; giving his assent to their acts of pretended legislation for quartering large bodies of armed troops among us;

For protecting them by a mock-trial from punishment for any murders which they should commit on the inhabitants of these states;

For cutting off our trade with all parts of the world;

For imposing taxes on us without our consent;

For depriving us of the benefits of trial by jury;

For transporting us beyond seas to be tried for pretended offenses;

For abolishing the free system of English laws in a neighboring province, establishing therein an arbitrary government, and enlarging its boundaries so as to render it at once an example and fit instrument for introducing the same absolute rule into these states;

For taking away our charters, abolishing our most valuable laws, and altering fundamentally the forms of our governments;

For suspending our own legislatures, and declaring themselves invested with power to legislate for us in all cases whatsoever.

He has abdicated government here, withdrawing his governors, and declaring us out of his allegiance and protection.

He has plundered our seas, ravaged our coasts, burnt our towns, and destroyed the lives of our people.

He is at this time transporting large armies of foreign mercenaries, to complete the works of death, desolation, and tyranny, already begun with circumstances of cruelty and perfidy unworthy the head of a civilized nation.

He has endeavored to bring on the inhabitants of our frontiers the merciless Indian savages, whose known rule of warfare is an undistinguished destruction of all ages, sexes, and conditions of existence.

He has incited treasonable insurrections of our fellow citizens, with the allurements of forfeiture and confiscation of our property.

He has constrained others, taken captives on the high seas, to bear arms against their country, to become the executioners of their friends and brethren, or to fall themselves by their hands.

He has waged cruel war against human nature itself, violating its most sacred rights of life and liberty in the persons of a distant people, who never offended him, captivating and carrying them into slavery in another hemisphere, or to incur miserable death in their transportation thither. This piratical warfare, the opprobrium of infidel *powers, is the warfare of the* Christian *king of Great Britain.* (Emphasis added) Determined to keep open a market where MEN should be bought and sold, he has prostituted his negative for suppressing every legislative attempt to prohibit or restrain this execrable commerce; and that this assemblage of horrors might want no fact of distinguished die, he is now exciting those very people to rise in arms among us, and to purchase that liberty of which *he* has deprived them, by murdering the people upon whom *he* also obtruded them: thus paying off former crimes committed against the *liberties* of one people, with crimes which he urges them to commit against the *lives* of another.

In every stage of these oppressions "we have petitioned for redress in the most humble terms." Our repeated petitions have been answered only by repeated injury. A prince whose character is thus marked by every act which may define a tyrant, is unfit to be the ruler of a people who mean to be free. Future ages will scarce believe that the hardiness of one man adventured, within the short compass of twelve years only, to lay a foundation, so broad and undisguised, for tyranny over a people fostered and fixed in principles of freedom.

Nor have we been wanting in attentions to our British brethren. We have warned them from time to time of attempts by their legislature to extend a jurisdiction over these our states. We have reminded them of the circumstances of our emigration and settlement here, no one of which could warrant so strange a pretension: that these were affected at the expense of our own blood and treasure, unassisted by the wealth or the strength of Great Britain: that in constituting indeed our several forms of government, we had adopted one common king, thereby laying a foundation for perpetual league and amity with them: but that submission to their parliament was no part of our constitution, nor ever in idea, if history may be credited: and we appealed to their native justice and magnanimity, as well as to the ties of our common kindred, to disavow these usurpations, which were likely to interrupt our condition and correspondence. They too have been deaf to the voice of justice and of consanguinity; and when occasions have been given them, by the regular course of their laws, of removing from their councils the disturbers of our harmony, they have by their free election reestablished them in power. At this very time, too, they are permitting their chief magistrate to send over not only soldiers of our common blood, but Scotch and foreign mercenaries to invade and destroy us. These facts have given the last stab to agonizing affection; and manly spirit bids us to renounce forever these unfeeling brethren. We must therefore endeavor to forget our former love for them, and to hold them as we hold the rest of mankind, enemies in war, in peace friends. We might have been a great and free people together; but a communication of grandeur and of freedom, it seems, is below their dignity. Be it so, since they will have it. The road to happiness and to glory is open to us too; we will climb it apart from them, and acquiesce in the necessity which denounces our eternal separation!

We therefore the Representatives of the United States of America in General Congress assembled, do, in the name and by the authority of the good people of these states, reject and renounce all allegiance and subjection to the kings of Great Britain, and all others who may hereafter claim by, through, or under them; we utterly dissolve all political connection which may heretofore have subsisted between us and the people or parliament of Great Britain; and finally we do assert and declare these colonies to be free and independent states, and that as free and independent states, they have full power to levy war, conclude peace, contract alliances, establish commerce, and to do all other acts and things which independent states may of right do. And for the support of this declaration, we mutually pledge to each other our lives, our fortunes, and our sacred honor.

Jefferson's Dilemma:

The Immorality of Slavery

—The Inferiority of Negroes

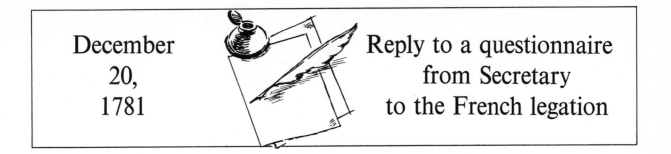
The Inferiority of Negroes

. . . DEEP-ROOTED prejudices entertained by the whites; ten thousand recollections, by the blacks, of the injuries they have sustained; new provocations; the real distinctions which nature has made; and many other circumstances, will divide us into parties, and produce convulsions, which will probably never end but in the extermination of the one or the other race. To these objections, which are political, may be added others, which are physical and moral. The first difference which strikes us is that of color. Whether the black of the negro resides in the reticular membrane between the skin, and scarf-skin, or in the scarf-skin itself; whether it proceeds from the color of the blood, the color of the bile, or from that of some other secretion, the difference is fixed in nature, and is as real as if its seat and cause were better known to us. And is this difference of no importance? Is it not the foundation of a greater or less share of beauty in the two races? Are not the fine mixtures of red and white, the expressions of every passion by greater or less suffusions of color in the one, preferable to that eternal monotony, which reigns in the countenances, that immovable veil of black which covers the emotions of the other race? Add to these, flowing hair, a more elegant symmetry of form, their own judgment in favor of the whites, declared by their preference of them, as uniformly as is the preference of the Oranootan for the black woman over those of his own species. The circumstance of superior beauty, is thought worthy attention in the propagation of our horses, dogs, and other domestic animals; why not in that of man? Besides those of color, figure, and hair, there are other physical distinctions proving a difference of race. They have less hair on the face and body. They secrete less by the kidneys, and more by the glands of the skin, which gives them a very strong and disagreeable odor. This greater degree of transpiration, renders them more tolerant of heat, and less so of cold than the whites. Perhaps, too, a difference of structure in the pulmonary apparatus, which a late ingenious experimentalist has discovered to be the principal regulator of animal heat, may have disabled them from extricating, in the act of inspiration, so much of that fluid from the outer air, or obliged them in expiration, to part with more of it. They seem to require less sleep. A black after hard labor through the day, will be induced by the slightest amusements to sit up till midnight, or later, though knowing he must be out with the first dawn of the morning.

They are at least as brave, and more adventuresome. But this may perhaps proceed from a want of forethought which prevents their seeing a danger till it be present. When present, they do not go through it with more coolness or steadiness than the whites. They are more ardent after their female; but love seems with them to be more an eager desire, than a tender delicate mixture of sentiment and sensation. Their griefs are transient. Those numberless afflictions, which render it doubtful whether heaven has given life to us in mercy or in wrath, are less felt, and sooner forgotten with them. In general, their existence appears to participate more of sensation than reflection. To this must be ascribed their disposition to sleep when abstracted from their diversions, and unemployed in labor. An animal whose body is at rest, and who does not reflect, must be disposed to sleep of course. Comparing them by their faculties of memory, reason, and imagination, it appears to me that in memory they are equal to the whites; in reason much inferior, as I think one could scarcely be found capable of tracing and comprehending the investigations of Euclid; and that in imagination they are dull, tasteless, and anomalous. It would be unfair to follow them

to Africa for this investigation. We will consider them here, on the same stage with the whites, and where the facts are not apocryphal on which a judgment is to be formed. It will be right to make great allowances for the difference of condition, of education, of conversation, of the sphere in which they move. Many millions of them have been brought to, and born in America. Most of them, indeed, have been confined to tillage, to their own homes, and their own society; yet many have been so situated, that they might have availed themselves of the conversation of their masters; many have been brought up to the handicraft arts, and from that circumstance have always been associated with the whites. Some have been liberally educated, and all have lived in countries where the arts and sciences are cultivated to a considerable degree, and all have had before their eyes samples of the best works from abroad. . . .

But never yet could I find that a black had uttered a thought above the level of plain narration; never saw even an elementary trait of painting or sculpture. In music they are more generally gifted than the whites with accurate ears for tune and time, and they have been found capable of imagining a small catch. Whether they will be equal to the composition of a more extensive run of melody, or of complicated harmony, is yet to be proved. Misery is often the parent of the most affecting touches in poetry. Among the blacks is misery enough, God knows, but no poetry. Love is the peculiar oestrum of the poet. Their love is ardent, but it kindles the senses only, not the imagination. Religion, indeed, has produced a Phyllis Whately; but it could not produce a poet. . . .

It is not their condition then, but nature, which has produced the distinction. Whether further observation will or will not verify the conjecture, that nature has been less bountiful to them in the endowments of the head, I believe that in those of the heart she will be found to have done them justice. That disposition to theft with which they have been branded, must be ascribed to their situation, and not to any depravity of the moral sense. The man in whose favor no laws of property exist, probably feels himself less bound to respect those made in favor of others. When arguing for ourselves, we lay it down as a fundamental, that laws, to be just, must give a reciprocation of right; that, without this, they are mere arbitrary rules of conduct, founded in force, and not in conscience; and it is a problem which I give to the master to solve, whether the religious precepts against the violation of property were not framed for him as well as his slave? And whether the slave may not as justifiably take a little from one who has taken all from him, as he may slay one who would slay him? That a change in the relations in which a man is placed should change his ideas of moral right or wrong, is neither new, nor peculiar to the color of the blacks. Homer tells us it was so two thousand six hundred years ago.

> . . . Odd. 17, 323.
> *Jove fix'd it certain,*
> *that whatever day*
> *Makes man a slave,*
> *Takes half his worth away.*

But the slaves of which Homer speaks were whites. Notwithstanding these considerations which must weaken their respect for the laws of property, we find among them numerous instances of the most rigid integrity, and as many as among their better instructed masters, of benevolence, gratitude, and unshaken fidelity. The opinion that they are inferior in the faculties of reason and imagination, must be hazarded with great diffidence. To justify a general conclusion, requires many observations, even where the subject may be submitted to the anatomical knife, to optical glasses, to analysis by fire or by solvents. How much more then where it is a faculty, not a substance, we are examining; where it eludes the research of all the senses; where the conditions of its existence are various and variously combined; where the effects of those which are present or absent bid defiance to calculation; let me add too, as a circumstance of great tenderness, where our conclusion would degrade a whole race of men from the rank in the scale of beings which their Creator may perhaps have given them. To our reproach it must be said, that though for a century and a half we have had under our eyes the races of black and of red men, they have never yet been viewed by us as subjects of natural history. I advance it, therefore, as a suspicion only, that the blacks, whether originally a distinct race, or made distinct by time and circumstances, are inferior to the whites in the endowments both of body and mind. . . .

The Immorality of Slavery

. . . THERE must doubtless be an unhappy influence on the manners of our people produced by the existence of slavery among us. The whole commerce between master and slave is a perpetual exercise of the most boisterous passions, the most unremitting despotism on the one part, and degrading submissions on the other. Our children see this, and learn to imitate it; for man is an imitative animal. This quality is the germ of all education in him. From his cradle to his grave he is learning to do what he sees others do. If a parent could find no motive either in his philanthropy or his self-love, for restraining the intemperance of passion towards his slave, it should always be a sufficient one that his child is present. But generally it is not sufficient. The parent storms, the child looks on, catches the lineaments of wrath, puts on the airs in the circle of smaller slaves, gives a loose to the worst of passions, and thus nursed, educated, and daily exercised in tyranny, cannot but be stamped by it with odious peculiarities. The man must be a prodigy who can retain his manners and morals undepraved by such circumstances. And with what execration should the statesman be loaded, who, permitting one half the citizens thus to trample on the rights of the other, transforms those into despots, and these into enemies, destroys the morals of the one part, and the *amor patriae* of the other. For if a slave can have a country in this world, it must be any other in preference to that in which he is born to live and labor for another; in which he must lock up the faculties of his nature, contribute as far as depends on his individual endeavors to the evanishment of the human race, or entail his own miserable condition on the endless generations proceeding from him. With the morals of the people, their industry also is destroyed. For in a warm climate, no man will labor for himself who can make another labor for him. This is so true, that of the proprietors of slaves a very small proportion indeed are ever seen to labor.

And can the liberties of a nation be thought secure when we have removed their only firm basis, a conviction in the minds of the people that these liberties are of the gift of God? That they are not to be violated but with his wrath? Indeed I tremble for my country when I reflect that God is just; that his justice cannot sleep forever; that considering numbers, nature and natural means only, a revolution of the wheel of fortune, and exchange of situation is among possible events; that it may become probable by supernatural interference! The Almighty has no attribute which can take side with us in such a contest. But it is impossible to be temperate and to pursue this subject through the various considerations of policy, of morals, of history natural and civil. We must be contented to hope they will force their way into every one's mind. I think a change already perceptible, since the origin of the present revolution. The spirit of the master is abating, that of the slave rising from the dust, his condition mollifying, the way I hope preparing, under the auspices of heaven, for a total emancipation, and that this is disposed, in the order of events, to be with the consent of the masters, rather than by their extirpation.

1783
Massachusetts

Commonwealth
Supreme Court
holds slavery
unconstitutional

The Quock Walker Case

. . . As to the doctrine of slavery and the right of Christians to hold Africans in perpetual servitude, and sell and treat them as we do our horses and cattle, that (it is true) has been heretofore countenanced by the Province Laws formerly, but nowhere is it expressly enacted or established. It has been a usage—a usage which took its origin from the practice of some of the European nations, and the regulations of British government respecting the then Colonies, for the benefit of trade and wealth. But whatever sentiments have formerly prevailed in this particular or slid in upon us by the example of others, a different idea has taken place with the people of America, more favorable to the natural rights of mankind, and to that natural, innate desire of Liberty, which with Heaven (without regard to color, complexion, or shape of noses—features) has inspired all the human race. And upon this ground our Constitution of Government, by which the people of this Commonwealth have solemnly bound themselves, sets out with declaring that all men are born free and equal—and that every subject is entitled to liberty, and to have it guarded by the laws, as well as life and property—and in short is totally repugnant to the idea of being born slaves. This being the case, I think the idea of slavery is inconsistent with our own conduct and Constitution . . .

Falconbridge Relates the

Horrors Aboard Slave Ships

After permission has been obtained for *breaking trade,* as it is termed, the captains go ashore, from time to time, to examine the Negroes that are exposed to sale, and to make their purchases. The unhappy wretches thus disposed of, are bought by the black traders at fairs, which are held for that purpose, at the distance of upwards of two hundred miles from the sea coast; and these fairs are said to be supplied from an interior part of the country. Many Negroes, upon being questioned relative to the places of their nativity, have asserted, that they have travelled during the revolution of several moons (their usual method of calculating time), before they have reached the places they were purchased by the black traders. At these fairs, which are held at uncertain periods, but generally every six weeks, several thousands are frequently exposed to sale, who had been collected from all parts of the country for a very considerable distance round. While I was upon the coast, during one of the voyages I made, the black traders brought down, in different canoes, from twelve to fifteen hundred Negroes, which had been purchased at one fair. They consisted chiefly of men and boys, the women seldom exceeding a third of the whole

number. From forty to two hundred Negroes are generally purchased at a time by the black traders, according to the opulence of the buyer; and consist of those of all ages, from a month to sixty years and upwards. Scarce any age or situation is deemed an exception, the price being proportionable. Women sometimes form a part of them, who happen to be so far advanced in their pregnancy, as to be delivered during their journey from the fairs to the coast; and I have frequently seen instances of deliveries on board ship. The slaves purchased at these fairs are only for the supply of the markets at Bonny, and Old and New Calabar.

There is great reason to believe, that most of the Negroes shipped off from the coast of Africa, are *kidnapped.* But the extreme care taken by the black traders to prevent the Europeans from gaining any intelligence of their modes of proceeding; the great distance inland from whence the Negroes are brought; and our ignorance of their language (with which, very frequently, the black traders themselves are equally unacquainted), prevent our obtaining such information on this head as we could wish. I have, however, by means of occasional inquiries, made through

1788
London

Ship's surgeon gives eyewitness account of slave trade evils

interpreters, procured some intelligence relative to the point, and such, as I think, puts the matter beyond a doubt.

From these I shall select the following striking instances: While I was in employ on board one of the slave ships, a Negro informed me that being one evening invited to drink with some of the black traders, upon his going away, they attempted to seize him. As he was very active, he evaded their design, and got out of their hands. He was, however, prevented from effecting his escape by a large dog, which laid hold of him, and compelled him to submit. These creatures are kept by many of the traders for that purpose; and being trained to the inhuman sport, they appear to be much pleased with it.

I was likewise told by a Negro woman that as she was on her return home, one evening, from some neighbours, to whom she had been making a visit by invitation, she was kidnapped; and, notwithstanding she was big with child, sold for a slave. This transaction happened a considerable way up the country, and she had passed through the hands of several purchasers before she reached the ship. A man and his son, according to their own information, were seized by professed kidnappers, while they were planting yams, and sold for slaves. This likewise happened in the interior parts of the country, and after passing through several hands, they were purchased for the ship to which I belonged.

It frequently happens that those who kidnap others are themselves, in their turns, seized and sold. A Negro in the West Indies informed me that after having been employed in kidnapping others, he had experienced this reverse. And he assured me that it was a common incident among his countrymen.

Continual enmity is thus fostered among the Negroes of Africa, and all social intercourse between them destroyed; which most assuredly would not be the case, had they not these opportunities of finding a ready sale for each other.

During my stay on the coast of Africa, I was an eye-witness of the following transaction: a black trader invited a Negro, who resided a little way up the country, to come and see him. After the entertainment was over, the trader proposed to his guest, to treat him with a sight of one of the ships lying in the river. The unsuspicious countryman readily consented, and accompanied the trader in a canoe to the side of the ship, which he viewed with pleasure and astonishment. While he was thus employed, some black traders on board, who appeared to be in the secret, leaped into the canoe, seized the unfortunate man, and dragging him into the ship, immediately sold him.

Previous to my being in this employ, I entertained a belief, as many others have done, that the kings and principal men *breed* Negroes for sale, as we do cattle. During the different times I was in the country, I took no little pains to satisfy myself in this particular; but notwithstanding I made many inquiries, I was not able to obtain the least intelligence of this being the case, which it is more than probable I should have done, had such a practise prevailed. All the information I could procure, confirms me in the belief, that to *kidnapping,* and to crimes (and many of these fabricated as a pretext), the slave trade owes its chief support.

The following instance tends to prove that the last mentioned artifice is often made use of. Several black traders, one of whom was a person of consequence, and exercised an authority somewhat similar to that of our magistrates, being in want of some particular kind of merchandise, and not having a slave to barter for it, they accused a fisherman, at the river Ambris, with extortion in the sale of his fish; and as they were interested in the decision, they immediately adjudged the poor fellow guilty, and condemned him to be sold. He was accordingly purchased by the ship to which I belonged, and brought on board.

As an additional proof that kidnapping is not only the general, but almost the sole mode, by which slaves are procured, the black traders, in purchasing them, choose those which are the roughest and most hardy; alleging that the smooth Negroes have been *gentlemen.* By this observation we may conclude they mean that nothing but fraud or force could have reduced these smooth-skinned gentlemen to a state of slavery.

It may not be here unworthy of remark, in order to prove that the wars among the Africans do not furnish the number of slaves they are supposed to do, that I never saw any Negroes with recent wounds; which must have been the consequence, at least with some of them, had they been taken in battle. And it being the particular province of the surgeon to examine the slaves when they are purchased, such a circumstance could not have escaped my observation. As a farther corroboration, it might be remarked, that on the Gold and Windward Coasts, where fairs are not held, the number of slaves procured at a time are usually very small.

The preparations made at Bonny by the black traders, upon setting out for the fairs which are held up the country, are very considerable. From twenty to thirty canoes, capable of containing thirty or forty Negroes each, are assembled for this purpose; and such goods put on board them as they expect will be wanted for the purchase of the number of slaves they intend to buy. When their loading is completed, they commence their voyage, with colours flying, and music playing; and in about ten or eleven days, they generally return to Bonny with full cargoes. As soon as the canoes arrive at the trader's landing-place, the purchased Negroes are cleaned, and oiled with palm-oil; and on the following day they are exposed to sale for the captains.

The black traders do not always purchase their slaves at the same rate. The speed with which the information of the arrival of ships upon the coast is conveyed to the fairs, considering it is in the interest of the traders to keep them ignorant, is really surprising. In a short time after the ships arrive upon the coast, especially if several make their appearance together, those who dispose of the Ne-

ABOARD A SLAVE SHIP   "... *they were frequently stowed so close as to admit of no other posture than lying on their sides. Neither will the height between decks, unless directly under the grating, permit them the indulgence of an erect posture; especially where there are platforms ...*"   (The Bettmann Archive)

groes at the fairs are frequently known to increase the price of them.

These fairs are not the only means, though they are the chief, by which the black traders on the coast are supplied with Negroes. Small parties of them, from five to ten, are frequently brought to the houses of the traders, by those who make a practise of kidnapping; and who are constantly employed in procuring a supply, while purchasers are to be found.

When the Negroes, whom the black traders have to dispose of, are shown to the European purchasers, they first examine them relative to their age. They then minutely inspect their persons, and inquire into the state of their health; if they are afflicted with any infirmity, or are deformed, or have bad eyes or teeth; if they are lame, or weak in their joints, or distorted in the back, or of a slender make, or are narrow in the chest; in short, if they have been, or are afflicted in any

manner, so as to render them incapable of much labour; if any of the foregoing defects are discovered in them, they are rejected. But if approved of, they are generally taken on board the ship the same evening. The purchaser has liberty to return on the following morning, but not afterwards, such as upon re-examination are found exceptionable.

The traders frequently beat those Negroes which are objected to by the captains, and use them with great severity. It matters not whether they are refused on account of age, illness, deformity, or for any other reason. At New Calabar, in particular, the traders have frequently been known to put them to death. Instances have happened at that place that the traders, when any of their Negroes have been objected to, have dropped their canoes under the stern of the vessel, and instantly beheaded them, in sight of the captain.

Upon the Windward Coast, another mode

of procuring slaves is pursued; which is, by what they term *boating;* a mode that is very pernicious and destructive to the crews of the ships. The sailors, who are employed in this trade, go in boats up the rivers, seeking for Negroes among the villages situated on the banks of them. But this method is very slow, and not always effectual. For, after being absent from the ship during a fortnight or three weeks, they sometimes return with only from eight to twelve Negroes. Numbers of these are procured in consequence of alleged crimes, which, as before observed, whenever any ships are upon the coast, are more productive than at any other period. Kidnapping, however, prevails here.

I have good reason to believe that of one hundred and twenty Negroes, which were purchased for the ship to which I then belonged, then lying at the river Ambris, by far the greater part, if not the whole, were kidnapped. This, with various other instances, confirms me in the belief that kidnapping is the fund which supplies the thousands of Negroes annually sold off these extensive Windward and other coasts, where boating prevails.

As soon as the wretched Africans, purchased at the fairs, fall into the hands of the black traders, they experience an earnest of those dreadful sufferings which they are doomed in future to undergo. And there is not the least room to doubt, but that even before they can reach the fairs, great numbers perish from cruel usage, want of food, travelling through inhospitable deserts, etc. They are brought from the places where they are purchased to Bonny, etc. in canoes; at the bottom of which they lie, having their hands tied with a kind of willow twigs, and a strict watch is kept over them. Their usage in other respects, during the time of the passage, which generally lasts several days, is equally cruel. Their allowance of food is so scanty, that it is barely sufficient to support nature. They are, besides, much exposed to the violent rains which frequently fall here, being covered only with mats that afford but a slight defence; and as there is usually water at the bottom of the canoes, from their leaking, they are scarcely ever dry.

Nor do these unhappy beings, after they become the property of the Europeans (from whom, as a more civilised people, more humanity might naturally be expected), find their situation in the least amended. Their treatment is no less rigorous. The men Negroes, on being brought aboard the ship, are immediately fastened together, two and two, by handcuffs on their wrists, and by irons rivetted on their legs. They are then sent down between the decks, and placed in an apartment partitioned off for that purpose. The women likewise are placed in a separate apartment between decks, but without being ironed. And an adjoining room, on the same deck, is besides appointed for the boys. Thus are they all placed in different apartments.

But at the same time, they are frequently stowed so close, as to admit of no other posture than lying on their sides. Neither will the height between decks, unless directly under the grating, permit them the indulgence of an erect posture; especially where there are platforms, which is generally the case. These platforms are a kind of shelf, about eight or nine feet in breadth, extending from the side of the ship towards the centre. They are placed nearly midway between the decks, at the distance of two or three feet from each deck. Upon these the Negroes are stowed in the same manner as they are on the deck underneath.

In each of the apartments are placed three or four large buckets, of a conical form, being near two feet in diameter at the bottom, and only one foot at the top, and in depth about twenty-eight inches; to which, when necessary, the Negroes have recourse. It often happens that those who are placed at a distance from the buckets, in endeavouring to get to them, tumble over their companions, in consequence of their being shackled. These accidents, although unavoidable, are productive of continual quarrels, in which some of them are always bruised. In this distressed situation, unable to proceed, and prevented from getting to the tubs, they desist from the attempt; and, as the necessities of nature are not to be repelled, ease themselves as they lie. This becomes a fresh source of broils and disturbances, and tends to render the condition of the poor captive wretches still more uncomfortable. The nuisance arising from these circumstances, is not unfrequently increased by the tubs being much too small for the purpose intended, and their being usually emptied but once every day. The rule for doing this, however, varies in different ships, according to the attention paid to the health and convenience of the slaves by the captain.

About eight o'clock in the morning the Negroes are generally brought upon deck. Their irons being examined, a long chain, which is locked to a ring-bolt, fixed in the deck, is run through the rings of the shackles of the men, and then locked to another ring-bolt, fixed also in the deck. By this means fifty or sixty, and sometimes more, are fastened to one chain, in order to prevent them from rising, or endeavouring to escape. If the weather proves favourable, they are permitted to remain in that situation till four or five in the afternoon, when they are disengaged from the chain, and sent down.

The diet of the Negroes, while on board, consists chiefly of horse beans, boiled to the consistence of a pulp; of boiled yams and rice, and sometimes a small quantity of beef or pork. The latter are frequently taken from the provisions laid in for the sailors. They sometimes make use of a sauce, composed of palm oil, mixed with flour, water, and pepper, which the sailors call *slabber sauce*. Yams are the favourite food of the Eboe, or Bight Negroes, and rice or corn, of those from the Gold and Windward Coasts; each preferring the produce of their native soil.

In their own country, the Negroes in general live on animal food and fish, with roots, yams, and Indian corn. The horse beans and rice, with which they are fed aboard ship, are chiefly taken from Europe. The latter, indeed, is sometimes purchased on the coast, being far superior to any other.

The Gold Coast Negroes scarcely ever refuse any food that is offered them, and they generally eat larger quantities of whatever is placed before them, than any other species of Negroes, whom they likewise excel in strength of body and mind. Most of the slaves have such an aversion to the horse beans, that unless they are narrowly watched, when fed upon deck, they will throw them overboard, or in each other's faces when they quarrel.

They are commonly fed twice a day, about eight o'clock in the morning, and four in the afternoon. In most ships they are only fed with their *own food* once a day. Their food is served up to them in tubs, about the size of a small water bucket. They are placed round these tubs in companies of ten to each tub, out of which they feed themselves with wooden spoons. These they soon lose, and when they are not allowed others, they feed themselves with their hands. In favourable weather they are fed upon deck, but in bad weather their food is given them below. Numberless quarrels take place among them during their meals; more especially when they are put upon short allowance, which frequently happens, if the passage from the coast of Guinea to the West India islands, proves of usual length. In that case, the weak are obliged to be content with a very scanty

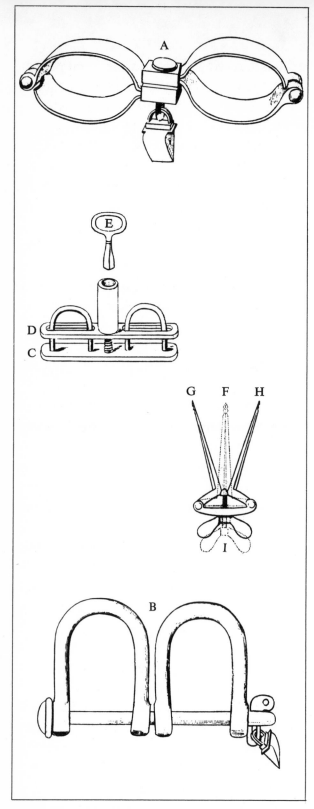

SECURELY BOUND   ". . . Negroes, on being brought aboard the ship are immediately fastened together, two and two, by handcuffs on their wrists, and by irons rivetted on their legs."

Implements of bondage and torture, as shown in Clarkson's Abolition of the Slave Trade;
A—Handcuffs; B—Leg Irons; C–E—Thumb Screws; F–I—A device to force open the mouth of a captive who refuses to eat.

portion. Their allowance of water is about half a pint each at every meal. It is handed round in a bucket, and given to each Negro in a pannekin, a small utensil with a straight handle, somewhat similar to a sauce-boat. However, when the ships approach the islands with a favourable breeze, they are no longer restricted.

Upon the Negroes refusing to take sustenance, I have seen coals of fire, glowing hot, put on a shovel, and placed so near their lips, as to scorch and burn them. And this has been accompanied with threats, of forcing them to swallow the coals, if they any longer persisted in refusing to eat. These means have generally had the desired effect. I have also been credibly informed that a certain captain in the slave trade poured melted lead on such of the Negroes as obstinately refused their food.

Exercise being deemed necessary for the preservation of their health, they are sometimes obliged to dance, when the weather will permit their coming on deck. If they go about it reluctantly, or do not move with agility, they are flogged; a person standing by them all the time with a cat-o'-nine-tails in his hand for that purpose. Their music, upon these occasions, consists of a drum, sometimes with only one head; and when that is worn out, they do not scruple to make use of the bottom of one of the tubs before described. The poor wretches are frequently compelled to sing also; but when they do so, their songs are generally, as may naturally be expected, melancholy lamentations of their exile from their native country.

The women are furnished with beads for the purpose of affording them some diversion. But this end is generally defeated by the squabbles which are occasioned, in consequence of their stealing them from each another.

On board some ships, the common sailors

are allowed to have intercourse with such of the black women whose consent they can procure. And some of them have been known to take the inconstancy of their paramours so much to heart, as to leap overboard and drown themselves. The officers are permitted to indulge their passions among them at pleasure, and sometimes are guilty of such brutal excesses as disgrace human nature.

The hardships and inconveniences suffered by the Negroes during the passage are scarcely to be enumerated or conceived. They are far more violently affected by the seasickness than the Europeans. It frequently terminates in death, especially among the women. But the exclusion of the fresh air is among the most intolerable. For the purpose of admitting this needful refreshment, most of the ships in the slave trade are provided, between the decks, with five or six air-ports on each side of the ship, of about six inches in length, and four in breadth; in addition to which, some few ships, but not one in twenty, have what they denominate *wind-sails*. But whenever the sea is rough and the rain heavy, it becomes necessary to shut these, and every other conveyance by which the air is admitted. The fresh air being thus excluded, the Negroes' rooms very soon grow intolerably hot. The confined air, rendered noxious by the effluvia exhaled from their bodies, and by being repeatedly breathed, soon produces fevers and fluxes, which generally carries off great numbers of them.

During the voyages I made, I was frequently a witness to the fatal effects of this exclusion of the fresh air. I will give one instance, as it serves to convey some idea, though a very faint one, of the sufferings of those unhappy beings whom we wantonly drag from their native country, and doom to perpetual labour and captivity. Some wet and blowing weather having occasioned the portholes to be shut, and the grating to be covered, fluxes and fevers among the Negroes ensued. While they were in this situation, my profession requiring it, I frequently went down among them, till at length their apartments became so extremely hot, as to be only sufferable for a very short time. But the excessive heat was not the only thing that rendered their situation intolerable. The deck, that is, the floor of their rooms, was so covered with the blood and mucus which had proceeded from them in consequence of the flux, that it resembled a slaughter-house. It is not in the power of the human imagination to picture to itself a situation more dreadful or disgusting. Numbers of the slaves having fainted, they were carried upon deck, where several of them died, and the rest were, with great difficulty, restored. It had nearly proved fatal to me also. The climate was too warm to admit the wearing of any clothing but a shirt, and that I had pulled off before I went down; notwithstanding which, by only continuing among them for about a quarter of an hour, I was so overcome with the heat, stench, and foul air, that I had nearly fainted; and it was not without assistance that I could get upon deck. The consequence was that I soon after fell sick of the same disorder, from which I did not recover for several months.

A circumstance of this kind sometimes repeatedly happens in the course of a voyage; and often to a greater degree than what has just been described; particularly when the slaves are much crowded, which was not the case at that time, the ship having more than a hundred short of the number she was to have taken in.

This devastation, great as it was, some few years ago was greatly exceeded on board a Liverpool ship. I shall particularise the circumstances of it, as a more glaring instance of an insatiable thirst for gain, or of less attention to the lives and happiness, even of that despised and oppressed race of mortals, the sable inhabitants of Africa, perhaps was never exceeded; though indeed several similar instances have been known.

This ship, though a much smaller ship than that in which the event I have just mentioned happened, took on board at Bonny, at least six hundred Negroes; but according to the information of the black traders, from whom I received the intelligence immediately after the ship sailed, they amounted to near *seven hundred*. By purchasing so great a number, the slaves were so crowded, that they were even obliged to lie one upon another. This occasioned such a mortality among them, that, without meeting with unusual bad weather, or having a longer voyage than common, nearly one half of them died before the ship arrived in the West Indies.

That the public may be able to form some idea of the almost incredible small space into which so large a number of Negroes were crammed, the following particulars of this ship are given. According to Liverpool custom she measured 235 tons. Her width across the beam, 25 feet. Length between the decks, 92 feet, which was divided into four rooms, thus:

Store room, in which there were
not any Negroes placed	15 feet

Negroes' rooms—

men's room	about	45 feet
women's ditto	about	10 feet
boys' ditto	about	22 feet
Total room for Negroes		77 feet*

* *Exclusive of the platform before described, from 8 to 9 feet in breadth, and equal in length to that of the rooms.*

It may be worthy of remark, that the ships in this trade are usually fitted out to receive only one-third women Negroes, or perhaps a smaller number, which the dimension of the room allotted for them, above given, plainly show, but in a greater disproportion.

One would naturally suppose that an attention to their own interest would prompt the owners of the Guinea ships not to suffer the captains to take on board a greater number of Negroes than the ship would allow room sufficient for them to lie with ease to themselves, or, at least, without rubbing against each other. However that may be, a more striking instance than the above, of avarice, completely and deservedly disappointed, was surely never displayed: for there is little room to doubt, but that in consequence of the expected premium usually allowed to the captains, of £6 per cent. sterling on the produce of the Negroes, this vessel was so thronged as to occasion such a heavy loss.

The place allotted for the sick Negroes is under the half deck where they lie on the bare planks. By this means, those who are emaciated, frequently have their skin, and even their flesh, entirely rubbed off, by the motion of the ship, from the prominent parts of the shoulders, elbows, and hips, so as to render the bones in those parts quite bare. And some of them, by constantly lying in the blood and mucus that had flowed from those afflicted with the flux, and which, as before observed, is generally so violent as to prevent their being kept clean, have their flesh much sooner rubbed off than those who have only to contend with the mere friction of the ship. The excruciating pain which the poor sufferers feel from being obliged to continue in such a dreadful situation, frequently for several weeks, in case they happen to live so long, is not to be conceived or described. Few, indeed, are ever able to withstand the fatal effects of it. The utmost skill of the surgeon is here ineffectual. If plaisters be applied, they are very soon displaced by the friction of the ship; and when bandages are used, the Negroes very soon take them off, and appropriate them to other purposes.

INSPECTION OF MERCHANDISE *". . . they first examine them relative to their age. They then minutely inspect their persons, and inquire into the state of their health; if they are afflicted with any infirmity, or are deformed, or have bad eyes or teeth; if they are lame, or weak in their joints, or distorted in the back, or of a slender make, or are narrow in the chest; in short, if they have been, or are afflicted in any manner, so as to render them incapable of much labour; if any of the foregoing defects are discovered in them, they are rejected."* (Library of Congress)

Falconbridge Relates the Horrors Aboard Slave Ships ☐ 51

The surgeon, upon going between decks, in the morning, to examine the situation of the slaves, frequently finds several dead; and among the men, sometimes a dead and living Negro fastened by their irons together. When this is the case, they are brought upon the deck, and being laid on the grating, the living Negro is disengaged, and the dead is thrown overboard.

It may not be improper here to remark that the surgeons employed in the Guinea trade are generally driven to engage in so disagreeable an employ by the confined state of their finances. An exertion of the greatest skill and attention could afford the diseased Negroes little relief, so long as the causes of their diseases, namely, the breathing of a putrid atmosphere and wallowing in their own excrements, remain. When once the fever and dysentery get to any height at sea, a cure is scarcely ever effected.

Almost the only means by which the surgeon can render himself useful to the slaves is by seeing that their food is properly cooked and distributed among them. It is true, when they arrive near the markets for which they are destined, care is taken to polish them for sale by an application of the lunar caustic to such as are afflicted with the yaws. This, however, affords but a temporary relief, as the disease most assuredly breaks out, whenever the patient is put upon a vegetable diet.

It has been asserted in favour of the captains in this trade, that the sick slaves are usually fed from their tables. The great number generally ill at a time, proves the falsity of such an assertion. Were even a captain *disposed* to do this, how could he feed half the slaves in his ship from his own table? for it is well known that *more than half* are often sick at a time. Two or three perhaps may be fed.

The loss of slaves, through mortality, arising from the causes just mentioned, are frequently very considerable. In the voyage lately referred to (not the Liverpool ship before-mentioned) one hundred and five, out of three hundred and eighty, died in the passage—a proportion seemingly very great, but by no means uncommon. One half, sometimes two-thirds, and even beyond that, have been known to perish. Before we left Bonny River, no less than fifteen died of fevers and dysenteries, occasioned by their confinement. On the Windward Coast, where slaves are procured more slowly, very few die, in proportion to the numbers which die at Bonny, and at Old and New Calabar, where they are obtained much faster; the latter being of a more delicate make and habit.

The havoc made among seamen engaged in this destructive commerce, will be noticed in another part; and will be found to make no inconsiderable addition to the unnecessary waste of life just represented.

As very few of the Negroes can so far brook the loss of their liberty, and the hardships they endure, as to bear them with any degree of patience, they are ever upon the watch to take advantage of the least negligence in their oppressors. Insurrections are frequently the consequence; which are seldom suppressed without much bloodshed. Sometimes these are successful, and the whole ship's company is cut off. They are likewise always ready to seize every opportunity for committing some act of desperation to free themselves from their miserable state; and notwithstanding the restraints under which they are laid, they often succeed.

While a ship, to which I belonged, lay in Bonny River, one evening, a short time before our departure, a lot of Negroes, consisting of about ten, was brought on board; when one of them, in a favourable moment, forced his way through the network on the larboard side of the vessel, jumped overboard and was supposed to have been devoured by the sharks.

During the time we were there, fifteen Negroes belonging to a vessel from Liverpool, found means to throw themselves into the river; very few were saved; and the residue fell a sacrifice to the sharks. A similar instance took place in a French ship while we lay there.

Circumstances of this kind are very frequent. On the coast of Angola, at the river Ambris, the following incident happened: During the time of our residing on shore, we erected a tent to shelter ourselves from the weather. After having been there several weeks, and being unable to purchase the number of slaves we wanted, through the opposition of another English slave vessel, we determined to leave the place. The night before our departure the tent was struck; which was no sooner perceived by some of the Negro women on board, than it was considered as a prelude to our sailing, and about eighteen of them, when they were sent between decks, threw themselves into the sea through one of the gun ports, the ship carrying guns between decks. They were all of them, however, excepting one, soon picked up; and that which was missing was, not long after, taken about a mile from the shore.

I once knew a Negro woman, too sensible of her woes, who pined for a considerable time, and was taken ill of a fever and dysentery; when, declaring it to be her determination to die, she refused all food and medical aid, and in about a fortnight after, expired. On being thrown overboard, her body was instantly torn to pieces by the sharks.

The following circumstances also came within my knowledge. A young female Negro, falling into a desponding way, it was judged necessary, in order to attempt her recovery, to send her on shore, to the hut of one of the black traders. Elevated with the prospect of regaining her liberty by this unexpected step, she soon recovered her usual cheerfulness; but hearing, by accident, that it was intended to take her on board the ship again, the poor young creature hung herself.

It frequently happens that the Negroes, on being purchased by the Europeans, become raving mad, and many of them die in that state, particularly the women. While I was one day ashore at Bonny, I saw a middle-aged stout woman, who had been brought down from a fair the preceding day, chained to the post of a black trader's door, in a state of furious insanity. On board a ship in Bonny River, I saw a young Negro woman chained to the deck, who had lost her senses, soon after she was purchased and taken on board. In a former voyage, on board a ship to which I belonged, we were obliged to confine a female Negro, of about twenty-three years of age, on her becoming a lunatic. She was afterwards sold during one of her lucid intervals.

One morning, upon examining the place allotted for the sick Negroes, I perceived that one of them, who was so emaciated as scarcely to be able to walk, was missing, and was convinced that he must have gone overboard in the night, probably to put a more expeditious period to his sufferings. And, to conclude on this subject, I could not help being sensibly affected, on a former voyage, at observing with what apparent eagerness a black woman seized some dirt from off an African yam, and put it into her mouth, seeming to rejoice at the opportunity of possessing some of her native earth.

From these instances I think it may be clearly deduced that the unhappy Africans are not bereft of the finer feelings, but have a strong attachment to their native country, together with a just sense of the value of liberty. And the situation of the miserable beings above described, more forcibly urges the necessity of abolishing a trade which is the source of such evils, than the most eloquent harangue, or persuasive arguments could do.

George Washington's

Plan for Manumission

IN THE NAME OF GOD AMEN

I George Washington of Mount Vernon —a citizen of the United States,—and lately President of the same, do make, ordain and declare this Instrument; which is written with my own hand and every page thereof subscribed with my name, to be my last Will & Testament, revoking all others. . . .

ITEM Upon the decease of my wife, it is my Will & desire that all the Slaves which I hold in *my own right,* shall receive their freedom. —To emancipate them during her life, would, tho' earnestly wished by me, be attended with such insuperable difficulties on account of their intermixture by Marriages with the Dower Negroes, as to excite the most painful sensations, if not disagreeable consequences from the latter, while both descriptions are in the occupancy of the same Proprietor; it not being in my power, under the tenure by which the Dower Negros are held, to manumit them—And whereas among those who will receive freedom according to this devise, there may be some, who from old age or bodily infirmities, and others who on

account of their infancy, that will be unable to support themselves; it is my Will and desire that all who come under the first & second description shall be comfortably cloathed & fed by my heirs while they live; —and that such of the latter description as have no parents living, or if living are unable, or unwilling to provide for them, shall be bound by the Court until they shall arrive at the age of twenty five years; —and in cases where no record can be produced, whereby their ages can be ascertained, the judgment of the Court upon its own view of the subject, shall be adequate and final. —The Negros thus bound, are (by their Masters or Mistresses) to be taught to read & write; and to be brought up to some useful occupation, agreeably to the Laws of the Commonwealth of Virginia, providing for the support of Orphan and other poor Children. —And I do hereby expressly forbid the Sale, or transportation out of the said Commonwealth of any Slave I may die possessed of, under any pretence whatsoever. —And I do moreover most pointedly, and most solemnly enjoin it upon my Executors hereafter named, or the Survivors of them, to see that *this* clause

respecting Slaves, and every part thereof be religiously fulfilled at the Epoch at which it is directed to take place; without evasion, neglect or delay, after the Crops which may then be on the ground are harvested, particularly as it respects the aged and infirm; —Seeing that a regular and permanent fund be established for their Support so long as there are subjects requiring it; not trusting to the uncertain provision to be made by individuals. —And to my Mulatto man William (calling himself William Lee) I give immediate freedom; or if he should prefer it (on account of the accidents which have befallen him, and which have rendered him incapable of walking or of any active employment) to remain in the situation he now is, it shall be optional in him to do so: In either case however, I allow him an annuity of thirty dollars during his natural life, which shall be independent of the victuals and cloaths he has been accustomed to receive, if he chuses the last alternative; but in full, with his freedom, if he prefers the first; —& this I give him as a testimony of my sense of his attachment to me, and for his faithful services during the Revolutionary War. —. . . .

Benjamin Banneker's Letter

to Thomas Jefferson

I am fully sensible of that freedom, which I take with you in the present occasion; a liberty which seemed to me scarcely allowable, when I reflected on that distinguished and dignified station in which you stand, and the almost general prejudice and prepossession, which is so prevalent in the world against those of my complexion.

I suppose it is a truth too well attested . . . to need a proof here, that we are a race of beings, who have long labored under the abuse and censure of the world; that we have long been looked upon with an eye of contempt; and that we have long been considered rather as brutish than human, and scarcely capable of mental endowments.

Sir, I hope I may safely admit . . . that you are a man less inflexible in sentiments of this nature, than many others; that you are measurably friendly, and well disposed towards us; and that you are willing and ready to lend your aid and assistance to our relief, from those many distresses, and numerous calamities, to which we are reduced.

. . . if this is founded in truth, I apprehend you will embrace every opportunity, to eradicate that train of absurd and false ideas and opinions, which so generally prevails with respect to us; and that your sentiments are concurrent with mine, which are, that one universal Father hath given being to us all; and that he hath not only made us all of one flesh, but that he hath also, without partiality, afforded us all the same sensations and endowed us all with the same faculties; and that however variable we may be in society or religion, however diversified in situation or color, we are all in the same family and stand in the same relation to him.

. . . if these are sentiments of which you are fully persuaded, I hope you cannot but acknowledge, that it is the indispensable duty of those, who maintain for themselves the rights of human nature, and who possess the obligations of Christianity, to extend their power and influence to the relief of every part of the human race, from whatever burden or oppression they may unjustly labor under . . .

. . . I have long been convinced, that if your love . . . for those inestimable laws, which preserved to you the rights of human nature, was founded on sincerity, you could not but be solicitous, that every individual, of whatever rank or distinction, might with you equally enjoy the blessings thereof; neither

could you rest satisfied short of the most active effusion of your exertions, in order to the promotion from any state of degradation, to which the unjustifiable cruelty and barbarism of men may have reduced them.

. . . I freely and cheerfully acknowledge, that I am of the African race, and in that color which is natural to them of the deepest dye; and it is under a sense of the most profound gratitude to the Supreme Ruler of the Universe, that I now confess to you, that I am not under that state of tyrannical thraldom, and inhuman captivity, to which too many of my brethren are doomed, but that I have abundantly tasted of the fruition of those blessings, which proceed from that free and unequalled liberty with which you are favored; and which, I hope, you will willingly allow you have mercifully received, from the immediate hand of that Being, from whom proceedeth every good and perfect Gift.

. . . suffer me to recall to your mind that time, in which the arms and tyranny of the British crown were exerted . . . in order to reduce you to a state of servitude: look back, I entreat you, on the variety of dangers to which you were exposed; reflect on that time, in which every human aid appeared unavail-

able, and in which even hope and fortitude wore the aspect of inability to the conflict, and you cannot but be led to a serious and grateful sense of your miraculous and providential preservation; you cannot but acknowledge, that the present freedom and tranquility . . . is the peculiar blessing of Heaven.

This, Sir, was a time when you clearly saw into the injustice of a state of slavery, and in which you had just apprehensions of the horror of its condition. . . . your abhorrence thereof was so excited, that you publicly held forth this true and invaluable doctrine, which is worthy to be recorded and remembered in all succeeding ages: 'We hold these truths to be self-evident, that all men are created equal; that they are endowed by their Creator with certain unalienable rights, and that among these are, life, liberty, and the pursuit of happiness.'

. . . tender feelings for yourselves had engaged you thus to declare, you were then impressed with proper ideas of the great violation of liberty, and the free possession of those blessings, to which you were entitled by nature; but, Sir, how pitiable is it to reflect, that although you were so fully convinced of the benevolence of the Father of Mankind,

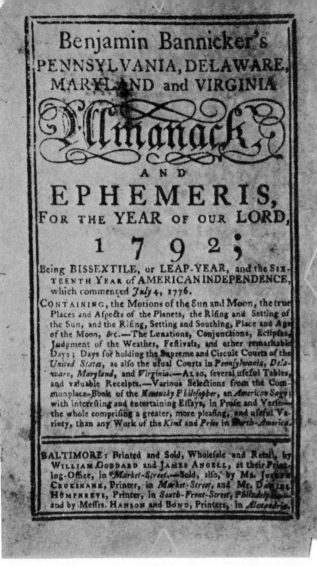

COVER—*Benjamin Bannicker's Almanack and Ephemeris*
(Schomburg Collection)

and of his equal and impartial distribution of these rights and privileges, which he hath conferred upon them, that you should at the same time counteract his mercies, in detaining by fraud and violence so numerous a part of my brethren, under groaning captivity, and cruel oppression, that you should at the same time be found guilty of that most criminal act, which you professedly detested in others, with respect to yourselves.

. . . I suppose that your knowledge of the situation of my brethren, is too extensive to need a recital here; neither shall I presume to prescribe methods by which they may be re-

lieved, otherwise than by recommending to you and all others, to wean yourselves from those narrow prejudices which you have imbibed with respect to them, and as Job proposed to his friends, 'put your soul in their souls' stead'; thus shall your hearts be enlarged with kindness and benevolence towards them; and thus shall you need neither the direction of myself or others, in what manner to proceed herein.

And now, Sir, although my sympathy and affection for my brethren hath caused my enlargement thus far, I ardently hope, that your candor and generosity will plead with you in my behalf, when I make known to you, that it was not originally my design; but having taken up my pen in order to direct to you, as a present, a copy of my Almanac, which I have calculated for the succeeding year, I was unexpectedly and unavoidably led thereto.

This calculation . . . is the product of my arduous study, in this most advanced stage of life; for having long had unbounded desires to become acquainted with the secrets of nature, I have had to gratify my curiosity herein through my own assiduous application to Astronomical Study, in which I need not recount to you the many difficulties and disadvantages which I have had to encounter.

And although I had almost declined to make my calculation for the ensuing year . . . yet finding myself under several engagements to Printers of this State, to whom I had communicated my design, on my return to my place of residence, I industriously applied myself thereto, which I hope I have accomplished with correctness and accuracy; a copy of which I have taken the liberty to direct to you, and which I humbly request you will favorably receive; . . . I choose to send it to you in manuscript . . . that thereby you might not only have an earlier inspection, but that you might also view it in my own hand writing.

Jefferson's Reply to Banneker

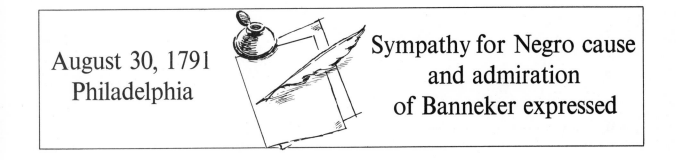

August 30, 1791
Philadelphia

Sympathy for Negro cause
and admiration
of Banneker expressed

Philadelphia, Aug. 30, 1791

Sir—

—I thank you sincerely for your letter of the 19th instant, and for the Almanac it contained. Nobody wishes more than I do to see such proofs as you exhibit, that nature has given to our black brethren talents equal to those of the other colours of men, and that the appearance of a want of them is owing only to the degraded condition of their existence both in Africa and America. I can add with truth that no one wishes more ardently to see a good system commenced for raising the condition both of their body and mind to what it ought to be, as fast as the imbecility of their present existence, and other circumstances which cannot be neglected, will admit. I have taken the liberty of sending your Almanac to Monsieur de Condorcet, Secretary of the Academy of Sciences at Paris, and member of the Philanthropic Society; because I considered it a document to which your whole colour had a right for their justification against the doubts which have been entertained of them.

I am, with great esteem, sir, your most obedient servant,

Tho. Jefferson

Richard Allen and Absalom Jones

Denounce Philadelphia Ingratitude

1794
Philadelphia

Elders of the
African Church
recall Negro valor
during cholera epidemic

I N consequence of a partial representation of the conduct of the people who were employed to nurse the sick, in the late calamitous state of the city of Philadelphia, we are solicited, by a number of those who feel themselves injured thereby, and by the advice of several respectable citizens, to step forward and declare facts as they really were; seeing that from our situation, on account of the charge we took upon us, we had it more fully and generally in our power, to know and observe the conduct and behavior of those that were so employed.

Early in September [1793], a solicitation appeared in the public papers, to the people of colour to come forward and assist the distressed, perishing, and neglected sick; with a kind of assurance, that people of our colour were not liable to take the infection. Upon which we and a few others met and consulted how to act on so truly alarming and melancholy an occasion. After some conversation, we found a freedom to go forth, confiding in him who can preserve in the midst of a burning fiery furnace, sensible that it was our duty to do all the good we could to our suffering fellow mortals. We set out to see where we could be useful. The first we visited was a man in Emsley's alley, who was dying . . .

We visited upwards of twenty families that day—they were scenes of woe indeed!

In order the better to regulate our conduct, we called on the mayor next day, to consult with him how to proceed, so as to be most useful. The first object he mentioned was a strict attention to the sick, and the procuring of nurses. This was attended to by Absalom Jones and William Gray; and, in order that the distressed might know where to apply, the mayor advertised the public that upon application to them they would be supplied. Soon after, the mortality increasing, the difficulty of getting a corpse taken away, was such, that few were willing to do it, when offered great rewards. The black people were looked to. We then offered our services in the public papers, by advertising that we would remove the dead and procure nurses. Our services were the production of real sensibility;—we sought not fee nor reward, until the increase of the disorder rendered our labour so arduous that we were not adequate to the service we had assumed. The mortality increasing rapidly, obliged us to call in the assistance of five—hired—men, in the awful discharge of interring the dead. They, with great reluctance, were prevailed upon to join us. It was very uncommon at this time, to find any one that would go near, much more, handle, a sick or dead person.

Mr. Carey . . . has observed, that, "for the honor of human nature, it ought to be recorded, that some of the convicts in the gaol, a part of the term of whose confinement had been remitted as a reward for their peaceable, orderly behavior, voluntarily offered themselves as nurses to attend the sick at Bush-hill; and have, in that capacity, conducted themselves with great fidelity," etc. Here it ought to be remarked, (although Mr. Carey hath not done it) that two thirds of the persons, who rendered these essential services, were people of colour, who, on the application of the elders of the African church, (who met to consider what they could do for the help of the sick) were liberated, on condition of their doing their duty of nurses at the hospital at Bush-hill; which they as voluntarily accepted to do, as they did faithfully discharge, this severe and disagreeable duty. —May the Lord reward them, both temporally and spiritually.

When the sickness became general, and several of the physicians died, and most of the survivors were exhausted by sickness or fatigue; that good man, Doctor [Benjamin] Rush, called us more immediately to attend upon the sick, knowing we could both bleed; he told us we could increase our utility, by attending to his instructions, and accordingly directed us where to procure medicine duly prepared, with proper directions how to administer them, and at what stages of the disorder to bleed, and when we found ourselves incapable of judging what was proper to be done, to apply to him, and he would, if able, attend them himself, or send Edward Fisher, his pupil, which he often did; and Mr. Fisher manifested his humanity, by an affectionate attention for their relief.—This has been no small satisfaction to us; for, we think, that

when a physician was not attainable, we have been the instruments, in the hand of God, for saving the lives of some hundreds of our suffering fellow mortals.

We feel ourselves sensibly aggrieved by the censorious epithets of many, who did not render the least assistance in the time of necessity, yet are liberal of their censure of us, for the prices paid for our services, when no one knew how to make a proposal to any one they wanted to assist them. At first we made no charge, but left it to those we served in removing their dead, to give what they thought fit—we set no price, until the reward was fixed by those we had served. After paying the people we had to assist us, our compensation is much less than many will believe.

We do assure the public, that *all* the money we have received, for burying, and for coffins which we ourselves purchased and procured, has not defrayed the expence of wages which we had to pay those whom we employed to assist us. . . . From this statement, for the truth of which we solemnly vouch, it is evident, and we sensibly feel the operation of the fact, that we are out of pocket . . . We feel ourselves hurt most by a partial, censorious paragraph, in Mr. Carey's second edition, of his account of the sickness . . . where he asperses the blacks alone, for having taken advantage of the distressed situation of the people. That some extravagant prices were paid, we admit; but how came they to be demanded? the reason is plain. It was with difficulty persons could be had to supply the wants of the sick, as nurses . . . It was natural for people in low circumstances to accept a voluntary, bounteous reward; especially under the loathsomeness of many of the sick, when nature shuddered at the thoughts of the infection, and the task assigned was aggravated by lunacy, and being left much alone with them. Had Mr. Carey been solicited to such an undertaking, for hire, Query, "what would *he* have demanded?" but Mr. Carey, although chosen a member of that band of worthies who have so eminently distinguished themselves by their labours, for the relief of the sick and helpless—yet, quickly after his election, left them to struggle with their arduous and hazardous task, by leaving the city. . . .

The bad consequences many of our colour apprehend from a partial relation of our conduct, are, that it will prejudice the minds of the people in general against us—because it is impossible that one individual, can have knowledge of all, therefore at some future day, when some of the most virtuous, that were upon most praiseworthy motives, induced to serve the sick, may fall into the service of a family that are strangers to him, or her, and it is discovered that it is one of those stigmatized wretches, what may we suppose will be the consequence? Is it not reasonable to think the person will be abhored, despised, and perhaps dismissed from employment, to their great disadvantage . . .

Mr. Carey pays William Gray and us a compliment; he says; our services and others of their colour, have been very great. &c By naming us, he leaves these others, in the hazardous state of being classed with those who are called the "vilest" . . . We have many unprovoked enemies, who begrudge us the liberty we enjoy, and are glad to hear of any complaint against our colour, be it just or unjust; in consequence of which we are more earnestly endeavouring all in our power, to warn, rebuke, and exhort our African friends, to keep a conscience void of offence towards God and man; and, at the same time, would not be backward to interfere, when stigmas or oppression appear pointed at, or attempted against them, unjustly; and, we are confident, we shall stand justified in the sight of the

candid and judicious, for such conduct.

Mr. Carey's first, second, and third editions, are gone forth into the world, and in all probability, have been read by thousands that will never read his fourth—consequently, any alteration he may hereafter make, in the paragraph alluded to, cannot have the desired effect, or atone for the past . . . Had Mr. Carey said, a number of white and black Wretches eagerly seized on the opportunity to extort from the distressed, and some few of both were detected in plundering the sick, it might extenuate, in a great degree, the having made mention of the blacks . . .

It is even to this day a generally received opinion in this city, that our colour was not so liable to the sickness as the whites. . . .

The public were informed that in the West Indies and other places where this terrible malady had been, it was observed the blacks were not affected with it. Happy would it have been for you, and much more so for us, if this observation had been verified by our experience.

When the people of colour had the sickness and died, we were imposed upon and told it was not with the prevailing sickness, until it became too notorious to be denied, then we were told some few died but not many. Thus were our services extorted *at the peril of our lives,* yet you accuse us of exhorting *a little money from you.*

The bill of mortality for the year 1793, published by Matthew Whitehead, and John Ormrod, Clerks, and Joseph Dolby, sexton, will convince any reasonable man that will examine it, that as many coloured people died in proportion as others. In 1792 there were 67 of our colour buried, and in 1793 it amounted to 305; thus the burials among us have increased more than fourfold, was not this in a great degree the effects of the services of the unjustly vilified black people?

Richard Allen and Absalom Jones

Speak Out Against Slavery

THE judicious part of mankind will think it unreasonable, that a superior good conduct is looked for, from our race, by those who stigmatize us as men, whose baseness is incurable, and may therefore be held in a state of servitude, that a merciful man would not deem a beast to; yet you try what you can to prevent our rising from the state of barbarism, you represent us to be in, but we can tell you, from a degree of experience, that a black man, although reduced to the most abject state human nature is capable of, short of real madness, can think, reflect, and feel injuries, although it may not be with the same degree of keen resentment and revenge, that you who have been and are our great oppressors, would manifest if reduced to the pitiable condition of a slave. We believe if you would try the experiment of taking a few black children, and cultivate their minds with the same care, and let them have the same prospect in view, as to living in the world, as you would wish for your own children, you would find them upon the trial, they were not inferior in mental endowments.

We do not wish to make you angry, but excite your attention to consider, how hateful slavery is in the sight of that God, who hath destroyed kings and princes, for their oppression of the poor slaves; Pharaoh and his princes with the posterity of King Saul, were destroyed by the protector and avenger of slaves. Would you not suppose the Israelites to be utterly unfit for freedom, and that it was impossible for them to attain to any degree of excellence? Their history shews how slavery had debased their spirits. Men must be wilfully blind and extremely partial, that cannot see the contrary effects of liberty and slavery upon the mind of man; we freely confess the vile habits often acquired in a state of servitude, are not easily thrown off; the example of the Israelite shews, who with all that Moses could do to reclaim them from it, still con-

tinued in their former habits more or less; and why will you look for better from us? Why will you look for grapes from thorns, or figs from thistles? It is in our posterity enjoying the same privileges with your own, that you ought to look for better things.

When you are pleaded with, do not you reply as Pharaoh did, "wherefore do ye Moses and Aaron, let the people from their work, behold the people of the land, now are many, and you make them rest from their burdens?" We wish you to consider, that God himself was the first pleader of the cause of slaves.

That God who knows the hearts of all men, and the propensity of a slave to hate his oppressor hath strictly forbidden it to his chosen people, "thou shalt not abhor an Egyptian, because thou wast a stranger in his land. Deut. xxiii. 7." The meek and humble Jesus, the great pattern of humanity, and every other virtue that can adorn and dignify men, hath commanded to love our enemies, to do good to them that hate and despitefully use us. We feel the obligations, we wish to impress them on the minds of our black brethren, and that we may all forgive you, as we wish to be forgiven; we think it a great mercy to have all anger and bitterness removed from our minds; we appeal to your own feelings, if it is not very disquieting to feel yourselves under the dominion of a wrathful disposition.

If you love your children, if you love your country, if you love the God of love, clear your hands from slaves, burden not your children or country with them. Our hearts have been sorrowful for the late bloodshed of the oppressors, as well as the oppressed, both appear guilty of each others blood, in the sight of him who said, he that sheddeth man's blood, by man shall his blood be shed.

Will you, because you have reduced us to the unhappy condition our colour is in, plead our incapacity for freedom, and our contented condition under oppression, as a sufficient cause for keeping us under the grievous yoke? We have shewn the cause of our incapacity, we will also shew, why we appear contented; were we to attempt to plead with our masters, it would be deemed insolence, for which cause they appear as contented as they can in your sight, but the dreadful insurrections they have made, when opportunity has offered, is enough to convince a reasonable man, that great uneasiness and not contentment, is the inhabitant of their hearts.

God himself hath pleaded their cause, he hath from time to time raised up instruments for that purpose, sometimes mean and contemptible in your sight; at other times he hath used such as it hath pleased him with whom you have not thought it beneath your dignity to contend, many add to your numbers, until the princes shall come forth from Egypt and Ethiopia stretch out her hand unto God.

The Importation of Slaves Prohibited

BE IT ENACTED, That from and after the first day of January, one thousand eight hundred and eight, it shall not be lawful to import or bring into the United States or the territories thereof from any foreign kingdom, place, or country, any negro, mulatto, or person of colour, as a slave, or to be held to service or labour.

. . . That no citizen of the United States, or any other person, shall, from and after the first day of January, in the year of our Lord one thousand eight hundred and eight, for himself, or themselves, or any other person whatsoever, either as master, factor, or owner, build, fit, equip, load or to otherwise prepare any ship or vessel, in any port or place within the jurisdiction of the United States, nor shall cause any ship or vessel to sail from any port or place within the same, for the purpose of procuring any negro, mulatto, or person of colour, from any foreign kingdom, place, or country, to be transported to any port or place whatsoever within the jurisdiction of the United States, to be held, sold, or disposed of as slaves, or to be held to service or labour: and if any ship or vessel shall be so fitted out for the purpose aforesaid, or shall be caused to sail so as aforesaid, every such ship or vessel, her tackle, apparel, and furniture, shall be forfeited to the United States, and shall be liable to be seized, prosecuted, and condemned in any of the circuit courts or district courts, for the district where the said ship or vessel may be found or seized . . .

If any citizen or citizens of the United States, or any person resident within the jurisdiction of the same, shall, from and after the first day of January, one thousand eight hundred and eight, take on board, receive or transport from any of the coasts or kingdoms of Africa, or from any other foreign kingdom, place, or country, any negro, mulatto, or person of colour in any ship or vessel, for the purpose of selling them in any port or place within the jurisdiction of the United States as slaves, or to be held to service or labour, or shall be in any ways aiding or abetting therein, such citizen or citizens, or person, shall severally forfeit and pay five thousand dollars. . . .

That if any person or persons whatsoever, shall, from and after the first day of January, one thousand eight hundred and eight, purchase or sell any negro, mulatto, or person, of colour, for a slave, or to be held to service or labour, who shall have been imported or brought from any foreign kingdom, place, or country, or from the dominions of any foreign state, immediately adjoining to the United States, after the last day of December, one thousand eight hundred and seven, knowing at the time of such purchase or sale, such negro, mulatto, or person of colour, was so brought within the jurisdiction of the United States, as aforesaid, such purchaser and seller shall severally forfeit and pay for every negro, mulatto, or person of colour, so purchased or sold as aforesaid, eight hundred dollars. . . .

That if any ship or vessel shall be found, from and after the first day of January, one thousand eight hundred and eight, in any river, port, bay, or harbor, or on the high seas, within the jurisdictional limits of the United States, or hovering on the coast thereof, having on board any negro, mulatto, or person of colour, for the purpose of selling them as slaves, or with intent to land the same, in any port or place within the jurisdiction of the United States, contrary to the prohibition of the act, every such ship or vessel, together with her tackle, apparel, and furniture, and the goods or effects which shall be found on board the same, shall be forfeited to the use of the United States, and may be seized, prosecuted, and condemned, in any court of the United States, having jurisdiction thereof. And it shall be lawful for the President of the United States, and he is hereby authorized, should he deem it expedient, to cause any of the armed vessels of the United States to be manned and employed to cruise on any part of the coast of the United States, or territories thereof, where he may judge attempts will be made to violate the provisions of this act, and to instruct and direct the commanders of armed vessels of the United States, to seize, take, and bring into any port of the United States all such ships or vessels, and moreover to seize, take, or bring into any port of the U.S. all ships or vessels of the U.S. wheresoever found on the high seas, contravening the provisions of this act. . . .

SECTION II

LET MY PEOPLE GO

Go down, Moses
  Way down in Egypt land,
Tell ole Pharaoh,
  Let my people go.

INTRODUCTION

THE YEARS FOLLOWING the ratification of the Constitution were eventful and fast moving. There was much to be done. Organization of the government took precedence and was accomplished at the quick pace the times required. George Washington, venerated soldier—hero of the late War of Independence—became the first President by unanimous vote. John Adams was Vice-President. Senators and Congressmen were elected to the national legislature. The Supreme Court was inducted with John Jay of New York as first Chief Justice. Members of the Cabinet were designated: Thomas Jefferson, Secretary of State; Alexander Hamilton, Secretary of the Treasury; Henry Knox, Secretary of War; and Edmund Randolph, Attorney General.

Fiscal problems left over from the war demanded, and received, high priority. By astute maneuvering, Alexander Hamilton put through a program that gave the nation essential revenues, established national credit and boosted public confidence in the Treasury's financial integrity. Despite his notable achievement, Hamilton was frequently opposed and this opposition eventually polarized and gave rise to the two-party political system. Hamilton and Adams were key figures in the autocratic, business-oriented Federalist party, and Jefferson and Madison were the leading spirits of the Republican party which claimed to speak for the common man. Necessary constitutional reforms were also made during this period. Two amendments were added to the Constitution. The first, Article XI, ratified January 8, 1798, provided the states with protection from "suits in law or equity;" and, the second, Article XII, ratified September 25, 1804, provided that the President and Vice-President should be elected on separate and distinct ballots. Other happenings suggest the excitement and tempo of the

nation's formative years.

The nation was thrilled with the hints of potential greatness contained in the reports of Captain Meriwether Lewis and William Clark returning from exploration of the Louisiana Territory and westward to the Pacific Ocean. The journals compiled by Lewis and Clark during their travels have become classics in the literature of exploration.

The nation was shocked and appalled that men high in the councils of government should resort to dueling to settle disagreements. Aaron Burr, a former Vice-President, and Alexander Hamilton, brilliant first Secretary of the Treasury, fought a duel with pistols at 10 paces that was fatal to Hamilton, and, for all intents and purposes, ended Burr's career.

The nation grew. Within a 30-year period 11 new states were admitted to the union: Vermont (1791), Kentucky (1792), Tennessee (1796), Ohio (1803), Louisiana (1812), Indiana (1816), Mississippi (1817), Illinois (1818), Alabama (1819), Maine (1820), and Missouri (1821). Louisiana and Missouri were the first states carved out of the Louisiana Territory. The Louisiana Purchase ranks high with the acquisition of the Island of Manhattan as a stupendous bargain. Purchased from France in 1803 at the phenomenally low price of $15,000,000, the Territory's more than 516,000,000 acres practically doubled the nation's size.

Though still young and not yet a world power, the nation was aggressively protective of its dignity. Interference by pirates with American ships which sailed the waters along North Africa's Barbary coast had long been a source of national irritation. In 1803, Thomas Jefferson, then President of the United States, determined that the nation would no longer pay tribute to the Barbary

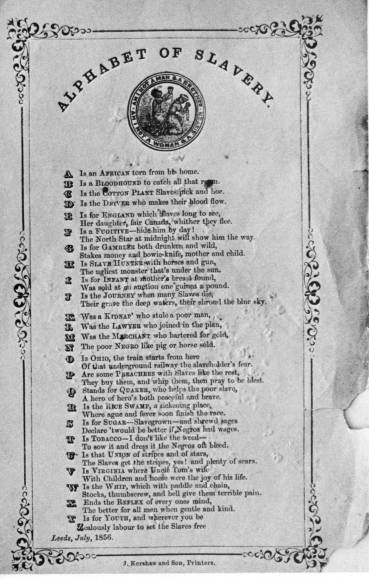

ALPHABET OF SLAVERY.

A Is an AFRICAN torn from his home.
B Is a BLOODHOUND to catch all that roam.
C Is the COTTON PLANT Slaves pick and hoe.
D Is the DRIVER who makes their blood flow.
E Is for ENGLAND which Slaves long to see,
  Her daughter, fair Canada, whither they flee.
F Is a FUGITIVE—hide him by day!
  The North Star at midnight will show him the way.
G Is for GAMBLER both drunken and wild,
  Stakes money and bowie-knife, mother and child.
H Is SLAVE HUNTER with horses and gun,
  The ugliest monster that's under the sun.
I Is for INFANT at mother's breast found,
  Was sold at an auction one guinea a pound.
J Is the JOURNEY when many Slaves die,
  Their grave the deep waters, their shroud the blue sky.
K Was a KIDNAP' who stole a poor man,
L Was the LAWYER who joined in the plan,
M Was the MERCHANT who bartered for gold,
N The poor NEGRO like pig or horse sold.
O Is OHIO, the train starts from here
  Of that underground railway the slaveholder's fear.
P Are some PREACHERS with Slaves like the rest,
  They buy them, and whip them, then pray to be blest.
Q Stands for QUAKER, who helps the poor slave,
  A hero of hero's both peaceful and brave.
R Is the RICE SWAMP, a sickening place,
  Where ague and fever soon finish the race.
S Is for SUGAR—Slavegrown—and shrewd sages
  Declare 'twould be better if Negros had wages.
T Is TOBACCO—I don't like the weed—
  To sow it and dress it the Negros oft bleed.
U Is that UNION of stripes and of stars,
  The Slaves get the stripes, yes! and plenty of scars.
V Is VIRGINIA where Uncle Tom's wife
  With Children and home were the joy of his life.
W Is the WHIP, which with paddle and chain,
  Stocks, thumbscrew, and bell give them terrible pain.
X Ends the REFLEX of every ones mind,
  The better for all men when gentle and kind.
Y Is for YOUTH, and wherever you be
Z Zealously labour to set the Slaves free

Leeds, July, 1856.

J. Kershaw and Son, Printers.

ALPHABET OF SLAVERY: *The shame and horror of slavery were portrayed graphically through the rhymed couplets of this widely circulated anti-slavery tract.* (Schomburg Collection)

Coast states. To assure safe passage, he dispatched a naval expedition which had the effect of ending pirate harassment.

The War of 1812 with Great Britain grew out of America's determination to sail unmolested in international waters. The special annoyance was the British custom of seizing American vessels and impressing American seamen into British naval service. The war ended without firmly resolving the issues that provoked it, but increased international respect for American rights. Later there would be war with Mexico which would end with Mexico's ceding a parcel in the Southwest, including what is now the state of California.

The wondrous new inventions of the period put America into the mainstream of the Industrial Revolution. In 1793, Eli Whitney designed the cotton gin, a device for removing seeds from cotton fibers. The cotton gin played an integral part in establishing the "Cotton Kingdom" in the South. In 1807, Robert Fulton sailed his boat, the *Clermont* on a five day voyage up the Hudson River, achieving speeds of nearly five miles an hour, thereby becoming the first functional and practical steam boat. The first American-made, steam-driven train began operating on a scheduled basis in December of 1830. Cyrus McCormick patented the grain harvesting machine which bears his name—"McCormick's Reaper"—in 1834, and in 1844, Samuel Morse transmitted the first experimental telegraphic message from Washington to Baltimore as he tapped out the exclamation: "What hath God wrought!"

In 1852 a new best seller appeared, causing Northerners to weep and Southerners to seethe as the author, Harriet Beecher Stowe, melodramatically detailed the shame of slavery. The book, *Uncle Tom's Cabin,* sold more than a million copies within a decade and became one of the most successful items of anti-slavery propaganda.

Despite the Act of 1807, prohibiting the importation of slaves into the United States after January 1, 1808, slavery did not decline. Although penalties could be imposed for buying and/or illegally importing slaves (Fine: $800 and up) or for equipping a slaving vessel (Fine: up to $20,000), in the period 1790 to 1860 the slave population grew from 657,000 to 4,000,000.

Like the prohibition amendment of the early twentieth century, the act did not significantly reduce the traffic in slaves. Rather the slavers, like the bootleggers of the next century, merely camouflaged their operations. In *From Slavery to Freedom,* John Hope Franklin notes that "from the beginning the law went unenforced." Stephen A. Douglas, as late as 1859, called attention to the fact that more slaves were imported that year than in any year before the ban on imports became effective.

Slavery had not always been profitable in the North and this economic consideration, coupled with humanitarian scruples, apparently spurred Northern movement toward emancipation. Under the respective State Constitutions of Vermont (1777), Massachusetts (1780), and New Hampshire (1784), programs of gradual emancipation were enacted in Pennsylvania (1780), Connecticut (1784), and Rhode Island (1784) which were followed later by New York (1799) and New Jersey (1804). The free Negro population of Maryland and Delaware increased steadily although those states had taken no action, constitutional or legislative, against slavery.

The *Act to prohibit the importation of Slaves* created a tight market for slaves and reintroduced the profit factor. Soon a combine of New England shipowners and businessmen from the Middle Atlantic and Upper South joined in profit-yielding adventures that violated the letter and spirit of the law. John Hope Franklin has observed that

> "The first underground railroad was not that carried on by the abolitionists to get Negro slaves to freedom but by the one carried on by merchants and others to introduce more Negroes into slavery."

Cotton became king in the deep South's agricultural economy with an almost insatiable appetite for slave laborers. In Benjamin Quarles' opinion:

> "Cotton was a powerful stimulant to slavery; the two seem to have been made for each other. . . ."

After 1854, open statements calling for the repeal of restrictions on the African slave trade were heard with increasing frequency. The South developed a rationale that defined slavery as consistent with *Natural Law*. The thesis was spelled out in the famous "Mud-Sill Speech" in the U.S. Senate by James H. Hammond of South Carolina, March 4, 1858. Hammond averred:

> In all social systems there must be a class to do the menial duties, to perform the drudgery of life. . . . a class requiring but a low order of intellect and but little skill. Its requisites are vigor, docility, fidelity. Such a class you must have, or you would not have that other class which leads progress, civilization, and refinement. It constitutes the very mud-sill of society and of political government; and you might as well attempt to build a house in the air, as to build either the one or the other, except on this mud-sill. Fortunately for the South, she found a race adapted to that purpose to her hand. A race inferior to her own, but eminently qualified in temper, in vigor, in docility, in capacity to stand the climate, to answer all her purposes. We use them for our purpose, and call them slaves. We found them slaves by the common 'consent of mankind,' which, according to Cicero, *'lex naturae est.'* The highest proof of what is Nature's law."

Hammond reminded the North that it too has a slave "mud-sill" which it mishandled with tragic results:

> "The difference between us is, that our slaves are hired for life and well compensated; there is no starvation, no begging, no want of employment among our people, and not too much employment either. Yours are hired by the day, not cared for, and scantily compensated, which may be proved in the most painful manner, at any hour in any street in any of your large towns. Why, you meet more beggars in one day, in any single street of the city of New York, than you would meet in a lifetime in the whole South. We do not think that whites should be slaves either by law or necessity. Our slaves are black, of another and inferior race. The *status* in which we

have placed them is an elevation. They are elevated from the condition in which God first created them, by being made our slaves. None of that race on the whole face of the globe can be compared with the slaves of the South. They are happy, content, unaspiring, and utterly incapable, from intellectual weakness, ever to give us any trouble by their aspirations."

The Hammond account does not find much support in the recollections of an ex-slave, Ben Simpson, whose narrative is preserved in *Lay My Burden Down, A Folk History of Slavery*, edited by B. A. Botkin. Simpson says:

". . . I's born in Georgia. . . . My father's name was Roger Stielszen, and my mother's name was Betty. Massa Earl Stielszen captures them in Africa and brung them to Georgia. He got kilt, and my sister and me went to his son. His son was a killer. He got in trouble there in Georgia and got him two good-stepping hosses and the covered wagon. Then he chains all he slaves round the necks and fastens the chains to the hosses and makes them walk all the way to Texas. My mother and my sister had to walk. Emma was my sister. Somewhere on the road it went to snowing, and Massa wouldn't let us wrap anything round our feet. We had to sleep on the ground, too, in all that snow.

". . . Mother, she give out on the way, 'bout the line of Texas. Her feet got raw and bleeding, and her legs swoll plumb out of shape. Then Massa, he just take out he gun and shot her, and whilst she lay dying he kicks her two-three times and say, 'Damn a nigger what can't stand nothing.' Boss, you know that man, he wouldn't bury my mother, just leave her laying where he shot her at. You know, then there wasn't no law 'gainst killing nigger slaves.

"He come plumb to Austin through that snow. He taken up farming and changes he name to Alex Simpson and changes our names, too. He cut logs and built he home on the side of them mountains. We never had no quarters. When nighttime come, he locks the chain round our necks and then locks it round a tree. Boss, our bed were the ground. All he feed us was raw meat and green corn. Boss, I et many a green weed. I was hungry. He never let us eat at noon, he worked us all day without stopping. We went naked, that the way he worked us. We never had any clothes.

"He brands us. He brand my mother before us left Georgia. Boss, that nearly kilt her. He brand her in the breast, then between the shoulders. He brand all us.

"My sister, Emma, was the only woman he have till he marries. Emma was wife of all seven Negro slaves. He sold her when she's 'bout fifteen, just before her baby was born. I never seen her since.

". . . We wore chains all the time. When we work, we drug them chains with us. At night he lock us to a tree to keep us from running off. He didn't have to do that. We were 'fraid to run. We knew he'd kill us. Besides he brands us, and they no way to git it off. It's put there with a hot iron. You can't git it off.

"If a slave die, Massa made the rest of us tie a rope round he feet and drag him off. Never buried one, it was too much trouble."

Simpson's remembrances of brutality are enlarged upon in Theodore Weld's documentary titled *American Slavery As It Is*. Dwight L. Dumond says "It is a book of horrors." Weld's introduction to the book constitutes a catalogue of human debasement:

"We will prove that the slaves in the United States are treated with barbarous inhumanity; that they are overworked, underfed, wretchedly clad and lodged, and have insufficient sleep; that they are often made to wear round their necks iron collars armed with prongs, to drag heavy chains and weights at their feet while working in the field, and to wear yokes, and bells, and iron horns; that they are often kept confined in the stocks day and night for weeks together, made to wear gags in their mouths for hours or days, have some of their front teeth torn out or broken off, that they may be easily detected when they run away; that they are frequently flogged with terrible severity, have red pepper rubbed into their lacerated flesh, and hot brine, spirits of turpentine, etc. poured over the gashes to increase the torture; that they are often stripped naked, their backs and limbs cut with knives, bruised and mangled by scores and hundreds of blows with the paddle, and terribly torn by the claws of cats, drawn over them by their tormentors; that they are often hunted with bloodhounds and shot down like beasts, or torn in pieces by dogs; that they are often suspended by the arms and whipped and beaten till they faint, and when, revived by restoratives, beaten again till they faint and sometimes till they die; that their ears are often cut off, their eyes knocked out, their bones broken, their flesh branded with red hot irons; that they are maimed, mutilated and burned to death over slow fires. . . . We will establish all these facts by the testimony of scores and hundreds of eye witnesses, by the testimony of *slaveholders* in all parts of the slave states, by slaveholding members of Congress and of state legislatures, by ambassadors to foreign courts, by judges, by doctors of divinity, and clergymen of all denominations, by merchants, mechanics, lawyers and physicians, by presidents and professors in college and professional seminaries, by planters, overseers and drivers. We shall show, not merely that such deeds are committed, but that they are frequent; not done in corners, but before the sun; not in one of the slave states, but in all of them; not perpetrated by brutal overseers and drivers merely, but by magistrates, by legislators, by professors of religion, by preachers of the gospel, by governors of states, by gentlemen of property and standing, and by delicate females moving in the highest circles of society."

The harsh and oppressive treatment meted out to the slaves by the slaveholders inevitably led to forms of individual and organized resistance. There are indications that at least 250 slave revolts transpired in the United States. Three of the organized revolts are well-known to history. In 1800 Gabriel Prosser headed a rebellion in Virginia. Denmark Vesey tried a similar—though logistically—improved rebellion. Then in 1831 came the important and singularly famous Nat Turner Revolt. Those who felt that the Negro had no deep instinct for liberty were confounded by these uprisings.

Another reaction to slavery as a social and moral ill found expression in a proliferation of anti-slavery societies. They included the Negro conventions, the Negro church as well as the many local offshoots of the American Anti-Slavery Society.

William Hamilton Refutes

Alleged Negro Inferiority

. . . THE proposition has been advanced by men who claim a pre-eminence in the learned world, that Africans are inferior to white men in the structure both of body and mind; the first member of this proposition is below our notice; the reasons assigned for the second are, that we have not produced any poets, mathematicians, or any to excel in any science whatever; our being oppressed and held in slavery forms no excuse, because, say they, among the Romans, their most excellent artists and greatest scientific characters were frequently their slaves, and that these on account of their ascendant abilities, arose to superior stations in the state; and they exultingly *tell* us that these slaves were white men. . . .

Among the Roman's it was only necessary for the slave to be manumitted, in order to be eligible to all the offices of state, together with the emoluments belonging thereto; no sooner was he free than there was open before him a wide field of employment for his ambition, and learning and abilities with merit, were as sure to meet with their reward in him, as in any other citizen. But what station above the common employment of craftsmen and labourers would we fill did we possess both learning and abilities; is there ought to enkindle in us one spark of emulation; must not he who makes any considerable advances under present circumstance be almost a prodigy: although it may be true we have not produced any to excel in arts and sciences, yet if our situation be properly considered, and the allowances made which ought to be, it will soon be perceived that we do not fall far behind those who boast of a superior judgment, we have produced some who have claimed attention, and whose works have been admired, yes in despight of all our embarresments our genious does sometimes burst forth from its incumbrance. . . .

. . . THESE thoughts were suggested by the promulgation of a late bill, before the Senate of Pennsylvania, to prevent the emigration of people of color into this state. It was not passed into a law at this session, and must in consequence lay over until the next, before when we sincerely hope, the white men, whom we should look upon as our protectors, will have become convinced of the inhumanity and impolicy of such a measure, and forbear to deprive us of those inestimable treasures, liberty and independence. This is almost the only state in the Union wherein the African race have justly boasted of rational liberty and the protection of the laws, and shall it now be said they have been deprived of that liberty, and publicly exposed for sale to the highest bidder? Shall colonial inhumanity that has marked many of us with shameful stripes, become the practice of the

erly and duly enforced. We wish not to screen the guilty from punishment, but with the guilty do not permit the innocent to suffer. If there are worthless men, there are also men of merit among the African race, who are useful members of Society. The truth of this let their benevolent institutions and the numbers clothed and fed by them witness. Punish the guilty man of color to the utmost limit of the laws, but sell him not to slavery! If he is in danger of becoming a public charge, prevent him! If he is too indolent to labor for his own subsistence, compel him to do so; but sell him not to slavery. By selling him you do not make him better, but commit a wrong, without benefiting the object of it or society at large. . . .

Has the God who made the white man and the black left any record declaring us a different species? Are we not sustained by the same power, supported by the same food, hurt by

James Forten of Philadelphia

people of Pennsylvania, while Mercy stands weeping at the miserable spectacle? People of Pennsylvania, descendants of the immortal Penn, doom us not to the unhappy fate of thousands of our countrymen in the Southern States and the West Indies; despise the traffic in blood, and the blessing of the African will forever be around you. Many of us are men of property, for the security of which we have hitherto looked to the laws of our blessed state, but should this become a law, our property is jeopardized, since the same power which can expose to sale an unfortunate fellow creature, can wrest from him those estates, which years of honest industry have accumulated. Where shall the poor African look for protection, should the people of Pennsylvania consent to oppress him? We grant there are a number of worthless men belonging to our color, but there are laws of sufficient rigor for their punishment, if prop-

the same wounds, wounded by the same wrongs, pleased with the same delights, and propagated by the same means? And should we not then enjoy the same liberty, and be protected by the same laws? We wish not to legislate, for our means of information and the acquisition of knowledge are, in the nature of things, so circumscribed, that we must consider ourselves incompetent to the task: but let us, in legislation be considered as men. It cannot be that the authors of our Constitution intended to exclude us from its benefits, for just emerging from unjust and cruel emancipation, their souls were too much affected with their own deprivations to commence the reign of terror over others. They knew we were deeper skinned than they were, but they acknowledged us as men, and found that many an honest heart beat beneath a dusky bosom. They felt that they had no more authority to enslave us, than

1813
Philadelphia

Inequities cited
in Pennsylvania bill
against Negro emigration

England had to tyrannize over them. They were convinced that if amenable to the same laws in our actions we should be protected by the same laws in our rights and privileges. Actuated by these sentiments they adopted the glorious fabric of our liberties, and declaring "all men" free, they did not particularize white and black, because they never supposed it would be made a question whether *we were men or not*. Sacred be the ashes, and deathless be the memory of those heroes who are dead; and revered be the persons and the

ties, as not only cruel in the extreme, but decidedly unconstitutional both as regards the letter and spirit of that glorious instrument. The same power which protects the white man, should protect the black.

The evils arising from the bill before our Legislature, so fatal to the rights of freemen, and so characteristic of European despotism, are so numerous, that to consider them all would extend these numbers further than time or my talent will permit me to carry them. The concluding paragraph of my last

Protests Negro "Registration"

characters of those who still exist and lift the thunders of admonition against the traffic in blood. . . .

Let us put a case, in which the law in question operates peculiarly hard and unjust.—I have a brother, perhaps, who resides in a distant part of the Union, and after a separation of years, actuated by the same fraternal affection which beats in the bosom of a white man, he comes to visit me. Unless that brother be registered in twenty-four hours after, and be able to produce a certificate of that effect, he is liable, according to the second and third sections of the bill, to a fine of twenty dollars, to arrest, imprisonment and sale. Let the unprejudiced mind ponder upon this, and then pronounce it the justifiable act of a free people, if he can. To this we trust our cause, without fear of the issue. The unprejudiced must pronounce any act tending to deprive a free man of his right, freedom and immuni-

utterance, states a case of peculiar hardship, arising from the second section of this bill, upon which I cannot refrain from making a few more remarks. The man of color receiving as a visitor any other person of color, is bound to turn informer, and rudely report to the Register, that a friend and brother has come to visit him for a few days, whose name he must take within twenty-four hours, or forfeit a sum which the iron hand of the law is authorized to rend from him, partly for the benefit of the Register. Who is this Register? A man, and exercising an office, where ten dollars is the fee for each delinquent, will probably be a cruel man and find delinquents where they really do not exist. The poor black is left to the merciless gripe of an avaricious Register, without an appeal, in the event, from his tyranny or oppression! O miserable race, born to the same hopes, created with the same feeling, and destined for the same goal, you are reduced by your fellow creatures below the brute. The dog is protected and pampered at the board of his master, while the poor African and his descendant, whether a Saint or a felon, is branded with infamy, registered as a slave, and we may expect shortly to find a law to prevent their increase, by taxing them according to numbers, and authorizing the Constables to seize and confine every one who dare to walk the streets without a collar on his neck!—What have the people of color been guilty of, that they more than others, should be compelled to register their houses, lands, servants and *children?* Yes, ye rulers of the black man's destiny, reflect upon this: our *children* must be registered, and bear about them a certificate, or be subject to imprisonment and fine. You, who are perusing this effusion of feeling, are you a parent? Have you children around whom your affections are bound, by those delightful bonds which none but a parent can know? Are they the delight of your prosperity, and the solace of your afflictions? If all this be true, to you we submit our cause. The parent's feeling cannot err. By your verdict will we stand or fall—by your verdict, live slaves or freeman. It is said that the bill does not extend to children, but the words of the bill are, "Whether as an *inmate, visitor, hireling, or tenant, in his or her house or room.*" Whether this does not embrace every soul that can be in a house, the reader is left to judge; and whether the father should be bound to register his child, even within the twenty-four hours after it is brought into the world, let the father's feelings determine. This is the fact, and our children sent on our lawful business, not having sense enough to understand the meaning of such proceedings, must show their certificate of registry or be borne to prison. The bill specifies neither age nor sex—designates neither the honest man or the vagabond—but like the fretted porcupine, his quills aim its deadly shafts promiscuously at all.

For the honor and dignity of our native state, we wish not to see this bill pass into a law. . . .

It is to be hoped that in our Legislature there is patriotism, humanity, and mercy sufficient to crush this attempt upon the civil liberty of freemen, and to prove that the enlightened body who have hitherto guarded their fellow creatures, without regard to the color of the skin, will still stretch forth the wings of protection to that race, whose persons have been the scorn, and whose calamities have been the jest of the world for ages. We trust the time is at hand when this obnoxious Bill will receive its death warrant, and freedom still remain to cheer the bosom of a man of color. . . .

—Are not men of color sufficiently degraded? Why then increase their degradation? It is a well known fact, that black people, upon certain days of public jubilee, dare not be seen after twelve o'clock in the day, upon the field to enjoy the times; for no sooner do the fumes of that potent devil, Liquor, mount into the brain, than the poor black is assailed like the destroying Hyena or the avaricious Wolf! I allude particularly to the *Fourth of July!*—Is it not wonderful, that the day set apart for the festival of liberty, should be abused by the advocates of freedom, in endeavoring to sully what they profess to adore. If men, though they know that the law protects all, will dare, in defiance of law, to execute their hatred upon the defenceless black, will they not by the passage of this bill, believe him still more a mark for their venom and spleen?—Will they not believe him completely deserted by authority, and subject to every outrage brutality can inflict—too surely they will, and the poor wretch will turn his eyes around to look in vain for protection. . . .

There are men among us of reputation and property, as good citizens as any men can be, and who, for their property, pay as heavy taxes as any citizens are compelled to pay.

All taxes, except personal, fall upon them, and still even they are not exempted from this degrading bill. The villainous part of the community, of all colors, we wish to see punished and retrieved as much as any people can. Enact laws to punish them severely, but do not let them operate against the innocent as well as the guilty. . . .

By the third section of this bill, which is its peculiar hardship, the police officers are authorized to apprehend any black, whether a vagrant or a man of reputable character, who cannot produce a certificate that he has been registered. He is to be arrayed before a justice, who is thereupon to commit him to prison!—The jailor is to advertise a Freeman, and at the expiration of six months, if no owner appear for this degraded black, he is to be *exposed to sale*, and if not sold to be confined at hard labor for seven years! ! —Man of feeling, read this!—No matter who, no matter where. The constable, whose antipathy generally against the black is very great, will take every opportunity of hurting his feelings!—Perhaps he sees him at a distance, and having a mind to raise the boys in hue and cry against him, exclaims, "Halloa! Stop the Negro!" The boys, delighting in the sport, immediately begin to hunt him, and immediately from a hundred tongues is heard the cry—*"Hoa, Negro, where is your Certificate!"*—Can anything be done more shocking to the principles of civil liberty! A person arriving from another state, ignorant of the existence of such a law, may fall a victim to its cruel oppression. But he is to be advertised, and if no owner appear—how can an owner appear for a man who is free and belongs to no one!—if no owner appear, he is exposed for sale!—Oh, inhuman spectacle: found in no unjust act, convicted of no crime, he is barbarously sold, like the produce of the soil, to the highest bidder, or what is still worse, for no crimes, without the inestimable privilege of a trial by his peers, doomed to the dreary walls of a prison for the term of seven

tedious years!—My God, what a situation is his! Search the legends of tyranny and find no precedent. No example can be found in all the reigns of violence and oppression, which have marked the lapse of time. It stands alone. It has been left for Pennsylvania to raise her ponderous arm against the liberties of the black, whose greatest boast has been that he resided in a state where civil liberty, and sacred justice were administered alike to all. . . .

The fifth section of this bill is also peculiarly hard, inasmuch as it prevents freemen from living where they please.—Pennsylvania has always been a refuge from slavery, and to this state the Southern black, when freed, has flown for safety. Why does he this? When masters in many of the Southern states, which they frequently do, free a particular black, unless the black leaves the state in so many hours, any person resident of the said state, can have him arrested and again sold to slavery:—The hunted black is obliged to flee, or remain and be again a slave. I have known persons of this description sold three times after being first emancipated. Where shall he go? Shut every state against him, and, like Pharaoh's kine, drive him into the sea.—Is there no spot on earth that will protect him! Against their inclination, his ancestors were forced from their homes by traders in human flesh, and even under such circumstances the wretched offspring are denied the protection you afford to brutes. . . .

I have done. My feelings are acute, and I have ventured to express them without intending either accusation or insult to any one. An appeal to the heart is my intention, and if I have failed, it is my great misfortune not to have had a power of eloquence sufficient to convince. But I trust the eloquence of nature will succeed, and that the law-givers of this happy Commonwealth will yet remain the Blacks' friend, and the advocates of Freemen.

James Forten of Philadelphia Protests Negro "Registration" □ 79

Resolutions Against

Proposed Colonization in Africa

Philadelphia, January 1817.

At a numerous meeting of the people of color, convened at Bethel church, to take into consideration the propriety of remonstrating against the contemplated measure, that is to exile us from the land of our nativity; James Forten was called to the chair, and Russell Parrott appointed secretary. The intent of the meeting having been stated by the chairman, the following resolutions were adopted, without one dissenting voice.

Whereas our ancestors (not of choice) were the first successful cultivators of the wilds of America, we their descendants feel ourselves entitled to participate in the blessings of her luxuriant soil, which their blood and sweat manured; and that any measure or system of measures, having a tendency to banish us from her bosom, would not only be cruel, but in direct violation of those principles, which have been the boast of this republic.

Resolved, That we view with deep abhorrence the unmerited stigma attempted to be cast upon the reputation of the free people of color, by the promoters of this measure, "that they are a dangerous and useless part of the community," when in the state of disfranchisement in which they live, in the hour of danger they ceased to remember their wrongs, and rallied around the standard of their country.

Resolved, That we never will separate ourselves voluntarily from the slave population in this country; they are our brethren by the ties of consanguinity, of suffering, and of wrong; and we feel that there is more virtue in suffering privations with them, than fancied advantages for a season.

Resolved, That without arts, without science, without a proper knowledge of government, to cast into the savage wilds of Africa the free people of color, seems to us the circuitous route through which they must return to perpetual bondage.

Resolved, That having the strongest confi-

January 1817
Philadelphia
and Richmond

Negroes
in Pennsylvania
and Virginia
avow their Americanism

dence in the justice of God, and philanthropy of the free states, we cheerfully submit our destinies to the guidance of Him who suffers not a sparrow to fall, without his special providence. . . .

At a meeting of a respectable portion of the free people of color of the city of Richmond, on Friday, January 24, 1817, William Bowler was appointed chairman, and Lentey Craw, secretary. The following preamble and resolution were read, unanimously adopted, and ordered to be printed.

Whereas a Society has been formed at the seat of government, for the purpose of colonizing, with their own consent, the free people of color of the United States; therefore, we, the free people of color of the city of Richmond, have thought it advisable to assemble together under the sanction of authority, for the purpose of making a public expression of our sentiments on a question in which we are so deeply interested. We perfectly agree with the Society, that it is not only proper, but would ultimately tend to the benefit and

advantage of a great portion of our suffering fellow creatures, to be colonized; but while we thus express our approbation of a measure laudable in its purposes, and beneficial in its designs, it may not be improper in us to say, that we prefer being colonized in the most remote corner of the land of our nativity, to being exiled to a foreign country—and whereas the president and board of managers of the said Society have been pleased to leave it to the entire discretion of Congress to provide a suitable place for carrying these laudable intentions into effect—Be it therefore

Resolved, That we respectfully submit to the wisdom of Congress whether it would not be an act of charity to grant us a small portion of their territory, either on the Missouri river, or any place that may seem to them most conducive to the public good and our future welfare, subject, however, to such rules and regulations as the government of the United States may think proper to adopt. . . .

The Tallmadge Amendment

February 13, 1819

. . . THAT the further introduction of slavery or involuntary servitude be prohibited, except for the punishment of crimes, whereof the party shall be duly convicted; and that all children of slaves, born within the said state, after the admission thereof into the Union, shall be free but may be held to service until the age of twenty-five years.

The Taylor Amendment

January 26, 1820

. . . MR. TAYLOR, of New York, proposed to amend the bill by incorporating in that section the following provision: ". . . And shall ordain and establish, that there shall be neither slavery nor involuntary servitude in the said State, otherwise than in the punishment of crimes, whereof the party shall have been duly convicted: Provided, always, That any person escaping into the same, from whom labor or service is lawfully claimed in any other State, such fugitive may be lawfully reclaimed, and conveyed to the person claiming his or her labor or service as aforesaid: And provided, also, That the said provision shall not be construed to alter the condition or civil rights of any person now held to service or labor in the said Territory."

The Thomas Amendment

February 17, 1820

. . . THAT, in all that territory ceded by France to the United States, under the name of Louisiana, . . . excepting only such part thereof as is included within the limits of the State contemplated by this act, slavery and involuntary servitude, otherwise than in punishment of crimes whereof the party shall have been duly convicted, shall be and is hereby forever prohibited: Provided always, That any person escaping into the same, from whom labor or service is lawfully claimed in any State or Territory of the United States, such fugitive may be lawfully reclaimed, and conveyed to the person claiming his or her labor or service, as aforesaid.

The great debate begins
on extension of
slavery into new states

The Missouri Compromise

Missouri Enabling Act

March 6, 1820

BE it enacted That the inhabitants of that portion of the Missouri territory included within the boundaries hereinafter designated, be, and they are hereby, authorized to form for themselves a constitution and state government, and to assume such name as they shall deem proper; and the said state, when formed, shall be admitted into the Union, upon an equal footing with the original states, in all respects whatsoever. . . .

. . . That all free white male citizens of the United States, who shall have arrived at the age of twenty-one years, and have resided in said territory three months previous to the day of election, and all other persons qualified to vote for representatives to the general assembly of the said territory, shall be qualified to be elected, and they are hereby qualified and authorized to vote, and choose representatives to form a convention. . . .

. . . That in all that territory ceded by France to the United States under the name of Louisiana . . . not included within the limits of the state, contemplated by this act, slavery and involuntary servitude, otherwise than in the punishment of crimes, whereof the parties shall have been duly convicted, shall be, and is hereby, forever prohibited: Provided always, That any person escaping into the same, from whom labour or service is lawfully claimed, in any state or territory of the United States, such fugitive may be lawfully reclaimed and conveyed to the person claiming his or her labour or service as aforesaid.

The Constitution of Missouri

July 19, 1820

. . . THE general assembly shall not have power to pass laws—

1. For the emancipation of slaves without the consent of their owners; or without paying them, before such emancipation, a full equivalent for such slaves so emancipated; and,

2. To prevent bona-fide immigrants to this State, or actual settlers therein, from bringing from any of the United States, or from any of their Territories, such persons as may there be deemed to be slaves, so long as any persons of the same description are allowed to be held as slaves by the laws of this State.

They shall have power to pass laws—

1. To prevent bona-fide immigrants to this State of any slaves who may have committed any high crime in any other State or Territory;

2. To prohibit the introduction of any slave for the purpose of speculation, or as an article of trade or merchandise;

3. To prohibit the introduction of any slave, or the offspring of any slave, who heretofore may have been, or who hereafter may be, imported from any foreign country into the United States, or any Territory thereof, in contravention of any existing statute of the United States; and,

4. To permit the owners of slaves to emancipate them, saving the right of creditors, where the person so emancipating will give security that the slave so emancipated shall not become a public charge.

It shall be their duty, as soon as may be, to pass such laws as may be necessary—

1. To prevent free negroes end (and) mulattoes from coming to and settling in this State, under any pretext whatsoever; and

2. To oblige the owners of slaves to treat them with humanity, and to abstain from all injuries to them extending to life or limb.

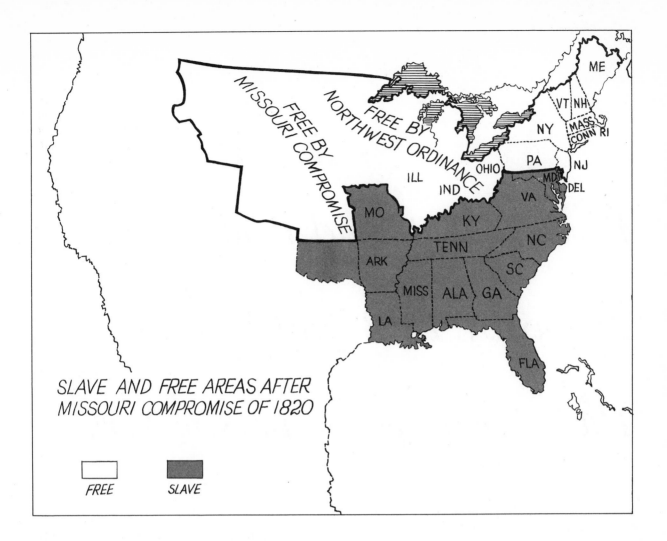

SLAVE AND FREE AREAS AFTER
MISSOURI COMPROMISE OF 1820

FREE   SLAVE

Resolution for the Admission of Missouri

March 2, 1821

RESOLVED, That Missouri shall be admitted into this union on an equal footing with the original states, in all respects whatever, upon the fundamental condition, that the fourth clause of the twenty-sixth section of the third article of the constitution submitted [by Missouri] to Congress, shall never be construed to authorize the passage of any law, and that no law shall be passed in conformity thereto, by which any citizen, of either of the states in this Union, shall be excluded from the enjoyment of any of the privileges and immunities to which such citizen is entitled under the constitution of the United States: Provided, That the legislature of the said state, by a solemn public act, shall declare the assent of the said state to the said fundamental condition, and shall transmit to the President of the United States, on or before the fourth Monday in November next, an authentic copy of the said act; upon the receipt whereof, the President, by proclamation, shall announce the fact; whereupon, and without any further proceeding on the part of Congress, the admission of the said state into this Union shall be considered as complete.

Reverend Nathaniel Paul,

Albany (N.Y.) Baptist Preacher,

Hails Emancipation in New York

... THE progress of emancipation, though slow, is nevertheless certain: It is certain, because that God who has made of one blood all nations of men, and who is said to be no respecter of persons, has so decreed; I therefore have no hesitation in declaring from this sacred place, that not only throughout the United States of America, but throughout every part of the habitable world where slavery exists, it will be abolished. However great may be the opposition of those who are supported by the traffic, yet slavery will cease. The lordly planter who has his thousands in bondage, may stretch himself upon his couch of ivory, and sneer at the exertions which are made by the humane and benevolent, or he may take his stand upon the floor of Congress, and mock the pitiful generosity of the east or west for

daring to meddle with the subject, and attempting to expose its injustice: he may threaten to resist all efforts for a general or a partial emancipation even to a dissolution of the union. But still I declare that slavery will be extinct; a universal and not a partial emancipation must take place; nor is the period far distant. The indefatigable exertions of the philanthropists in England to have it abolished in their West India Islands, the recent revolutions in South America, the catastrophe and exchange of power in the Isle of Hayti, the restless disposition of both master and slave in the southern states, the constitution of our government, the effects of literary and moral instruction, the generous feelings of the pious and benevolent, the influence and spread of the holy religion of the cross of Christ, and the irrevocable decrees of Almighty God, all combine their efforts and

July 5, 1827
Albany,
New York

New York's
abolition of
slavery celebrated

with united voice declare, that the power of tyranny must be subdued, the captive must be liberated, the oppressed go free, and slavery must revert back to its original chaos of darkness, and be forever annihilated from the earth. Did I believe that it would always continue, and that man to the end of time would be permitted with impunity to usurp the same undue authority over his fellow, I would disallow any allegiance or obligation I was under to my fellow creatures, or any submission that I owed to the laws of my country; I would deny the superintending power of divine providence in the affairs of this life; I would ridicule the religion of the Saviour of the world, and treat as the worst of men the ministers of an everlasting gospel; I would consider my Bible as a book of false and delusive fables, and commit it to the flames; nay, I would still go farther; I would at once confess myself an atheist, and deny the existence of a holy God. But slavery will cease, and the equal rights of man will be universally acknowledged. Nor is its tardy progress any argument against its final accomplishment. But do I hear it loudly responded, —this is but a mere wild fanaticism, or at best but the misguided conjecture of an untutored descendant of Africa. Be it so. I confess my ignorance, and bow with due deference to my superiors in understanding; but if in this case I err, the error is not peculiar to myself; if I wander, I wander in a region of light from whose political hemisphere the sun of liberty pours forth his refulgent rays, around which dazzle the star-like countenances of Clarkson, Wilberforce, Pitt, Fox and Grenville, Washington, Adams, Jefferson, Hancock and Franklin; if I err, it is their sentiments that have caused me to stray. . . .

Freedom's Journal,

First Negro Newspaper, Appears

March 16, 1827

FREEDOM'S JOURNAL.

" RIGHTEOUSNESS EXALTETH A NATION."

CORNISH & RUSSWURM,
Editors & Proprietors. NEW-YORK, FRIDAY, MARCH 16, 1827. VOL. I. NO. 1.

TO OUR PATRONS.

IN presenting our first number to our Patrons, we feel all the diffidence of persons entering upon a new and untried line of business. But a moment's reflection upon the noble objects, which we have in view by the publication of this Journal; the expediency of its appearance at this time, when so many schemes are in action concerning our people—encourage us to come boldly before an enlightened publick. For we believe, that a paper devoted to the dissemination of useful knowledge among our brethren, and to their moral and religious improvement, must meet with the cordial approbation of every friend to humanity.

The peculiarities of this Journal, render it important that we should advertise to the world the motives by which we are actuated, and the objects which we contemplate.

We wish to plead our own cause. Too long have others spoken for us. Too long has the publick been deceived by misrepresentations, in things which concern us dearly, though in the estimation of some mere trifles; for though there are many in society who exercise towards us benevolent feelings; still (with sorrow we confess it) there

works of trivial importance, we shall consider it a part of our duty to recommend to our young readers, such authors as will not only enlarge their stock of useful knowledge, but such as will also serve to stimulate them to higher attainments in science.

We trust also, that through the columns of the FREEDOM'S JOURNAL, many practical pieces, having for their bases, the improvement of our brethren, will be presented to them, from the pens of many of our respected friends, who have kindly promised their assistance.

It is our earnest wish to make our Journal a medium of intercourse between our brethren in the different states of this great confederacy: that through its columns an expression of our sentiments, on many interesting subjects which concern us, may be offered to the publick: that plans which apparently are beneficial may be candidly discussed and properly weighed; if worthy, receive our cordial approbation; if not, our marked disapprobation.

Useful knowledge of every kind, and every thing that relates to Africa, shall find a ready admission into our columns; and as that vast continent becomes daily more known, we trust that many things will come to light, proving

narrative which they have published; the establishment of the republic of Hayti after years of sanguinary warfare; its subsequent progress in all the arts of civilization; and the advancement of liberal ideas in South America, where despotism has given place to free governments, and where many of our brethren now fill important civil and military stations, prove the contrary.

The interesting fact that there are FIVE HUNDRED THOUSAND free persons of colour, one half of whom might peruse, and the whole be benefitted by the publication of the Journal; that no publication, as yet, has been devoted exclusively to their improvement—that many selections from approved standard authors, which are within the reach of few, may occasionally be made—and more important still, that this large body of our citizens have no public channel—all serve to prove the real necessity, at present, for the appearance of the FREEDOM'S JURNAL.

It shall ever be our desire so to conduct the editorial department of our paper as to give offence to none of our patrons; as nothing is farther from us than to make it the advocate of any partial views, either in politics or religion. What few days we can number, have been devoted to the improvement of our breth-

March 16, 1827
New York City

Editor-Publishers,
Samuel Cornish
and John B. Russwurm,
announce their policies

In presenting our first number to our Patrons, we feel all the diffidence of persons entering upon a new and untried line of business. But a moment's reflection upon the noble objects, which we have in view by the publication of this Journal; the expediency of its appearance at this time, when so many schemes are in action concerning our people —encourage us to come boldly before an enlightened publick. For we believe, that a paper devoted to the dissimination of useful knowledge among our brethren, and to their moral and religious improvement, must meet with the cordial approbation of every friend to humanity.

The peculiarities of this Journal, renders it important that we should advertise to the world our motives by which we are actuated, and the objects which we contemplate.

We wish to plead our own cause. Too long have others spoken for us. Too long has the publick been deceived by misrepresentations, in things which concern us dearly, though in the estimation of some mere trifles; for though there are many in society who exercise towards us benevolent feelings; still (with sorrow we confess it) there are others who make it their business to enlarge upon the least trifle, which tends to the discredit of any person of colour; and pronounce anathemas and denounce our whole body for the misconduct of this guilty one. We are aware that there are many instances of vice among us, but we avow that it is because no one has taught its subjects to be virtuous; many instances of poverty, because no sufficient efforts accommodated to minds contracted by slavery, and deprived of early education have been made, to teach them how to husband their hard earnings, and to secure to themselves comfort.

Education being an object of the highest importance to the welfare of society, we shall endeavour to present just and adequate views of it, and to urge upon our brethren the necessity and expediency of training their children, while young, to habits of industry, and thus forming them for becoming useful members of society. . . .

Though not desiring of dictating, we shall feel it our incumbent duty to dwell occasionally upon the general principles and rules of economy. . . .

The civil rights of a people being of the greatest value, it shall ever be our duty to vindicate our brethren, when oppressed; and to lay the case before the publick. We shall also urge upon our brethren, (who are qualified by the laws of the different states) the expediency of using their elective franchise; and of making an independent use of the same. We wish them not to become the tools of party.

And as much time is frequently lost, and wrong principles instilled, by the perusal of works of trivial importance, we shall consider it a part of our duty to recommend to our young readers, such authors as will not only enlarge their stock of useful knowledge, but such as will also serve to stimulate them to higher attainments in science.

We trust also, that through the columns of the FREEDOM'S JOURNAL, many practical pieces, having for their bases, the improvement of our brethren, will be presented to them, from the pens of many of our respected friends, who have kindly promised their assistance.

It is our earnest wish to make our Journal a medium of intercourse between our brethren in the different states of this great confederacy: that through its columns an expression of our sentiments, on many interesting subjects which concern us, may be offered to the publick: that plans which apparently are beneficial may be candidly discussed and properly weighed; if worth, receive our cordial approbation; if not, our marked disapprobation.

Useful knowledge of every kind, and everything that relates to Africa, shall find a ready admission into our columns; and as that vast continent becomes daily more known, we trust that many things will come to light, proving that the natives of it are neither so ignorant nor stupid as they have generally been supposed to be.

And while these important subjects shall occupy the columns of the FREEDOM'S JOURNAL, we would not be unmindful of our brethren who are still in the iron fetters of bondage. They are our kindred by all the ties of nature; and though but little can be effected by us, still let our sympathies be poured forth . . .

From the press and the pulpit we have suffered much by being incorrectly represented. Men whom we equally love and admire have not hesitated to represent us disadvantageously, without becoming personally acquainted with the true state of things, nor discerning between virtue and vice among us. . . .

In the spirit of candor and humility we intend by a simple representation of facts to lay our case before the public, with a view to arrest the progress of prejudice, and to shield ourselves against the consequent evils. We wish to conciliate all and to irritate none, yet we must be firm and unwavering in our principles, and persevering in our efforts.

If ignorance, poverty and degradation have hitherto been our unhappy lot; has the Eternal decree gone forth, that our race alone are to remain in this state, while knowledge and civilization are shedding their enlivening rays over the rest of the human family? The recent travels of Denham and Clapperton in the interior of Africa, and the interesting narrative which they have published; the establishment of the republic of Hayti after years of sanguinary warfare; its subsequent progress in all the arts of civilization; and the advancement of liberal ideas in South America, where despotism has given place to free governments, and where many of our brethren now fill important civil and military stations, prove the contrary.

It shall ever be our desire so to conduct the editorial department of our paper as to give offence to none of our patrons; as nothing is farther from us than to make it the advocate of any partial views, either in politics or religion. What few days we can number, have been devoted to the improvement of our brethren; and it is our earnest wish that the remainder may be spent in the same delightful service.

In conclusion, whatever concerns us as a people, will ever find a ready admission into the FREEDOM'S JOURNAL, interwoven with all the principal news of the day.

The interesting fact that there are FIVE HUNDRED THOUSAND free persons of colour, one half of whom might peruse, and the whole be benefitted by the publication of the Journal; that no publication, as yet, has been devoted exclusively to their improvement— that many selections from approved standard authors, which are within the reach of few, may occasionally be made—and more important still, that this large body of our citizens have no public channel—all serve to prove the real necessity, at present, for the appearance of the FREEDOM'S JOURNAL.

Freedom's Journal

Reports a Lynching

Tuscaloosa, Alabama, June 20, 1827

Horrid Occurrence.—Some time during the last week one of those outrageous transactions—and we really think, disgraceful to the character of civilized man, took place near the north east boundary line of Perry, adjoining Bibb and Autanga counties. The circumstances we are informed by a gentleman from that county, are— That a Mr. McNeily having lost some clothing or some other property, of no great value, the slave of a neighboring planter was charged with the theft. McNeily, in company with his brother, found the Negro driving his master's wagon, they seized him, and either did or were about to chastise him, when the Negro stabbed McNeily, so that he died in an hour afterwards; the Negro was taken before a Justice of the Peace, who, after serious deliberation, waived his authority—perhaps through fear, as the crowd of persons from the above counties had collected to the number of seventy or eighty, near Mr. People's (the justice) house. He acted as President of the mob, and put the vote, when it was decided he should be immediately executed by being *burnt to death*—then the sable culprit was led to a tree and tied to it, and a large quantity of pine knots collected and placed around him, and the fatal torch was applied to the pile, even against the remonstrances of several gentlemen who were present; and the miserable being was in a short time consumed to ashes. An inquest was held over the remains and the Sheriff of Perry county, with a company of about twenty men, repaired to the neighborhood where this barbarous act took place, to secure those concerned, but with what success we have not heard, but we hope he will succeed in bringing the perpetrators of so highhanded a measure to account to their country for their conduct in this affair. This is the second Negro who has been thus put to death, without Judge or Jury in that county.

Minutes

of the

First

Negro Convention

At a Convention held by adjournments from the 20th day of September, to the 24th of the same inclusive, 1830, in accordance with a public notice issued on behalf of the coloured citizens of Philadelphia, and addressed to their brethren throughout the U. States, inviting them to assemble by delegation, in Convention, to be held in the city of Philadelphia, on the 20th day of September, 1830, and signed on behalf, by the Rev. Bishop *Allen, Cyrus Black, Junius C. Morel, Benjamin Paschall*, jr., & *James Cornish*—

The delegation accordingly met in Bethel church, on the 20th of September, at 10 o'clock A. M. and after a chaste and appropriate prayer by the venerable Bishop *Allen*, the Convention was organized by electing

Rt. Rev. Richard Allen, *President.*
Dr. Belfast Burton, of Philadelphia,
and Austin Steward of Rochester, N.Y.
Vice Presidents
Junius C. Morel, of Philadelphia,
Secretary
and Robert Cowley, of Maryland,
Assistant Secretary.

On motion it was *Resolved,* That this Convention do recommend the formation of a Parent Society; and that immediately after its organization, to appoint a general corresponding Agent, to reside at or near the intended purchase in Upper Canada.

On motion it was *Resolved,* That this Convention enjoins and requires of each of its members to use their utmost influence in the formation of societies, *auxiliary* to the Parent Society about being established in the city of Philadelphia; and also to instruct the auxiliary societies when formed, to send delegates to the next General Convention.

On motion it was *Resolved,* That the next General Convention shall be composed of delegates appointed by the Parent Society and its auxiliaries: provided always, that the number of delegates from each society, shall not exceed five, and all other places, where there are no auxiliaries, are hereby invited to send one delegate.

On motion it was *Resolved,* That this Convention address the Free People of Colour throughout the United States, and publish in one of the daily papers of this city.

On motion it was *Resolved,* That the Convention do adjourn at the invitation of one of the managers of the Lombard-street Free School for colored children. The Convention were highly gratified at the order, regularity and improvement discoverable in the various departments, among a collection of children, Their specimens in writing, needle-work, &c. &c made a deep impression on the Convention, with a desire that the People of Colour

September
20-24,
1830
Philadelphia

Pioneer
protest organization
launches program
for Negro advancement

may availingly appreciate every extended opportunity for their improvement in the various situations where they may reside.

On motion, the House adjourned *sine die*.

Rt. Rev. Richard Allen, President
Junius C. Morel, Secretary

The following Delegates
composed the Convention, viz.

Pennsylvania—Rev. Richard Allen, Dr. Belfast Burton, Cyrus Black, Junius C. Morel, Benjamin Paschall, jr., James Cornish, Wm. S. Whipper, Peter Gardiner, John Allen, James Newman, Charles H. Leveck, Frederick A. Hinton.
New-York—Austin Steward, Jos. Adams, George L. Brown.
Connecticut—Scipio C. Augustus.
Rhode Island—George C. Willis, Alfred Niger.
Maryland—James Deavour, Hezekiah Grice, Aaron Willoon, Robert Cowley.
Delaware—Abraham D. Shad.
Virginia—Arthur M. Waring, Wm. Duncan, James West, jr.

Honorary Members.

Robert Brown, William Rogers, John Bowers, Richard Howell, Daniel Peterson, Charles Shorts, of Pennsylvania; Leven Williams, of New-York; James P. Walker, of Maryland; John Arnold, of New-Jersey; Sampson Peters, of New-Jersey; Rev. Anthony Campbell, of

Delaware; Don Carlos Hall, of Delaware. . . .

ADDRESS

*To the Free People of Colour
of these United States*

Brethren, Impressed with a firm and settled conviction, and more especially being taught by that inestimable and invaluable instrument, namely, the Declaration of Independence, that all men are born free and equal, and consequently are endowed with unalienable rights, among which are the enjoyments of life, liberty and the pursuits of happiness.

Viewing these as incontrovertable facts, we have been led to the following conclusions; that our forlorn and deplorable situation earnestly and loudly demands of us to devise and pursue all legal means for the speedy elevation of ourselves and brethren to the scale and standing of men.

And in pursuit of this great object, various ways and means have been resorted to; among others, the African Colonization Society is the most prominent. Not doubting the sincerity of many friends who are engaged in that cause; yet we beg leave to say, that it does not assist in this benevolent and important work.

To encourage our brethren earnestly to co-operate with us, we offer the following, viz. 1st. Under that government no invidious distinction of colour is recognized, but there we shall be entitled to all the rights, privileges and immunities of other citizens. 2d. That the language, climate, soil, and productions are similar to those in this country. 3d. That land of the best quality can be purchased at the moderate price of one dollar and fifty cents per acre, by the one hundred acres. 4th. The market for different kinds of produce raised in that colony, is such as to render a suitable reward to the industrious farmer, equal in our opinion to that of the United States. And lastly, as the erections of buildings must necessarily claim the attention of the emigrants, we would invite the mechanics from our large cities to embark in the enterprise; the advancement of architecture depending much on their exertions, as they must consequently take with them the arts and improvements of our well regulated communities.

It will be much to the advantage of those who have large families, and desire to see them happy and respected, to locate themselves in a land where the laws and prejudices of society will have no effect in retarding their advancement to the summit of civil and religious improvement. There the diligent student will have ample opportunity to reap the reward due to industry and perseverance; whilst those of moderate attainments, if properly nurtured, may be enabled to take their stand as men in the several offices and situations necessary to promote union, peace, order and tranquility. It is to these we must look for the strength and spirit of our future prosperity.

Before we close, we would just remark, that it has been a subject of deep regret to this convention, that we as a people, have not availingly appreciated every opportunity placed within our power by the benevolent efforts of the friends of humanity in elevating our condition to the rank of freemen. That our mental and physical qualities have not been more actively engaged in pursuits more lasting, is attributable in a great measure to a want of unity among ourselves; whilst our only stimulus to action has been to become domestics, which at best is but a precarious and degraded situation.

It is to obviate these evils, that we have recommended our views to our fellow-citizens in the foregoing instrument, with a desire of raising the moral and political standing of ourselves; and we cannot devise any plan more likely to accomplish this end, than by encouraging agriculture and mechanical arts: for by the first, we shall be enabled to act with a degree of independence, which as yet has fallen to the lot of but few among us; and the faithful pursuit of the latter, in connection with the sciences, which expand and ennoble the mind, will eventually give us the standing and condition we desire.

To effect these great objects, we would earnestly request our brethren throughout the United States, to co-operate with us, by forming societies *auxiliary* to the Parent Institution; about being established in the city of Philadelphia, under the patronage of the General Convention. And we further recommend to our friends and brethren, who reside in places where, *at present,* this may be impracticable, so far to aid us, by contributing to the funds of the Parent Institution; and, if disposed, to appoint one delegate to represent them in the next Convention; to be held in Philadelphia the first Monday in June next, it being fully understood, that organized societies be at liberty to send any number of delegates not exceeding *five*.

Signed by order of the Convention,
Rev. Richard Allen, *President,*
Senior Bishop of the
African Methodist Episcopal Churches.
Junius C. Morel, *Secretary*

THE LIBERATOR, *First Edition*

. . . DURING my recent tour for the purpose of exciting the minds of the people by a series of discourses on the subject of slavery, every place that I visited gave fresh evidence of the fact, that a greater revolution in public sentiment was to be effected in the free states —and particularly in New England—than at the south. I found contempt more bitter, opposition more active, detraction more relentless, prejudice more stubborn, and apathy more frozen, than among slave owners themselves. Of course, there were individual exceptions to the contrary. This state of things afflicted, but did not dishearten me. I determined, at every hazard, to lift up the standard of emancipation in the eyes of the nation, within sight of Bunker Hill and in the birth place of liberty. That standard is now unfurled; and long may it float, unhurt by the spoliations of time or the missiles of a desperate foe—yea, till every chain be broken, and every bondman set free! Let Southern oppressors tremble—let their secret abettors tremble—let their Northern apologists tremble—let all the enemies of the persecuted blacks tremble.

. . . I shall not array myself as the political partisan of any man. In defending the great cause of human rights, I wish to derive the assistance of all religions and of all parties.

Assenting to the "self evident truth" maintained in the American Declaration of Independence, . . . I shall strenuously contend for the immediate enfranchisement of our slave population. In Park-Street Church, on the Fourth of July, 1829, in an address on slavery, I unreflectingly assented to the popular but pernicious doctrine of gradual abolition. I seize this opportunity to make a full and unequivocal recantation, and thus publicly to ask pardon of my God, of my country, and of my brethren the poor slaves, for having uttered a sentiment so full of timidity, injustice and absurdity. A similar recantation, from my pen, was published in the Genius of Universal Emancipation at Baltimore, in September, 1829. My conscience is now satisfied.

I am aware, that many object to the severity of my language; but is there not cause for severity? I will be as harsh as truth, and as uncompromising as justice. On this subject, I do not wish to think, or speak, or write, with moderation. No! No! Tell a man whose house is on fire, to give a moderate alarm; tell him to moderately rescue his wife from the hands of the ravisher; tell the mother to gradually extricate her babe from the fire into which it has fallen;—but urge me not to use moderation in a cause like the present. I am in earnest—I will not equivocate—I will not excuse—I will not retreat a single inch—AND I WILL BE HEARD. . . .

William Lloyd Garrison

Philadelphia Negroes Petition

To the Honorable the Senate and House of Representatives of the Commonwealth of Pennsylvania:

The memorial of the people of color of the city of Philadelphia and its vicinity, respectfully showeth:

That they have learned with deep regret that two resolutions have passed the House of Representatives of this commonwealth, directing the committee of the judiciary to inquire—First, into the expediency of passing a law to protect the citizens of this commonwealth against the evils arising from the emigration of free blacks from other states into Pennsylvania—and, secondly, into the expediency of repealing so much of the Acts of Assembly passed on the 27th of March, 1820, and the 25th of March, 1826, as relates to fugitives from labor from other states, and of giving full effect to the act of Congress of the 12th of February, 1793, relative to such fugitives.

At the same time that your memorialists entertain the most perfect respect for any expression of sentiment emanating from so high a source as one of the legislative bodies of Pennsylvania, they cannot but lament, that at a moment when all mankind seem to be struggling for freedom, and endeavoring to throw off the shackles of political oppression, the constituted authorities of this great state should entertain a resolution which has a tendency to abridge the liberties heretofore accorded to a race of men confessedly oppressed. Our country asserts for itself the glory of being the freest upon the surface of the globe. She wrested that freedom, while yet in her infancy, by force of arms, at the expense of infinite blood and treasure, from a gigantic and most powerful adversary. She proclaimed freedom to all mankind—and offered her soil as a refuge to the enslaved of all nations. The brightness of her glory was radiant, but one dark spot still dimmed its lustre.

January 1832
Philadelphia

Protest: Restricted
Negro emigration
and diluted protection
of fugitive slaves

the Pennsylvania Legislature

Domestic slavery existed among a people who had themselves disdained to submit to a master. Many of the states of this union hastened to wipe out this blot: and foremost in the race was Pennsylvania. In less than four years after the declaration of independence by the act of 1st March, 1780, she abolished slavery within her limits, and from that time her avowed policy has been to enlarge and beautify this splendid feature in her system—to preserve unimpaired the freedom of all men, whatever might be the shade of complexion with which it may have pleased the *Almighty* to distinguish them. . . . "It is not for us to enquire," says the beautiful preamble to the act of 1780, . . . "why, in the creation of mankind, the inhabitants of the several parts of the earth were distinguished by a difference in feature or complexion—it is sufficient for us to know that all are the work of an Almighty hand." And from that day to the present, Pennsylvania has acted upon a principle,

that among those whom the same Almighty hand has formed, the hand of man should not presume to make a difference. And why, we respectfully ask, is this distinction now to be proclaimed for the first time in the code of Pennsylvania? Why are her borders to be surrounded by a wall of iron, against freemen, whose complexions fall below the wavering and uncertain shades of white? For this is the only criterion of admission or exclusion which the resolutions indicate. It is not to be asked, is he brave—is he honest—is he just— is he free from the stain of crime—but is he black—is he brown—is he yellow—is he other than white?

This is the criterion by which Pennsylvania, who for fifty years has indignantly rejected the distinction, who daily receives into her bosom all men, from all nations, is now called upon to reject from her soil, such portions of a banished race of freemen, born within view of her own mountains, as may seek within her limits a place of rest. We respectfully ask, is not this the spirit of the first resolution? And why, we repeat, shall this abandonment of the principles of your honorable forefathers *now* first take place in Pennsylvania? Have the rights we now possess been abused? The domestic history of Pennsylvania answers these questions in the negative. . . . Your memorialists are aware that prejudice has recently been exalted against them by unfounded reports of their concurrence in promoting servile insurrections. With the feeling of honest indignation, inspired by conscious innocence, they repel the slander. They feel themselves to be citizens of Pennsylvania. Many of them were descended from ancestors, who were raised with yours on this soil, to which they feel bound by the strongest ties. As children of the state, they look to it as a guardian and a protector, and in common with you feel the necessity of maintaining law and order, for the promotion of the commonweal. Equally unfounded is the charge, that this population fills the almshouses with paupers—and increases, in an undue proportion, the public burdens. We appeal to the facts and documents which accompany this memorial, as giving abundant refutation to an error so injurious to our character.

Unsupportable as your memorialists conceive the first resolution to be, the second, which proposes the repeal of so much of the laws of 1820 and 1826, as relates to fugitives from labor, is still more abhorrent to their feelings. What, let us ask, is the substance of these portions of the acts in question? Simply to take from aldermen and justices of the peace, the power of deciding upon the liberty or slavery of a man. The power is still reserved to them to issue a warrant, and cause the arrest of a suspected fugitive from labor. But the determination of his fate, a question almost as momentous as that of life or death, is referred to the intelligence and discretion of judges. And is this a defect in our laws? Is it a defect, that before a man, a husband, a father, shall be torn from the bosom of his family and consigned to chains —and doomed to hopeless slavery, he shall be heard before a judge? Is this provision of our laws a stain upon our statute book? Rather let us ask, was it not derogatory to the character of the commonwealth of Pennsylvania, that she should ever have prized liberty so lightly, as to permit officers, whom to this day she does not suffer to pass upon matters of property beyond one hundred dollars, (and even then subject to the right of appeal,) whose powers were formerly limited to one fifth of that sum—to decide by their voice the permanent and irrevocable fate of a human being? Now that this enormity has ceased to overshadow the land, we can scarcely credit that it ever existed. We can with difficulty persuade ourselves to believe that in this free and powerful state, it ever could have been, that a man should be seized without a warrant, dragged to the office of any magistrate whom the oppressor might choose to select— and from thence, at his bidding, be consigned to slavery—such was the law—such, we earnestly pray, may it never be again. Pennsylvania has revolted from the flagrant injustice. She has taken one step in advance. She has said, a justice of the peace shall not pass upon the liberty of a man; a justice of the peace shall not bear a freeholder from his house, a father from his family. No authority less than that of a judge shall inflict this blow. And is this not enough? . . . Is it not, we respectfully ask, far too great a concession to the spirit of slavery, that we should suffer even our judges to officiate as the instruments for the assertion of her claims? Compare the condition of a judge in this commonwealth, with that of a judge of the very nation from which we have wrested our own liberties. Let a man of the deepest jet be brought before him, and it is the glorious prerogative of that judge to exclaim, "Your feet are on English soil— therefore you are free!"

While here, in this republican land, which has again and again proclaimed the equality of rights of all men, the judge, the American judge, the Pennsylvania judge, himself a freeman, is bound by our laws, tied down hand and foot, obliged to stifle the beatings of his own heart, to keep down his own indignant spirit, and sentence a fellow being to chains and to the lash. Is not this a sufficient sacrifice at the altar of slavery? Would it not be just, is it not due to the honor of the state, do not the constitution of the state and the declaration of rights demand, that instead of the retrograde step now proposed, another be made in *advance,* and that the decision *of a jury* should be required upon so high a question as the liberty of a man? We respectfully submit it to your honorable bodies, that if the authorities of this state are to be employed in such unhappy matters they should be obliged to call to their aid the same means of attaining to a rightful decision, as are secured to us in all other transactions of life, *a jury of twelve men*—and why should this not be? Should the most elevated individual in this community demand of the humblest and lowliest black man, five hundred and thirty-four cents, that humble and lowly man may place his cause under the protection of a jury. Then shall he be denied this privilege, when that which is dearer to him than his life, is demanded by his adversary? Your memorialists do not ask you to interfere with those rights of property which are claimed under the constitution, by our fellow citizens of other states. They simply and most respectfully ask, that if the aid of the officers of this commonwealth be invoked, if the judiciary of this state be called upon to enforce what is termed the right of property in human beings, that they shall be permitted to lend their aid only under such checks and guards, as are consistent with the feelings of this state, with the spirit and letter of her constitution, and with the whole tenor of our code of laws.

In conclusion, your memorialists most earnestly pray, for the sake of humanity, for the honor of the community, in the name of freedom, they most earnestly pray, that your honorable bodies will reject, if offered for your adoption, any measures such as those which appear to be contemplated by the resolutions referred. And your memorialists will ever pray, &c

Signed in behalf of a numerous meeting of the people of color, held in the city of Philadelphia, on the — day of January, 1832.

JAMES FORTEN, *Chairman*

William Whipper, ⎫
⎬ *Secretaries.*
Robert Purvis, ⎭

Rev. Nathaniel Paul Protests

Mistreatment of Lady Educator

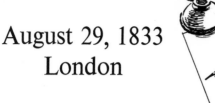
SIR— Through the medium of the American newspapers, I have seen your name, and the names of your worthy coadjutors, and have read your noble and praiseworthy deeds, in regard to the establishment of a school in your town, conducted by one Miss Prudence Crandall, for the instruction of young ladies of color! And believing that acts so patriotic, so republican, so Christian-like in their nature, as yours, against the unpardonable attempts of this fanatical woman, should not be confined to one nation or continent, but that the WORLD should know them, and learn and profit thereby;—I have thought proper to do all in my power to spread your fame, that your works may be known at least throughout this country. Nor will you marvel at my magnanimity when I inform you that I am, myself, a native of New-England, and consequently *proud* of whatever may emanate from her sons, calculated to exalt them in the eyes of the world.

And as I have been for some months past and still am engaged in travelling and delivering lectures upon the state of slavery as it exists in the United States, and the condition of the free people of color there, it will afford me an excellent opportunity of making this whole affair known; nor shall I fail to im-

prove it. Yes, sir, Britons shall know that there are men in America, and whole towns of them, too, who are not so destitute of true heroism but that they can assail a helpless woman, surround her house by night, break her windows, and drag her to prison, for the treasonable act of teaching females of color to read! ! !

Already is the State of Connecticut indebted to me for my gratuitous services since I have been in this country, in her behalf; especially the city of *New-Haven,* and its worthy Mayor. Their magnanimous conduct in regard to the establishment of a college for colored youth in that place, I have spread from "Dan to Beersheba;"—and Dennis Kimberly may rest assured that the name of Benedict Arnold does not stand higher in the estimation of the American people than *his* does in England! It is my intention, sir, to give you an equal elevation.

I shall make no charge for the service I may render you. Nevertheless, if you think I am truly deserving, and ought to have a compensation, whatever you may feel it your duty to give, you will please to hand it over to the Treasurer of the "American Colonization Society," of which, I understand, you are a member and an advocate.

Constitution of the

American Anti-Slavery Society

and Its Declaration of Sentiments

Whereas the Most High God "hath made of one blood all nations of men to dwell on all the face of the earth," and hath commanded them to love their neighbors as themselves; and whereas, our National Existence is based upon this principle, as recognized in the Declaration of Independence, "that all mankind are created equal, and that they are endowed by their Creator with certain inalienable rights, among which are life, liberty, and the pursuit of happiness"; and whereas, after the lapse of nearly sixty years, since the faith and honor of the American people were pledged to this avowal, before Almighty God and the world, nearly one-sixth part of the nation are held in bondage by their fellow-citizens; and whereas, Slavery is contrary to the principles of natural justice, of our republican form of government, and of the Christian religion, and is destructive of the prosperity of the country, while it is endangering the peace, union, and liberties of the States; and whereas, we believe it the duty and interest of the masters immediately to emancipate their slaves, and that no scheme of expatriation, either voluntary or by compulsion, can remove this great and increasing evil; and whereas, we believe that it is practicable, by appeals to the consciences, hearts, and interests of the people, to awaken a public sentiment throughout the nation that will be opposed to the continuance of Slavery in any part of the Republic, and by effecting the speedy abolition of Slavery, prevent a general convulsion; and whereas, we believe we owe it to the oppressed, to our fellow-citizens who hold slaves, to our whole country, to posterity, and to God, to do all that is lawfully in our power to bring about the extinction of Slavery, we do hereby agree,

December
4,
1833
Philadelphia

The
anti-slavery
movement formalized

with a prayerful reliance on the Divine aid, to form ourselves into a society, to be governed by the following Constitution:—

ART. I—This Society shall be called the AMERICAN ANTI-SLAVERY SOCIETY.

ART. II—The object of this Society is the entire abolition of Slavery in the United States. While it admits that each State, in which Slavery exists, has, by the Constitution of the United States, the exclusive right to legislate in regard to its abolition in said State, it shall aim to convince all our fellow-citizens, by arguments addressed to their understandings and consciences, that Slave-holding is a heinous crime in the sight of God, and that the duty, safety, and best interests of all concerned, require its immediate abandonment, without expatriation. The Society will also endeavor, in a constitutional way to influence Congress to put an end to the domestic Slave trade, and to abolish Slavery in all those portions of our common country which come under its control, especially in the District of Columbia,—and likewise to prevent the extension of it to any State that may be hereafter admitted to the Union.

ART. III—This Society shall aim to elevate the character and condition of the people of color, by encouraging their intellectual, moral, and religious improvement, and by removing public prejudice, that thus they may, according to their intellectual and moral worth, share an equality with the whites, of civil and religious privileges; but this Society will never, in any way, countenance the oppressed in vindicating their rights by resorting to physical force.

ART. IV—Any person who consents to the principles of this Constitution, who contributes to the funds of this Society, and is not a Slaveholder, may be a member of this Society, and shall be entitled to vote at the meetings. . . .

DECLARATION OF SENTIMENTS

The convention assembled in the city of Philadelphia, to organize a National Anti-Slavery Society, promptly seize the opportunity to promulgate the following Declaration of Sentiments . . .

We have met together for the achievement of an enterprise, without which that of our fathers is incomplete; and which, for its magnitude, solemnity, and probable results upon the destiny of the world, as far transcends theirs as moral truth does physical force. . . .

Their grievances, great as they were, were trifling in comparison with the wrongs and sufferings of those for whom we plead. Our fathers were never slaves—never bought and sold like cattle—never shut out from the light of knowledge and religion—never subjected to the lash of brutal taskmasters.

But those, for whose emancipation we are striving—constituting at the present time at least one-sixth part of our countrymen—are recognized by law, and treated by their fellow-beings, as brute beasts; are plundered daily of the fruits of their toil without redress; really enjoy no constitutional nor legal protection from licentious and murderous outrages upon their persons; and are ruthlessly torn asunder—the tender babe from the arms of its frantic mother—the heartbroken wife from her weeping husband—at the caprice or pleasure of irresponsible tyrants. For the crime of having a dark complexion, they suffer the pangs of hunger, the infliction of stripes, the ignominy of brutal servitude. They are kept in heathenish darkness by laws expressly enacted to make their instruction a criminal offence.

These are the prominent circumstances in the condition of more than two million people, the proof of which may be found in thousands of indisputable facts, and in the laws of the slave-holding States.

Hence we maintain—that, in view of the civil and religious privileges of this nation, the guilt of its oppression is unequalled by any other on the face of the earth; and, therefore, that it is bound to repent instantly, to undo the heavy burdens, and to let the oppressed go free. . . .

It is piracy to buy or steal an native African, and subject him to servitude. Surely, the sin is as great to enslave an American as an African.

Therefore we believe and affirm—that there is no difference, in principle, between the African slave trade and American slavery:

That every American citizen, who detains a human being in involuntary bondage as his property, is, according to Scripture, (Ex. xxi, 16,) a man-stealer.

That the slaves ought instantly to be set free, and brought under the protection of law:

That if they had lived from the time of Pharaoh down to the present period, and had been entailed through successive generations, their right to be free could never have been alienated, but their claims would have constantly risen in solemnity:

That all those laws which are now in force, admitting the right of slavery, are therefore, before God, utterly null and void; being an audacious usurpation of the Divine prerogative, a daring infringement on the law of nature, a base overthrow of the very foundations of the social compact, a complete extinction of all the relations, endearments and obligations of mankind, and a presumptuous transgression of all the holy commandments; and that therefore they ought instantly to be abrogated.

We further believe and affirm—that all persons of color, who possess the qualifications which are demanded of others, ought to be admitted forwith to the enjoyment of the same privileges, and the exercise of the same prerogatives, as others; and that the paths of preferment, of wealth and of intelligence, should be opened as widely to them as to persons of a white complexion.

We maintain that no compensation should be given to the planters emancipating their slaves:

Because it would be a surrender of the great fundamental principle, that man cannot hold property in man:

Because slavery is a crime, and therefore is not an article to be sold:

Because the holders of slaves are not the just proprietors of what they claim; freeing the slave is not depriving them of property, but restoring it to its rightful owner; it is not wronging the master, but righting the slave—restoring him to himself:

Because immediate and general emancipation would only destroy nominal, not real property; it would not amputate a limb or break a bone of the slaves, but by infusing motives into their breasts, would make them doubly valuable to the masters as free laborers; and

Because, if compensation is to be given at all, it should be given to the outraged and guiltless slaves, and not to those who have plundered and abused them.

We regard as delusive, cruel and dangerous, any scheme of expatriation which pretends to aid, either directly or indirectly, in the emancipation of the slaves, or to be a substitute for the immediate and total abolition of slavery.

We fully and unanimously recognise the sovereignty of each State, to legislate exclusively on the subject of the slavery which is tolerated within its limits; we concede that Congress, under the present national compact, has no right to interfere with any of the slave States, in relation to this momentous subject:

But we maintain that Congress has a right, and is solemnly bound, to suppress the domestic slave trade between the several States, and to abolish slavery in those portions of our territory which the Constitution has placed under its exclusive jurisdiction.

We also maintain that there are, at the present time, the highest obligations resting upon the people of the free States to remove slavery by moral and political action, as prescribed in the Constitution of the United States. They are now living under a pledge of their tremendous physical force, to fasten the galling fetters of tyranny upon the limbs of millions in the Southern States; they are liable to be called at any moment to suppress a general insurrection of the slaves; they authorize the slave owner to vote for three-fifths of his slaves as property, and thus enable him to perpetuate his oppression; they support a standing army at the South for its protection; and they seize the slave, who has escaped into their territories, and send him back to be tortured by an outraged master or a brutal driver. This relation to slavery is criminal, and full of danger: *IT MUST BE BROKEN UP.* . . .

David Ruggles,

New York Bookseller,

Refutes an Anti-Abolitionist

ABOLITIONISTS do not wish "amalgamation:" I do not wish it, nor does any colored man or woman of my acquaintance, nor can instances be adduced where a desire was manifested by any colored person; but I deny that "intermarriages" between "whites and blacks are unnatural," and hazard nothing in giving my opinion that if *"amalgamation"* should become popular Dr. R. would not be the last to vindicate it, practically too if *expedient*. How utterly vain and futile are the following remarks, "The fact that no white person ever did consent to marry a Negro without having previously forfeited all character with the whites, and that even profligate sexual intercourse between the races, everywhere meets with the execration of the respectable and virtuous among the whites, as the most despicable form of licentiousness; is of itself irrefragable proof that *equality* in any aspect in this country, is neither practicable nor desirable. Criminal amalgamation may and does exist among the most degraded of the species, but Americans (what a patriot!) will never yield the sanction of law and religion to an equality so incongruous and unnatural."

Now "that no white person never did con-

sent to marry a Negro without having previously forfeited all character with the respectable and virtuous among the whites," *is not true,* unless it is true that a man's "character" depends upon the color of his skin; if it does, which of the two races would "forfeit all character" by intermarrying, the white or the colored? The whites have robbed us (the blacks) for centuries—they made Africa bleed rivers of blood!—they have torn husbands from their wives—wives from their husbands—parents from their children—children from their parents—brothers from their sisters—sisters from their brothers, and bound them in chains—forced them into holds of vessels—subjected them to the most unmerciful tortures: starved and murdered, and doomed them to endure the horrors of slavery! Still, according to Dr. Reese's logic, the whites have virtuous "characters" and we are *brutes!*

"Deem our nation brutes no longer,
Till some reason you can find,
Worthier to regard, and stronger,
Than the color of our kind!
Slaves of gold! Whose sordid dealings
Tarnish all your boasted powers,

Prove that *ye* have human feelings,
Ere ye proudly question ours!"

. . . . "Would you be willing to marry a black wife," is a question often asked by colonizationists to members of the A.S. [Anti-Slavery] Society. Were I a white man, or was the question reversed and put to me, my reply would be—you had better put your question to colonizationists at the south, who have been so long in a process of training. Why insult gentlemen with a silly, "quirkish," nonsensical interrogative, loped off from the fag ends of extremity. Every man that can read and has sense sufficient to put two ideas together without losing one, knows what the Abolitionists mean when they speak of elevating us "according to our equal rights." But why is it that it seems to you so "repugnant" to marry your sons and daughters to colored persons? Simply because public opinion is against it. *Nature* teaches no such "repugnance," but experience has taught me that education only does. Do children feel and exercise that prejudice towards colored persons? Do not colored and white children play together promiscuously until the white is taught to despise the colored? . . . .

My dear brother, Rev. Bishop Reese, M.D. closes his famous exigesis by submitting his conclusions to the citizens and christians of America, pretty sure that no "sophistry can evade them." I now submit my criticism to the same candid public, entirely regardless whether *sophistry* evade them or not, but challenging the truth to search them. If there be anything of importance in the review which I have not noticed, it was not because the thing itself was impregnable, nor because I was not equal to the siege, but, as I stated before, because my limits did not permit a comment upon every error in my brother's deviating course. But as it is, I submit it to the candor of a generous public, and should *public sentiment* condemn the work, should it be thought out of place and *inexpedient* by any of my friends—should it gain for me frowns and reproaches instead of laurels— one thing I know, posterity will requite my wrongs, and when the "extinguisher" of Dr. David M. Reese shall itself have been extinguished in death, and sunk down—down —in the long eternal sleep of oblivion, my little book, pregnant with truth, shall survive the revolution of ages, and give even Dr. Reese himself a reluctant IMMORTALITY!

South Carolina Resolutions

on Abolitionist Propaganda

RESOLVED, That the formation of the abolition societies, and the acts and doings of certain fanatics, calling themselves abolitionists, in the non-slaveholding states of this confederacy, are in direct violation of the obligations of the compact of the union, dissocial, and incendiary in the extreme.

. . . That no state having a just regard for her own peace and security can acquiesce in a state of things by which such conspiracies are engendered within the limits of a friendly state, united to her by the bonds of a common league of political association, without either surrendering or compromising her most essential rights.

. . . That the Legislature of South Carolina, having every confidence in the justice and friendship of the non-slaveholding states, announces to her co-states her confident expectation, and she earnestly requests that the governments of these states will promptly and effectually suppress all those associations within their respective limits, purporting to be abolition societies, and that they will make it highly penal to print, publish, and distribute newspapers, pamphlets, tracts and pictorial representations calculated and having an obvious tendency to excite slaves of the southern states to insurrection and revolt.

. . . That, regarding the domestic slavery of the southern states as a subject exclusively within the control of each of the said states, we shall consider every interference, by any other state of the general government, as a direct and unlawful interference, to be resisted at once, and under every possible circumstance.

. . . In order that a salutary negative may be put on the mischievous and unfounded assumption of some of the abolitionists—the non-slaveholding states are requested to disclaim by legislative declaration, all right, either on the part of themselves or the government of the United States, to interfere in any manner with domestic slavery, either in the states, or in the territories where it exists.

. . . That we should consider the abolition of slavery in the District of Columbia, as a violation of the rights of the citizens of that District, derived from the implied conditions on which that territory was ceded to the general government, and as an usurpation to be at once resisted as nothing more than the commencement of a scheme of much more extensive and flagrant injustice.

. . . That the legislature of South Carolina, regards with decided approbation, the measures of security adopted by the Post Office Department of the United States, in relation to the transmission of incendiary tracts. But if this highly essential and protective policy, be counteracted by congress, and the United States mail becomes a vehicle for the transmission of the mischievous documents, with which it was recently freighted, we, in this contingency, expect that the Chief Magistrate of our state, will forthwith call the legislature together, that timely measures may be taken to prevent its traversing our territory.

Resolutions of African Methodist

Episcopal Church Annual Conference

September 5, 1840

Social action program adopted by the "Pittsburgh" district

WE, the members of this Conference, are fully satisfied that the principles of the gospel are arrayed against all sin, and that it is the duty of all Christians to use their influence and energies against all systems that rudely trample under foot the claims of justice and the sacred principles of revelation. And, whereas, slavery pollutes the character of the church of God, and makes the Bible a sealed book to thousands . . . Therefore,

Resolved, on motion, That we will aid, by our prayers, those pious persons whom God has raised up to plead the cause of the dumb, until every fetter shall be broken and all men enjoy the liberty which the gospel proclaims.

Resolved, on motion, That, whereas education is one of the principal means of creating in our minds those noble feelings which prompt us to the practice of piety, virtue, and temperance, and is calculated to elevate us above the condition of brutes, by assimilating us to the image of our Maker, we therefore recommend to all our preachers to enjoin undeviating attention to its promotion, and earnestly request all our people to neglect no opportunity of advancing it, by pledging our-

selves to assist them as far as it is in our power.

Resolved, on motion, That we hereby recommend to all our preachers, in their labors to promote the cause of temperance, to hold up the principle of total abstinence from (as a beverage) all intoxicating drinks, as the true and safe rule for all consistent friends of temperance to go by, and is in accordance with our discipline and the resolutions of our former annual conferences.

Resolved, on motion, That a sermon be preached, quarterly, on all our circuits and stations, by our preachers, on the subjects of temperance and moral reform; and the preacher in charge who neglects to attend to that duty, or see that it is attended to, shall be amenable to the next annual conference.

Resolved, on motion, That there be four sermons preached in the year, in all our churches and congregations, for the purpose of encouraging the cause of education and Sabbath schools among our people; and that a collection be taken up, where there are Sabbath schools established, at those times, for the special aid of those schools.

November 1841
Long Island,
New York

Negro teachers
summoned to conference
on Negro advancement

Announcement of

New York Teachers' Meeting

To the Colored Freeman of Long Island, for a convention to be held at Jamaica, Queen's County, November 25th, 1841, at 10½ o'clock, A.M., for devising means more effectually to advance the cause of education and temperance, and also for co-operating with our disfranchised brethren throughout the State, in petitioning for the right of suffrage.

—Brethren, come! The cause of Education calls loudly upon you to come. Hundreds of children that are now shut out from the blessings of Education, call loudly upon you to come. If there ever was a time that called for united action, it is now. If there ever was a time for colored freemen to show their love of liberty, their hatred of ignorance, and determination to be free and enlightened, it is now! We want *union* and *action*. The man who draws back, and refuses to give heed to a call for such noble purposes, plainly shows himself to be an enemy to the greatest earthly blessings conferred by the Creator on his creatures. Come, brethren, refuse not the voice that calls you together for such noble purposes. It is the voice of Liberty, of Education, and of Temperance. Inactivity is criminal! Come from old Suffolk! Our noble, active and enterprising brethren of Kings, they must come! They of Queens must not stay at home! Come from the borders of the blue waters of the Atlantic—from the shores of the Long Island Sound! Let a general rally be made, and let there be a delegate from every town and village, and from every society in the Island. Remember that the first county convention held in this State was held on the Island, and the first State convention was appointed by the freemen of the Island; and now let us give an impetus to the cause of Education! Again we say, come! Let none refuse but those who are enemies to the prosperity and happiness of their people.

Charles Lenox Remond

Addresses

Massachusetts Legislative

Committee

Against Segregation in Travel

An early denunciation
of the
"Jim Crow" railroad car

Mr. Chairman, and Gentlemen of the Committee: In rising at this time, and on this occasion, being the first person of color who has ever addressed either of the bodies assembling in this building, I should, perhaps, in the first place, observe that, in consequence of the many misconstructions of the principles and measures of which I am the humble advocate, I may in like manner be subject to similar misconceptions from the moment I open my lips in behalf of the prayer of the petitioners for whom I appear, and therefore feel I have the right at least to ask, at the hands of this intelligent Committee, an impartial hearing; and that whatever prejudices they may have imbibed, be eradicated from their minds, if such exist. I have, however, too much confidence in their intelligence, and too much faith in their determination to do their duty as the representatives of this Commonwealth, to presume they can be actuated by partial motives. Trusting, as I do, that the day is not distant, when, on all questions touching the rights of the citizens of this State, men shall be considered great only as they are good—and not that it shall be told, and painfully experienced, that, in this country, this State, aye, this city, the Athens of America, the rights, privileges and immunities of its citizens are measured by complexion, or any other physical peculiarity or conformation, especially such as over which no man has any control. Complexion can in no sense be construed into crime, much less be rightfully made the criterion of rights. Should the people of color, through a revolution of Providence, become a majority, to the last I would oppose it upon the same principle; for, in either case, it would be equally reprehensible and unjustifiable—alike to be condemned and repudiated. It is JUSTICE I stand here to claim, and not FAVOR for either complexion.

And now, sir, I shall endeavor to confine my remarks to the same subject which has occupied the attention of the Committee thus far, and to stand upon the same principle which has been so ably and so eloquently maintained and established by my esteemed friend, Mr. [Wendell] Phillips.

Our right to citizenship in this State has been acknowledged and secured by the allowance of the elective franchise and consequent taxation; and I know of no good reason, if admitted in this instance, why it should be denied in any other.

With reference to the wrongs inflicted and injuries received on railroads, by persons of color, I need not say they do not end with the termination of the route, but, in effect, tend to discourage, disparage and depress this class of citizens. All hope of reward for upright conduct is cut off. Vice in them becomes a virtue. No distinction is made by the community in which we live. The most vicious is treated as well as the most respectable, both in public and private.

. . . it is said we all look alike. If this is true, it is not true that we all behave alike. There is a marked difference; and we claim a recognition of this difference.

In the present state of things, they find God's provisions interfered with in such a way, by these and kindred regulations, that virtue may not claim her divinely appointed rewards. Color is made to obscure the brightest endowments, to degrade the fairest character, and to check the highest and most praiseworthy aspirations . . .

The grievances of which we complain, be assured, sir, are not imaginary, but real—not local, but universal—not occasional, but continual, every day matter of fact things—and have become, to the disgrace of our common country, matter of history. . . .

There is a marked difference between social and civil rights. It has been well and justly remarked, by my friend Mr. [Wendell] Phillips, that we all claim the privilege of selecting our society and associations; but, in civil rights, one man has not the prerogative to define rights for another. For instance, sir, in public conveyances, for the rich man to usurp the privileges to himself, to the injury of the poor man, would be submitted to in no well regulated society. And such is the position suffered by persons of color. On my arrival home from England, I went to the railway station, to go to Salem, being anxious to see my parents and sisters as soon as possible—asked for a ticket—paid 50 cents for it, and was pointed to the American designation car. Having previously received information of the regulations, I took my seat peaceably, believing it better to suffer wrong than do wrong. I felt then, as I felt on many occasions prior to leaving home, unwilling to descend so low as to bandy words with the superintendents, or contest my rights with conductors, or any others in the capacity of servants of any stage or steamboat company, or rail-road corporation; although I never, by any means, gave evidence that, by my submission, I intended to sanction usages which would derogate from uncivilized, much less long and loud professing and high pretending America.

Bear with me while I relate an additional occurrence. On the morning after my return home, I was obliged to go to Boston again, and on going to the Salem station I met two friends, who enquired if I had any objection to their taking seats with me. I answered, I should be most happy. They took their seats accordingly, and soon afterwards one of them remarked to me—"Charles, I don't know if they will allow us to ride with you." It was some time before I could understand what they meant, and, on doing so, I laughed—feeling it to be a climax to every absurdity I had heard attributed to Americans. To say nothing of the wrong done those friends, and the insult and indignity offered me by the appearance of the conductor, who ordered the friends from the car in a somewhat harsh manner—they immediately left the carriage.

On returning to Salem some few evenings afterwards, Mr. Chase, the superintendent on this road, made himself known to me by recalling bygone days and scenes, and then enquired if I was not glad to get home after so long an absence in Europe. I told him I was glad to see my parents and family again, and this was the only object I could have, unless he thought I should be glad to take a hermit's life in the great pasture; inasmuch as I never felt to loathe my American name so much as since my arrival. He wished to know my reasons for the remark. I immediately gave them, and wished to know of him, if, in the event of his having a brother with red hair, he should find himself separated while traveling because of this difference, he should deem it just. He could make no reply. I then wished to know if the principle was not the same; and if so, there was an insult implied by his question.

In conclusion, I challenged him as the instrument inflicting the manifold injuries upon all not colored like himself to the presentation of an instance in any other Christian or unchristian country, tolerating usages at once so disgraceful, unjust and inhuman. What if some few of the West or East India planters and merchants should visit our liberty-loving country, with their colored wives—how would he manage? Or, if R. M. Johnson, the gentleman who has been elevated to the second office in the gift of the people, should be travelling from Boston to Salem, if he was prepared to separate him from his wife or daughters. [Involuntary burst of applause, instantly restrained.]

Sir, it happens to be my lot to have a sister a few shades lighter than myself; and who knows, if this state of things is encouraged, whether I may not on some future occasion be mobbed in Washington Street, on the supposition of walking with a white young lady! [Suppressed indications of sympathy and applause.]

Gentlemen of the Committee, these distinctions react in all their wickedness—to say nothing of their concocted and systematized odiousness and absurdity—upon those who instituted them; and particularly so upon those who are illiberal and mean enough to practise them.

Mr. Chairman, if colored people have abused any rights granted them, or failed to exhibit due appreciation of favors bestowed, or shrunk . . . dangers or responsibility, let it be made to appear. Or if our country contains a population to compare with them in loyalty and patriotism, circumstances duly considered, I have it yet to learn. The history of our country must ever testify in their behalf. In view of these and many additional considerations, I unhesitatingly assert their claim, on the naked principle of merit, to every advantage set forth in the Constitution of this Commonwealth.

Finally, Mr. Chairman, there is in this and other States a large and growing colored population, whose residence in your midst has not been from choice (let this be understood and reflected upon), but by the force of circumstances over which they never had control. Upon the heads of their oppressors and calumniators be the censure and responsibility. If to ask at your hands redress for injuries, and protection in our rights and immunities, as citizens, is reasonable, and dictated alike by justice, humanity and religion, you will not reject, I trust, the prayer of your petitioners. . . .

Prigg vs. The Commonwealth of Pennsylvania

*The Majority Opinion
Delivered by Mr. Justice Story*

This is a writ of error to the Supreme Court of Pennsylvania, brought under the 25th section of the Judiciary Act of 1789, for the purpose of revising the judgement of that court, in a case involving the construction of the Constitution and laws of the United States. The facts are briefly these: the plaintiff in error was indicted . . . for having, . . . taken and carried away from that county to the State of Maryland, a certain negro woman, named Margaret Morgan, with a design and intention of selling and disposing of, and keeping her as a slave or servant for life, contrary to a statute of Pennsylvania, passed on the 26th of March 1826. That statute . . . provides, that if any person or persons shall from and after the passing of the act, by force and violence take and carry away . . . and shall by fraud and false pretense seduce . . . any negro or mulatto from any part of that Common-

wealth . . . on conviction thereof, [shall] be deemed guilty of a felony, and shall forfeit, and pay a sum not less than five hundred, nor more than one thousand dollars; . . . and shall be confined and kept to hard labor . . .

The plaintiff in error pleaded not guilty to the indictment; and at the trial the jury found a special verdict, which, in substance, states, that the negro woman, Margaret Morgan was a slave for life, and held to labor and service . . . to a certain Margaret Ashmore, a citizen of Maryland; that the slave escaped and fled from Maryland into Pennsylvania in 1832; that the plaintiff in error . . . caused the said negro woman to be taken . . . as a fugitive from labor by a State constable under a warrant from a Pennsylvania magistrate; that the said negro woman was thereupon brought before the said magistrate who refused to take further cognizance of the case; and thereupon the plaintiff . . . did . . . carry away the said negro woman and her children out of Pennsylvania into Maryland. . . . The special verdict further finds, that one of the children was born in Pennsylvania,

more than a year after the said Negro woman had fled and escaped from Maryland . . .

The question arising in the case as to the constitutionality of the statute of Pennsylvania, has been most elaborately argued at the bar. The counsel for the plaintiff have contended that the statute of Pennsylvania is unconstitutional; First, because Congress has the exclusive power of legislation upon the subject matter under the constitution of the United States, and under the act of the 12th of February, 1793, which was passed in pursuance thereof; second, that if this power is not exclusive in Congress, still the concurrent power of the State Legislatures is suspended by the actual exercise of the power by Congress; and third, that if not suspended, still the statute of Pennsylvania, in all its provisions applicable to this case, is in direct collision with the act of Congress, and therefore is unconstitutional and void. The counsel for Pennsylvania maintain the negative of all these points.

The remaining question is, whether the power of legislation upon this subject is exclusive in the national government, or concurrent in the States, until it is exercised by Congress. In our opinion it is exclusive; . . .

In the first place it is material to state . . . that the right to seize and retake fugitive slaves and the duty to deliver them up, in whatever State of the Union they may be found, and of course the corresponding power of Congress to use the appropriate means to enforce the right and duty, derive their whole validity and obligation exclusively from the Constitution of the United States . . . Under the Constitution it is recognized as an absolute and positive right and duty, pervading the whole Union with an equal and supreme force, uncontrolled and uncontrollable by State sovereignty or State legislation. It is therefore in a just sense a new and positive right, independent of comity, confined to no territorial limits, and bounded by no State institutions or policy. The natural inference deducible from this consideration certainly is, in the absence of any positive delegation of power to the State Legislatures, that it belongs to the legislative department of the national government, to which it owes its origin and its establishment. . . .

In the next place, the nature of the provision and the objects to be attained by it require that it should be controlled by one and the same will, and act uniformly by the same system of regulations throughout the Union. . . .

It is scarcely conceivable that the slaveholding States would have been satisfied with leaving to the legislation of the non-slaveholding States a power of regulation, in the absence of that of Congress, which would or might practically amount to a power to destroy the rights of the owner . . . On the other hand, construe the right of legislation as exclusive in Congress, and every evil and every danger vanishes. The right and duty are then co-extensive and uniform in remedy and operation throughout the whole Union. The owner has the same security, and the same remedial justice, and the same exemption from State regulation and control, through however many States he may pass with his fugitive slave in his possession. . . .

These are some of the reasons but by no means all upon which we hold the power of legislation on this subject to be exclusive in Congress. To guard, however, against any possible misconstruction of our views, it is proper to state that we are by no means to be understood, in any manner whatsoever to doubt or to interfere with the police power belonging to the States in virtue of their general sovereignty. That police power extends over all subjects within the territorial limits of the States, and has never been conceded to the United States . . . But such regulations can never be permitted to interfere with or to obstruct the just rights of the owner to reclaim his slave, derived from the Constitution of the United States, or with the remedies prescribed by Congress to aid and enforce the same.

Upon these grounds we are of opinion that the act of Pennsylvania upon which this indictment is founded, is unconstitutional and void . . .

Judgement reversed. . . .

Mr. Justice M'Lean's Dissent

. . . The slave is found in the State where every man, black or white, is presumed to be free; and this State, to preserve the peace of its citizens, and its soil and jurisdiction from acts of violence, has prohibited the forcible abduction of persons of color. Does this law conflict with the Constitution? It clearly does not in its terms . . .

No conflict can arise between the act of Congress and this State law. The conflict can only arise between the forcible acts of the master and the law of the State. The master exhibits no proof of right to the services of the slave, but seizes him and is about to remove him by force. I speak only of the force exerted on the slave. The law of the State presumes him to be free and prohibits his removal. Now, which shall give way, the master or the State? The law of the State does in no case discharge, in the language of the Constitution, the slave from the service of his master.

It is a most important police regulation. And if the master violate it, is he not amenable? The offense consists in the abduction of a person of color. And this is attempted to be justified upon the simple ground that the slave is property. That a slave is property must be admitted. The State law is not violated by the seizure of the slave by the master, for this is authorized by the act of Congress; but by removing him out of the State by force, and without proof of right, which the act does not authorize. Now, is not this an act which a State may prohibit? The important point is, shall the presumption of right set up by the master, unsustained by proof, or the presumption which arises from the laws and institutions of the State, prevail. This is the true issue. The sovereignty of the State is on one side, and the asserted interest of the master on the other. That interest is protected by the paramount law, and a special, a summary, and an effectual mode of redress is given. But this mode is not pursued, and the remedy is taken into his own hands, by the master.

The presumption of the State that the colored person is free may be erroneous in fact; and if so, there can be no difficulty in proving it. But may not the assertion of the master be erroneous also; and if so, how is his act of force to be remedied? The colored person is taken, and forcibly conveyed beyond the jurisdiction of the State. This force, not being authorized by the act of Congress nor by the Constitution, may be prohibited by the State. As the act covers the whole power in the Constitution, and carries out, by special enactments, its provisions, we are, in my judgement, bound by the act. We can no more, under such circumstances, administer a remedy under the Constitution in disregard of the act than we can exercise a commercial or other power in disregard of an act of Congress on the same subject.

This view respects the rights of the master and the rights of the State. It neither jeopards nor retards the reclamation of the slave. It removes all State action prejudicial to the rights of the master; and recognizes in the State a power to guard and protect its own jurisdiction, and the peace of its citizens . . .

Prigg vs. The Commonwealth of Pennsylvania □ 119

Henry Highland Garnet

Urges Slave "Resistance"

Brethren and Fellow Citizens:—Your brethren of the North, East, and West have been accustomed to meet together in National Conventions, to sympathize with each other, and to weep over your unhappy condition. In these meetings we have addressed all classes of the free, but we have never, until this time, sent a word of consolation and advice to you. We have been contented in sitting still and mourning over your sorrows, earnestly hoping that before this day your sacred liberty would have been restored. But, we have hoped in vain. Years have rolled on, and tens of thousands have been borne on streams of blood and tears, to the shores of eternity. While you have been oppressed, we have also been partakers with you; nor can we be free while you are enslaved. We, therefore, write to you as being bound with you.

Many of you are bound to us, not only by the ties of a common humanity, but we are connected by the more tender relations of parents, wives, husbands, children, brothers, and sisters, and friends. As such we most affectionately address you.

Slavery has fixed a deep gulf between you and us, and while it shuts out from you the relief and consolation which your friends would willingly render, it affects and persecutes you with a fierceness which we might not expect to see in the fiends of hell. But still the Almighty Father of mercies has left to us a glimmering ray of hope, which shines out like a lone star in a cloudy sky. Mankind are becoming wiser, and better—the oppressor's power is fading, and you, every day, are becoming better informed, and more numerous. Your grievances, brethren, are many. . . .

Two hundred and twenty-seven years ago, the first of our injured race were brought to the shores of America. They came not with glad spirits to select their homes in the New World. They came not with their own consent, to find an unmolested enjoyment of the blessings of this fruitful soil. The first dealings they had with men calling themselves Christians, exhibited to them the worst features of corrupt and sordid hearts; and convinced them that no cruelty is too great, no villainy and no robbery too abhorrent for even enlightened men to perform, when influenced by avarice and lust. Neither did they come flying upon the wings of Liberty, to a land of freedom. But they came with broken hearts, from their beloved native land, and were doomed to unrequited toil and deep degradation. Nor did the evil of their bondage end at their emancipation by death. Succeeding generations inherited their chains, and millions have come from eternity into time, and have returned again to the world of

spirits, cursed and ruined by American slavery.

The propagators of the system, or their immediate ancestors, very soon discovered its growing evil, and its tremendous wickedness, and secret promises were made to destroy it. The gross inconsistency of a people holding slaves, who had themselves "ferried o'er the wave" for freedom's sake, was too apparent to be entirely overlooked. The voice of Freedom cried, "Emancipate yourselves." Humanity supplicated with tears for the deliverance of the children of Africa. Wisdom urged her solemn plea. The bleeding captive plead his innocence, and pointed to Christianity who stood weeping at the cross. Jehovah frowned upon the nefarious institution, and thunderbolts, red with vengeance, struggled to leap forth to blast the guilty wretches who maintained it. But all was in vain. Slavery had stretched its dark wings of death over the land, the Church stood silently by—the priests prophesied falsely, and the people loved to have it so. Its throne is established, and now it reigns triumphant.

Nearly three millions of your fellow-citizens are prohibited by law and public opinion, (which in this country is stronger than law,) from reading the Book of Life. Your intellect has been destroyed as much as possible, and every ray of light they have attempted to shut out from your minds. The oppressors themselves have become involved in the ruin. They have become weak, sensual, and rapacious—they have cursed you—they have cursed themselves—they have cursed the earth which they have trod.

The colonists threw the blame upon England. They said that the mother country entailed the evil upon them, and that they would rid themselves of it if they could. The world thought they were sincere, and the philanthropic pitied them. But time soon tested their sincerity.

In a few years the colonists grew strong, and severed themselves from the British Government. Their independence was declared, and they took their station among the sovereign powers of the earth. The declaration was a glorious document. Sages admired it, and the patriotic of every nation reverenced the God-like sentiments which it contained. When the power of Government returned to their hands, did they emancipate the slaves? No; they rather added new links to our chains. Were they ignorant of the principles of Liberty? Certainly they were not. The sentiments of their revolutionary orators fell in burning eloquence upon their hearts, and with one voice they cried, Liberty or Death. Oh what a sentence was that! It ran from soul to soul like electric fire, and nerved the arm of thousands to fight in the holy cause of Freedom. Among the diversity of opinions that are entertained in regard to physical resistance, there are but a few found to gainsay that stern declaration. We are among those who do not. Slavery! How much misery is comprehended in that single word. What mind is there that does not shrink from its direful effects? Unless the image of God be obliterated from the soul, all men cherish the love of Liberty. The nice discerning political economist does not regard the sacred right more than the untutored African who roams in the wilds of Congo. Nor has the one more right to the full enjoyment of his freedom than the other. In every man's mind the good seeds of liberty are planted, and he who brings his fellow down so low, as to make him contented with a condition of slavery, commits the highest crime against God and man. Brethren, your oppressors aim to do this. They endeavor to make you as much like brutes as possible. When they have blinded the eyes of your mind—when they have embittered the sweet waters of life—then, and not till then, has American slavery done its perfect work.

To such degradation it is sinful in the extreme for you to make voluntary submission. The divine commandments you are in duty bound to reverence and obey. If you do not obey them, you will surely meet with the displeasure of the Almighty. He requires you to love him supremely, and your neighbor as yourself—to keep the Sabbath day holy—to search the Scriptures—and bring up your children with respect for his laws, and to worship no other God but him. But slavery sets all these at nought, and hurls defiance in the face of Jehovah. The forlorn condition in which you are placed, does not destroy your moral obligation to God. You are not certain of heaven, because you suffer yourselves to remain in a state of slavery, where you cannot obey the commandments of the Sovereign of the universe. If the ignorance of slavery is a passport to heaven, then it is a blessing, and no curse, and you should rather desire its perpetuity than its abolition. God will not receive slavery, nor ignorance, nor any other state of mind, for love and obedience to him. Your condition does not absolve you from your moral obligation. The diabolical injustice by which your liberties are cloven down, NEITHER GOD, NOR ANGELS, OR JUST MEN, COMMAND YOU TO SUFFER FOR A SINGLE MOMENT. THEREFORE IT IS YOUR SOLEMN AND IMPERATIVE DUTY TO USE EVERY MEANS, BOTH MORAL, INTELLECTUAL, AND PHYSICAL THAT PROMISES SUCCESS. . . .

Brethren, it is as wrong for your lordly oppressors to keep you in slavery, as it was for the man thief to steal our ancestors from the coast of Africa. You should therefore now use the same manner of resistance, as would have been just in our ancestors when the bloody foot-prints of the first remorseless soul-thief was placed upon the shores of our fatherland. The humblest peasant is as free in the sight of God as the proudest monarch that ever swayed a sceptre. Liberty is a spirit sent out from God, and like its great Author, is no respecter of persons.

Brethren, the time has come when you must act for yourselves. It is an old and true saying that, "if hereditary bondmen would be free, they must themselves strike the blow." You can plead your own cause, and do the work of emancipation better than any others. The nations of the world are moving in the great cause of universal freedom, and some of them at least will, ere long, do you justice. . . . Look around you, and behold the bosoms of your loving wives heaving with untold agonies! Hear the cries of your poor children! Remember the stripes your fathers bore. Think of the torture and disgrace of your noble mothers. Think of your wretched sisters, loving virtue and purity, as they are driven into concubinage and are exposed to the unbridled lusts of incarnate devils. Think of the undying glory that hangs around the ancient name of Africa—and forget not that you are native born American citizens, and as such, you are justly entitled to all the rights that are granted to the freest. Think how many tears you have poured out upon the soil which you have cultivated with unrequited toil and enriched with your blood; and then go to your lordly enslavers and tell them plainly, that you *are determined to be free.*

. . . If they then commence the work of death, they, and not you, will be responsible for the consequences. You had better all die —*die immediately,* than live slaves and entail your wretchedness upon your posterity. If you would be free in this generation, here is your only hope. However much you and all of us may desire it, there is not much hope of redemption without the shedding of blood. If you must bleed, let it all come at once— rather *die freemen, than live to be slaves.* . . .

You will not be compelled to spend much time in order to become inured to hardships. From the first moment that you breathed the air of heaven, you have been accustomed to nothing else but hardships. The heroes of the American Revolution were never put upon harder fare than a peck of corn and a few herrings per week. You have not become enervated by the luxuries of life. Your sternest energies have been beaten out upon the anvil of severe trial. Slavery has done this, to make you subservient, to its own purposes; but it has done more than this, it has prepared you for any emergency. . . .

Fellow men! Patient sufferers! behold your dearest rights crushed to the earth! See your sons murdered, and your wives, mothers and sisters doomed to prostitution. In the name of the merciful God, and by all that life is worth, let it no longer be a debatable question

whether it is better to choose *Liberty or death.* . . .

Brethren, arise, arise! Strike for your lives and liberties. Now is the day and the hour. Let every slave throughout the land do this, and the days of slavery are numbered. You cannot be more oppressed than you have been—you cannot suffer greater cruelties than you have already. *Rather die freemen than live to be slaves.* Remember that you are FOUR MILLIONS!

It is in your power so to torment the God-cursed slaveholders that they will be glad to let you go free. If the scale was turned, and black men were the masters and white men the slaves, every destructive agent and element would be employed to lay the oppressor low. Danger and death would hang over their heads day and night. Yes, the tyrants would meet with plagues more terrible than those of Pharaoh. But you are a patient people. You act as though, you were made for the special use of these devils. You act as though your daughters were born to pamper the lusts of your masters and overseers. And worse than all, you tamely submit while your lords tear your wives from your embraces and defile them before your eyes. In the name of God, we ask, are you men? Where is the blood of your fathers? Has it all run out of your veins? Awake, awake; millions of voices are calling you! Your dead fathers speak to you from their graves. Heaven, as with a voice of thunder, calls on you to arise from the dust.

Let your motto be resistance! *resistance!* RESISTANCE! No oppressed people have ever secured their liberty without resistance. What kind of resistance you had better make, you must decide by the circumstances that surround you, and according to the suggestion of expediency. Brethren, adieu! Trust in the living God. Labor for the peace of the human race, and remember that you are FOUR MILLIONS.

Henry Highland Garnet Urges Slave "Resistance" □ 123

Editorial in the Inaugural

Edition of the **North Star**

TO OUR OPPRESSED COUNTRYMEN

We solemnly dedicate the *North Star* to the cause of our long oppressed and plundered fellow countrymen. May God bless the offering to your good! It shall fearlessly assert your rights, faithfully proclaim your wrongs, and earnestly demand for you instant and even-handed justice. Giving no quarter to slavery at the South, it will hold no truce with oppressors at the North. While it shall boldly advocate emancipation for our enslaved brethren, it will omit no opportunity to gain for the nominally free, complete enfranchisement. Every effort to injure or degrade you or your cause—originating wheresoever, or with whomsoever—shall find in it a constant, unswerving and inflexible foe.

We shall energetically assail the ramparts of Slavery and Prejudice, be they composed of church or state, and seek the destruction of every refuge of lies, under which tyranny may aim to conceal and protect itself.

Among the multitude of plans proposed and opinions held, with reference to our cause and condition, we shall try to have a mind of our own, harmonizing with all as far as we can, and differing from any and all where we must, but always discriminating between men and measures. We shall cordially approve every measure and effort calculated to advance your sacred cause, and strenuously oppose any which in our opinion may tend to retard its progress. In regard to our position, on questions that have unhappily divided the friends of freedom in this country, we shall stand in our paper where we have ever stood on the platform. Our views written shall accord with our views spoken, earnestly seeking peace with all men, when it can be secured without injuring the integrity of our movement, and never shrinking from conflict or division when summoned to vindicate truth and justice.

While our paper shall be mainly Anti-Slavery, its columns shall be freely opened to the candid and decorous discussions of all measures and topics of a moral and humane character, which may serve to enlighten, improve, and elevate mankind. Temperance, Peace, Capital Punishment, Education,—all subjects claiming the attention of the public mind may be freely and fully discussed here.

While advocating your rights, the *North Star* will strive to throw light on your duties: while it will not fail to make known your virtues, it will not shun to discover your faults. To be faithful to our foes it must be faithful to ourselves, in all things.

Remember that we are one, that our cause is one, and that we must help each other, if we would succeed. We have drunk to the dregs the bitter cup of slavery; we have worn the heavy yoke; we have sighed beneath our

December 3, 1847
Rochester,
New York

Frederick Douglass
dedicates his newspaper
to cause of Negro

bonds, and writhed beneath the bloody lash; —cruel mementoes of our oneness are indelibly marked in our living flesh. We are one with you under the ban of prejudice and proscription—one with you under the slander of inferiority—one with you in social and political disfranchisement. What you suffer, we suffer; what you endure, we endure. We are indissolubly united, and must fall or flourish together.

We feel deeply the solemn responsibility which we have now assumed. We have seriously considered the importance of the enterprise, and have now entered upon it with full purpose of heart. We have nothing to offer in the way of literary ability to induce you to encourage us in our laudable undertaking. You will not expect or require this at our hands. The most that you can reasonably expect, or that we can safely promise, is, a paper of which you need not be ashamed. Twenty-one years of severe bondage at the South, and nine years of active life at the North, while it has afforded us the best possible opportunity for storing our mind with much practical and important information, has left us little time for literary pursuits or attainments. We have yet to receive the advantage of the first day's schooling. In point of education, birth and rank, we are one with yourselves, and of yourselves. What we are, we are not only without help, but against

trying opposition. Your knowledge of our history for the last seven years makes it unnecessary for us to say more on this point. What we have been in your cause, we shall continue to be; and not being too old to learn, we may improve in many ways. Patience and Perseverance shall be our motto.

We shall be the advocates of learning, from the very want of it, and shall most readily yield the deference due to men of education among us; but shall always bear in mind to accord most merit to those who have labored hardest, and overcome most, in the praiseworthy pursuit of knowledge, remembering "that the whole need not a physician, but they that are sick," and that "the strong ought to bear the infirmities of the weak."

Brethren, the first number of the paper is before you. It is dedicated to your cause. Through the kindness of our friends in England, we are in possession of an excellent printing press, types, and all other materials necessary for printing a paper. Shall this gift be blest to our good, or shall it result in our injury? It is for you to say. With your aid, co-operation and assistance, our enterprise will be entirely successful. We pledge ourselves that no effort on our part shall be wanting, and that no subscriber shall lose his subscription—"The *North Star* Shall Live."

The North Star, December 3, 1847

Editorial in the Inaugural Edition □ 125

Clay's Resolutions on Slavery

in the Territories

and the District of Columbia

I T being desirable, for the peace, concord, and harmony of the Union of these States, to settle and adjust amicably all existing questions of controversy between them arising out of the institution of slavery upon a fair, equitable and just basis: therefore,

. . . Resolved, That California, with suitable boundaries, ought, upon her application to be admitted as one of the States of this Union, without the imposition by Congress of any restriction in respect to the exclusion or introduction of slavery within those boundaries.

. . . That as slavery does not exist by law and is not likely to be introduced into any of the [Mexico] territory . . . by the United States . . . it is inexpedient for Congress to provide by law either for its introduction into, or exclusion from, any part of the said territory; and that appropriate territorial governments ought to be established by Congress in all of the said territory, not assigned as the boundaries of the proposed State of California, without the adoption of any restriction or condition on the subject of slavery.

. . . That it is inexpedient to abolish slavery in the District of Columbia whilst that institution continues to exist in the State of Maryland, without the consent of that State, without the consent of the people of the District, and without just compensation to the owners of slaves within the District.

. . . But . . . That it is expedient to prohibit, within the District, the slave trade in slaves brought into it from States or places beyond the limits of the District, either to be sold therein as merchandise, or to be transported to other markets without the District of Columbia.

. . . That more effectual provision ought to be made by law, according to the requirement of the constitution, for the restitution and delivery of persons bound to service and labor in any State, who may escape into any other State or Territory in the Union. And,

. . . That Congress has no power to promote or obstruct the trade in slaves between the slaveholding States; but that the admission or exclusion of slaves brought from one into another of them, depends exclusively upon their own particular laws.

1850

The Compromise of 1850:
Act of 1793 strengthened;
slavery in capital ended

Fugitive Slave Act

An Act to amend, and supplementary to, the Act entitled "An Act respecting Fugitives from Justice, and Persons escaping from the Service of their Masters," approved—[February 12, 1793].

. . . That it shall be the duty of all marshals and deputy marshals to obey and execute all warrants and precepts issued under provisions of this act, when to them directed; and should any marshal or deputy marshal refuse to receive such warrant, or other process, when tendered, or to use all proper means diligently to execute the same, he shall, on conviction thereof, be fined in the sum of one thousand dollars, to the use of such claimant, . . . and after arrest . . . should such fugitive escape, whether with or without the assent of such marshal or his deputy, such marshal shall be liable, on his official bond, to be prosecuted for the benefit of such claimant, for the full value of the service or labor of said fugitive in the State, Territory, or District whence he escaped: and the better to enable the said commissioners, when thus appointed, to execute their duties faithfully and efficiently, in conformity with the requirements of the Constitution of the United States and of this act, they are hereby authorized and empowered, within their counties respectively, to appoint, . . . any one or more suitable persons, from time to time, to execute all such warrants and other process as may be issued by them in the lawful performance of their respective duties; with authority to such commissioners, or the persons to be appointed by them, to execute process as aforesaid, to summon and call to their aid the bystanders, or 'posse comitatus' of the proper county, when necessary to ensure a faithful observance of the Clause of the Constitution referred to, in conformity with the provisions of this act; and all good citizens are hereby commanded to aid and assist in the prompt and efficient execution of this law, whenever their services may be required, as aforesaid, for that purpose; and said warrants shall run, and be executed by said officers, anywhere in the State within which they are issued.

. . . when a person held to service or labor in any State or Territory of the United States, has heretofore or shall hereafter escape into another State or Territory of the United States, the person or persons to whom such service or labor may be due, . . . may pursue and reclaim such fugitive person, either by procuring a warrant from some one of the courts, judges, or commissioners aforesaid, of the proper circuit, district, or county, for the apprehension of such fugitive from service or labor, or by seizing and arresting such fugitive, where the same can be done without process, and by taking, or causing such person to be taken, forthwith before such court, judge, or commissioner, . . . or by other satisfactory testimony, duly taken and certified by . . . and with proof, also by affidavit, of the identity of the person whose service or labor is claimed to be due as aforesaid, that the person so arrested does in fact owe service or labor to the person or persons claiming him or her, in the State or Territory from which such fugitive may have escaped as aforesaid, and that said person escaped, to make out and deliver to such claimant, his or her agent or attorney, a certificate setting forth the substantial facts as to the service or labor due from such fugitive to the claimant, and of his or her escape from the State or Territory . . . such claimant, . . . to use such reasonable force and restraint as may be necessary, under the circumstances of the case, to take and remove such fugitive person back to the State or Territory whence he or she may have escaped as aforesaid. In no trial or hearing under this act shall the testimony of

such alleged fugitive be admitted in evidence; and the certificates in this and the first (fourth) section mentioned, shall be conclusive of the right of the person or persons in whose favor granted, to remove such fugitive to the State or Territory from which he escaped, and shall prevent all molestation of such person or persons by any process issued by any court, judge, magistrate, or other person whomsoever.

. . . any persons who shall knowingly and willingly obstruct, hinder, or prevent such claimant, his agent or attorney, or any person or persons lawfully assisting him, her, or them, from arresting such a fugitive from service or labor, either with or without process as aforesaid, or shall rescue, or attempt to rescue, such fugitive from service or labor, from the custody of such claimant, . . . or other person or persons lawfully assisting as aforesaid, when so arrested, . . . or shall aid, abet, or assist such person so owing service or labor as aforesaid, directly or indirectly, to escape from such claimant, . . . or shall harbor or conceal such fugitive, so as to prevent the discovery and arrest of such person, after notice or knowledge of the fact that such person was a fugitive from service or labor . . . shall, for either of said offences be subject to a fine not exceeding one thousand dollars, and imprisonment not exceeding six months . . . ; and shall moreover forfeit and pay, by way of civil damages to the party injured by such illegal conduct, the sum of one thousand dollars, for each fugitive so lost a aforesaid . . . .

. . . That, upon affidavit made by the claimant of such fugitive, . . . that he has reason to apprehend that such fugitive will be rescued by force from his or their possession before he can be taken beyond the limits of the State in which the arrest is made, it shall be the duty of the officer making the arrest to retain such fugitive in his custody, and to remove him to the State whence he fled, and there deliver him to said claimant, his agent, or attorney. And to this end, the officer aforesaid is hereby authorized and required to employ so many persons as he may deem necessary to overcome such force, and to retain them in his service so long as circumstances may require . . .

. . . when any person held to service or labor in any State or Territory, or in the District of Columbia, shall escape therefrom, the party to whom such service or labor shall be due, . . . may apply to any court of record therein, . . . and make satisfactory proof to such court, . . . of the escape aforesaid, and that the person escaping owed service or labor to such party. Whereupon the court shall cause a record to be made of the matters so proved, and also a general description of the person so escaping, with such convenient certainty as may be; and a transcript of such record, . . . being produced in any other State, Territory, or district in which the person so escaping may be found, . . . shall be held and taken to be full and conclusive evidence of the fact of escape, and that the service or labor of the person escaping is due to the party in such record mentioned. And upon the production by the said party of other and further evidence if necessary, either oral or by affidavit, in addition to what is contained in the said record of the identity of the person escaping, he or she shall be delivered up to the claimant. And the said court, commissioner, judge, or other person authorized by this act to grant certificates to claimants of fugitives, shall, upon the production of the record and other evidences aforesaid, grant to such claimant a certificate of his right to take any such person identified and proved to

be owing service or labor as aforesaid, which certificates shall authorize such claimant to seize or arrest and transport such person to the State or Territory from which he escaped.

Act Abolishing the Slave Trade in the District of Columbia

September 20, 1850

An Act to suppress the Slave Trade in the District of Columbia.

Be it enacted . . . That from and after January 1, 1851, it shall not be lawful to bring into the District of Columbia any slave whatever, for the purpose of being sold, or for the purpose of being placed in depot, to be subsequently transferred to any other State or place to be sold as merchandize. And if any slave shall be brought into the said District by its owner, or by the authority or consent of its owner, contrary to the provisions of this act, such slave shall thereupon become liberated and free.

. . . That it shall and may be lawful for each of the corporations of the cities of Washington and Georgetown, from time to time, and as often as may be necessary, to abate, break up, and abolish any depot or place of confinement of slaves brought into the said District as merchandize, contrary to the provisions of this act, by such appropriate means as may appear to either of the said corporations expedient and proper. And the same power is hereby vested in the Levy Court of Washington County, if any attempt shall be made, within its jurisdictional limits, to establish a depot or place of confinement for slaves brought into the said District as merchandize for sale contrary to this act.

The Georgia Platform
on the Extension of Slavery Question

| 1850 Milledgeville, Georgia | Southern reaction to federal interference with slavery voiced |

To the end that the position of the State may be clearly apprehended by her Confederates of the South and of the North, and that she may be blameless of all future consequences—

Be it resolved by the people of Georgia in Convention assembled, . . . That we hold the American Union secondary in importance only to the rights and principles it was designed to perpetuate. That past associations, present fruition, and future prospects, will bind us to it so long as it continues to be the safe-guard of those rights and principles.

. . . That if the thirteen original Parties to the Compact, bordering the Atlantic in a narrow belt, while their separate interests were in embryo, their peculiar tendencies scarcely developed, their revolutionary trials and triumphs still green in memory, found Union impossible without compromise, the thirty-one of this day may well yield somewhat in the conflict of opinion and policy, to preserve that Union which has extended the sway of Republican Government over a vast wilderness to another ocean, and proportionately advanced their civilization and national greatness.

. . . That in this spirit the State of Georgia has maturely considered the action of Congress, embracing . . . the suppression of the slave-trade in the District of Columbia,

and the extradition of fugitive slaves, and . . . the rejection of propositions to exclude slavery from the Mexican Territories, and to abolish it in the District of Columbia; and, whilst she does not wholly approve, will abide by it as a permanent adjustment of this sectional controversy.

. . . That the State of Georgia, in the judgement of this Convention, will and ought to resist, . . . any future Act of Congress abolishing Slavery in the District of Columbia, without the consent and petition of the slave-holders thereof, or any Act abolishing Slavery in places within the slave-holding States, purchased by the United States for the erection of forts, magazines, arsenals, dock-yards, navy-yards, and other like purposes; or in any Act suppressing the slave-trade between slave-holding States; or in any refusal to admit as a State any Territory applying because of the existence of Slavery therein; or in any Act prohibiting the introduction of slaves into the Territories of Utah and New Mexico; or in any Act repealing or materially modifying the laws now in force for the recovery of fugitive slaves.

. . . That it is the deliberate opinion of this Convention, that upon the faithful execution of the Fugitive Slave Bill by the proper authorities, depends the preservation of our much loved Union.

Resolutions of the Nashville Convention Opposing Congressional Control of Slavery

. . . Resolved, That the territories of the United States belong to the people of the several States of this Union as their common property. That the citizens of the several States have equal rights to migrate with their property to these territories, and are equally entitled to the protection of the federal government in the enjoyment of that property so long as the territories remain under the charge of that government.

. . . That Congress has no power to exclude from the territory of the United States any property lawfully held in the States of the Union, and any act which may be passed by Congress to effect this result is a plain violation of the Constitution of the United States. . . .

. . . That to protect property existing in the several States of the Union, the people of these States invested the federal government with the powers of war and negotiation and of sustaining armies and navies, and prohibited to State authorities the exercise of the same powers. They made no discrimination in the protection to be afforded or the description of the property to be defended, nor was it allowed to the federal government to determine what should be held as property. Whatever the States deal with as property the federal government is bound to recognize and defend as such. Therefore it is the sense of this Convention that all acts of the federal government which tend to denationalize property of any description recognized in the Constitution and laws of the States, or that

1850

Equitable partition of territories suggested by Southern moderates

discriminate in the degree and efficiency of the protection to be afforded to it, or which weaken or destroy the title of any citizen upon American territories, are plain and palpable violations of the fundamental law under which it exists.

. . . That the slaveholding States cannot and will not submit to the enactment by Congress of any law imposing onerous conditions or restraints upon the rights of masters to remove with their property into the territories of the United States, or to any law making discrimination in favor of the proprietors of other property against them. . . .

. . . That the performance of its duties, upon the principle we declare, would enable Congress to remove the embarrassment in which the country is now involved. The vacant territories of the United States, no longer regarded as prizes for sectional rapacity and ambition, would be gradually occupied by inhabitants drawn to them by their interests and feelings. The institutions fitted to them would be naturally applied by governments formed on American ideas, and approved by the deliberate choice of their constituents.

The community would be educated and disciplined under a republican administration in habits of self government, and fitted for an association as a State, and to the enjoyment of a place in the confederacy. . . .

. . . That a recognition of this principle would deprive the questions between Texas and the United States of their sectional character and would leave them for adjustment, without disturbance from sectional prejudices and passions, . . .

. . . That in the event a dominant majority shall refuse to recognize the great constitutional rights we assert, and shall continue to deny the obligations of the Federal Government to maintain them, it is the sense of this convention that the territories should be treated as property, and divided between the sections of the Union, so that the rights of both sections be adequately secured in their respective shares. . . .

. . . That it is the opinion of this Convention that this controversy should be ended, either by a recognition of the constitutional Rights of the Southern people, or by an equitable partition of the territories. . . .

"What to the Slave is the Fourth of July?"

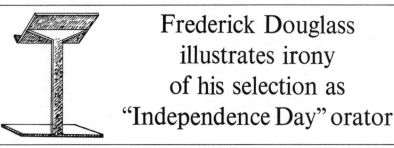

July 4, 1852
Rochester,
New York

Frederick Douglass
illustrates irony
of his selection as
"Independence Day" orator

Fellow Citizens: Pardon me, and allow me to ask, why am I called upon to speak here today? What have I or those I represent to do with your national independence? Are the great principles of political freedom and of natural justice, embodied in that Declaration of Independence, extended to us? And am I, therefore, called upon to bring our humble offering to the national altar, and to confess the benefits, and express devout gratitude for the blessings resulting from your independence to us?

Would to God, both for your sakes and ours, that an affirmative answer could be truthfully returned to these questions. Then would my task be light, and my burden easy and delightful. For who is there so cold that a nation's sympathy could not warm him? Who so obdurate and dead to the claims of gratitude, that would not thankfully acknowledge such priceless benefits? Who so stolid and selfish that would not give his voice to swell the halleluiahs of a nation's jubilee, when the chains of servitude had been torn from his limbs? I am not that man.

. . . I say it with a sad sense of disparity between us. I am not included within the pale of this glorious anniversary! Your high independence only reveals the immeasurable distance between us. The blessings in which you this day rejoice are not enjoyed in common. The rich inheritance of justice, liberty, prosperity, and independence bequeathed by your fathers is shared by you, not by me. The sunlight that brought life and healing to you has brought stripes and death to me. This Fourth of July is *yours,* not *mine. You* may rejoice, *I* must mourn. To drag a man in fetters into the grand illuminated temple of liberty, and call upon him to join you in joyous anthems, were inhuman mockery and sacrilegious irony. Do you mean, citizens, to mock me, by asking me to speak today? If so, there is a parallel to your conduct. And let me warn you, that it is dangerous to copy the example of a nation whose crimes, towering up to heaven, were thrown down by the breath of the Almighty, burying that nation in irrecoverable ruin. I can today take up the lament of a peeled and woe-smitten people.

"By the rivers of Babylon, there we sat down. Yes! We wept when we remembered

Zion. We hanged our harps upon the willows in the midst thereof. For there they that carried us away captive, required of us a song; and they who wasted us, required of us mirth, saying, Sing us one of the songs of Zion. How can we sing the Lord's song in a strange land? If I forget thee, O Jerusalem, let my right hand forget her cunning. If I do not remember thee, let my tongue cleave to the roof of my mouth."

Fellow citizens, above your national, tumultuous joy, I hear the mournful wail of millions, whose chains, heavy and grievous yesterday, are today rendered more intolerable by the jubilant shouts that reach them. If I do forget, if I do not remember those bleeding children of sorrow this day, "may my right hand forget her cunning, and may my tongue cleave to the roof of my mouth!" To forget them, to pass lightly over their wrongs, and to chime in with the popular theme, would be treason most scandalous and shocking, and would make me a reproach before God and the world. My subject, then, fellow citizens, is "American Slavery." I shall see this day and its popular characteristics from the slave's point of view. Standing here, identified with the American bondman, making his wrongs mine, I do not hesitate to declare, with all my soul, that the character and conduct of this nation never looked blacker to me than on this Fourth of July. Whether we turn to the declarations of the past, or to the professions of the present, the conduct of the nation seems equally hideous and revolting. America is false to the past, false to the present, and solemnly binds herself to be false to the future. Standing with God and the crushed and bleeding slave on this occasion, I will, in the name of humanity, which is outraged, in the name of liberty, which is fettered, in the name of the Constitution and the Bible, which are disregarded and trampled upon, dare to call in question and to denounce, with all the emphasis I can command, everything that serves to perpetuate slavery—the great sin and shame of America! "I will not equivocate; I will not excuse"; I will use the severest language I can command, and yet not one word shall escape me that any man, whose judgment is not blinded by prejudice, or who is not at heart a slaveholder, shall not confess to be right and just.

But I fancy I hear some of my audience say it is just in this circumstance that you and your brother Abolitionists fail to make a favorable impression on the public mind. Would you argue more and denounce less, would you persuade more and rebuke less, your cause would be much more likely to succeed. But, I submit, where all is plain there is nothing to be argued. What point in

the anti-slavery creed would you have me argue? On what branch of the subject do the people of this country need light? Must I undertake to prove that the slave is a man? That point is conceded already. Nobody doubts it. The slave-holders themselves acknowledge it in the enactment of laws for their government. They acknowledge it when they punish disobedience on the part of the slave. There are seventy-two crimes in the State of Virginia, which, if committed by a black man (no matter how ignorant he be), subject him to the punishment of death; while only two of these same crimes will subject a white man to like punishment. What is this but the acknowledgment that the slave is a moral, intellectual, and responsible being? The manhood of the slave is conceded. It is admitted in the fact that Southern statute-books are covered with enactments, forbidding, under severe fines and penalties, the teaching of the slave to read and write. When you can point to any such laws in reference to the beasts of the field, then I may consent to argue the manhood of the slave. When the dogs in your streets, when the fowls of the air, when the cattle on your hills, when the fish of the sea, and the reptiles that crawl, shall be unable to distinguish the slave from a brute, then I will argue with you that the slave is a man!

For the present it is enough to affirm the equal manhood of the Negro race. Is it not astonishing that, while we are plowing, planting, and reaping, using all kinds of mechanical tools, erecting houses, constructing bridges, building ships, working in metals of brass, iron, copper, silver, and gold; that while we are reading, writing, and cyphering, acting as clerks, merchants, and secretaries, having among us lawyers, doctors, ministers, poets, authors, editors, orators, and teachers; that while we are engaged in all the enterprises common to other men—digging gold in California, capturing the whale in the Pacific, feeding sheep and cattle on the hillside, living, moving, acting, thinking, planning, living in families as husbands, wives, and children, and above all, confessing and worshipping the Christian God, and looking hopefully for life and immortality beyond the grave—we are called upon to prove that we are men?

Would you have me argue that man is entitled to liberty? That he is the rightful owner of his own body? You have already declared it. Must I argue the wrongfulness of slavery? Is that a question for republicans? Is it to be settled by the rules of logic and argumentation, as a matter beset with great difficulty, involving a doubtful application of the principle of justice, hard to understand? How should I look today in the presence of Americans, dividing and subdividing a discourse, to show that men have a natural right to freedom, speaking of it relatively and positively, negatively and affirmatively? To do so would be to make myself ridiculous, and to offer an insult to your understanding. There is not a man beneath the canopy of heaven who does not know that slavery is wrong *for him*.

What! Am I to argue that it is wrong to make men brutes, to rob them of their liberty, to work them without wages, to keep them ignorant of their relations to their fellow men, to beat them with sticks, to flay their flesh with the last, to load their limbs with irons, to hunt them with dogs, to sell them at auction, to sunder their families, to knock out their teeth, to burn their flesh, to starve them into obedience and submission to their masters? Must I argue that a system thus marked with blood and stained with pollution is wrong? No; I will not. I have better employment for my time and strength than such arguments would imply.

What, then, remains to be argued? Is it that slavery is not divine; that God did not establish it; that our doctors of divinity are mistaken? There is blasphemy in the thought. That which is inhuman cannot be divine. Who can reason on such a proposition? They that can, may; I cannot. The time for such argument is past.

At a time like this, scorching irony, not convincing argument, is needed. Oh! had I the ability, and could I reach the nation's ear, I would today pour out a fiery stream of biting ridicule, blasting reproach, withering sarcasm, and stern rebuke. For it is not light that is needed, but fire; it is not the gentle shower, but thunder. We need the storm, the whirlwind, and the earthquake. The feeling of the nation must be quickened; the conscience of the nation must be roused; the propriety of the nation must be startled; the hypocrisy of the nation must be exposed; and its crimes against God and man must be denounced.

What to the American slave is your Fourth of July? I answer, a day that reveals to him more than all other days of the year, the gross injustice and cruelty to which he is the constant victim. To him your celebration is a sham; your boasted liberty an unholy license; your national greatness, swelling vanity; your sounds of rejoicing are empty and heartless; your denunciation of tyrants, brass-fronted impudence; your shouts of liberty and equality, hollow mockery; your prayers and hymns, your sermons and thanksgivings, with all your religious parade and solemnity, are to him mere bombast, fraud, deception, impiety, and hypocrisy—a thin veil to cover up crimes which would disgrace a nation of savages. . . .

Robert Purvis

Protests

Segregated Education

November 4, 1853 Philadelphia

Payment of "outrageous" school tax refused

You called yesterday for the tax upon my property in this Township, which I shall pay, excepting the "School Tax." I object to the payment of this tax, on the ground that my rights as a citizen, and my feelings as a man and a parent, have been grossly outraged in depriving me, in violation of law and justice, of the benefits of the school system which this tax was designed to sustain. I am perfectly aware that all that makes up the character and worth of the citizens of this township look upon the proscription and exclusion of my children from the Public School as illegal, and an unjustifiable usurpation of my right. I have borne this outrage ever since the innovation upon the usual practice of admitting *all* the children of the Township into the Public Schools, and at considerable expense, have been obliged to obtain the services of private teachers to instruct my children, while my school tax is greater, with a single exception, than that of any other citizen of the township.

It is true, (and the outrage is made but the more glaring and insulting,) I was informed by a *pious Quaker* director, with a sanctifying grace, imparting, doubtless, an unctuous glow to his *saintly* prejudices, that a school in the village of Mechanicsville was appropriated for *"thine."* The miserable shanty, with all its appurtenances, on the very line of the township, to which this *benighted* follower of George Fox alluded, is, as you know, the most flimsy and ridiculous sham which any tool of a skin-hating aristocracy could have resorted to, to cover or protect his servility. To submit by voluntary payment of the demand is too great an outrage upon nature, and, with a spirit, thank God, unshackled by this, or any other wanton and cowardly act, I shall resist this tax, which, before the unjust exclusion, had always afforded me the highest gratification in paying. With no other than the best feeling towards yourself, I am forced to this unpleasant position, in vindication of my rights and personal dignity . . .

The Sentencing

of Mrs. Douglass

for Teaching

Negro Children

to Read

. . . Upon an indictment found against you for assembling with negroes to instruct them to read and write, and for associating with them in an unlawful assembly, you were found guilty, and a mere nominal fine imposed. . . . The Court is not called on to vindicate the policy of the law in question, for so long as it remains upon the statute book, and unrepealed, public and private justice and morality require that it should be respected and sustained. There are persons, I believe, in our community, opposed to the policy of the law in question. They profess to believe that universal intellectual culture is necessary to religious instruction and education, and that such culture is suitable to a state of slavery; and there can be no misapprehension as to your opinion on the subject, judging from the indiscreet freedom with which you spoke of your regard for the colored race in general. Such opinions in the present state of our society I regard as manifestly mischievous. It is not true that our slaves cannot be taught religious and moral duty, without being able to read the Bible and use the pen . . .

A valuable report or document recently published in the city of New York by the Southern Aid Society sets forth many valuable and important truths upon the condition of the Southern slaves, and the utility of moral and religious instruction, apart from a knowledge of books. I recommend the careful perusal of it to all whose opinions concur with your own. It shows that a system of catechetical instruction, with a clear and simple exposition of Scripture, has been employed with gratifying success; that the slaves of the South are peculiarly susceptible of good religious influences. Their mere residence among a Christian people has wrought a great and happy change in their condition: they have been raised from the night of heathenism to the light of Christianity, and thousands of

1853
Norfolk,
Virginia

Judge Baker awards
maximum punishment
to foster respect
for Virginia slave code

them have been brought to a saving knowledge of the Gospel.

Of the one hundred millions of the negro race, there cannot be found another so large a body as the three millions of slaves in the United States, at once so intelligent, so inclined to the Gospel, and so blessed by the elevating influence of civilization and Christianity. Occasional instances of cruelty and oppression, it is true, may sometimes occur, and probably will ever continue to take place under any system of laws; but this is not confined to wrongs committed upon the negro; wrongs are committed and cruelty practiced in a like degree by the lawless white man upon his own color; and while the negroes of our own town and State are known to be surrounded by most of the substantial comforts of life, and invited both by precept and example to participate in proper, moral and religious duties, it argues, it seems to me, a sickly sensibility towards them to say their persons, and feelings, and interests are not sufficiently respected by our laws, . . .

. . . The first legislative provision upon this subject was introduced in the year 1831, immediately succeeding the bloody scenes of the memorable Southampton insurrection; and that law being found not sufficiently penal to check the wrongs complained of, was reenacted with additional penalties in the year of 1848, which last mentioned act, after several years' trial and experience, has been re-affirmed by adoption, and incorporated into our present code. After these several and repeated recognitions of the wisdom and propriety of the said act, it may well be said that bold and open opposition to it is a matter not to be slightly regarded. . . .

There might have been no occasion for such enactments in Virginia, or elsewhere, on the subject of negro education, but as a matter of self-defense against the schemes of Northern incendiaries, and the outcry against holding our slaves in bondage. Many now living well remember how, and when, and why the anti-slavery fury began, and by what means its manifestations were made public. Our mails were clogged with abolition pamphlets and inflammatory documents, to be distributed among our Southern negroes to induce them to cut our throats. . . . These, however, were not the only means resorted to by the Northern fanatics to stir up insubordination among our slaves. They scattered far and near pocket handkerchiefs, and other similar articles, with frightful engravings, and printed over with anti-slavery nonsense, with the view to work upon the feeling and ignorance of our negroes. . . . Under such circumstances there was but one measure of protection for the South, and that was adopted. . . . In vindication of the policy and justness of our laws, which every individual should be taught to respect, the judgment of the Court is, in addition to the proper fine and costs, that you be imprisoned for the period of one month. . . .

The Sentencing of Mrs. Douglass ☐ 139

Appeal of the Independent Democrats

Against the Nebraska Slavery Bill

As Senators and Representatives in the Congress of the United States it is our duty to warn our constituents, whenever imminent danger menaces the freedom of our institutions or the permanency of the Union.

Such danger, as we firmly believe, now impends, and we earnestly solicit your prompt attention to it.

At the last session of Congress a bill for the organization of the Territory of Nebraska passed the House of Representatives by an overwhelming majority. That bill was based on the principle of excluding slavery from the new Territory. It was not taken up for consideration in the Senate and consequently failed to become law.

At the present session a new Nebraska bill has been reported by the Senate Committee on Territories, which, should it unhappily receive the sanction of Congress, will open all the unorganized Territories of the Union to the ingress of slavery.

We arraign this bill as a gross violation of a sacred pledge; as a criminal betrayal of precious rights; as part and parcel of an atrocious plot to exclude from a vast unoccupied region immigrants from the Old World and free laborers from our own States, and convert it into a dreary region of despotism, inhabited by masters and slaves. . . .

The original settled policy of the United States, clearly indicated by the Jefferson proviso of 1784 and the Ordinance of 1787, was

non-extension of slavery.

In 1818, . . . the inhabitants of the Territory of Missouri applied to Congress for authority to form a State Constitution, and for admission into the Union. There were, at that time, in the whole territory acquired from France, outside of the State of Louisiana, not three thousand slaves.

There was no apology, in the circumstances of the country, for the continuance of slavery. The original national policy was against it, and not less the plain language of the treaty under which the territory had been acquired from France.

It was proposed, therefore, to incorporate in the bill authorizing the formation of a State government, a provision requiring that the constitution of the new State should contain an article providing for the abolition of existing slavery, and prohibiting the further introduction of slaves.

This provision was vehemently and pertinaciously opposed, but finally prevailed in the House of Representatives by a decided vote. In the Senate it was rejected, and—in consequence of the disagreement between the two Houses—the bill was lost.

At the next session of Congress, the controversy was renewed with increased violence. It was terminated at length by a compromise. Missouri was allowed to come into the Union with slavery; but a section was inserted in the act authorizing her admission, excluding

slavery forever from all the territory acquired from France, not included in the new State, lying north of 36° 30′ . . .

The question of the constitutionality of this prohibition was submitted by President Monroe to his cabinet. John Quincy Adams was then Secretary of State; John C. Calhoun was Secretary of War; William H. Crawford was Secretary of the Treasury; and William Wirt was Attorney-General. Each of these eminent gentlemen—three of them being from the slave States—gave a written opinion, affirming its constitutionality, and thereupon the act received the sanction of the President himself, also from a Slave State.

Nothing is more certain in history than the fact that Missouri could not have been admitted as a slave State had not certain members from the free States been reconciled to the measure by incorporation of this prohibition into the act of admission. Nothing is more certain than that this prohibition has been regarded and accepted by the whole country as a solemn compact against the extension of slavery . . . The same act—let it be ever remembered—which authorized the formation of a constitution by the State, without a clause forbidding slavery, consecrated, beyond question and beyond honest recall, the whole remainder of the Territory to freedom and free institutions forever. For more than thirty years—during more than half of our national existence under our pres-

ent Constitution—this compact has been universally regarded and acted upon as inviolable American law. In conformity with it, Iowa was admitted as a free State and Minnesota has been organized as a free Territory. . . .

. . . it is now deliberately proposed to repeal this prohibition, by implication or directly—the latter certainly the manlier way—and thus to subvert the compact, and allow slavery in all the yet unorganized territory. . . .

It is said that Nebraska sustains the same relations to slavery as did the territory acquired from Mexico prior to 1850, and that the pro-slavery clauses of the bill are necessary to carry into effect the compromise of that year. . . .

The statesmen whose powerful support carried the Utah and New Mexico acts never dreamed that their provisions would be ever applied to Nebraska . . .

These pretenses, therefore, that the territory covered by the positive prohibition of 1820, sustains a similar relation to slavery with that acquired from Mexico, covered by no prohibition except that of disputed constitutional or Mexican law, and that the Compromises of 1850 require the incorporation of the pro-slavery clauses of the Utah and New Mexico Bill in the Nebraska Act, are mere inventions, designed to cover from public reprehension meditated bad faith. Were he living now, no one would be more forward,

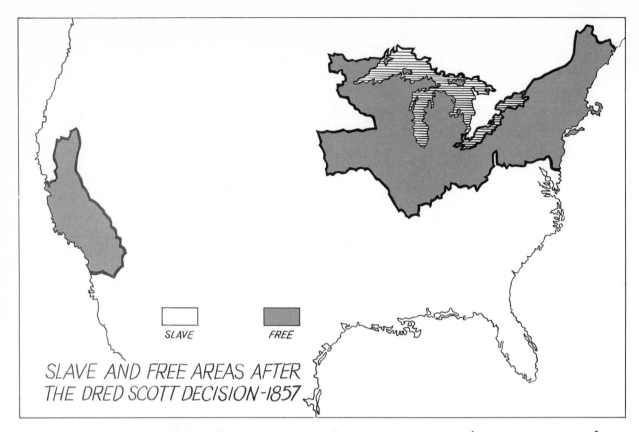

SLAVE AND FREE AREAS AFTER
THE DRED SCOTT DECISION·1857

more eloquent, or more indignant in his denunciation of that bad faith, than Henry Clay, the foremost champion of both compromises . . .

We confess our total inability properly to delineate the character or describe the consequences of this measure. . . .

We appeal to the people. We warn you that the dearest interests of freedom and the Union are in imminent peril. Demagogues may tell you that the Union can be maintained only by submitting to the demands of slavery. We tell you that the Union can only be maintained by the full recognition of the just claims of freedom and man. The Union was formed to establish justice and secure the blessings of liberty. When it fails to accomplish these ends it will be worthless, and when it becomes worthless it cannot long endure.

We entreat you to be mindful of that fundamental maxim of Democracy—EQUAL RIGHTS AND EXACT JUSTICE FOR ALL MEN. Do not submit to become agents in extending legalized oppression and systematized injus-

tice over a vast territory yet exempt from these terrible evils. . . .

Whatever apologies may be offered for the toleration of slavery in the States, none can be offered for its extension into Territories where it does not exist, and where that extension involves the repeal of ancient law and the violation of solemn compact. Let all protest, earnestly and emphatically, . . . against this enormous crime.

For ourselves, we shall resist it by speech and vote, and with all the abilities which God has given us. Even if overcome in the impending struggle, we shall not submit. We shall go home to our constituents, erect anew the standard of freedom, and call on the people to come to the rescue of the country from the domination of slavery. We will not despair; for the cause of human freedom is the cause of God.

S. P. Chase   Edward Wade
Charles Sumner   Gerritt Smith
J. R. Giddings   Alexander De Witt

The Kansas-Nebraska Act

May 30, 1854

The Missouri Compromise overthrown as both states admitted without restrictions on slavery

An Act to Organize the Territories of Nebraska and Kansas.

Be it enacted . . . , That all that part of the territory of the United States . . . by the name of the Territory of Nebraska; . . . when admitted as a State or States, the said Territory, or any portion of the same, shall be received into the Union with or without slavery, as their constitution may prescribe at the time of their admission: . . .

And be it further enacted, . . . That the Constitution, and all laws of the United States which are not locally inapplicable, shall have the same force and effect within the said Territory of Nebraska as elsewhere within the United States, except the eighth section of the act preparatory to the admission of Missouri into the Union, approved March 6, 1820, which, being inconsistent with the principle of non-intervention by Congress with slavery in the States and Territories, as recognized by the legislation of eighteen hundred and fifty, commonly called

the Compromise Measures, is hereby declared inoperative and void; it being the true intent and meaning of this act not to legislate slavery into any Territory or State, nor to exclude it therefrom, but to leave the people thereof perfectly free to form and regulate their domestic institutions in their own way, subject only to the Constitution of the United States: *Provided,* That nothing herein contained shall be construed to revive or put in force any law or regulation which may have existed prior to the act of March 6, 1820, either protecting, establishing, prohibiting, or abolishing slavery . . .

. . . And be it further enacted, That all that part of the Territory of the United States . . . by the name of the Territory of Kansas; . . . when admitted as a State or States, the said Territory, or any portion of the same, shall be received into the Union with or without slavery, as their constitution may prescribe at the same time of their admission. . . .

Massachusetts Personal Liberty Act

*A*n Act to protect the Rights and Liberties of the People of the Commonwealth of Massachusetts.

. . . The meaning of the one hundred and eleventh chapter of the Revised Statutes is hereby declared to be, that every person imprisoned or restrained of his liberty is entitled, as of right and of course, to the writ of *habeas corpus,* except in the cases mentioned in the second section of that chapter.

. . . The writ of *habeas corpus* may be issued by the supreme judicial court, the court of common pleas, by any justice's court or police court of any town or city, by any court of record, or by any justice of either of said courts, or by any judge of probate; and it may be issued by any justice of the peace, if no magistrate above named is known to said justice of the peace to be within five miles of the place where the party is imprisoned or restrained, and it shall be returnable before the supreme judicial court, or any one of the justices thereof, whether the court may be in session or not. . . .

. . . If any claimant shall appear to demand the custody or possession of the person for whose benefit such writ is sued out, such claimant shall state in writing the facts on which he relies, with precision and certainty; and neither the claimant of the alleged fugitive, nor any person interested in his alleged obligation to service or labor, nor the alleged fugitive, shall be permitted to testify at the trial of the issue; and no confessions, admissions or declarations of the alleged fugitive against himself shall be given in evidence. Upon every question of fact involved in the issue, the burden of proof shall be on the claimant, and the facts alleged and necessary to be established, must be proved by the testimony of at least two credible witnesses, or other legal evidence equivalent thereto, and by the rules of evidence known and secured by the common law; and no *ex parte* deposition or affidavit shall be received in proof in behalf of the claimant, and no presumption shall arise in favor of the claimant from any proof that the alleged fugitive or any of his ancestors had actually been held as a slave, without proof that such holding was legal.

. . . If any person shall remove from the limits of this Commonwealth, or shall assist in removing therefrom, or shall come into the Commonwealth with the intention of removing or of assisting in the removing therefrom, or shall procure or assist in procuring to be so removed, any person being in the peace thereof who is not "held to service and labor" by the "party" making "claim", or who has not "escaped" from the "party" making "claim" within the meaning of those words in the constitution of the United States,

May 21, 1855
Boston

The federal
Fugitive Slave Act's
provisions nullified by
Mass. legislature

on the pretence that such person is so held or has so escaped, or that his "service" or "labor" is so "due" or with the intent to subject him to such "service or labor," he shall be punished by a fine of not less than one thousand, nor more than five thousand dollars, and by imprisonment in the State Prison not less than one, nor more than five years. . . .

. . . Any person who shall grant any certificate under or by virtue of the acts of congress, mentioned in the preceding section, shall be deemed to have resigned any commission from the Commonwealth which he may possess, his office shall be deemed vacant, and he shall be forever thereafter ineligible to any office of trust, honor or emolument under the laws of this Commonwealth.

. . . Any person who shall act as counsel or attorney for any claimant of any alleged fugitive from service or labor, under or by virtue of the acts of congress mentioned in the ninth section of this act, shall be deemed to have resigned any commission from the Commonwealth that he may possess, and he shall be thereafter incapacitated from appearing as counsel or attorney in the courts of this Commonwealth . . .

. . . Any person holding any judicial office under the constitution or laws of this Commonwealth, who shall continue, for ten days after the passage of this act, to hold the office of United States commissioner, or any office . . . which qualifies him to issue any

warrant or other process . . . under the [Fugitive Slave Acts] shall be deemed to have violated good behavior, to have given reason for the loss of public confidence, and furnished sufficient ground either for impeachment or for removal by address.

. . . Any sheriff, deputy sheriff, jailer, coroner, constable, or other officer of this Commonwealth, or the police of any city or town, or any district, county, city or town officer, or any officer or other member of the volunteer militia of this Commonwealth, who shall hereafter arrest . . . any person for the reason that he is claimed or adjudged to be a fugitive from service or labor, shall be punished by fine . . . and by imprisonment. . . .

. . . The volunteer militia of the Commonwealth shall not act in any manner in the seizure . . . of any person for the reason that he is claimed or adjudged to be a fugitive from service or labor. . . .

. . . No jail, prison, or other place of confinement belonging to, or used by, either the Commonwealth of Massachusetts or any county therein, shall be used for the detention or imprisonment of any person accused or convicted of any offense created by (the Federal Fugitive Slave Acts) . . . or accused or convicted of obstructing or resisting any process, warrant, or order issued under either of said acts, or of rescuing, or attempting to rescue, any person arrested or detained under any of the provisions of either of the said acts. . . .

Dred Scott vs. *Sandford*

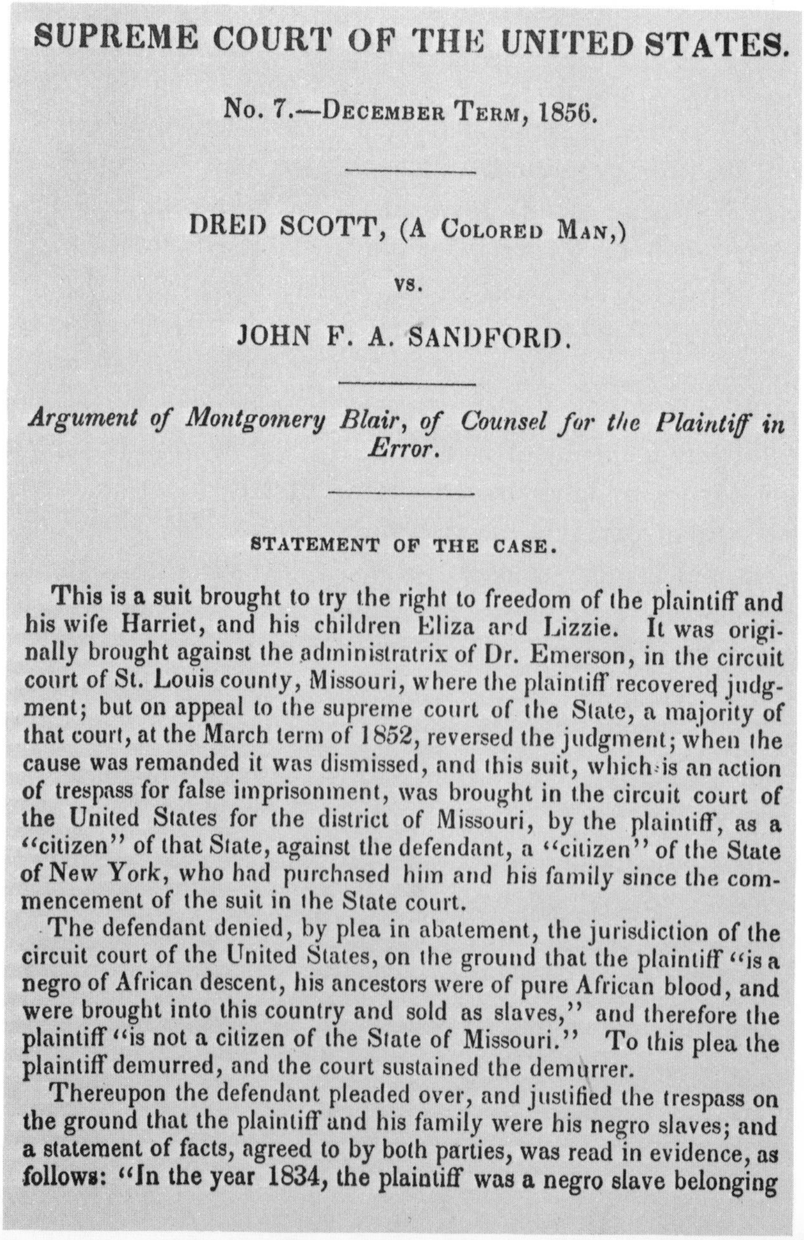

SUPREME COURT OF THE UNITED STATES.

No. 7.—December Term, 1856.

DRED SCOTT, (A Colored Man,)

vs.

JOHN F. A. SANDFORD.

Argument of Montgomery Blair, of Counsel for the Plaintiff in Error.

STATEMENT OF THE CASE.

This is a suit brought to try the right to freedom of the plaintiff and his wife Harriet, and his children Eliza and Lizzie. It was originally brought against the administratrix of Dr. Emerson, in the circuit court of St. Louis county, Missouri, where the plaintiff recovered judgment; but on appeal to the supreme court of the State, a majority of that court, at the March term of 1852, reversed the judgment; when the cause was remanded it was dismissed, and this suit, which is an action of trespass for false imprisonment, was brought in the circuit court of the United States for the district of Missouri, by the plaintiff, as a "citizen" of that State, against the defendant, a "citizen" of the State of New York, who had purchased him and his family since the commencement of the suit in the State court.

The defendant denied, by plea in abatement, the jurisdiction of the circuit court of the United States, on the ground that the plaintiff "is a negro of African descent, his ancestors were of pure African blood, and were brought into this country and sold as slaves," and therefore the plaintiff "is not a citizen of the State of Missouri." To this plea the plaintiff demurred, and the court sustained the demurrer.

Thereupon the defendant pleaded over, and justified the trespass on the ground that the plaintiff and his family were his negro slaves; and a statement of facts, agreed to by both parties, was read in evidence, as follows: "In the year 1834, the plaintiff was a negro slave belonging

FIRST PAGE — *Dred Scott* (a colored man) v. *John F. A. Sandford: Argument of Montgomery Blair, Scott's counsel.* (Harvard Law School Library)

Supreme Court dictum: Slaves are property

*[Chief Justice Taney
delivered the decision of the Court]*

. . . There are two leading questions presented by the record:

1. Had the Circuit Court of the United States jurisdiction to hear and determine the case between these parties? And.

2. If it had jurisdiction, is the judgment it has given erroneous or not?

The plaintiff in error, who was also the plaintiff in the court below, was, with his wife and children, held as slaves by the defendant, in the State of Missouri, and he brought this action in the Circuit Court of the United States for that district, to assert the title of himself and his family to freedom.

The declaration is . . . that he and the defendant are citizens of different States; that is, that he is a citizen of Missouri, and the defendant a citizen of New York.

The defendant pleaded in abatement to the jurisdiction of the court, that the plaintiff was not a citizen of the State of Missouri, as alleged in his declaration, being a negro of African descent whose ancestors were of pure African blood, and who were brought into this country and sold as slaves. . . .

That plea denies the right of the plaintiff to sue in a court of the United States, for the reasons therein stated.

If the question raised by it is legally before us, and the court should be of the opinion that the facts stated in it disqualify the plaintiff from becoming a citizen, in the sense in which that word is used in the Constitution of the United States, then the judgment of the Circuit Court is erroneous, and must be reversed. . . .

The question is simply this: Can a negro, whose ancestors were imported into this country, and sold as slaves, become a member of the political community formed and brought into existence by the Constitution of the United States, and as such become entitled to all the rights, and privileges, and immunities, guarantied by that instrument to the citizen? One of which rights is the privilege of suing in a court of the United States in the cases specified in the Constitution.

It will be observed, that the plea applies to that class of persons only whose ancestors were negroes of the African race, and imported into this country, and sold and held as slaves. . . . And this being the only matter in dispute on the pleadings, the court must be understood as speaking in this opinion of that class only, that is of persons who are the descendants of Africans who were imported into this country and sold as slaves. . . .

The words "people of the United States" and "citizens" are synonymous terms, and mean the same thing. They both describe the political body who, according to our republican institutions, form the sovereignty, and who hold the power and conduct the government through their representatives. They are what we familiarly call the "sovereign people," and every citizen is one of this people, and a constituent member of this sovereignty. The question before us is, whether the class of persons described in the plea in abatement compose a portion of this people, and are constituent members of this sovereignty? We think they are not, and they are not included, and were not intended to be included, under the word "citizens" in the Constitution, and can, therefore, claim none of the rights and privileges which that instrument provides for and secures to citizens of the United States. . . .

It is very clear, therefore, that no State can, by any Act or law of its own, passed since the adoption of the Constitution, introduce a new member into the political community created by the Constitution of the United States. It cannot make him a member of this community by making him a member of its own. And for the same reason it cannot introduce any person, or description of persons, who were not intended to be embraced in this new political family, which the Constitution brought into existence, but were intended to be excluded from it.

The question then arises, whether the provisions of the Constitution, in relation to the personal rights and privileges to which the citizen of a State should be entitled,

embraced the negro African race, at that time in this country, or who might afterwards be imported, who had then or should afterwards be made free in any State; and to put it in the power of a single State to make him a citizen of the United States, and endue him with the full rights of citizenship in every other State without their consent. . . .

The court think the affirmative of these propositions cannot be maintained. And if it cannot, the plaintiff in error could not be a citizen of the State of Missouri, within the meaning of the Constitution of the United States, and, consequently, was not entitled to sue in its courts.

It is true, every person, and every class and description of persons, who were at the time of the adoption of the Constitution recognized as citizens in the several States, became also citizens of this new political body; but none other; it was formed by them, and for them and their posterity, but for no one else. And the personal rights and privileges guarantied to the citizens of this new sovereignty were intended to embrace those only who were then members of the several state communities, or who should afterwards, by birthright or otherwise, become members, according to the provisions of the Constitution and the principles on which it was founded. . . .

In the opinion of the court, the legislation and histories of the times, and the language used in the Declaration of Independence, show, that neither the class of persons who have been imported as slaves, nor their descendants, whether they had become free or not, were then acknowledged as a part of the people, nor intended to be included in the general words used in that memorable instrument. . . .

They had for more than a century before been regarded as beings of an inferior order; and altogether unfit to associate with the white race, either in social or political relations; and so far inferior that they had no rights which the white man was bound to respect; and that the negro might justly and lawfully be reduced to slavery for his benefit. . . . This opinion was at that time fixed and universal in the civilized portion of the white race. It was regarded as an axiom in morals as well as in politics, which no one thought of disputing, or supposed to be open to dispute; . . .

But there are two clauses in the Constitution which point directly and specifically to the negro race as a separate class of persons, and show clearly that they were not regarded as a portion of the people or citizens of the Government then formed.

One of these clauses reserves to each of the thirteen States the right to import slaves until the year 1808, if he thinks it proper. And the importation which it thus sanctions was unquestionably of persons of the race of which we are speaking, as the traffic in slaves in the United States had always been confined to them. And by the other provision the States pledge themselves to each other to maintain the right of property of the master, by delivering up to him any slave who may have escaped from his service, and be found within their respective territories. . . . And these two provisions show, conclusively, that neither the description of persons therein referred to, nor their descendants, were embraced in any of the other provisions of the Constitution; . . .

But it is said that a person may be a citizen, and entitled to that character, although he does not possess all the rights which may belong to other citizens; as, for example, the right to vote, or to hold particular offices; and that yet, when he goes into another State, he is entitled to be recognized there as a citizen, although the State may measure his rights by the rights which it allows to persons of a like character or class, resident in the State, and refuse to him the full rights of citizenship.

This argument overlooks the language of the provision in the Constitution of which we are speaking.

Undoubtedly, a person may be a citizen, that is, a member of the community who form the sovereignty, although he exercises no share of the political power, and is incapacitated from holding particular offices. . . .

So, too, a person may be entitled to vote by the law of the State, who is not a citizen even of the State itself. . . . And the State may give the right to free negroes and mulattoes, but that does not make them citizens of the State, and still less of the United States. And the provision in the Constitution giving privileges and immunities in other States, does not apply to them.

Neither does it apply to a person who, being the citizen of a State, migrates to another State. For then he becomes subject to the laws of the State in which he lives, and he is no longer a citizen of the State from which he removed. And the State in which he resides may then, unquestionably, determine his status or condition, and place him among the class of persons who are not recognized as citizens, but belong to an inferior and subject race; and may deny him the privileges and immunities enjoyed by its citizens. . . .

. . . But if he ranks as a citizen of the State to which he belongs, within the meaning of the Constitution of the United States, then, whenever he goes into another State, the Constitution clothes him, as to the rights of person, with all the privileges and immunities which belong to citizens of the State. And if persons of the African race are citizens of a state, and of the United States, they would be entitled to all of these privileges and immunities in every State, and the State could not restrict them; for they would hold these privileges and immunities, under the paramount authority of the Federal Government, and its courts would be bound to maintain and enforce them. . . .

And upon a full and careful consideration of the subject, the court is of opinion that, upon the facts stated in the plea in abatement, Dred Scott was not a citizen of Missouri within the meaning of the Constitution of the United States, and not entitled as such to sue in its courts; and, consequently, that the Circuit Court had no jurisdiction of the case, and that the judgment on the plea in abatement is erroneous. . . .

We proceed, therefore, to inquire whether the facts relied on by the plaintiff entitled him to his freedom. . . .

In considering this part of the controversy, two questions arise: 1st. Was he, together with his family, free in Missouri by reason of the stay in the territory of the United States hereinbefore mentioned? And 2d, If they were not, is Scott himself free by reason of his removal to Rock Island, in the State of Illinois, as stated in the above admissions?

We proceed to examine the first question.

The Act of Congress, upon which the plaintiff relies, declares that slavery and involuntary servitude, except as a punishment for crime, shall be forever prohibited in all that part of the territory ceded by France, under the name of Louisiana, which lies north of thirty-six degrees thirty minutes latitude, and not included within the limits of Missouri. And the difficulty which meets us at the threshold of this part of the inquiry is, whether Congress was authorized to pass this law under any of the powers granted to it by the Constitution; for if the authority is not given by that instrument, it is the duty of this court to declare it void and inoperative, and incapable of conferring freedom upon any one who is held as a slave under the laws of any one of the States.

The counsel for the plaintiff has laid much stress upon that article in the Constitution which confers on Congress the power "to dispose of and make all needful rules and regulations respecting the territory or other property belonging to the United States;" but, in the judgment of the court, that provision has no bearing on the present controversy, and the power there given, whatever it may be, is confined, and was intended to be confined, to the territory which at that time belonged to, or was claimed by the United States, and was within their boundaries . . . and can have no influence upon a territory afterwards acquired from a foreign Government. It was a special provision for a known and particular territory, and to meet a present emergency, and nothing more. . . .

But the power of Congress over the person or property of a citizen can never be a mere discretionary power under our Constitution and form of Government. The powers of the

Government and the rights and privileges of the citizen are regulated and plainly defined by the Constitution itself. And when the Territory becomes a part of the United States, the Federal Government enters into possession in the character impressed upon it by those who created it. It enters upon it with its powers over the citizen strictly defined, and limited by the Constitution, from which is derives its own existence, and by virtue of which alone it continues to exist and act as a Government and sovereignty. It has no power of any kind beyond it; . . . .

. . . An Act of Congress which deprives a person of the United States of his liberty or property merely because he came himself or brought his property into a particular Territory of the United States, and who had committed no offense against the laws, could hardly be dignified with the name of due process of law. . . .

. . . if the Constitution recognizes the right of property of the master in a slave, and makes no distinction between that description of property and other property owned by a citizen, no tribunal, acting under the authority of the United States, whether it be legislative, executive, or judicial, has a right to draw such a distinction, or deny to it the benefit of the provisions and guarantees which have been provided for the protection of private property against the encroachments of the Government.

Now . . . the right of property in a slave is distinctly and expressly affirmed in the Constitution. The right to traffic in it, like an ordinary article of merchandise and property, was guaranteed to the citizens of the United States, in every State that might desire it, for twenty years. And the Government in express terms is pledged to protect it in all future time, if the slave escapes from his owner . . . And no word can be found in the Constitution which gives Congress a greater power over slave property, or which entitles property of that kind to less protection than property of any other description. The only power conferred is the power coupled with the duty of guarding and protecting the owner in his rights.

Upon these considerations, it is the opinion of the court that the Act of Congress which prohibited a citizen from holding and owning property of this kind in the territory of the United States north of the line therein mentioned, is not warranted by the Constitution, and is therefore void; and that neither Dred Scott himself, nor any of his family, were made free by being carried into this territory; even if they had been carried there by the owner, with the intention of becoming a permanent resident. . . .

Upon the whole, therefore, it is the judgment of this court, that it appears by the record before us that the plaintiff in error is not a citizen of Missouri, in the sense in which that word is used in the Constitution; and that the Circuit Court of the United States, for that reason, had no jurisdiction in the case, and could give no judgment in it. . . .

Its judgment for the defendant must, consequently, be reversed, and a mandate issued directing the suit to be dismissed for want of jurisdiction.

WAYNE, J., NELSON, J., GRIER, J., DANIEL, J., CAMPBELL, J., and CATRON, J., filed separate concurring opinions. MCLEAN, J. and CURTIS, J. dissented.

SECTION III

THE WALLS CAME TUMBLIN' DOWN

Joshua fit the battle of Jericho
Jericho, Jericho
Joshua fit the battle of Jericho
And the walls came tumblin' down.

INTRODUCTION

WHEN, IN 1857, Chief Justice Roger B. Taney handed down the Dred Scott decision, he let loose concepts that would long plague the Nation. His definition of the Negro as an inferior being in the eyes of the law provoked a debate that has not yet been settled; and his overthrow of the Missouri Compromise set the stage for war between the States.

The "irrepressible conflict" became unavoidable with Abraham Lincoln's victory (180 of 303 electoral votes) in the election of 1860. Lincoln offered the South an olive branch in his first inaugural address:

> "The government will not assail you. You can have no conflict without being yourselves the aggressors. . . .

> "We are not enemies but friends. We must not be enemies. Though passion may have strained, it must not break our bonds of affection. . . ."

However, the new president's attempts at conciliation were too late. The South had already moved in the direction of conflict and turned deaf ears to Lincoln's placating statements.

South Carolina took the first step. Immediately after the election, the state cited Lincoln's antipathy to slavery, and withdrew from the Union. Mississippi, Florida, Alabama, Georgia, Louisiana and Texas followed soon after. By February 1861 these states had formed the Confederate States of America. Jefferson Davis, who had represented Mississippi in the United States Senate, became the first President. He justified secession by describing Northern sentiment against slavery, concluding:

> ". . . the labor of African slaves was and is indispensable. . . .

THE CONTRABAND

FREEDOM FIGHTER: *The evolution of a Negro from slave to war-disabled veteran is shown above and on the following pages. These illustrations are from a post Civil War issue of* Harper's Weekly.

> "With interests of such overwhelming magnitude imperiled, the people of the Southern States were driven by the conduct of the North to the adoption of some course of action to avert the danger with which they were openly menaced. . . ."

The battle was joined on April 12, 1861—just one month and eight days after Lincoln's inauguration—when South Carolina troops bombarded Fort Sumter in Charleston harbor. Support of Union retaliatory action came even from Lincoln's old rival, Stephen A.

THE RECRUIT

Ulysses S. Grant. The war had seen over three million men called to the colors of the North and South. Fatalities numbered 620,000. The triumph of the Constitution and the principle of *union* exacted one other toll from the Nation: on Good Friday, April 14, 1865, Abraham Lincoln, United States Commander in Chief, was assassinated by John Wilkes Booth, a crazed actor. After firing the fatal shot Booth declared: "The South is avenged."

The war had invigorating impact on the economy of the North. Manufacturing concerns, particularly those engaged in war supplies, thrived and grew rich. To the South, however, the war brought economic ruin. The old plantations and their aristocratic overlords became part of a vanishing civilization. The West continued to grow, and the Homestead Act of 1862—providing that 160 acres of public land would become the property of anyone who cultivated it for five years—stimulated the expansion. Four years after the War, from the East to the West, the nation had been linked by railroads.

Women, too, achieved new status during the War. They were used with good effect by both the North and the South as spies. They served as military nurses, directors of recreation, schoolteachers, fund-raisers for charities and social workers to those experiencing personal upheaval in the wake of war.

Socially, the most significant result of the War was Negro emancipation. Slavery's abolition, however, was not a gift bestowed upon the Negro. He, too, had participated in the realization of his freedom. *Freedom to the Free,* described the Freedmen's Memorial statue of Lincoln and noted that the artist was criticized because he first "represented the slave kneeling in a completely passive position, receiving his freedom at the hands of Lincoln, his liberator." In the final rendering, the slave is shown exerting his strength to break the chains of slavery.

For a time it looked as though the Negro would play no part in securing his freedom. His appeals for enlistment in the armed forces were refused by Northern state militias and by the War Department. In the South, however, he was pressed into service by the Con-

Douglas, who declared: "There can be but two parties, the party of patriots and the party of traitors."

War necessitated a stand on the part of the remaining Southern States. Accordingly, Virginia, Arkansas, Tennessee and North Carolina entered the Confederacy. The Union-sympathizing Western counties of Virginia left the state and became West Virginia. Missouri, Kentucky, Maryland and Delaware continued as members of the Union.

What was expected to be a short war lengthened into four years. On Palm Sunday, April 9, 1865, Confederate General Robert E. Lee surrendered to the Union's General

federate Army and the governors of six Southern States. He became the vital cog in the South's "home front" effort.

The Emancipation Proclamation, as a tactic to induce Southern slaves to run away, proved highly effective. And, as the War stretched on, the Proclamation's provisions for the enlistment of freed Negroes proved the answer to Northern problems of conscription. Negroes filled state quotas; they became highly acceptable substitutes for Northern white draftees looking for a way out.

Equality was not an inducement to Negro volunteers. Compared with the white soldiers, Negroes realized that:

> their pay would be lower,
> their period of service longer,
> the promotions slower,
> their weapons less perfect,
> their medical treatment inferior, and
> their safety less sure if captured.

Still, because this was their fight too, some 180,000 volunteered for the Union Army and 38,000 gave their lives in battle. (The proud Fifty-Fourth Massachusetts Regiment served one year without pay in protest against the disparate treatment.) Lauded by Secretary Stanton as "among the bravest of the brave, performing deeds of daring and shedding their blood with a heroism unsurpassed by soldiers of any other race," the Negro soldier is due credit for helping to assure the Union's survival and freedom for his race.

Negro sailors were no less valiant. Of the Navy's total strength of 118,000 men, some 29,000 were Negroes. One of the War's most daring naval exploits was engineered by Robert Smalls, a young slave from South Carolina, assigned to the all-Negro crew aboard a Confederate gunboat, the *Planter*. During the night, while the white officers of the ship were ashore visiting their homes, Smalls smuggled his relatives aboard, built up a head of steam, and flying the Confederate flag, sailed for the open sea. He headed the ship toward the Union Navy's blockade and surrendered it to the Union as a "gift from the Confederacy."

When the War ended, the Negro stood expectantly on the threshold of a new era. With the adoption of the Thirteenth Amendment in December, 1865, he exulted:

> *Free at last!*
> *Free at last!*
> *Thank God a-mighty*
> *I'm free at last!*

A new era had indeed dawned. William Lloyd Garrison, the abolitionist editor, saw it as a period during which the important job of "making the freedmen in every sense a free man and citizen" would be undertaken. That job remains to be completed.

THE VETERAN

PORTRAIT—JOHN BROWN
(Print Room, New York Public Library)

John Brown's Speech

After Being

Adjudged Guilty of Treason

November
2,
1859
Virginia

Foe of slavery denies
treason and murder
and restates
righteousness of abolition

I have, may it please the Court, a few words to say.

In the first place, I deny everything but what I have all along admitted,—the design on my part to free the slaves. I intended certainly to have made a clean thing of that matter, as I did last winter, when I went into Missouri and there took slaves without the snapping of a gun on either side, moved them through the country, and finally left them in Canada. I designed to have done the same thing again, on a larger scale. That was all I intended. I never did intend murder, or treason, or the destruction of property, or to excite or incite slaves to rebellion, or to make insurrection.

I have another objection; and that is, it is unjust that I should suffer such a penalty. Had I interfered in the manner which I admit has been fairly proved (for I admire the truthfulness and candor of the greater portion of the witnesses who have testified in this case),—had I so interfered in behalf of the rich, the powerful, the intelligent, the so-called great, or in behalf of any of their friends,—either father, mother, brother, sister, wife, or children, or any of that class,—and suffered and sacrificed what I have in this interference, it would have been all right; and every man in this court would have deemed it an act worthy of reward rather than punishment.

This court acknowledges, as I suppose, the validity of the law of God. I see a book kissed here which I suppose to be the Bible, or at least the New Testament. That teaches me that all things whatsoever I would that men should do to me, I should do even so to them. It teaches me, further, to "remember them that are in bonds, as bound with them." I endeavored to act to that instruction. I say, I am yet too young to understand that God is any respecter of persons. I believe that to have interfered as I have done—as I have always freely admitted I have done—in behalf of His despised poor, was not wrong, but right. Now, if it is deemed necessary that I should forfeit my life for the furtherance of the ends of justice, and mingle my blood further with the blood of my children and with the blood of millions in this slave country whose rights are disregarded by wicked, cruel, and unjust enactments,—I submit; so let it be done!

Let me say one word further.

. . . But I feel no consciousness of guilt. I have stated from the first what was my intention, and what was not. I never had any design against the life of any person, nor any disposition to commit treason, or excite slaves to rebel, or make any general insurrection. I never encouraged any man to do so, but always discouraged any idea of that kind.

Let me say, also, a word in regard to the statements made by some of those connected with me. I hear it has been stated by some of them that I have induced them to join me. But the contrary is true. I do not say this to injure them, but as regretting their weakness. There is not one of them but joined me of his own accord, and the greater part of them at their own expense. A number of them I never saw, and never had a word of conversation with, till the day they came to me; and that was for the purpose I have stated.

Now I have done.

John Brown's Speech After Being Adjudged Guilty of Treason   ☐   157

The Correspondence of

Mrs. Logue,
The Slaveholder's Letter
February 20, 1860

To Jarm:—I now take my pen to write you a few lines, to let you know how we all are. I am a cripple, but I am still able to get about. The rest of the family are all well. Cherry is as well as common. I write you these lines to let you know the situation we are in,—partly in consequence of your running away and stealing Old Rock, our fine mare. Though we got the mare back, she never was worth much after you took her;—and, as I now stand in need of some funds, I have determined to sell you, and I have had an offer for you, but did not see fit to take it. If you will send me one thousand dollars, and pay for the old mare, I will give up all claim I have to you. Write to me as soon as you get these lines, and let me know if you will accept my proposition. In consequence of your running away, we had to sell Abe and Ann and twelve acres of land; and I want you to send me the money, that I may be able to redeem the land that you was the cause of our selling, and on receipt of the above-named sum of money, I will send you your bill of sale. If you do not comply with my request, I will sell you to some one else, and you may rest assured that the time is not far distant when things will be changed with you. Write to me as soon as you get these lines. Direct your letter to Bigbyville, Maury County, Tennessee. You had better comply with my request.

I understand that you are a preacher. As the Southern people are so bad you had better come and preach to your old acquaintances. I would like to know if you read your Bible. If so, can you tell what will become of the thief if he does not repent? and, if the blind lead the blind, what will the consequence be? I deem it unnecessary to say much more at present. A word to the wise is sufficient. You know where the liar has his part. You know that we reared you as we reared our own children; that you was never abused, and that shortly before you ran away, when your master asked if you would like to be sold, you said you would not leave him to go with anybody.

a Slave-owner

and Her

Former Slave

The Rev. Mr. Loguen,
The Fugitive Slave's Reply
March 28, 1860

Mrs. Sarah Logue: Yours of the 20th of February is duly received, and I thank you for it. It is a long time since I heard from my poor old mother, and I am glad to know that she is yet alive, and, as you say, "as well as common." What that means, I don't know. I wish you had said more about her.

You are a woman; but, had you a woman's heart, you never could have insulted a brother by telling him you sold his only remaining brother and sister, because he put himself beyond your power to convert him into money.

You sold my brother and sister, Abe and Ann, and twelve acres of land, you say, because I ran away. Now you have the unutterable meanness to ask me to return and be your miserable chattel, or in lieu thereof, send you $1000 to enable you to redeem the *land*, but not to redeem my poor brother and sister! If I were to send you money, it would be to get my brother and sister, and not that you should get land. You say you are a *cripple*, and doubtless you say it to stir my pity, for you knew I was susceptible in that direction. I do pity you from the bottom of my heart. Nevertheless, I am indignant beyond the power of words to express, that you should be so sunken and cruel as to tear the hearts I love so much all in pieces; that you should be willing to impale and crucify us all, out of compassion for your poor *foot* or *leg*. Wretched woman! Be it known to you that I value my freedom, to say nothing of my mother, brothers and sisters, more than your whole body; more, indeed, than my own life; more than all the lives of all the slaveholders and tyrants under heaven.

You say you have offers to buy me, and that you shall sell me if I do not send you $1000, and in the same breath and almost in the same sentence, you say, "You know we raised you as we did our own children." Woman, did you raise your *own children* for the market? Did you raise them for the whipping-post? Did you raise them to be driven off, bound to a coffle in chains? Where are my poor bleeding brothers and sisters? Can you tell? Who was it that sent them off into sugar and cotton fields, to be kicked and cuffed, and whipped, and to groan and die; and where no kin can hear their groans, or attend and sympathize at their dying bed, or follow in their funeral? Wretched woman! Do you say *you* did not do it? Then I reply, your husband did, and *you* approved the deed —and the very letter you sent me shows that your heart approves it all. Shame on you!

But, by the way, where is your husband? You don't speak of him. I infer, therefore, that he is dead, that he has gone to his great account, with all his sins against my poor family upon his head. Poor man! gone to meet the spirits of my poor, outraged and murdered people, in a world where Liberty and Justice are *Masters*.

But you say I am a thief, because I took the old mare along with me. Have you got to learn that I had a better right to the old mare, as you call her, than Mannasseth Logue had to me? Is it a greater sin for me to steal his horse, than it was for him to rob my mother's cradle, and steal me? If he and you infer that I forfeit all my rights to you, shall not I infer that you forfeit all your rights to me? Have you got to learn that human rights are mutual and reciprocal, and if you take my liberty and life, you forfeit your own liberty and life? Before God and high heaven, is there a law for one man which is not a law for every other man?

If you or any other speculator on my body and rights, wish to know how I regard my rights, they need but come here, and lay their hands on me to enslave me. Did you think to terrify me by presenting the alternative to give my money to you, or give my body to slavery? Then let me say to you, that I meet the proposition with unutterable scorn and contempt. The proposition is an outrage and an insult. I will not budge one hair's breadth. I will not breathe a shorter breath, even to save me from your persecutions. I stand among a free people, who, I thank God, sympathize with my rights, and the rights of mankind; and if your emissaries and venders come here to re-enslave me, and escape the unshrinking vigor of my own right arm, I trust my strong and brave friends, in this city and State, will be my rescuers and avengers.

Lincoln's Proposals

PORTRAIT—ABRAHAM LINCOLN
(Print Room, New York Public Library)

1862

Presidential plans
for gradual and just
"abolishment" of slavery

for Compensated Emancipation

Message to Congress

March 6, 1862

FELLOW-CITIZENS OF THE SENATE AND HOUSE OF REPRESENTATIVES:—I recommend the adoption of a joint resolution by your honorable bodies which shall be substantially as follows:

"Resolved, That the United States ought to co-operate with any State which may adopt gradual abolishment of slavery, giving to such State pecuniary aid, to be used by such State, in its discretion, to compensate for the inconveniences, public and private, produced by such change of system."

If the proposition contained in the resolution does not meet the approval of Congress and the country, there is the end; but if it does command such approval, I deem it of importance that the States and people immediately interested should be at once distinctly notified of the fact, so that they begin to consider whether to accept or reject it. The Federal Government would find its highest interest in such a measure, as one of the most efficient means of self-preservation. The leaders of the existing insurrection entertain the hope that this government will ultimately be forced to acknowledge the independence of some part of the disaffected region, and

. . . I recommend the adoption of the following resolution and articles amendatory to the Constitution of the United States:

Resolved by the Senate and House of Representatives of the United States of America, in Congress assembled, (two thirds of both Houses concurring), That the following articles be proposed to the Legislatures (or conventions) of the several States as amendments to the Constitution of the United States, all or any of which articles, when ratified by three fourths of the said Legislatures (or conventions), to be valid as part or parts of the said Constitution, viz:

. . . Every State wherein slavery now exists which shall abolish the same therein at any time or times before the 1st day of January, A.D. 1900, shall receive compensation from the United States as follows, to wit:

The President of the United States shall deliver to every such State bonds of the United States bearing interest at the rate of —per cent per annum to an amount equal to the aggregate sum of—for each slave shown to have been therein by the Eighth Census of the United States, said bonds to be delivered to such State by instalments or in one parcel at the completion of the abolishment, accordingly as the same shall have been gradual or at one time within such State; and interest shall begin to run upon any such bond only from the proper time of its delivery as aforesaid. Any State having received bonds as aforesaid and afterwards reintroducing or tolerating slavery therein shall refund to the United States the bonds so received, or the value thereof, and all interest paid thereon.

that all the slave States north of such part will then say, "The Union for which we have struggled being already gone, we now choose to go with the Southern section." To deprive them of this hope substantially ends the rebellion, and the initiation of emancipation completely deprives them of it as to all the States initiating it. The point is not that all the States tolerating slavery would initiate emancipation; but that, while the offer is equally made to all, the more northern shall by such initiation make it certain to the more southern that in no event will the former ever join the latter in their proposed confederacy. I say "initiation" because, in my judgment, gradual and not sudden emancipation is better for all. In the mere financial or pecuniary view, any member of Congress with the census tables and treasury reports before him can readily see for himself how very soon the current expenditures of this war would purchase, at fair valuation, all the slaves in any named State. Such a proposition on the part of the General Government sets up no claim of a right by Federal authority to interfere with slavery within State limits, referring, as it does, the absolute control of the subject in each case to the State and its people immediately interested. . . .

. . . All slaves who shall have enjoyed actual freedom by the chances of the war at any time before the end of the rebellion shall be forever free; but all owners of such who shall not have been disloyal shall be compensated for them at the same rates as is provided for the States adopting abolishment of slavery, but in such way that no slave shall be twice accounted for.

. . . Congress may appropriate money and otherwise provide for colonizing free colored persons with their own consent at any place or places without the United States.

I beg indulgence to discuss these proposed articles at some length. Without slavery the rebellion could never have existed; without slavery it could not continue.

Among the friends of the Union there is great diversity of sentiment and policy in regard to slavery and the African race amongst us. Some would perpetuate slavery; some would abolish it suddenly and without compensation; some would abolish it gradually and with compensation; some would remove the freed people from us, and some would retain them with us; and there are yet other minor diversities. Because of these diversities we waste much strength in struggles among ourselves. By mutual concession we should harmonize and act together. This would be compromise, but it would be compromise among the friends and not with the enemies of the Union. . . . If the plan shall be adopted, it is assumed that emancipation will follow, at least in several of the States.

The emancipation will be unsatisfactory to the advocates of perpetual slavery, but the length of time should greatly mitigate their dissatisfaction. The time spares both races from the evils of sudden derangement —in fact, from the necessity of any derangement—while most of those whose habitual course of thought will be disturbed by the measure will have passed away before its consummation. They will never see it. Another class will hail the prospect of emancipation, but will deprecate the length of time. They will feel that it gives too little to the now living slaves. But it really gives them much. It saves them from the vagrant destitution which must largely attend immediate emancipation in localities where their numbers are very great, and it gives the inspiring assurance that their posterity shall be free forever. . . .

The plan would, I am confident, secure peace more speedily and maintain it more permanently than can be done by force alone, while all it would cost, considering amounts and manner of payment and times of payment, would be easier paid than will be the additional cost of the war if we rely solely upon force. . . . it would cost no blood at all.

Fellow-citizens, *we* can not escape history. We of this Congress and this administration will be remembered in spite of ourselves. No personal significance or insignificance can spare one or another of us. The fiery trial through which we pass will light us down in honor or dishonor to the latest generation. We *say* we are for the Union. The world will not forget that we say this. We know how to save the Union. The world knows we do know how to save it. We, even *we here*, hold the power and bear the responsibility. In *giving* freedom to the *slave* we *assure* freedom to the *free*. . . . We shall nobly save or meanly lose the last, best hope of earth. . . . The way is plain, peaceful, generous, just—a way which if followed the world will forever applaud and God must forever bless.

ABRAHAM LINCOLN.

William Wells Brown

Presses for Negro Participation

in the Civil War

. . . ONE of the first things that I heard when I arrived in the free States—and it was the strangest thing to me that I heard—was, that the slaves cannot take care of themselves. I came off without any education. Society did not take me up; I took myself up. (Laughter.) I did not ask society to take me up. All I asked of the white people was, to get out of the way, and give me a chance to come from the South to the North. That was all I asked, and I went to work with my own hands. And that is all I demand for my brethren of the South to-day—that they shall have an opportunity to exercise their own physical and mental abilities. Give them that, and I will leave the slaves to take care of themselves, and be satisfied with the result.

Now, Mr. President, I think that the present contest has shown clearly that the fidelity of the black people of this country to the cause of freedom is enough to put to shame every white man in the land who would think of driving us out of the country, provided freedom shall be proclaimed. I remember well, when Mr. Lincoln's proclamation went forth, calling for the first 75,000 men, that among the first to respond to that call were the colored men. A meeting was held in Boston, crowded as I never saw a meeting before; meetings were held in Rhode Island and Connecticut, in New York and Philadelphia, and throughout the West, responding to the President's call. Although the colored men in many of the free States were disfranchised, abused, taxed without representation, their children turned out of the schools, nevertheless, they went on, determined to try to discharge their duty to the country, and to save it from the tyrannical power of the slaveholders of the South. But the cry went forth—"We won't have the

Speech asserts Negro's
capacity for self-care
if given opportunity

Negroes; we won't have anything to do with them; we won't fight with them; we won't have them in the army, nor about us." Yet scarcely had you got into conflict with the South, when you were glad to receive the news that contrabands brought. (Applause.) The first telegram announcing any news from the disaffected district commences with—"A contraband just in from Maryland tells us" so much. The last telegram, in to-day's paper, announces that a contraband tells us so much about Jefferson Davis and Mrs. Davis and the little Davises. (Laughter.) The nation is glad to receive the news from the contraband. We have an old law with regard to the mails, that a Negro shall not touch the mails at all; and for fifty years the black man has not had the privilege of touching the mails of the United States with his little finger; but we are glad enough now to have the Negro bring the mail in his pocket! The first thing asked of a contraband is—"Have you got a newspaper?—what's the news?" And the news is greedily taken in, from the lowest officer or soldier in the army, up to the Secretary of War. They have tried to keep the Negro out of the war, but they could not keep him out, and now they drag him in, with his news, and are glad to do so. General Wool says the contrabands have brought the most reliable news. Other Generals say their information can be relied upon. The Negro is taken as a pilot to guide the fleet of General Burnside through the inlets of the South. (Applause.) The black man welcomes your armies and your fleets, takes care of your sick, is ready to do anything, from cooking up to shouldering a musket; and yet these would-be patriots and professed lovers of the land talk about driving the Negro out!

Greeley and Lincoln

Exchange Views on Slavery

Greeley's Open Letter:
The Prayer of Twenty Millions

To Abraham Lincoln,
President of the United States:

Dear Sir: I do not intrude to tell you—for you must know already—that a great proportion of those who triumphed in your election, and all who desire the unqualified suppression of the rebellion now desolating our country, are sorely disappointed and deeply pained by the policy you seem to be pursuing with regard to the slaves of rebels. I write only to set succinctly and unmistakably before you what we require, what we think we have a right to expect, and of what we complain.

We require of you, as the first servant of the Republic, charged especially and preëminently with this duty, that you EXECUTE THE LAWS. . . .

We think you are strangely and disastrously remiss in the discharge of your official and imperative duty with regard to the emancipating provisions of the new Confiscation Act. Those provisions were designed to fight Slavery with Liberty. They prescribe that men loyal to the Union, and willing to shed their blood in her behalf, shall no longer be held, with the nation's consent, in bondage to persistent, malignant traitors, who for twenty years have been plotting and for sixteen months have been fighting to divide and destroy our country. Why these traitors should be treated with tenderness by you, to the prejudice of the dearest rights of loyal men, we cannot conceive.

We think you are unduly influenced by the councils, the representations, the menaces, of certain fossil politicians hailing from the Border Slave States. Knowing well that the heartily, unconditionally loyal portion of the white citizens of those States do not expect nor desire that Slavery shall be upheld to the prejudice of the Union. . . . we ask you to consider that Slavery is everywhere the inciting cause and sustaining base of treason: the most slaveholding sections of Maryland and Delaware being this day, though under the Union flag, in full sympathy with the rebellion, while the free labor portions of Tennessee and of Texas, though writhing under the bloody heel of treason, are unconquerably loyal to the Union. . . . It seems to us the most obvious truth, that whatever strengthens or fortifies Slavery in the Border States strengthens also treason, and drives home the wedge intended to divide the Union. Had you, from the first, refused to recognize in those States, as here, any other than unconditional loyalty—that which

August
19, 22,
1862

Tribune's Publisher
provokes famous
"I would save the Union"
statement of purpose

stands for the Union, whatever may become of Slavery—those States would have been, and would be, far more helpful and less troublesome to the defenders of the Union. . . .

We think timid counsels in such a crisis calculated to prove perilous, and probably disastrous. It is the duty of a Government so wantonly, wickedly assailed by rebellion as ours has been, to oppose force to force in a defiant, dauntless spirit. It cannot afford to temporize with traitors, nor with semi-traitors. It must not bribe them to behave themselves, nor make them fair promises in the hope of disarming their causeless hostility. Representing a brave and highspirited people, it can afford to forfeit any thing else better than its own self-respect, or their admiring confidence. . . .

We complain that the Union cause has suffered, and is now suffering immensely, from mistaken deference to rebel Slavery. Had you, sir, in your Inaugural Address, unmistakably given notice that, in case the rebellion already commenced, were persisted in, and your efforts to preserve the Union and enforce the laws should be resisted by armed force, *you would recognize no loyal person as rightfully held in Slavery by a traitor,* we believe the rebellion would therein have received a staggering if not fatal blow. . . .

Had you then proclaimed that rebellion would strike the shackles from the slaves of every traitor, the wealthy and the cautious would have been supplied with a powerful inducement to remain loyal. . . .

We complain that the Confiscation Act which you approved is habitually disregarded by your Generals, and that no word of rebuke for them from you has yet reached the public ear. Fremont's Proclamation and Hunter's Order favoring Emancipation were promptly annulled by you; while Halleck's Number Three, forbidding fugitives from slavery to rebels to come within his lines—an order as unmilitary as inhuman, and which received the hearty approbation of every traitor in America—with scores of like tendency, have never provoked even your remonstrance . . . And finally, we complain that you, Mr. President, elected as a Republican, knowing well what an abomination Slavery is, and how emphatically it is the core and essence of this atrocious rebellion, seem never to interfere with these atrocities, and never give a direction to your military subordinates, which does not appear to have been conceived in the interest of Slavery rather than of Freedom. . . .

On the face of this wide earth, Mr. President, there is not one disinterested, determined, intelligent champion of the Union cause who does not feel that all attempts to put down the rebellion and at the same time uphold its inciting cause are preposterous and futile . . . and that every hour of deference to Slavery is an hour of added and deepened peril to the Union. . . .

I close as I began with the statement that what an immense majority of the loyal millions of your countrymen require of you is a frank, declared, unqualified, ungrudging execution of the laws of the land, . . . We cannot conquer ten millions of people united in solid phalanx against us, powerfully aided by Northern sympathizers and European allies. We must have scouts, guides, spies, cooks, teamsters, diggers, and choppers from the blacks of the South, whether we allow them to fight for us or not, or we shall be baffled and repelled. As one of the millions who would gladly have avoided this struggle at any sacrifice but that of principle and honor, but who now feel that the triumph of the Union is indispensable not only to the existence of our country but to the well-being of mankind, I entreat you to render a hearty and unequivocal obedience to the law of the land.

Yours, Horace Greeley.

New - York, August 19, 1862.

President Lincoln's Answer

Executive Mansion,
Washington, August 22, 1862.
Hon. Horace Greeley:

Dear Sir: I have just read yours of the nineteenth, addressed to myself through the New York *Tribune.* If there be in it any statements or assumptions of fact which I may know to be erroneous, I do not now and here controvert them. If there be in it any

inferences which I may believe to be falsely drawn, I do not now and here argue against them. If there be perceptible in it an impatient and dictatorial tone, I waive it in deference to an old friend, whose heart I have always supposed to be right.

As to the policy I "seem to be pursuing," as you say, I have not meant to leave any one in doubt.

I would save the Union. I would save it the shortest way under the Constitution. The sooner the National authority can be restored, the nearer the Union will be "the Union as it was." If there be those who would not save the Union unless they could at the same time *save* Slavery, I do not agree with them. If there be those who would not save the Union unless they could at the same time *destroy* Slavery, I do not agree with them. My paramount object in this struggle *is* to save the Union, and is *not* either to save or destroy Slavery. If I could save the Union without freeing *any* slave, I would do it; and if I could save it by freeing *all* the slaves, I would do it; and if I could do it by freeing some and leaving others alone, I would also do that. What I do about Slavery and the colored race, I do because I believe it helps to save this Union; and what I forbear, I forbear because I do *not* believe it would help to save the Union. I shall do *less* whenever I shall believe what I am doing hurts the cause, and I shall do *more* whenever I shall believe doing more will help the cause. I shall try to correct errors when shown to be errors; and I shall adopt new views so fast as they shall appear to be true views. I have here stated my purpose according to my view of *official* duty, and I intend no modification of my oft-expressed *personal* wish that all men, everywhere, could be free.

Yours,
A. Lincoln.

The Emancipation Proclamation

By the President of the United States of America:

A Proclamation

Whereas on the 22d day of September, A.D. 1862, a proclamation was issued by the President of the United States, containing, among other things, the following, to wit:

"That on the 1st day of January, A.D. 1863, all persons held as slaves within any State or designated part of a State the people whereof shall then be in rebellion against the United States shall be then, thenceforward, and forever free; and the executive government of the United States, including the military and naval authority thereof, will recognize and maintain the freedom of such persons and will do no act or acts to repress such persons, or any of them, in any efforts they may make for their actual freedom.

"That the executive will on the 1st day of January aforesaid, by proclamation, designate the States and parts of States, if any, in which the people thereof, respectively, shall then be in rebellion against the United States; and the fact that any State or the people thereof shall on that day be in good faith represented in the Congress of the United States by members chosen thereto at elections wherein a majority of the qualified voters of such States shall have participated shall, in the absence of strong countervailing testimony, be deemed conclusive evidence that such State and the people thereof are not then in rebellion against the United States."

Now, therefore, I, Abraham Lincoln, President of the United States, by virtue of the power in me vested as Commander-in-Chief of the Army and Navy of the United States in time of actual armed rebellion against the authority and government of the United States, and as a fit and necessary war measure for suppressing said rebellion, do, on this 1st day of January, A.D. 1863, and in accordance with my purpose so to do, publicly proclaimed for the full period of one hundred days from the first day above mentioned, order and designate as the States and parts of States wherein the people thereof, respectively, are this day in rebellion against the United States the following, to wit:

Arkansas, Texas, Louisiana . . . Mississippi, Alabama, Florida, Georgia, South Carolina, North Carolina, and Virginia (except the forty-eight counties designated as West Virginia, . . .)

And by virtue of the power and for the purpose aforesaid, I do order and declare that all persons held as slaves within the said designated States and parts of States are, and henceforward shall be, free; and that the Executive Government of the United States, including the military and naval authorities thereof, will recognize and maintain the freedom of said persons.

And I hereby enjoin upon the people so declared to be free to abstain from all violence, unless in necessary self-defense; and I recommend to them that, in all cases when allowed, they labor faithfully for reasonable wages.

And I further declare and make known that such persons of suitable condition will be received into the armed service of the United States to garrison forts, positions, stations, and other places, and to man vessels of all sorts in said service.

And upon this act, sincerely believed to be an act of justice, warranted by the Constitution upon military necessity, I invoke the considerate judgment of mankind and the gracious favor of Almighty God.

SECTION IV

THE WILDERNESS OF EMANCIPATION

*And the children said
... Would to God we had died
by the hand of the Lord
in the land of Egypt,
when we sat by the flesh pots,
and when we did
eat bread to the full;
for ye have brought us
forth into this wilderness...*

Exodus 16: 2

In his second inaugural address, delivered a month before Lee's surrender to Grant, Lincoln eloquently projected the coming job of reconstruction:

> "With malice toward none, with charity for all, with firmness in the right as God gives us to see the right, let us strive on to finish the work we are in, to bind up the nation's wounds, to care for him who shall have borne the battle and for his widow and his orphan, to do all which may achieve and cherish a just and lasting peace among ourselves and with all nations."

Reconstruction would be fraught with difficulties. The War left the South weakened and disorganized. Great numbers of emancipated Negroes would have to surmount overnight the problems of illiteracy and limited skills. Lincoln's successor, Andrew Johnson, was ambivalent about the exercise of federal authority and inept in his dealings with Congress.

The political problems of the post-war years were foreshadowed in 1864 when Congress rejected the principles of Lincoln's Proclamation of Amnesty and Reconstruction.

Lincoln viewed the South's rebellion as the action of individual citizens rather than the states and thus it was within the powers of the President to bring the rebellious states back into the Union. The Proclamation gave "full pardon" to "all persons who have, directly or by implication, participated in the . . . rebellion, except as hereinafter excepted." The pardon provided "restoration of all rights of property except as to slaves and in property cases where rights of third parties shall have intervened." The persons excepted were functionaries of the Confederacy. The other pre-condition to pardon was an oath of allegiance to the United States. When one-tenth of a rebellious state's 1860 population had taken the oath, a state government might then be organized. With regard to the Negro, the proclamation merely provided executive permissiveness in the restored state's plans:

". . . any provision which may be adopted by such State government in relation to the freed people of such State which shall recognize and declare their permanent freedom, provide for their education, and which may yet be consistent as a temporary arrangement with their present condition as a laboring, landless, and homeless class, will not be objected to by the National Executive."

Congress retaliated by refusing to seat representatives from the reconstructed states, and offered the Wade-Davis Bill as a substitute for Presidential Reconstruction. Designated as "an act to guarantee to certain States whose Governments have been usurped or overthrown, a Republican Form of Government," the bill provided that new governments might be organized by a "majority of the persons enrolled in the state" who had sworn their loyalty—past, present and future—to the United States. Lincoln let the bill go unsigned (pocket-veto). The authors of the bill denounced the veto, asserting that: "A more studied outrage on the legislative authority of the people has never been perpetrated."

The day Andrew Johnson took office a long Congressional recess started. During Congress' absence, Johnson implemented the Lincoln plan for Reconstruction, making only minimal changes. When he addressed Congress on December 16, 1865, restoration of the states was an accomplished fact. But the struggle between Congress and the President for direction of Reconstruction policy had just begun.

The early delegations from the reconstituted states included many former officials of the Confederacy. This was a signal to Radical Republicans in Congress of the need for a thoroughgoing investigation of Negro suffrage and other problems of reconstruction. Much of the legislation of the period grew out of the findings of a Joint Committee of Fifteen headed by Thaddeus Stevens. The Radical strength in both houses after the election of 1866 was seen as a rebuff to Johnson and a mandate to Congress to set the tone of

INTRODUCTION

Reconstruction.

During the Radicals' political ascendancy they produced the First Reconstruction Act which divided the old Confederacy into five military districts and made readmission of "rebel" states contingent upon its extension of voting rights to Negroes and the states' ratification of the Fourteenth Amendment. The Act was strengthened by subsequent legislation and the Fifteenth Amendment.

The war between Johnson and Congress reached its climax when the President (his term nearly over) was impeached following his removal of Edwin Stanton as Secretary of War in violation of the Tenure of Office Act. Congress failed by only one vote in handing Johnson the supreme rebuff, removal from office.

The successful Civil War General, Ulysses S. Grant, was elected President in 1868. The popular vote was close and the Negro vote was decisive. Grant was not a great President and his two-term administration was marred by scandal and corruption.

Reconstruction—a turbulent, short-lived epoch—ended in 1877 with the election of Rutherford B. Hayes, a Republican. His Democratic opponent, Samuel J. Tilden, received a majority of the popular vote. Although in Florida, Louisiana, Oregon and South Carolina the returns were contested, Tilden needed only one electoral vote to claim the election. A special fifteen-man Electoral Commission—five members each of the House, the Senate and the Supreme Court—was appointed. Politically they divided into eight Republicans and seven Democrats and their votes were invariably partisan. Democratic acceptance of the vote was obtained by Republican promises to remove the troops occupying the South and to name a Southerner to the Cabinet. In this instance political promises were scrupulously observed.

From the fires of Civil War and Reconstruction a new colossus of modern times, the United States of America, was forged. The last frontier gave way to settlers and the national area stretched from "sea to shining sea." Agriculture yielded first place to bustling industry, as natural resources, technical

HOPE BETRAYED: *Federal funds intended to ease the Negro's progress toward first-class citizenship were often appropriated for other purposes, including the pockets of professed friends of the Negro.*

(Harper's Weekly)

THE "PRACTICAL" POLITICIAN'S LOVE FOR THE NEGRO.

enlightenment, manpower and machinery were joined with ever-growing success. Traditional isolationism made room for greater participation in international affairs, spurred on by the need of a larger marketplace for American industrial abundance and investment capital. By the end of the 19th century, America, long regarded as an infant among world powers, seemed suddenly mature.

The Negro's response to the rapid maturation which was forced upon him in this era is at once a proud and shameful chapter in American history. Emancipation made him a *displaced* person, in Lincoln's words: "a laborless, landless and homeless class." Reconstruction made him a *whole* person and enfranchised him. The Negro made himself a man. Some nourishment, of course, came from sources outside his person. The Freedmen's Bureau, the abolitionists, Northern religious groups and philanthropic organizations are highest among the resources available to the Negro in those moments when he needed assistance.

Negro progress during the era was evaluated by James A. Garfield while still a Congressman from Ohio. He remarked:

"... Dullness of intellect, a low state of morals, a want of thrift and foresight—all these were the inevitable results of generations of slavery, which afforded no incentive to the development of those qualities that make citizens independent, intelligent, and self-reliant. If the negroes had lost the passion for acquiring property, if they had shown themselves unwilling to work, neither liberty nor suffrage could have saved them. . . . But the evidences are increasing on every hand that they are sucessfully solving the problem of their own future, by a commendable degree of industry, and by very earnest efforts to educate their children. In these efforts they are outstripping the class known in the days of slavery as 'the poor whites.' . . . their thirst for knowledge has not been quenched. . . .

"They are acquiring property far more rapidly than their white neighbors expected. In the Freedmen's Savings Bank alone, the failure of which was so calamitous, they had deposited surplus earnings to the amount of three millions of dollars. They are gradually becoming owners of real estate and of comfortable homes. In one county of South Carolina they are now paying $300,000 of taxes per annum; and this is neither an isolated nor an exaggerated example. In short, they are gradually gaining those two elements of power, 'intelligence and wealth,' which Senator Thurman says will in the long run control the politics of a community."

The happy ending foreseen by Garfield cannot, however, close this chapter. To the ugly pages written by prejudices belongs the last word. The pages have gloomy headings: "Black Codes," the birth of the Ku Klux Klan, segregation achieved through "Jim Crow" laws, and Negro disfranchisement. Collaborators, no doubt unwitting, were the Northerners who abandoned the Negro to pursue the easy profits afforded by vibrant economy, the Republican withdrawal of federal troops from the South, and Supreme Court antipathy to Negro rights.

Mr. Justice Brown, on behalf of the majority, pronounced the benediction in *Plessy* v. *Ferguson* (1896) as he intoned:

"We consider the underlying fallacy of the plaintiff's argument to consist in the assumption that the enforced separation of the two races stamps the colored race with a badge of inferiority . . . that social prejudices may be overcome by legislation, and that equal rights cannot be secured to the negro except by an enforced commingling of the two races. . . . Legislation is powerless to eradicate racial instincts or to abolish distinctions based upon physical differences. . . ."

This lithograph, circa 1886, illustrates achievements of Negroes after the Emancipation Proclamation. Of particular note is the emphasis placed on higher education. (The Bettmann Archive)

Resolution of the

Illinois

State Legislature

in Opposition

to the

Emancipation

Proclamation

RESOLVED: That the emancipation proclamation of the President of the United States is as unwarrantable in military as in civil law; a gigantic usurpation, at once converting the war, professedly commenced by the administration for the vindication of the authority of the constitution, into the crusade for the sudden, unconditional and violent liberation of 3,000,000 negro slaves; a result which would not only be a total subversion of the Federal Union but a revolution in the social organization of the Southern States, the immediate and remote, the present and far-reaching consequences of which to both races cannot be contemplated without the most dismal foreboding of horror and dismay. The proclamation invites servile insurrection as an element in this emancipation crusade—a means of warfare, the inhumanity and diabolism of which are without example in civilized warfare, and which we denounce, as an uneffaceable disgrace to the American people.

January 7, 1863
Illinois

Northern abuse
of Lincoln
for "gigantic usurpation"

A Negro Eyewitness Describes

Anti-Negro Violence in Detroit

. . . THE present state of affairs in relation to the colored people is one of great perplexity, and is not only so on account of the South, but also in the North.

There certainly is something mysterious about [Negroes]. On the one hand they are being mobbed, and everything that is sacred to a people to make a country or home dear are denied them, in many of the large Northern cities. And on the other hand they are marching off to the call of the Government as if they were sharing all the blessings of the most favored citizens!

And it is equally mysterious to see the bitter opposition that a class of men, professing loyalty to the Government of the United States, should have against the colored soldier . . .

But one thing the colored man knows, that the class of men of the same politics as those South are doing the mobbing North; . . .

Whatever, therefore, our treatment may be, so far as the rage of the enemies of freedom may be; whatever, through cowardice, a ruthless mob of men may inflict upon our people, [Negroes] will not be deterred from the duty they owe to their God, themselves and posterity, to do all they possibly can to undo the heavy burdens and let the oppressed go free! . . . they too well know that the way to glory is the way of suffering; therefore they desire to bear a good part in the battlefield rather than to be always exposed to such outrages as slavery entails, . . .

The mob, in its first appearance to me, was a parcel of fellows running up Lafayette street after two or three colored men. They then returned back, and in a short time I saw a tremendous crowd coming up Croghan street on drays, wagons, and foot, with kegs of beer on their wagons, and rushed for the prison. Here they crowded thick and heavy. After this, while I was standing on the corner, with half a dozen other gentlemen, a rifle ball came whistling over our heads. After which we heard several shots, . . . In a short time after this there came one fellow . . . saying, "I am shot in the thigh." And

another came with his finger partly shot off. A few minutes after that another ruffian came down, saying: "If we are got to be killed up for Negroes then we will kill every one in this town." A very little while after this we could hear them speaking up near the jail, and appeared to be drinking, but I was unable to hear what they said. This done, they gave a most fiendish yell and started down Beaubien street. On reaching Croghan street, a couple of houses west on Beaubien street, they commenced throwing, and before they reached my residence, clubs, brick, and missiles of every description flew like hail. Myself and several others were standing on the side-walk, but were compelled to hasten in and close our doors, while the mob passed my house with their clubs and bricks flying into my windows and doors, sweeping out light and sash!

They then approached my door in large numbers, where I stood with my gun, and another friend with an axe, but on seeing us, they fell back. They approached four times determined to enter my door, but I raised my gun at each time and they fell back. In the meantime part of the mob passed on down Beaubien street. After the principle part had passed, I rushed up my stairs looking to see what they were doing, and heard the shattering of windows and slashing of boards. In a few moments I saw them at Whitney Reynolds, a few doors below Lafayette street. Mr. Reynolds is a cooper; had his shop and residence on the same lot, and was the largest colored cooper establishment in the city—employing a number of hands regular.

I could see from the windows men striking with axe, spade, clubs, &c., just as you could see men thrashing wheat. A sight the most revolting, to see innocent men, women, and children, all without respect to age or sex, being pounded in the most brutal manner.

Sickened with the sight, I sat down in deep solicitude in relation to what the night would bring forth; for to human appearance it seemed as if Satan was loose, and his children were free to do whatever he might direct without fear of the city authority. . . .

A Negro Eyewitness Describes Anti-Negro Violence in Detroit □ 177

Sgt. Carney (CMH) Tells About Himself

October 13, 1863
Morris Island,
South Carolina

Simple origins set down
by a winner
of the nation's highest
military decoration

Dear Sir—Complying with your request, I send you the following history, pertaining to my birth, parentage, social and religious experience and standing; in short, a concise epitome of my life. I undertake to perform it in my poor way:

I was born in Norfolk, Va., in 1840; my father's name was William Carney; my mother's name before her marriage was Ann Dean; she was the property of one Major Carney, but, at his death, she, with all his people, was by his will made *free*. In my fourteenth year, when I had no work to do, I attended a private and secret school kept in Norfolk by a minister. In my fifteenth year I embraced the gospel; at that time I was also engaged in the coasting trade with my father.

In 1850, I left the sea for a time, and my father set out to look for a place to live in peace and freedom. He first stopped in Pennsylvania—but he rested not there; the black man was *not secure* on the soil where the Declaration of Independence was written. He went far. Then he visited the empire State —great New York—whose chief ambition seemed to be for commerce and gold, and with her unceasing struggle for supremacy she heard not the slave; she only had time to spurn the man with a sable skin, and make him feel that he was an alien in his native land.

At last he set his weary feet upon the sterile rocks of "Old Massachusetts." The very air he breathed put enthusiasm into his spirit. O, yes, he found a refuge from oppression in the old Bay State. He selected as his dwelling-place the city of New Bedford, where "Liberty Hall" is a sacred edifice. Like the Temple of Diana which covered the virgins from harm in olden time, so old Liberty Hall in New Bedford protects the oppressed slave of the 19th Century. After stopping a short time, he sent for his family, and there they still dwell. I remained in the city with the family, pursuing the avocation of a jobber of work for stores, and at such places as I could find employment. I soon formed connection with a church under charge of the Rev. Mr. Jackson, now chaplain of the 55th Mass. Volunteers.

Previous to the formation of colored troops, I had a strong inclination to prepare myself for the ministry; but when the country called for *all persons,* I could best serve my God by serving my country and my oppressed brothers. The sequel is short—*I enlisted for the war.*

I am your humble and obedient servant,
WILLIAM H. CARNEY
Sergeant Co. C, 54th Mass. Vols.

January 1, 1864
Tennessee

Jubilation
matched by
patriotic service
recommended

Sentiments of the Colored People

of Memphis on the First Anniversary

of the Emancipation Proclamation

. . . WE hail with feelings of joy and gratitude to Almighty God, that we have the exalted privilege of meeting together, for the purpose of offering tribute and honor to one of the most magnanimous and brilliant chapters written in the nineteenth century.

. . . we greet the dawn of this beautiful and ever memorable day; and we trust that our children will cherish it until truth, and honor shall cease to be revered among the civilized nations of the earth.

. . . the respect to his excellency, the President of the United States, and the admiration we cherish for the gallant army and navy that have borne their glittering arms, backed by their courageous hearts, in triumph over hundreds of battle-fields, call upon us today to pledge ourselves as colored men to fill the ranks made vacant by our colored brothers, who have fallen so bravely upon the various fields of strife.

. . . we recommend every colored man, capable of performing military duty, both North and South, to enlist forthwith in the army and navy of the United States, where he can successfully perform his duty to his God, his country, and his fellow-men.

. . . As this is our country, and we are citizens of the United States, . . . therefore we are willing to defend them with life and limb; and after protecting them with our guns, we humbly pray God that there may be generosity enough left to protect us in our native land.

. . . we recommend the colored people everywhere in the United States to stand by the Government, to be true to the stars and stripes.

. . . we recommend the benevolent associations of the North to send us teachers, who are known to be our true and devoted friends.

. . . we recommend the teachers to bring their tents with them, ready for erection in the field, by the roadside, or in the fort, . . .

Congress Establishes

the Freedmen's Bureau

*An Act
to establish a Bureau
for the Relief
of Freedmen and Refugees*

Be it enacted, That there is hereby established in the War Department, to continue during the present war of rebellion, and for one year thereafter, a bureau of refugees, freedmen, and abandoned lands, to which shall be committed, as hereinafter provided, the supervision and management of all abandoned lands, and the control of all subjects relating to refugees and freedmen from rebel states, or from any district of country within the territory embraced in the operations of the army, under such rules and regulations as may be prescribed by the head of the bureau and approved by the President. The said bureau shall be under the management and con-

Care and protection
provided for freedmen,
refugees
and abandoned land

trol of a commissioner to be appointed by the President, . . .

. . . That the Secretary of War may direct such issues of provisions, clothing, and fuel, as he may deem needful for the immediate and temporary shelter and supply of destitute and suffering refugees and freedmen and their wives and children, under such rules and regulations as he may direct.

. . . That the President may, . . . appoint an assistant commissioner for each of the states declared to be in insurrection, not exceeding ten in number, who shall, under the direction of the commissioner, aid in the execution of the provisions of this act; . . . And any military officer may be detailed and assigned to duty under this act without increase of pay or allowances. . . .

. . . That the commissioner, under the direction of the President, shall have authority to set apart, for the use of loyal refugees and freedmen, such tracts of land within the insurrectionary states as shall have been abandoned, or to which the United States shall have acquired title by confiscation or sale, or otherwise, and to every male citizen, whether refugee or freedman, as aforesaid, there shall be assigned not more than forty acres of such land, and the person to whom it was so assigned shall be protected in the use and enjoyment of the land for the term of three years at an annual rent not exceeding six per centum upon the value of such land, as it was appraised by the state authorities in the year eighteen hundred and sixty, for the purpose of taxation, and in case no such appraisal can be found, then the rental shall be based upon the estimated value of the land in said year, to be ascertained in such manner as the commissioner may by regulation prescribe. At the end of said term, or at any time during said term, the occupants of any parcels so assigned may purchase the land and receive such title thereto as the United States can convey, upon paying therefor the value of the land, . . .

The "Black Code" of Mississippi

*. . . B*e it enacted, . . . That all freedmen, free negroes, and mulattoes may sue and be sued, implead and be impleaded, in all the courts of law and equity of this State, and may acquire personal property, and choses in action, by descent or purchase, and may dispose of the same in the same manner and to the same extent that white persons may: *Provided,* That the provisions of this section shall not be so construed as to allow any freedman, free negro, or mulatto to rent or lease any lands or tenements except in incorporated cities or towns, in which places the corporate authorities shall control the same. . . .

. . . All freedmen, free negroes, or mulattoes who do now and have herebefore lived and cohabited together as husband and wife shall be taken and held in law as legally married, and the issue shall be taken and held as legitimate for all purposes; that it shall not be lawful for any freedman, free negro, or mulatto to intermarry with any white person; nor for any white person to intermarry with any freedman, free negro, or mulatto; and any person who shall so intermarry, shall be deemed guilty of felony, and on conviction thereof shall be confined in the State penitentiary for life; and those shall be deemed freedmen, free negroes, and mulattoes who are of pure negro blood, and those descended from a negro to the third generation, inclusive, though one ancestor in each generation may have been a white person.

. . . In addition to cases in which freedmen, free negroes, and mulattoes are now by law competent witnesses, freedmen, free negroes, or mulattoes shall be competent in civil cases, when a party or parties to the suit, either plaintiff or plaintiffs, defendant or defendants, and a white person or white persons, is or are the opposing party or parties, plaintiff or plaintiffs, defendant or defendants. They shall also be competent witnesses in all criminal prosecutions where the crime charged is alleged to have been committed by a white person upon or against the person or property of a freedman, free negro, or mulatto: *Provided,* that in all cases said witnesses shall be examined in open court, on the stand; except, however, they may be examined before the grand jury, and shall in all cases be subject to the rules and tests of the common law as to competency. . . .

. . . All contracts for labor made with freedmen, free negroes, and mulattoes for a longer period than one month shall be in writing, and in duplicate, attested and read to said freedmen, free negro, or mulatto by a beat, city or county officer, or two disinterested white persons of the county in which the labor is to be performed, of which each

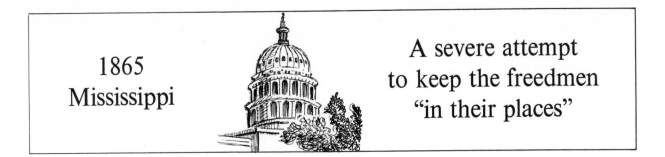

1865
Mississippi

A severe attempt
to keep the freedmen
"in their places"

party shall have one; and said contracts shall be taken and held as entire contracts, and if the laborer shall quit the service of the employer before the expiration of his term of service, without good cause, he shall forfeit his wages for that year up to the time of quitting.

. . . Every civil officer shall, and every person may, arrest and carry back to his or her legal employer any freedman, free negro, or mulatto who shall have quit the service of his or her employer before the expiration of his or her term of service without good cause; and said officer and person shall be entitled to receive for arresting and carrying back every deserting employe aforesaid the sum of five dollars, and ten cents per mile from the place of arrest to the place of delivery; and the same shall be paid by the employer, and held as a set-off for so much against the wages of said deserting employe: *Provided,* that said arrested party, after being so returned, may appeal to the justice of the peace or member of the board of police of the county, who, on notice to the alleged employer, shall try summarily whether said appellant is legally employed by the alleged employer, and has good cause to quit said employer; either party shall have the right of appeal to the county court, pending which the alleged deserter shall be remanded to the alleged employer or otherwise disposed of, as shall be right and just. . . .

. . . If any person shall persuade or attempt to persuade, entice, or cause any freedman, free negro, or mulatto to desert from the legal employment of any person before the expiration of his or her term of service, or shall knowingly employ any such deserting freedman, free negro, or mulatto, or shall knowingly give or sell to any such deserting freedman, free negro, or mulatto, any food, raiment, or other thing, he or she shall be guilty of a misdemeanor, and, upon conviction, shall be fined not less than twenty-five dollars and not more than two hundred dollars and the costs; and if said fine and costs shall not be immediately paid, the court shall sentence said convict to not exceeding two months' imprisonment in the county jail, and he or she shall moreover be liable to the party injured in damages: *Provided,* if any person shall, or shall attempt to persuade, entice, or cause any freedman, free negro, or mulatto to desert from any legal employment of any person, with the view to employ said freedman, free negro, or mulatto without the limits of this State, such person, on conviction, shall be fined not less than fifty dollars, and not more than five hundred dollars and costs; and if said fine and costs shall not be immediately paid, the court shall sentence said convict to not exceeding six months imprisonment. . . .

The "Black Code" of Mississippi   ☐   183

The Thirteenth Amendment

RATIFIED DECEMBER 18, 1865

. . . Neither slavery nor involuntary servitude, except as a punishment for crime whereof the party shall have been duly convicted, shall exist within the United States, or any place subject to their jurisdicton.

. . . Congress shall have power to enforce this article by appropriate legislation.

The First Reconstruction Act

An Act to provide for the more efficient Government of the Rebel States

Whereas no legal State governments or adequate protection for life or property now exists in the rebel States of Virginia, North Carolina, South Carolina, Georgia, Mississippi, Alabama, Louisiana, Florida, Texas, and Arkansas; and whereas it is necessary that peace and good order should be enforced in said States until loyal and republican State governments can be legally established: Therefore,

Be it enacted, That said rebel States shall be divided into military districts and made subject to the military authority of the United States. . . .

. . . That it shall be the duty of the President to assign to the command of each of said districts an officer of the army, not below the rank of brigadier-general, and to detail a sufficient military force to enable such officer to perform his duties and enforce his authority within the district to which he is assigned.

. . . That it shall be the duty of each officer assigned as aforesaid, to protect all persons in their rights of persons and property, to suppress insurrection, disorder, and violence, and to punish, or cause to be

March 2, 1867

Congress provides
military rule
pending reconstitution of
loyal state governments

punished, all disturbers of the public peace and criminals; . . . and all interference under color of State authority with the exercise of military authority under this act, shall be null and void.

. . . That all persons put under military arrest by virtue of this act shall be tried without unnecessary delay, and no cruel or unusual punishment shall be inflicted, and no sentence of any military commission or tribunal hereby authorized, affecting the life or liberty of any person, shall be executed until it is approved by the officer in command of the district, and the laws and regulations for the government of the army shall not be affected by this act, except in so far as they conflict with its provisions: *Provided,* That no sentence of death under the provisions of this act shall be carried into effect without the approval of the President.

. . . That when the people of any one of said rebel States shall have formed a constitution of government in conformity with the Constitution of the United States in all respects, framed by a convention of delegates elected by the male citizens of said State, twenty-one years old and upward, of whatever race, color, or previous condition, who have been resident in said State for one year previous to the day of such election, except such as may be disfranchised for participation in the rebellion or for felony at common law, and when such constitution shall provide that the elective franchise shall be enjoyed by all such persons as have the qualifications herein stated for electors of delegates, and when such constitution shall be ratified by a majority of the persons voting on the question of ratification who are qualified as electors for delegates, and when such consti-

tution shall have been submitted to Congress for examination and approval, and Congress shall have approved the same, and when said State, by a vote of its legislature elected under said constitution, shall have adopted the amendment to the Constitution of the United States, proposed by the Thirty-ninth Congress, and known as article fourteen, and when said article shall have become a part of the Constitution of the United States said State shall be declared entitled to representation in Congress, and senators and representatives shall be admitted therefrom on their taking the oath prescribed by law, and then and thereafter the preceding sections of this act shall be inoperative in said State: *Provided,* That no person excluded from the privilege of holding office by said proposed amendment to the Constitution of the United States, shall be eligible to election as a member of the convention to frame a constitution for any of said rebel States, nor shall any such person vote for members of such convention.

. . . That, until the people of said rebel States shall be by law admitted to representation in the Congress of the United States, any civil governments which may exist therein shall be deemed provisional only, and in all respects subject to the paramount authority of the United States . . . and in all elections to any office under such provisional governments all persons shall be entitled to vote, and none others, who are entitled to vote, under the provisions of . . . this act; and no persons shall be eligible to any office under any such provisional governments who would be disqualified from holding office under the provisions of the third *article* of said constitutional amendment. [The Fourteenth Amendment]

The Fourteenth Amendment

RATIFIED JULY 28, 1868

. . . All persons born or naturalized in the United States, and subject to the jurisdiction thereof, are citizens of the United States and of the State wherein they reside. No State shall make or enforce any law which shall abridge the privileges or immunities of citizens of the United States; nor shall any State deprive any person of life, liberty, or property, without due process of law; nor deny to any person within its jurisdiction the equal protection of the laws.

. . . Representatives shall be apportioned among the several States according to their respective numbers, counting the whole number of persons in each State, excluding Indians not taxed. But when the right to vote at any election for the choice of electors for President and Vice President of the United States, Representatives in Congress, the Executive and Judicial officers of a State, or the members of the Legislature thereof, is denied to any of the male inhabitants of such State, being twenty-one years of age, and citizens of the United States, or in any way abridged, except for participation in rebellion, or other crime, the basis of representation therein shall be reduced in the proportion which the number of such male citizens shall bear to the whole number of male citizens twenty-one years of age in such State.

. . . No person shall be a Senator or Representative in Congress, or elector of President and Vice President, or hold any office, civil or military, under the United States, or under any State, who, having previously taken an oath, as a member of Congress, or as an officer of the United States, or as a member of any State legislature, or as an executive or judicial officer of any State, to support the Constitution of the United States, shall have engaged in insurrection or rebellion against the same, or given aid or comfort to the enemies thereof. But Congress may by a vote of two-thirds of each House, remove such disability.

. . . The validity of the public debt of the United States, authorized by law, including debts incurred for payment of pensions and bounties for services in suppressing insurrection or rebellion, shall not be questioned. But neither the United States nor any State shall assume or pay any debt or obligation incurred in aid of insurrection or rebellion against the United States, or any claim for the loss or emancipation of any slave; but all such debts, obligations and claims shall be held illegal and void.

. . . The Congress shall have power to enforce, by appropriate legislation, the provisions of this article.

KKK Rules of Order

APPELLATION

This Organization shall be styled and denominated, the Order of the ***.

CREED

We, the Order of the * * *, reverentially acknowledge the majesty and supremacy of the Divine Being, and recognize the goodness and providence of the same. And we recognize our relation to the United States Government, the supremacy of the Constitution, the Constitutional Laws, thereof, and the Union of States thereunder.

CHARACTER AND OBJECTS OF THE ORDER

This is an institution of Chivalry, Humanity, Mercy and Patriotism; embodying in its genius and its principles all that is chivalric in conduct, noble in sentiment, generous in manhood, and patriotic in purpose; its peculiar objects being

First: To protect the weak, the innocent, and the defenceless, from the indignities, wrongs, and outrages of the lawless, the violent, and the brutal; to relieve the injured and oppressed; to succor the suffering and unfortunate, and especially the widows and orphans of Confederate Soldiers.

Second: To protect and defend the Constitution of the United States, and all laws passed in conformity thereto, and to protect the States and the people thereof from all invasion from any source whatever.

Third: To aid and assist in the execution of all constitutional laws, and to protect the people from unlawful seizure, and from trial except by their peers in conformity to the laws of the land. . . .

ELIGIBILITY FOR MEMBERSHIP

SECTION 1. No one shall be presented for admission into the Order until he shall have first been recommended by some friend or intimate who *is* a member, to the Investigating Committee, (which shall be composed of the Grand Cyclops, the Grand Magi, and the Grand Monk,) and who shall have investigated his antecedents and his past and present standing and connections; and after such investigation, shall have pronounced him competent and worthy to become a member. *Provided,* no one shall be presented for admission into, or become a member of, this Order who shall not have attained the age of eighteen years.

SECTION 2. No one shall become a member of this Order unless he shall *voluntarily* take the following oaths or obligations, and shall *satisfactorily* answer the following interrogatories, while kneeling, with his right hand raised to heaven, and his left hand resting on the Bible:

PRELIMINARY OBLIGATION

"I_____solemnly swear or affirm that I will never reveal any thing that I may this day (or night) learn concerning the Order of the * * *, and that I will true answer

make to such interrogatories as may be put to me touching my competency for admission into the same. So help me God."

INTERROGATORIES TO BE ASKED:

1st. Have you ever been rejected, upon application for membership in the * * *, or have you ever been expelled from the same?

2d. Are you now, or have you ever been, a member of the Radical Republican party, or either of the organizations known as the "Loyal League" and the "Grand Army of the Republic?"

3d. Are you opposed to the principles and policy of the Radical Republican party, and to the "Loyal League," and the "Grand Army of the Republic," so far as you are informed of the character and purposes of those organizations?

4th. Did you belong to the Federal army during the late war, and fight against the South during the existence of the same?

5th. Are you opposed to negro equality, both social and political?

6th. Are you in favor of a white man's government in this country?

7th. Are you in favor of Constitutional liberty, and a Government of equitable laws instead of a Government of violence and oppression?

8th. Are you in favor of maintaining the Constitutional rights of the South?

9th. Are you in favor of the re-enfranchisement and emancipation of the white men of the South, and the restitution of the Southern people to all their rights, alike proprietary, civil, and political?

10th. Do you believe in the inalienable right of self-preservation of the people against the exercise of arbitrary and unlicensed power?

If the foregoing interrogatories are satisfactorily answered, and the candidate desires to go further (after something of the character and nature of the Order has thus been indicated to him) and to be admitted to the benefits, mysteries, secrets and purposes of the Order, he shall then be required to take the following final oath or obligation. But if said interrogatories are not satisfactorily answered, or the candidate declines to proceed further, he shall be discharged, after being solemnly admonished by the initiating officer of the deep secrecy to which the oath already taken has bound him, and that the extreme penalty of the law will follow a violation of the same.

FINAL OBLIGATION

"I_____of my own free will and accord, and in the presence of Almighty God, do solemnly swear or affirm, that I will never reveal to any one not a member of the Order of the * * *, by any intimation, sign, symbol, word or act, or in any other manner whatever, any of the secrets, signs, grips, passwords, or mysteries of the Order of the * * *, or that I am a member of the same, or that I know any one who *is* a member; and that I will abide by the Prescript and Edicts of the Order of the * * *. So help me God. . . ."

ÉTATS-UNIS. — Réception, au Congrès de Washington, de M. Hiram Revels, sénateur nègre élu par l'État de Mississipi. — (Voir page 266.)

FRENCH CARTOON HAILS FIRST NEGRO SENATOR   *"United States—Mr. Hiram Revels, Negro Senator elected from the State of Mississippi, presents his credentials to the Congress in Washington."* From L'Illustration, *April, 1870.*   (Picture Collection, New York Public Library)

First Negro Senator

Makes His First Speech to the Senate

March 16, 1870

Hiram Revels assumes responsibility as exponent of "well-being of my race"

Mr. President, I rise at this particular juncture in the discussion . . . with feelings which perhaps never before entered into the experience of any member of this body. I rise, too, with misgivings as to the propriety of lifting my voice at this early period after my admission into the Senate. Perhaps it were wiser for me, so inexperienced in the details of senatorial duties, to have remained a passive listener in the progress of this debate; but when I remember that my term is short, and that the issues with which this bill is fraught are momentous in their present and future influence upon the well-being of my race, I would seem indifferent to the importance of the hour and recreant to the high trust imposed upon me if I hesitated to lend my voice on behalf of the loyal people of the South. I therefore waive all thoughts as to the propriety of taking a part in this discussion. When questions arise which bear upon the safety and protection of the loyal white and colored population of those States lately in rebellion I cannot allow any thought as to mere propriety to enter into my consideration of duty. The responsibility of being the exponent of such a constituency as I have the honor to represent are fully appreciated by me. I bear about me daily the keenest sense of their weight, and that feeling prompts me now to lift my voice for the first time in the Council Chamber of the nation; and, sir, I stand today on this floor to appeal for protection from the strong arm of the Government for her loyal children, irrespective of color and race, who are citizens of the southern States. . . .

I am well aware, sir, that the idea is abroad that an antagonism exists between the whites and blacks, that that race which the nation raised from the degradation of slavery, and endowed with the full and unqualified rights and privileges of citizenship, are intent upon power, at whatever price it can be gained. It has been the well-considered purpose and aim of a class not confined to the South to spread this charge over the land, and their efforts are as vigorous to day to educate the people of this nation into that belief as they were at the close of the war. It was not uncommon to find this same class, even during the rebellion, prognosticating a servile war. It may have been that "the wish was father to the thought." And, sir, as the recognized representative of my downtrodden people, I deny the charge, and hurl it back into the teeth of those who make it, and who, I believe, have not a true and conscientious desire to further the interests of the whole South. Certainly no one possessing any personal knowledge of the colored population of my own or other States need be reminded of the noble conduct of that people under the most trying circumstances in the history of the late war, when they were beyond the protection of the Federal forces. While the confederate army pressed into its ranks every white male capable of bearing arms, the mothers, wives, daughters, and sisters of the southern soldiers were left defenseless and in the power of the blacks, upon whom the chains of slavery were still riveted; and to bind those chains the closer was the real issue for which so much life and property was sacrificed.

And now, sir, I ask, how did that race act? Did they in those days of confederate weakness and impotence evince the malignity of which we hear so much? Granting, for the sake of argument, that they were ignorant and besotted, which I do not believe, yet with all their supposed ignorance and credulity they in their way understood as fully as you or I the awful import of the contest. They knew if the gallant corps of national soldiers were beaten back and their flag trailed in the dust that it was the presage of still heavier bondage. They longed, too, as their fathers did before them, for the advent of that epoch over which was shed the hallowed light of inspiration itself. They desired, too, with their fathers, to welcome the feet of the stranger shod with the peaceful preparation of good news. Weary years of bondage had told their tale of sorrow to the court of Heaven. In the councils of the great Father of all they knew the adjudication of their case, albeit delayed for years, in which patient suffering had nearly exhausted itself, would in the end bring to them the boon for which they sighed—God's most blessed gift to His creatures—the inestimable boon of liberty. They waited, and they waited patiently. In the absence of their masters they protected the virtue and chastity of defenseless women. Think, sir, for a moment, what the condition of this land would be today if the slave population had risen in servile insurrection against those who month by month were fighting to perpetuate that institution which brought to them all the evils of which they complained. Where would have been the security for property, female chastity, and childhood's innocence? . . .

Mr. President, I maintain that the past record of my race is a true index of the feelings which today animate them. They bear toward their former masters no revengeful thoughts, no hatreds, no animosities. They aim not to elevate themselves by sacrificing one single interest of their white fellow-citizens. They ask but the rights which are theirs by God's universal law, and which are the natural out-growth, the logical sequence of the condition in which the legislative enactments of this nation have placed them. They appeal to you and to me to see that they receive that protection which alone will enable them to pursue their daily avocations with success and enjoy the liberties of citizenship on the same footing with their white neighbors and friends. I do not desire simply to defend my own race from unjust and unmerited charges, but I also desire to place upon record an expression of my full and entire confidence in the integrity of purpose with which I believe the President, Congress, and the Republican party will meet these questions so prolific of weal or woe, not only to my own people, but to the whole South. They have been, so far as I can read the history of the times, influenced by no spirit of petty tyranny. The poet has well said that—

"It is excellent
To have a giant's strength, but it is tyrannous
To use it like a giant."

And how have they used that power lodged in them by the people? In acts of cruelty and oppression toward those who sought, to rend in twain this goodly fabric of our fathers, the priceless heritage of so much hardship and endurance in revolutionary times? Let the reconstruction enactments answer the interrogation. No poor words of mine are needed to defend the wise and beneficent legislation which has been extended alike to white and colored citizens. The Republican party is not inflamed, as some would fain have the country believe, against the white population of the South. Its borders are wide enough for all truly loyal men to find within them peace and repose from the din and discord of angry faction. And be that loyal man white or black, that great party of our Republic will, if consistent with the record it has already made for posterity, throw around him the same impartial security in his pursuit of liberty and happiness. If a certain class at the South had accepted in good faith the benevolent overtures which were offered to them with no niggard hand today would not find our land still harassed with feuds and contentions.

I remarked, Mr. President, that I rose to plead for protection for the defenseless race who now send their delegation to the seat of Government to sue for that which this Congress alone can secure to them. And here let me say further, that the people of the North owe to the colored race a deep obligation which it is no easy matter to fulfill. When the Federal armies were thinned by death and disaster, and somber clouds overhung the length and breadth of the Republic, and the very air was pregnant with the rumors of foreign interference—in those dark days of defeat, whose memories even yet haunt us as an ugly dream, from what source did our nation in its seeming death throes gain additional and new-found power? It was the sable sons of the South that valiantly rushed to the rescue, and but for their intrepidity and ardent daring many a northern fireside would miss today paternal counsels or a brother's love.

Sir, I repeat the fact that the colored race saved to the noble women of New England and the middle States men on whom they lean today for security and safety. Many of my race, the representatives of these men on the field of battle, sleep in the countless graves of the South. If those quiet resting-places of our honored dead could speak today what a mighty voice, like to the rushing of a mighty wind, would come up from those sepulchral homes! Could we resist the eloquent pleadings of their appeal? Ah, sir, I think that this question of immediate and ample protection for the loyal people of Georgia would lose its legal technicalities, and we would cease to hesitate in our provisions for their instant relieve. Again, I regret this delay on other grounds. The taunt is frequently flung at us that a Nemesis more terrible than the Greek personation of the anger of the gods awaits her hour of direful retribution. We are told that at no distant day a great uprising of the American people will demand that the reconstruction acts of Congress be undone and blotted forever from the annals of legislative enactment. I inquire, sir, if this delay in affording protection to the loyalists . . . does not lend an uncomfortable significancy to this boasting sneer with which we so often meet? Delay is perilous at best; for it is as true in legislation as in physics, that the longer we procrastinate to apply the proper remedies the more chronic becomes the malady that we seek to heal.

"The land wants such
As dare with rigor execute the laws.
Her festered members
must be lanced and tented.
He's a bad surgeon that for pity spares
The part corrupted till the gangrene spread
And all the body perish. He that's merciful
Unto the bad is cruel to the good."

The Fifteenth Amendment

RATIFIED MARCH 30, 1870

. . . The right of citizens of the United States to vote shall not be denied or abridged by the United States or by any State on account of race, color, or previous condition of servitude—

. . . The Congress shall have power to enforce this article by appropriate legislation—

"Ku Klux Klan" Act

An Act

*to enforce the Provisions
of the Fourteenth Amendment to the
Constitution of the United States,
and for other Purposes*

*B*e it enacted . . . , That any person who, under color of any law, statute, ordinance, regulation, custom, or usage of any State, shall subject, or cause to be subjected, any person within the jurisdiction of the United States to the deprivation of any rights, privileges, or immunities secured by the Constitution of the United States, shall, any such law, statute, ordinance, regulation, custom, or usage of the State to the contrary notwithstanding, be liable to the party injured in any action at law, suit in equity, or other proper proceeding for redress; such proceeding to be prosecuted in the several district or circuit courts of the United States, with and subject to the same rights of appeal, review upon error, and other remedies provided in like cases in such courts, under the provisions of the [Civil Rights Act of 1866], and the other remedial laws of the United States. . . .

. . . That if two or more persons within any State or Territory of the United States

April 20, 1871

Enforcement
of Fourteenth Amendment
legislated

shall conspire together to overthrow, or to put down, or to destroy by force the government of the United States, or to levy war against the United States, or to oppose by force the authority of the government of the United States, or by force, intimidation, or threat to prevent, hinder, or delay the execution of any law of the United States, or by force to seize, take, or possess any property of the United States contrary to the authority thereof, or by force, intimidation, or threat to prevent any person from accepting or holding any office or trust or place of confidence under the United States, or from discharging the duties thereof, or by force, intimidation, or threat to induce any officer of the United States to leave any State, district, or place where his duties as such officer might lawfully be performed, or to injure him in his person or property on account of his lawful discharge of the duties of his office, or to injure his person while engaged in the lawful discharge of the duties of his office, or to injure his property so as to molest, interrupt, hinder, or impede him in the discharge of his official duty, or by force, intimidation, or threat to deter any party or witness in any court of the United States from attending such court, or from testifying in any matter pending in such court fully, freely, and truthfully, or to injure any such party or witness in his person or property on account of his having so attended or testified, or by force, intimidation, or threat to influence the verdict, presentment, or indictment, of any juror or grand juror in any court of the United States, or to injure such juror in his person or property on account of any verdict, presentment, or indictment lawfully assented to by him, or on account of his being or having been such juror, or shall conspire together, or go in disguise upon the public highway or upon the premises of another for the

purpose, either directly or indirectly, of depriving any person or any class of persons of the equal protection of the laws, or of equal privileges or immunities under the laws, or for the purpose of preventing or hindering the constituted authorities of any State from giving or securing to all persons within such State the equal protection of the laws, or shall conspire together for the purpose of in any manner impeding, hindering, obstructing, or defeating the due course of justice in any State or Territory, with intent to deny to any citizen of the United States the due and equal protection of the laws, or to injure any person in his person or his property for lawfully enforcing the right of any person or class of persons to the equal protection of the laws, or by force, intimidation, or threat to prevent any citizen of the United States lawfully entitled to vote from giving his support or advocacy in a lawful manner towards or in favor of the election of any lawfully qualified person as an elector of President or Vice-President of the United States, or as a member of the Congress of the United States, or to injure any such citizen in his person or property on account of such support or advocacy, each and every person so offending shall be deemed guilty of a high crime, and, upon conviction thereof in any district or circuit court of the United States or district or supreme court of any Territory of the United States having jurisdiction of similar offences, shall be punished by a fine not less than five hundred nor more than five thousand dollars, or by imprisonment, with or without hard labor, as the court may determine, for a period of not less than six months nor more than six years, as the court may determine, or by both such fine and imprisonment as the court shall determine. . . .

. . . That in all cases where insurrection, domestic violence, unlawful combinations, or conspiracies in any State shall so obstruct or hinder the execution of the laws thereof, and of the United States, as to deprive any portion or class of the people of such State of any of the rights, privileges, or immunities, or protection, named in the Constitution and secured by this act, and the constituted authorities of such State shall either be unable to protect, or shall, from any cause, fail in or refuse protection of the people in such rights, such facts shall be deemed a denial by such State of the equal protection of the laws to which they are entitled under the Constitution of the United States; and . . . it shall be lawful for the President, and it shall be his duty to take such measures, by the employment of the militia or the land and naval forces of the United States, or of either, or by other means, as he may deem necessary for the suppression of such insurrection, domestic violence, or combinations. . . .

. . . That whenever in any State or part of a State the unlawful combinations named in the preceding section of this act shall be organized and armed, and so numerous and powerful as to be able, by violence, to either overthrow or set at defiance the constituted authorities of such State, and of the United States within such State, or when the constituted authorities are in complicity with, or shall connive at the unlawful purposes of, such powerful and armed combinations; and whenever, by reason of either or all of the causes aforesaid, the conviction of such offenders and the preservation of the public safety shall become in such district impracticable, in every such case such combinations shall be deemed a rebellion against the government of the United States, and during the continuance of such rebellion, and within the limits of the district which shall be so under the sway thereof, such limits to be prescribed by proclamation, it shall be lawful for the President of the United States, when in his judgment the public safety shall require it, to suspend the privileges of the writ of habeas corpus, to the end that such rebellion may be overthrown: *Provided,* That all the provisions of the second section of [the Habeas Corpus Act of March 3, 1863], which relate to the discharge of prisoners other than prisoners of war, and to the penalty for refusing to obey the order of the court, shall be in full force so far as the same are applicable to the provisions of this section: *Provided further,* That the President shall first have made proclamation, as now provided by law, commanding such insurgents to disperse: *And provided also,* That the provisions of this section shall not be in force after the end of the next regular session of Congress.

. . . That no person shall be a grand or petit juror in any court of the United States upon any inquiry, hearing, or trial of any suit, proceeding, or prosecution based upon or arising under the provisions of this act who shall, in the judgment of the court, be in complicity with any such combination or conspiracy; and every such juror shall, before entering upon any such inquiry, hearing, or trial, take and subscribe an oath in open court that he has never, directly or indirectly, counselled, advised, or voluntarily aided any such combination or conspiracy. . . .

. . . That any person or persons, having knowledge that any of the wrongs conspired to be done and mentioned in the second section of this act are about to be committed, and having power to prevent or aid in preventing the same, shall neglect or refuse to do so, and such wrongful act shall be committed, such person or persons shall be liable to the person injured . . . for all damages caused by any such wrongful act which such first-named person or persons by reasonable diligence could have prevented. . . .

Heroism of Negro Troops

January 6, 1874

Civil War general
reports to Congress
on fearlessness
of Negro troops

On the 29th day of September, 1864, I was ordered by the commanding general officer of the armies to cross the James River at two points and attack the enemy's line of works, one in the center of their line, Fort Harrison, the other a strong work guarding their left flank at New Market Heights. I went myself with the colored troops to attack the enemy at New Market Heights, which was the key to the enemy's flank on the north side of James River. That work was a redoubt built on the top of a hill of some considerable elevation, then running down into a marsh: in that marsh was a brook, then rising again to a plain which gently rolled away toward the river.

On that plain, when the flash of dawn was breaking, I placed a column of three thousand colored troops in close column by divisions, right in front, with guns at "right-shoulder shift." I said "that work must be taken by the weight of your column; no shot must be fired;" and as the sun rose up in the heavens the order was given, "Forward, march;" and they marched forward steadily as if on parade—went down the hill, across the marsh, and as they got into the brook they came within the range of the enemy's fire, which vigorously opened upon them. Oh, it was a moment of intense anxiety; but they formed again as they reached firm ground, marching steadily on with closed ranks under the enemy's fire until the head of the column reached the first line of the abatis, some 150

yards from the enemy's works. Then the axmen ran to the front to cut away the obstructions of defense, while one thousand men of the enemy, with their artillery concentrated, poured from the redoubt a heavy fire upon the head of the column hardly wider than the Clerk's desk.

The axmen go down under the murderous fire, other strong hands grasp the ax in their stead, and the abatis is cut away. Again at double-quick the column goes forward to within 50 yards of the fort, to meet there another line of abatis. The column halts, and there a very fire of hell is pouring on them. The abatis resists and holds; the head of the column seems literally to melt away under the rain of shot and shell; the flags of the leading regiments go down, but a brave black hand seizes the colors—they are up again, and wave their starry light over the storm of battle. Again the axmen fall, but strong hands and willing hearts seize the heavy, sharpened trees and drag them away, and the column rushes forward and with a shout which now rings in my ear go over that redoubt like a flash, and the enemy never stop running for 4 miles.

It became my painful duty, sir, to follow the track of that charging column, and there in a space not wider than the Clerk's desk and 300 yards long lay the dead bodies of five hundred and forty-three of my colored comrades, slain in defense of their country, who had laid down their lives to uphold its flag and its honor as a willing sacrifice.

*An act
to protect all citizens
in their civil and legal rights*

WHEREAS it is essential to just government we recognize the equality of all men before the law, and hold that it is the duty of government in its dealings with the people to mete out equal and exact justice to all, of whatever nativity, race, color, or persuasion, religious or political; and it being the appropriate object of legislation to enact great fundamental principles into law: Therefore,

Be it enacted, That all persons within the jurisdiction of the United States shall be entitled to the full and equal enjoyment of the accommodations, advantages, facilities, and privileges of inns, public conveyances on land or water, theaters, and other places of public amusement; subject only to the conditions and limitations established by law, and applicable alike to citizens of every race and color, regardless of any previous condition of servitude.

. . . That any person who shall violate the foregoing section by denying to any citizen, except for reasons by law applicable to citizens of every race and color, and regardless of any previous condition of servitude, the full enjoyment of any of the accommodations, advantages, facilities, or privileges in said section enumerated, or by aiding or inciting such denial, shall, for every such offense, forfeit and pay the sum of five hundred dollars to the person aggrieved thereby, . . . and shall also, for every such offense, be deemed guilty of a misdemeanor, and, upon conviction thereof, shall be fined not less than five hundred nor more than one thousand dollars, or shall be imprisoned not less than thirty days nor more than one year. . .

. . . That the district and circuit courts of the United States shall have, exclusively of the courts of the several States, cognizance of all crimes and offenses against, and violations of, the provisions of this act . . .

. . . That no citizen possessing all other qualifications which are or may be prescribed by law shall be disqualified for service as grand or petit juror in any court of the United States, or of any State, on account of race, color, or previous condition of servitude; and any officer or other person charged with any duty in the selection or summoning of jurors who shall exclude or fail to summon any citizen for the cause aforesaid shall, on conviction thereof, be deemed guilty of a misdemeanor, and be fined not more than five thousand dollars.

. . . That all cases arising under the provisions of this act . . . shall be renewable by the Supreme Court of the United States. . . .

The Civil Rights Act

March 1, 1875

Equality
of all men
before law
exacted

Grant's Proclamation

to Deter Terrorism

By the President of the United States of America

A Proclamation

WHEREAS it has been satisfactorily shown to me that insurrection and domestic violence exist in several counties of the State of South Carolina, and that certain combinations of men against law exist in many counties of said State, known as "rifle clubs," who ride up and down by day and night in arms, murdering some peaceable citizens and intimidating others, which combinations, though forbidden by the laws of the State, cannot be controlled or suppressed by the ordinary course of justice;

And whereas it is provided in the Constitution of the United States that the United States shall protect every state in this Union, on application of the Legislature, or of the executive when the Legislature cannot be convened, against domestic violence;

And whereas by laws in pursuance of the above it is provided (in the laws of the United States) that in all cases of insurrection in any State (or of obstruction to the laws thereof) it shall be lawful for the President of the United States, on application of the Legislature of such State, or of the executive when the Legislature cannot be convened, to call forth the militia of any other State or States, or to employ such part of the land and naval forces as shall be judged necessary for the purpose of suppressing such insurrection or causing the laws to be duly executed.

And whereas the Legislature of said State is not now in session and cannot be convened in time to meet the present emergency, and the executive of said State, under section 4 of Article IV of the Constitution of the United States, and the laws passed in pursuance thereof, has therefore made due appli-

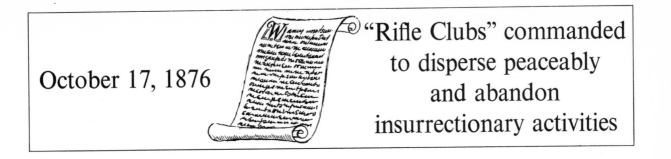

October 17, 1876

"Rifle Clubs" commanded to disperse peaceably and abandon insurrectionary activities

cation to me in the premises for such part of the military force of the United States as may be necessary and adequate to protect said State and the citizens thereof against domestic violence, and to enforce the due execution of the laws;

And whereas it is required that, whenever it may be necessary, in the judgment of the President, to use the military force for the purpose aforesaid, he shall forthwith, by proclamation, command such insurgents to disperse and retire peaceably to their respective homes within a limited time:

Now, therefore, I, Ulysses S. Grant, President of the United States, do hereby make proclamation, and command all persons engaged in said unlawful and insurrectionary proceedings to disperse and retire peaceably to their respective abodes within three days from this date, and hereafter abandon said

combinations and submit themselves to the laws and constituted authorities of said State.

And I invoke the aid and the co-operation of all good citizens thereof to uphold the laws and preserve the public peace.

In witness whereof I have hereunto set my hand and caused the seal of the United States to be affixed.

Done at the city of Washington this 17th day of October, A.D. 1876, and of the Independence of the United States one hundred and one.

U. S. GRANT

[Seal]

By the President:
JOHN L. CADWALADER,
Acting Secretary of State

Mrs. Selina Wallis

Tells the Senate

How Her Husband Was Murdered

Question: You live in Copiah County, do you?

Answer: Yes, sir.

Q: You are the widow of Thomas Wallis?

A: Yes, sir.

Q: Thomas Wallis was killed, was he?

A: Yes, sir.

Q: When?

A: Friday morning before the election.

Q: Friday morning before the last election?

A: Yes, sir.

Q: Who killed him?

A: I don't know.

Q: Tell the committee what you saw in regard to the matter.

A: The men came there to my gallery and hailed.

Q: How many men?

A: I don't know sir, how many there was.

Q: A dozen?

A: I think there were more than a dozen.

Q: Twenty?

A: I reckon; I couldn't tell how many there was.

Q: Did they come on horseback?

A: Yes, sir.

Q: Did they have guns?

A: Yes, sir.

Q: What time of the day was it?

A: It wasn't in the day; it was in the night.

Q: What time in the night?

A: It must have been between one and two o'clock.

Q: You and your husband were in the house.

A: Yes, sir.

Q: In bed?

A: Yes, sir.

Q: Who else was in the house?

A: None but my baby and my other little son in that end of the house I was in.

Q: What did you first hear?

A: They hailed, and I heard them when they hailed.

Q: What did they do?

A: They called and told him to get up and open the door and kindle a light, and he was trying to kindle a light up and couldn't kindle it up as quick as they wanted, and they told him to make haste; he told them to give him a little time, and they said "damn little time," and they told him to open the door, and I told them the door wasn't fastened, and they shoved it once, and it didn't shove open because a chair

Widow testifies that she
saw Thomas Wallis killed
by night riders

was against it, and they shoved it again, and that time it flew wide open and knocked the chair from behind it, and two come in, and, as well as I could see, there was about five or six on the gallery; I couldn't tell how many there was—me in the house and them out-of-doors.

Q: What did they do after they got in?

A: They asked Tom who he was, and he told them he was Wallis; they asked him which one of the Wallises, and he told them old man Wallis; they asked him what was his given name, and he told them Tom Wallis; then they told him he was the man that they was after; that they had a writ for him. But when they hailed, my other son asked them who it was, my son that was in the little back room, and he said it was the sheriff from Brookhaven; he said, "which Sheriff?" and he told him "Mr. Cummings from Brookhaven." When Tommy told them he was Tom Wallis, they said he was the man they was after; he said, "All right, you are the very one I am after," and Tom says, "All right"; and when they said they had a writ, one of them pulled a line out of his pocket and started to put it over his

neck.

Q: A rope, you mean?

A: Yes, sir. When he went to put it over, he throwed up his hand and said, "Hold on, gentlemen;" and as soon as he said that, one of them shot him. Then they hollered to them that was outside to come in, and they came in from the gallery and pulled him out, and when they got him to the door, his axe was lying at the door, and he catched at the axe, and got hold of the handle.

Q: Who did, Thomas?

A: Yes, sir. And another one shot, and he shot sort of up inside of the house and it went through the ceiling of the house, and another one shot and it went up through the gallery and up in the top of the house, and another one shot right through the door and that went through his neck.

Q: It went through your arm and through his neck?

A: Yes, sir.

Q: And then he was dead?

A: Yes, sir; he fell right on my dress-tail behind.

Q: How long did they stay there?

A: They didn't stay a minute after they shot him.

Q: Did they do anything more?

A: They just went and jumped right on their horses and went right off.

Q: Are there many colored people living around in that neighborhood?

A: Yes, sir; right smart.

Q: Did they threaten them?

A: Yes, sir.

Q: What did they do, take to the woods?

A: Yes, sir.

Q: How long did they stay away from their houses at night?

A: Two or three weeks.

Q: Do you know where they went to?

A: To the woods, most of them did.

Q: Where did you stay?

A: Sometimes in the woods and sometimes over to my sister's house.

Q: How long was your arm sore?

A: It ain't quite well yet.

Q: Which arm was it?

A: The left arm. I can't do a thing with my arm now.

Q: How many children have you?

A: . . . I think I got nine.

Q: How many at home with you there?

A: I ain't got but two.

Q: What did you do with them when you were sleeping out in the woods?

A: Carried them with me.

Q: What did you do with your wounded arm?

A: I carried it with me.

Q: Did you have anybody to take care of it?

A: No, sir; nobody but my baby.

Q: How many nights did you sleep out of the house?

A: Four weeks.

Q: Do you know whether they visited your house again?

A: They came the night before the election again. They didn't go in the house that time; they came out in the road and shot all over the house, and all around, and went right on up the road.

Q: Firing the guns?

A: Yes, sir.

Q: How many times should you say they fired?

A: I don't know; I couldn't tell you that.

Q: Were they firing around there occasionally?

A: Yes, sir . . .

Q: Was your husband a Republican?

A: Yes, sir.

Q: Did he take an interest in politics? Did he generally vote?

A: Yes, sir.

Booker T. Washington's Address

at the Opening of the

Cotton States' Exposition

Mr. President and Gentlemen of the Board of Directors and Citizens:

One third of the population of the South is of the Negro race. No enterprise seeking the material, civil, or moral welfare of this section can disregard this element of our population and reach the highest success. I but convey to you, Mr. President and Directors, the sentiment of the masses of my race when I say that in no way have the value and manhood of the American Negro been more fittingly and generously recognized than by the managers of this magnificent Exposition at every stage of its progress. It is a recognition that will do more to cement the friendship of the two races than any occurrence since the dawn of our freedom.

Not only this, but the opportunity here afforded will awaken among us a new era of industrial progress. Ignorant and inexperienced, it is not strange that in the first years of our new life we began at the top instead of at the bottom; that a seat in Congress or the State Legislature was more sought than real estate or industrial skill; that the political convention or stump speaking had more attractions than starting a dairy farm or truck garden.

A ship lost at sea for many days suddenly sighted a friendly vessel. From the mast of the unfortunate vessel was seen a signal: "Water, water; we die of thirst!" The answer from the friendly vessel at once came back: "Cast down your bucket where you are." A second time the signal, "Water, water; send us water!" ran up from the distressed vessel, and was answered: "Cast down your bucket where you are." And a third and fourth signal for water was answered: "Cast down your bucket where you are." The captain of the distressed vessel, at last heeding the injunction, cast down his bucket, and it came up full of fresh, sparkling water from the mouth of the Amazon River. To those of my race who

September 18, 1895 Atlanta

Controversial "Atlanta Compromise" speech by Tuskegee founder depend on bettering their condition in a foreign land, or who underestimate the importance of cultivating friendly relations with the Southern white man, who is their next door neighbor, I would say: "Cast down your bucket where you are"—cast it down in making friends in every manly way of the people of all races by whom we are surrounded.

Cast it down in agriculture, mechanics, in commerce, in domestic service, and in the professions. And in this connection it is well to bear in mind that whatever other sins the South may be called to bear, when it comes to business, pure and simple, it is in the South that the Negro is given a man's chance in the commercial world, and in nothing is this Exposition more eloquent than in emphasizing this chance. Our greatest danger is, that in the great leap from slavery to freedom we may overlook the fact that the masses of us are to live by the productions of our hands, and fail to keep in mind that we shall prosper in proportion as we learn to dignify and glorify common labor, and put brains and skill into the common occupations of life; shall prosper in proportion as we learn to draw the line between the superficial and the substantial, the ornamental gewgaws of life and the useful. No race can prosper till it learns that there is as much dignity in tilling a field as in writing a poem. It is at the bottom of life we must begin, and not at the top. Nor should we permit our grievances to overshadow our opportunities.

To those of the white race who look to the incoming of those of foreign birth and strange tongue and habits for the prosperity of the South, were I permitted, I would repeat what I say to my own race, "Cast down your bucket where you are." Cast it down among the 8,000,000 Negroes whose habits you know, whose fidelity and love you have tested in days when to have proved treacherous meant the ruin of your firesides. Cast down your bucket among these people who have, without strikes and labor wars, tilled your fields, cleared your forests, builded your railroads and cities, and brought forth treasures from the bowels of the earth, and helped make possible this magnificent representation of the progress of the South. Casting down your bucket among my people, helping and encouraging them as you are doing on these grounds, and, with education of head, hand and heart, you will find that they will buy your surplus land, make blossom the waste places in your fields, and run your factories. While doing this, you can be sure in the future, as in the past, that you and your families will be surrounded by the most patient, faithful, law-abiding, and unresentful people that the world has seen.

As we have proved our loyalty to you in the past, in nursing your children, watching by the sick bed of your mothers and fathers, and often following them with tear-dimmed eyes to their graves, so in the future, in our humble way, we shall stand by you with a devotion that no foreigner can approach, ready to lay down our lives, if need be, in defense of yours, interlacing our industrial, commercial, civil, and religious life with yours in a way that shall make the interests of both races one. In all things that are purely social we can be as separate as the fingers, yet one as the hand in all things essential to mutual progress.

There is no defense or security for any of us except in the highest intelligence and development of all. If anywhere there are efforts tending to curtail the fullest growth of the Negro, let these efforts be turned into stimulating, encouraging, and making him the most useful and intelligent citizen. Effort or means so invested will pay a thousand per cent interest. These efforts will be twice blessed—"blessing him that gives and him that takes."

There is no escape through law of man or God from the inevitable:

"The laws of changeless justice bind
Oppressor with oppressed;
And close as sin and suffering joined
We march to fate abreast."

Nearly sixteen millions of hands will aid you in pulling the load upwards, or they will pull against you the load downwards. We shall constitute one-third and more of the ignorance and crime of the South, or one-third its intelligence and progress; we shall contribute one-third to the business and industrial prosperity of the South, or we shall prove a veritable body of death, stagnating, depressing, retarding every effort to advance the body politic.

Gentlemen of the Exposition, as we present to you our humble effort at an exhibition of our progress, you must not expect overmuch. Starting thirty years ago with ownership here and there in a few quilts and pumpkins and chickens (gathered from miscellaneous sources), remember the path that has led from these to the invention and production of agricultural implements, buggies, steam engines, newspapers, books, statuary, carving, paintings, the management of drug stores and banks, has not been trodden without contact with thorns and thistles. While we take pride in what we exhibit as a result of our independent efforts, we do not for a moment forget that our part in this exhibition would fall far short of your expectations but for the constant help that has come to our educational life, not only from the Southern States, but especially from Northern philanthropists, who have made their gifts a constant stream of blessing and encouragement.

The wisest among my race understand that the agitation of questions of social equality is the extremist folly, and that progress in the enjoyment of all the privileges that will come to us must be the result of severe and constant struggle rather than of artificial forcing. No race that has anything to contribute to the markets of the world is long in any degree ostracized. It is important and right that all privileges of the law be ours, but it is vastly more important that we be prepared for the exercise of those privileges. The opportunity to earn a dollar in a factory just now is worth infinitely more than the opportunity to spend a dollar in an opera house.

In conclusion, may I repeat that nothing in thirty years has given us more hope and encouragement, and drawn us so near to you of the white race, as this opportunity offered by the Exposition; and here bending, as it were, over the altar that represents the results of the struggles of your race and mine, both starting practically empty-handed three decades ago, I pledge that, in your effort to work out the great and intricate problem which God has laid at the doors of the South, you shall have at all times the patient, sympathetic help of my race; only let this be constantly in mind that, while from representations in these buildings of the product of field, of forest, of mine, of factory, letters, and art, much good will come, yet far above and beyond material benefits will be that higher good, that let us pray God will come, in a blotting out of sectional differences and racial animosities and suspicions, in a determination to administer absolute justice, in a willing obedience among all classes to the mandates of law. This, coupled with our material prosperity, will bring into our beloved South a new heaven and a new earth.

Plessy vs. Ferguson

THIS case turns upon the constitutionality of an act of the General Assembly of the State of Louisiana, passed in 1890, providing for separate railway carriages for the white and colored races. . . .

The first section of the statute enacts "that all railway companies carrying passengers in their coaches in this State, shall provide equal but separate accommodations for the white, and colored races, by providing two or more passenger coaches for each passenger train, or by dividing the passenger coaches by a partition so as to secure separate accommodations: *Provided,* That this section shall not be construed to apply to street railroads. No person or persons, shall be admitted to occupy seats in coaches, other than, the ones, assigned, to them on account of the race they belong to."

By the second section it was enacted "that the officers of such passenger trains shall have power and are hereby required to assign each passenger to the coach or compartment used for the race to which such passenger belongs; any passenger insisting on going into a coach or compartment to which by race he does not belong, shall be liable to a fine of twenty-five dollars, or in lieu thereof to imprisonment for a period of not more than twenty days in the parish prison, and any

officer of any railroad insisting on assigning a passenger to a coach or compartment other than the one set aside for the race to which said passenger belongs, shall be liable to a fine of twenty-five dollars, or in lieu thereof to imprisonment for a period of not more than twenty days in the parish prison; and should any passenger refuse to occupy the coach or compartment to which he or she is assigned by the officer of such railway, said officer shall have power to refuse to carry such passenger on his train, and for such refusal neither he nor the railway company which he represents shall be liable for damages in any of the courts of this State."

The third section provides penalties for the refusal or neglect of the officers, directors, conductors and employes of railway companies to comply with the act, with a proviso that "nothing in this act shall be construed as applying to nurses attending children of the other race." . . .

The information filed in the criminal District Court charged in substance that Plessy, being a passenger between two stations within the State of Louisiana, was assigned by officers of the company to the coach used for the race to which he belonged, but he insisted upon going into a coach used by the race to which he did not belong. . . .

The petition for the writ of prohibition averred that petitioner was seven eighths Caucasian and one eighth African blood; that the mixture of colored blood was not discernible in him, and that he was entitled to every right, privilege and immunity secured to citizens of the United States of the white race; and that, upon such theory, he took possession of a vacant seat in a coach where passengers of the white race were accommodated, and was ordered by the conductor to vacate said coach and take a seat in another assigned to persons of the colored race, and having refused to comply with such demand he was forcibly ejected with the aid of a police officer, and imprisoned in the parish jail to answer a charge of having violated the above act.

The constitutionality of this act is attacked upon the ground that it conflicts both with the Thirteenth Amendment of the Constitution, abolishing slavery, and the Fourteenth Amendment, which prohibits certain restrictive legislation on the part of the States.

. . . That it does not conflict with the Thirteenth Amendment, which abolished slavery and involuntary servitude, except as a punishment for crime, is too clear for argument. Slavery implies involuntary servitude—a state of bondage; the ownership of mankind as a chattel. . . .

. . . in the *Civil Rights cases* . . . it was said that the act of a mere individual, the owner of an inn, a public conveyance or place of amusement, refusing accommodations to colored people, cannot be justly regarded as imposing any badge of slavery or servitude upon the applicant, but only as involving an ordinary civil injury, properly cognizable by the laws of the State, and presumably subject to redress by those laws until the contrary appears. "It would be running the slavery argument into the ground," said Mr. Justice Bradley, "to make it apply to every act of discrimination which a person may see fit to make as to the guests he will entertain, or as to the people he will take into his coach or cab or car, or admit to his concert or theatre, or deal with in other matters of intercourse or business."

A statute which implies merely a legal distinction between the white and colored races —a distinction which is founded in the color of the two races, and which must always exist so long as white men are distinguished from the other race by color—has no tendency to destroy the legal equality of the two races, or reëstablish a state of involuntary servitude. . . .

. . . By the Fourteenth Amendment, all

persons born or naturalized in the United States, and subject to the jurisdiction thereof, are made citizens of the United States and of the State wherein they reside; and the States are forbidden from making or enforcing any law which shall abridge the privileges or immunities of citizens of the United States, or shall deprive any person of life, liberty or property without due process of law, or deny to any person within their jurisdiction the equal protection of the laws.

The proper construction of this amendment was first called to the attention of this court in the *Slaughter-house cases . . .* which involved, however, not a question of race, but one of exclusive privileges. The case did not call for any expression of opinion as to the exact rights it was intended to secure to the colored race, but it was said generally that its main purpose was to establish the citizenship of the negro; to give definitions of citizenship of the United States and of the States, and to protect from the hostile legislation of the States the privileges and immunities of citizens of the United States, as distinguished from those of citizens of the States.

The object of the amendment was undoubtedly to enforce the absolute equality of the two races before the law, but in the nature of things it could not have been intended to abolish distinctions based upon color, or to enforce social, as distinguished from political equality . . . laws permitting, and even requiring, their separation in places where they are liable to be brought into contact do not necessarily imply the inferiority of either race to the other, and have been generally, if not universally, recognized as within the competency of the state legislatures in the exercise of their police power. The most common instance of this is connected with the establishment of separate schools for white and colored children, which has been held to be a valid exercise of the legislative power even by courts of States where the political rights of the colored race have been longest and most earnestly enforced. . . .

Laws forbidding the intermarriage of the two races may be said in a technical sense to interfere with the freedom of contract, and yet have been universally recognized as within the police power of the State. . . .

So far, then, as a conflict with the Fourteenth Amendment is concerned, the case reduces itself to the question whether the statute of Louisiana is a reasonable regulation, and with respect to this there must necessarily be a large discretion on the part of the legislature. In determining the question of reasonableness it is at liberty to act with reference to the established usages, customs and traditions of the people, and with a view to the promotion of their comfort, and the preservation of the public peace and good order. Gauged by this standard, we cannot say that a law which authorizes or even requires the separation of the two races in public conveyances is unreasonable, or more obnoxious to the Fourteenth Amendment than the acts of Congress requiring separate schools for colored children in the District of Columbia, the constitutionality of which does not seem to have been questioned, or the corresponding acts of state legislatures.

We consider the underlying fallacy of the plaintiff's argument to consist in the assumption that the enforced separation of the two races stamps the colored race with a badge of inferiority. If this be so, it is not by reason of anything found in the act, but solely because the colored race chooses to put that construction upon it. The argument necessarily assumes that if, as has been more than once the case, and is not unlikely to be so again, the colored race should become the dominant power in the state legislature, and should enact a law in precisely similar terms, it would thereby relegate the white race to an inferior position. We imagine that the white race, at least, would not acquiesce in this assumption. The argument also assumes that social prejudices may be overcome by legislation, and that equal rights cannot be secured to the negro except by an enforced commingling of the two races. We cannot accept this proposition. If the two races are to meet upon terms of social equality, it must be the result of natural affinities, a mutual appreciation of each other's merits and a voluntary consent of individuals. . . . Legislation is powerless to eradicate racial instincts or to abolish distinctions based upon physical differences, and the attempt to do so can only result in accentuating the difficulties of the present situation. If the civil and political rights of both races be equal one cannot be inferior to the other civilly or politically. If one race be inferior to the other socially, the Constitution of the United States cannot put them upon the same plane.

Mr. Justice Harlan's Dissent

. . . In respect of civil rights, common to all citizens, the Constitution of the United States does not, I think, permit any public authority to know the race of those entitled to be protected in the enjoyment of such rights. Every true man has pride of race, and under appropriate circumstances when the rights of others, his equals before the law, are not to be affected, it is his privilege to express such pride and to take such action based upon it as to him seems proper. But I deny that any legislative body or judicial tribunal may have regard to the race of citizens when the civil rights of those citizens are involved. . . .

The white race deems itself to be the dominant race in this country. And so it is, in prestige, in achievements, in education, in wealth and in power. So, I doubt not, it will continue to be for all time, if it remains true to its great heritage and holds fast to the principles of constitutional liberty. But in view of the Constitution, in the eye of the law, there is in this country no superior, dominant, ruling class of citizens. There is no caste here. Our Constitution is color-blind, and neither knows nor tolerates classes among citizens. In respect of civil rights, all citizens are equal before the law. The humblest is the peer of the most powerful. The law regards man as man, and takes no account of his surroundings or of his color when his civil rights as guaranteed by the supreme law of the land are involved. It is, therefore, to be regretted that this high tribunal, the final expositor of the fundamental law of the land, has reached the conclusion that it is competent for a State to regulate the enjoyment by citizens of their civil rights solely upon the basis of race. . . .

The arbitrary separation of citizens, on the basis of race, while they are on a public highway, is a badge of servitude wholly inconsistent with the civil freedom and the equality before the law established by the Constitution.

If evils will result from the commingling of the two races upon public highways established for the benefit of all, they will be infinitely less than those that will surely come from state legislation regulating the enjoyment of civil rights upon the basis of race. We boast of the freedom enjoyed by our people above all other peoples. But it is difficult to reconcile that boast with a state of the law which, practically, puts the brand of servitude and degradation upon a large class of our fellow-citizens, our equals before the law. The thin disguise of "equal" accommodations for passengers in railroad coaches will not mislead any one. . . .

Artist's conception of Congressman George White addressing the House of Representatives.

The Last Negro in Congress Says "Goodbye"

... **M**R. Chairman, there are others on this committee and in this House who are far better prepared to enlighten the world with their eloquence as to what the agriculturists of this country need than your humble servant. I therefore resign to more competent minds the discussion of this bill. I shall consume the remainder of my time in reverting to measures and facts that have in them more weighty interests to me and mine . . . —matters of life and existence.

I want to enter a plea for the colored man, the colored woman, the colored boy, and the colored girl of this country. I would not thus digress from the question at issue and detain the House in a discussion of the interests of this particular people at this time but for the constant and the persistent efforts of certain gentlemen upon this floor to mold and rivet public sentiment against us as a people and to lose no opportunity to hold up the unfortunate few who commit crimes and depredations and lead lives of infamy and shame, as other races do, as fair specimens of representatives of the entire colored race. . . . an opportunity to answer some of the statements made by gentlemen from different States . . . was denied me; and I therefore must embrace this opportunity to say, out of season, perhaps, that which I was not permitted to say in season.

January 29, 1901

Congressman White's valedictory statement predicts Negro's return to federal legislature

In the catalogue of members of Congress in this House perhaps none have been more persistent in their determination to bring the black man into disrepute and, with a labored effort, to show that he was unworthy of the right of citizenship than my colleague from North Carolina, Mr. KITCHIN. . . . During the first session of this Congress, while the Constitutional amendment was pending in North Carolina, he labored long and hard to show that the white race was at all times and under all circumstances superior to the negro by inheritance if not otherwise, and . . . that an illiterate negro was unfit to participate in making the laws of a sovereign State and the administration and execution of them; but an illiterate white man living by his side, with no more or perhaps not as much property, with no more exalted character, no higher thoughts of civilization, no more knowledge of the handicraft of government, had by birth, because he was white, inherited some peculiar qualification . . . that entitled him to vote, though he knew nothing whatever of letters. It is true, in my opinion, that men brood over things at times which they would have exist until they fool themselves and actually, sometimes honestly, believe that such things do exist.

I would like to call the gentleman's attention to the fact that the Constitution of the United States forbids the granting of any title of nobility to any citizen thereof, and while it does not in letters forbid the inheritance of this superior caste, I believe in the fertile imagination of the gentleman promulgating it, his position is at least in conflict with the spirit of that organic law of the land . . .

If the gentleman to whom I have referred will pardon me, I would like to advance the statement that the musty records of 1868, filed away in the archives of Southern capitals, as to what the negro was thirty-two years ago, is not a proper standard by which the negro living on the threshold of the twentieth century should be measured. Since that time we have reduced the illiteracy of the race at least 45 per cent. We have written and published near 500 books. We have nearly 300 newspapers, 3 of which are dailies. We have now in practice over 2,000 lawyers and a corresponding number of doctors. We have accumulated over $12,000,000 worth of school property and about $40,000,000 worth of church property. We have about 140,000 farms and homes, valued at in the neighborhood of $750,000,000, and personal property valued at about $170,000,000. We have raised about $11,000,000 for educational purposes, and the property per capita for every colored man, woman, and child in the United States is estimated at $75.

We are operating successfully several banks, commercial enterprises among our people in the Southland, including 1 silk mill and 1 cotton factory. We have 32,000 teachers in the schools of the country . . . We have over 600,000 acres of land in the South alone. The cotton produced, mainly by black labor, has increased from 4,669,770 bales in 1860 to 11,235,000 in 1899. All this we have done under the most adverse circumstances. We have done it in the face of lynching, burning at the stake, with the humiliation of "Jim Crow" cars, the disfranchisement of our male citizens, slander and degradation of our women, with the factories closed against us, no negro permitted to be conductor on the railway cars, whether run through the streets of our cities or across the prairies of our great country, no negro permitted to run as engineer on a locomotive, most of the mines closed against us. Labor unions—carpenters, painters, brick masons, machinists, hackmen, and those supplying nearly every conceivable avocation of livelihood have banded themselves together to better their condition, but, with few exceptions, the black face has been left out. . . . With all these odds against us, we are forging our way ahead, slowly, perhaps, but surely. You may tie us and then taunt us for a lack of bravery, but one day we will break the bonds. You may use our labor for two and a half centuries and then taunt us for our poverty, but let me remind you we will not always remain poor. You may withhold even the knowledge of how to read God's word and learn the way from earth to glory and then taunt us for our ignorance, but we would remind you that there is plenty of room at the top, and we are climbing.

After enforced debauchery, with the many kindred horrors incident to slavery, it comes with ill grace from the perpetrators of these deeds to hold up the shortcomings of some of our race to ridicule and scorn.

. . . Mr. Chairman, before concluding my remarks I want to submit a brief recipe for the solution of the so-called American negro problem. He asks no special favors, but simply demands that he be given the same chance for existence, for earning a livelihood, for raising himself in the scales of manhood and womanhood that are accorded to kindred nationalities. Treat him as a man; go into his home and learn of his social conditions; learn of his cares, his troubles, and his hopes for the future; gain his confidence; open the doors of industry to him; let the word "negro," "colored," and "black" be stricken from all the organizations enumerated in the federation of labor.

Help him to overcome his weaknesses, punish the crime-committing class by the courts of the land, measure the standard of the race by its best material, cease to mold prejudicial and unjust public sentiment against him, and my word for it, he will learn to support, hold up the hands of, and join in with that political party, that institution, whether secular or religious, in every community where he lives, which is destined to do the greatest good for the greatest number. Obliterate race hatred, party prejudice, and help us to achieve nobler ends, greater results, and become more satisfactory citizens to our brother in white.

This, Mr. Chairman, is perhaps the negroes' temporary farewell to the American Congress; but let me say, Phoenix-like he will rise up some day and come again. These parting words are in behalf of an outraged, heart-broken, bruised, and bleeding, but God-fearing people, faithful, industrious, loyal people—rising people, full of potential force.

Mr. Chairman, in the trial of Lord Bacon, when the court disturbed the counsel for the defendant, Sir Walter Raleigh raised himself up to his full height and, addressing the court, said:

SIR, I AM PLEADING FOR THE LIFE OF A HUMAN BEING.

The only apology that I have to make for the earnestness with which I have spoken is that I am pleading for the life, the liberty, the future happiness, and manhood suffrage for one-eighth of the entire population of the United States. [*Loud applause.*]

FRANCHISE.

AND NOT THIS MAN?"

SECTION V

BOUND FOR THE PROMISED LAND

On Jordan's stormy banks I stand
And cast a wishful eye
To Canaan's fair and happy land
Where my possessions lie.
I am bound for the promised land
I am bound for the promised land
Oh, who will come and go with me
I am bound for the promised land.

UNWELCOME: *Turn of the century prospects were hardly optimistic for the Negro. "In the gloomy overcast of the new century's dawn neither life, liberty nor the pursuit of happiness seemed secure to the Negro."*
(Harper's Weekly)

THE RISE OF SOCIAL AND ECONOMIC *progressivism* accompanied the advent of the twentieth century in America. Women, working men, "small-business" men and juveniles received the attention of a group of reformers and social workers and paved the way for the massive social security programs undertaken in the 1930's.

The period following the Civil War saw many attempts at organizing labor, but labor's growth was halting and, often, violence accompanied the maturation process. State militia and federal troops were required to quell violence in the Railway Strike of 1877. The Haymarket Riot of 1886 grew out of a general strike sponsored by the Knights of Labor for an eight-hour work day. The Homestead Strike of 1892 resulted in the death of seven men, killed in a battle between workers and 300 private guards representing the Carnegie Steel Company. In the Pullman Strike of 1894, President Grover Cleveland intervened and assigned the Army of the United States to move the mails. Since that time organized labor has become a powerful force in American life, and the cause of the working man is championed in every contemporary political party platform.

Women's rights have had a similarly dramatic history in America. The women's suffrage movement in this country was led by many of the same group of women who spearheaded the drive to abolish slavery. Suffrage was first extended to women by Wyoming when it achieved statehood in 1889. Gradually other states gave women the vote, and in 1920, under the Nineteenth Amendment, women entered the national electorate. Contemporaneously, increasing support has been gained for an Equal Rights Amendment, intended to remove *all* discriminatory obstacles to the participation of women in *all* aspects of American life.

The Sherman Anti-Trust Act of 1890 has been followed by numerous laws and court cases aimed at removing the abuses of business "bigness." The national posture in this area has been marked by ambivalence, expressed in the Supreme Court's supple doctrine that "the law does not make mere size an offense." Through the efforts of various private agencies and governmental regulatory commissions, codes of business ethics protecting the consumer and extending the life of small business have evolved.

Programs of child welfare have existed since colonial days, but have taken their longest strides in twentieth century America. The emphasis in these programs has shifted from the placement of orphaned children in almshouses or with private persons; as indentured servants or apprentices—to the provision of a healthy environment in which children may grow toward responsible adult citizenship. Children receive the attention of White House conferences, the Children's Bureau of the Federal Department of Health, Education and Welfare, state, county and municipal agencies, as well as myriad child-serving social service agencies. Child labor is controlled by federal law, and special children's courts seek to curtail juvenile delinquency through preventive and corrective treatment.

The twentieth century also elevated America to the rank of number one among world powers. In the decades following the Civil War, United States interest in world affairs broadened, and provincialism atrophied. American delegates participated in the discussions of the Hague Conferences of 1899 (at which the Permanent Court of International Cooperation was established) and 1907 (which issued a declaration disavowing the use of force to collect international debts).

The United States was also a member of the London Conference (1908–09) which devised a code of naval warfare that obtained until World War II. In China, 1900, the State Department fostered the "Open Door" policy and, that same year, joined with other Western nations to suppress the "Boxer Rebellion"—a Chinese uprising against non-Oriental residents. American relations with the Far East included Japan, and the Russo-Japanese War (1904–05) was settled through the good offices of President Theodore Roosevelt.

America's path to world supremacy was cleared by World War I. Alone among the world's powers, the United States came out of the war in a stronger position than upon entering the conflict. The monarchy of Austria-Hungary was vanquished; Germany was defeated; Russia was beset by revolution; and France, Great Britain and Italy were enfeebled and debt-ridden. On the other hand, when the war ended, the United States had liquidated her debts and became chief international creditor.

Triumphs in World War II and dramatic breakthroughs in nuclear armaments made it appear for a time that American supremacy was incontrovertible. When the United Nations evolved, America's was a dominant voice. Yet the United States' moral leadership in U.N. debate has been debilitated by her inability to show resolute action that would secure full justice and equality to certain minorities—non-whites, especially Negroes.

Prospects for the Negro were less optimistic in 1900. One lone Negro remained in Congress, and his tenure would soon end. His impending departure gave chilling testimony to the awful effectiveness of post Civil War schemes to reverse the progress of the Negro. In the gloomy overcast of the new century's dawn, neither *life, liberty nor the pursuit of happiness* seemed secure to the Negro.

Life was jeopardized by lynch mobs whose victims in 1900 totaled 115. Of these, 107 were Negroes. *Liberty* was illusive, walled off in various guises including grandfather clauses, poll taxes, and literacy tests. *The pursuit of happiness* became mere rhetoric as *Plessy* v. *Ferguson* gave judicial recognition to alleged Negro inferiority and permitted the roadblocks of "Jim Crow" and discrimination to impede both the Negro's and America's march toward democracy's fulfillment. Yet this forlorn period produced a generation called the "New Negro" and provoked a dialogue whose ramifications would spread from the Negro community, throughout the American society and ultimately into the world's consciousness.

The dialogue started slowly, in Atlanta,

PORTRAIT — BOOKER TALIAFERRO WASHINGTON

Georgia, where on September 18, 1895, Booker T. Washington compared the plight of the Negro to a ship's crew "lost at sea." Like a friendly vessel which answered the lost ship's appeal for water, Washington advised the Negro: "Cast down your bucket where you are." Advocating industrial training in preference to higher learning, economic security in preference to intellectual attainment and conciliation in preference to agitation for social equality, Washington concluded:

"The wisest among my race understand that the agitation of questions of social equality is the extremist folly, and that progress in the enjoyment of all the privileges that will come to us must be the result of severe and constant struggle rather than of artificial forcing. No race that has anything to contribute to the markets of the world is long in any degree ostracized. It is important and right that all privileges of the law be ours, but it is vastly more important that we be prepared for the exercise of those privileges. The opportunity to earn a dollar in a factory just now is worth infinitely more than the opportunity to spend a dollar in an opera house."

Washington's speech enjoyed wide acclaim in the nation's press and its accommodating practicality was welcomed by Southern as well as Northern white businessmen and politicians. Tuskegee Institute received sufficient gifts from philanthropists to remove the accustomed threat of financial crisis. Theodore Roosevelt invited Washington to dinner at the White House. And his white admirers, in a familiar process, proclaimed Washington Negro leader supreme.

The Negro community had other reactions to the Washington proposal. It was castigated as a "compromise" and a disservice to the Negro cause in many private conversations. Few, however, gave public expression to their sentiments; Washington's broad power and influence was a potent deterrent. Some dared speak out. The most effective rebuttal was offered by Dr. W. E. B. DuBois. In a magazine piece "Of Booker T. Washington and Others"—later included in his celebrated volume *The Souls of Black Folk*—DuBois named Washington "the most distinguished Southerner since Jefferson Davis." After submitting the Washington "Atlanta Compromise" to merciless scrutiny and evaluation DuBois concluded:

"So far as Mr. Washington preaches Thrift, Patience, and Industrial Training for the masses, we must hold up his hands and strive with him' . . . But so far as Mr. Washington apologizes for injustice, North or South, does not rightly value the privilege and duty of voting, belittles the emasculating effects of caste distinctions, and opposes the higher training and ambition of our brighter minds,— so far as he, the South, or the Nation, does this,—we must unceasingly and firmly oppose them."

Both programs—Washington's and DuBois'—went forward. Industrial schools proliferated in the North and in the South for Negro and for white students. Simultaneously, increasing numbers of Negroes entered American universities to obtain degrees in the arts and sciences, and starting with the Niagara Movement, lineal ancestor of the NAACP, protest organizations have sprung up to alleviate the social injustices dealt the Negro.

Though they do not necessarily all agree on objectives or strategy, they all share a common purpose: to speed the day when the Negro and other minorities will come to the end of a road called *Freedom*.

PORTRAIT — WILLIAM EDWARD BURGHARDT DuBOIS

Dr. DuBois' Affirmation of Faith

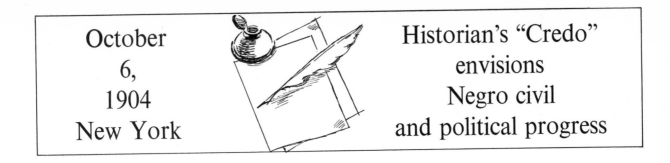

October
6,
1904
New York

Historian's "Credo"
envisions
Negro civil
and political progress

I BELIEVE in God who made of one blood all races that dwell on earth. I believe that all men, black and brown, and white, are brothers, varying, through Time and Opportunity, in form and gift and feature, but differing in no essential particular, and alike in soul and in the possibility of infinite development.

Especially do I believe in the Negro Race; in the beauty of its genius, the sweetness of its soul, and its strength in that meekness which shall inherit this turbulent earth.

I believe in pride of race and lineage itself; in pride of self so deep as to scorn injustice to other selves; in pride of lineage so great as to despise no man's father; in pride of race so chivalrous as neither to offer bastardy to the weak nor beg wedlock of the strong, knowing that men may be brothers in Christ, even though they be not brothers-in-law.

I believe in Service—humble reverent service, from the blackening of boots to the whitening of souls; for Work is Heaven, Idleness Hell, and Wages is the "Well done!" of the Master who summoned all them that labor and are heavy laden, making no distinction between the black sweating cotton-hands of Georgia and the First Families of Virginia, since all distinction not based on deed is devilish and not divine.

I believe in the Devil and his angels, who wantonly work to narrow the opportunity of struggling human beings, especially if they be black, who spit in the faces of the fallen, strike them that cannot strike again, believe the worst and work to prove it, hating the image which their Maker stamped on a brother's soul.

I believe in the Prince of Peace. I believe that War is Murder. I believe that armies and navies are at bottom the tinsel and braggadocio of oppression and wrong; and I believe that the wicked conquest of weaker and darker nations by nations white and stronger but foreshadows the death of that strength.

I believe in Liberty for all men; the space to stretch their arms and their souls; the right to breathe and the right to vote, the freedom to choose their friends, enjoy the sunshine and ride on the railroads, uncursed by color; thinking, dreaming, working as they will in a kingdom of God and love.

I believe in the training of children black even as white; the leading out of little souls into the green pastures and beside the still waters, not for pelf or peace, but for Life lit by some large vision of beauty and goodness and truth. . . .

Finally, I believe in Patience—patience with the weakness of the Weak and the strength of the Strong, the prejudice of the Ignorant and the ignorance of the Blind; patience with the tardy triumph of Joy and the mad chastening of Sorrow—patience with God.

Dr. DuBois' Affirmation of Faith   ☐   223

The Niagara Movement

Sets Forth Its Principles

Progress: The members of the conference, known as the Niagara Movement, assembled in annual meeting at Buffalo, July 11th, 12th and 13th, 1905, congratulate the Negro-Americans on certain undoubted evidences of progress in the last decade, particularly the increase of intelligence, the buying of property, the checking of crime, the uplift in home life, the advance in literature and art, and the demonstration of constructive and executive ability in the conduct of great religious, economic and educational institutions.

Suffrage: At the same time, we believe that this class of American citizens should protest emphatically and continually against the curtailment of their political rights. We believe in manhood suffrage; we believe that no man is so good, intelligent or wealthy as to be entrusted wholly with the welfare of his neighbor.

Civil Liberty: We believe also in protest against the curtailment of our civil rights. All American citizens have the right to equal treatment in places of public entertainment according to their behavior and deserts.

Economic Opportunity: We especially complain against the denial of equal opportunities to us in economic life; in the rural districts of the South this amounts to peonage and virtual slavery; all over the South it tends to crush labor and small business enterprises;

and everywhere American prejudice, helped often by iniquitous laws, is making it more difficult for Negro-Americans to earn a decent living.

Education: Common school education should be free to all American children and compulsory. High school training should be adequately provided for all, and college training should be the monopoly of no class or race in any section of our common country. We believe that, in defense of our own institutions, the United States should aid common school education, particularly in the South, and we especially recommend concerted agitation to this end. We urge an increase in public high school facilities in the South, where the Negro-Americans are almost wholly without such provisions. We favor well-equipped trade and technical schools for the training of artisans, and the need of adequate and liberal endowment for a few institutions of higher education must be patent to sincere well-wishers of the race.

Courts: We demand upright judges in courts, juries selected without discrimination on account of color and the same measure of punishment and the same efforts at reformation for black as for white offenders. We need orphanages and farm schools for dependent children, juvenile reformatories for delinquents, and the abolition of the

dehumanizing convict-lease system.

Public Opinion: We note with alarm the evident retrogression in this land of sound public opinion on the subject of manhood rights, republican government and human brotherhood, and we pray God that this nation will not degenerate into a mob of boasters and oppressors, but rather will return to the faith of the fathers, that all men were created free and equal, with certain unalienable rights.

Health: We plead for health—for an opportunity to live in decent houses and localities, for a chance to rear our children in physical and moral cleanliness.

Employers and Labor Unions: We hold up for public execration the conduct of two opposite classes of men: The practice among employers of importing ignorant Negro-American laborers in emergencies, and then affording them neither protection nor permanent employment; and the practice of labor unions in proscribing and boycotting and oppressing thousands of their fellow-toilers, simply because they are black. These methods have accentuated and will accentuate the war of labor and capital, and they are disgraceful to both sides.

Protest: We refuse to allow the impression to remain that the Negro-American assents to inferiority, is submissive under oppression and apologetic before insults. Through helplessness we may submit, but the voice of protest of ten million Americans must never cease to assail the ears of their fellows, so long as America is unjust.

Color-Line: Any discrimination based simply on race or color is barbarous, we care not how hallowed it be by custom, expediency or prejudice. Differences made on account of ignorance, immorality, or disease are legitimate methods of fighting evil, and against them we have no word of protest; but discriminations based simply and solely on physical peculiarities, place of birth, color of skin, are relics of that unreasoning human savagery of which the world is and ought to be thoroughly ashamed.

"Jim Crow" Cars: We protest against the "Jim Crow" car, since its effect is and must be to make us pay first-class fare for third-class accommodations, render us open to insults and discomfort and to crucify wantonly our manhood, womanhood and self-respect.

Soldiers: We regret that this nation has never seen fit adequately to reward the black soldiers who, in its five wars, have defended their country with their blood, and yet have been systematically denied the promotions which their abilities deserve. And we regard as unjust, the exclusion of black boys from the military and naval training schools.

War Amendments: We urge upon Congress the enactment of appropriate legislation for securing the proper enforcement of those articles of freedom, the thirteenth, fourteenth and fifteenth amendments of the Constitution of the United States.

Oppression: We repudiate the monstrous doctrine that the oppressor should be the sole authority as to the rights of the oppressed. The Negro race in America stolen, ravished and degraded, struggling up through difficulties and oppression, needs sympathy and receives criticism; needs help and is given hindrance, needs protection and is given mob-violence, needs justice and is given charity, needs leadership and is given cowardice and apology, needs bread and is given a stone. This nation will never stand justified before God until these things are changed.

The Church: Especially are we surprised and astonished at the recent attitude of the church of Christ—of an increase of a desire to bow to racial prejudice, to narrow the bounds of human brotherhood, and to segregate black men to some outer sanctuary. This is wrong, unchristian and disgraceful to the twentieth century civilization.

Agitation: Of the above grievances we do not hesitate to complain, and to complain loudly and insistently. To ignore, overlook, or apologize for these wrongs is to prove ourselves unworthy of freedom. Persistent manly agitation is the way to liberty, and toward this goal the Niagara Movement has started and asks the cooperation of all men of all races.

Help: At the same time we want to acknowledge with deep thankfulness the help of our fellowmen from the Abolitionist down to those who today still stand for equal opportunity and who have given and still give of their wealth and of their poverty for our advancement.

Duties: And while we are demanding, and ought to demand, and will continue to demand the rights enumerated above, God forbid that we should ever forget to urge corresponding duties upon our people:

The duty to vote.

The duty to respect the rights of others.

The duty to work.

The duty to obey the laws.

The duty to be clean and orderly.

The duty to send our children to school.

The duty to respect ourselves,

    even as we respect others.

This statement, complaint and prayer we submit to the American people, and Almighty God.

The Birth of the NAACP

<table>
<tr>
<td>February
12,
1909
New York City</td>
<td></td>
<td>The founding call
to all believers to
renew struggle for civil
and political liberty</td>
</tr>
</table>

THE celebration of the Centennial of the birth of Abraham Lincoln, widespread and grateful as it may be, will fail to justify itself if it takes no note of and makes no recognition of the colored men and women to whom the great emancipator labored to assure freedom. Besides a day of rejoicing, Lincoln's birthday in 1909 should be one of taking stock of the nation's progress since 1865.

How far has it lived up to the obligations imposed upon it by the Emancipation Proclamation? How far has it gone in assuring to each and every citizen, irrespective of color, the equality of opportunity and equality before the law, which underlie our American institutions and are guaranteed by the Constitution?

If Mr. Lincoln could revisit this country in the flesh, he would be disheartened and discouraged. He would learn that on January 1, 1909, Georgia had rounded out a new confederacy by disfranchising the Negro, after the manner of all the other Southern States. He would learn that the Supreme Court of the United States, supposedly a bulwark of American liberties, had refused every opportunity to pass squarely upon this disfranchisement of millions, by laws avowedly discriminatory and openly enforced in such manner that the white men may vote and

black men be without a vote in their government; he would discover, therefore, that taxation without representation is the lot of millions of wealth-producing American citizens, in whose hands rests the economic progress and welfare of an entire section of the country.

He would learn that the Supreme Court, according to the official statement of one of its own judges in the Berea College case, has laid down the principle that if an individual State chooses, it may "make it a crime for white and colored persons to frequent the same market place at the same time, or appear in an assemblage of citizens convened to consider questions of a public or political nature in which all citizens, without regard to race, are equally interested."

In many states Lincoln would find justice enforced, if at all, by judges elected by one element in a community to pass upon the liberties and lives of another. He would see the black men and women, for whose freedom a hundred thousand of soldiers gave their lives, set apart in trains, in which they pay first-class fares for third-class service, and segregated in railway stations and in places of entertainment; he would observe that State after State declines to do its elementary duty in preparing the Negro through education for the best exercise of citizenship.

Added to this, the spread of lawless attacks upon the Negro, North, South, and West—even in the Springfield made famous by Lincoln—often accompanied by revolting brutalities, sparing neither sex nor age nor youth, could but shock the author of the sentiment that "government of the people, by the people, for the people, shall not perish from the earth."

Silence under these conditions means tacit approval. The indifference of the North is already responsible for more than one assault upon democracy, and every such attack reacts as unfavorably upon whites as upon blacks. Discrimination once permitted cannot be bridled; recent history in the South shows that in forging chains for the Negroes the white voters are forging chains for themselves. "A house divided against itself cannot stand"; this government cannot exist half-slave and half-free any better today than it could in 1861.

Hence we call upon all the believers in democracy to join in a national conference for the discussion of present evils, the voicing of protests, and the renewal of the struggle for civil and political liberty.

Jane Addams [Chicago]
Samuel Bowles [Springfield *Republican*]
Professor W. L. Bulkley [New York]
Harriet Stanton Blatch [New York]
Ida Wells Barnett [Chicago]
E. H. Clement [Boston]
Kate Claghorn [New York]
Professor John Dewey [New York]
Dr. W. E. B. DuBois [Atlanta]
Mary E. Dreier [Brooklyn]
Dr. John L. Elliott [New York]
William Lloyd Garrison [Boston]
Rev. Francis J. Grimké [Washington, D.C.]
William Dean Howells [New York]
Rabbi Emil G. Hirsch [Chicago]
Rev. John Haynes Holmes [New York]
Professor Thomas C. Hall [New York]
Hamilton Holt [New York]
Florence Kelley [New York]
Rev. Frederick Lynch [New York]
Helen Marot [New York]
John E. Milholland [New York]
Mary E. McDowell [Chicago]
Professor J. G. Merrill [Connecticut]
Dr. Henry Moskowitz [New York]
Leonora O'Reilly [New York]
Mary W. Ovington [New York]
Rev. Dr. Charles H. Parkhurst [New York]

Louis F. Post [Chicago]
Rev. Dr. John P. Peters [New York]
Dr. Jane Robbins [New York]
Charles Edward Russell [New York]
Joseph Smith [Boston]
Anna Garlin Spencer [New York]
William M. Salter [Chicago]
J. G. Phelps Stokes [New York]
Judge Wendell Stafford [Washington]
Helen Stokes [Boston]
Lincoln Steffens [Boston]
President Thwing [Western Reserve University]
Professor W. I. Thomas [Chicago]
Oswald Garrison Villard [New York *Evening Post*]
Rabbi Stephen S. Wise [New York]
Bishop Alexander Walters [New York]
Dr. William H. Ward [New York]
Horace White [New York]
William English Walling [New York]
Lillian D. Wald [New York]
Dr. J. Milton Waldron [Washington, D.C.]
Mrs. Rodman Wharton [Philadelphia]
Susan P. Wharton [Philadelphia]
President Mary E. Woolley [Mt. Holyoke College]
Professor Charles Zueblin [Boston]

The Urban League Emerges

1910
New York City

Consolidation of three
organizations effected
to better serve
Negroes in the cities

THIS organization is the result of the intense patriotism of a group of unusual men and women of both races, who in New York City in 1906 met at the call of William H. Baldwin, then President of the Long Island Railroad and President of the General Education Board.

These persons were primarily interested in the industrial welfare of Negroes in New York and realized then, as we do now, that there can be no sure solution of the problems of race relations as long as our industrial problems are intensified by the racial aspects. Negroes, then as now, but with probably more disastrous results, were with difficulty able to find work for which they were fitted or had a bent. Labor unions discriminated against them, employers consulted the attitudes of their white employees before taking on Negro workers, and sometimes justified their personal disinclination based on prejudice to give Negroes work by ascribing imaginary unwillingness on the part of their white employees to work with Negro fellow-workers. This group of valiant believers in the rights of men and in the responsibilities which rested on those of more vision and more intelligence began immediately to study

the industrial needs of Negroes, and to seek new openings for those most fit. This group called themselves the Committee for Improving the Industrial Conditions of Negroes.

Almost simultaneously, in the same year with the meeting of this group, Miss Frances Kellor, a worker with immigrant white women, called together a group of men and women of both races to whom she told the story of the difficulties she had experienced in trying to get work for colored girls who were coming into New York and Philadelphia by coastwise steamers from the South. The only difference between the problems of these girls and the problems of the white girls was that there was at least a sympathetic community waiting to give the white girls a chance in the new country while with the colored girls, neither the white community nor the colored community was sympathetic in a definite way with their hopes and aspirations. They were met very often at the steamers and trains by unscrupulous representatives of employment agencies, both white and colored, who exploited them in a most inhuman way. They were frequently placed at work in houses of ill-fame. They were given jobs paying wages far less than they had been led to expect when they left the South. Sometimes there was no work at all for them, with no one meeting them to give a welcome of any kind in the new city.

Withal, it was a very discouraging situation. A committee was formed called the League for the Protection of Colored Women. This name was criticized by many colored leaders who felt that Negro women did not need protection, but it was in no way a misnomer. Protection was just what they needed. Encouragement and a new hope followed as the next step in the process of adjustment. These two organizations—The Committee for Improving the Industrial Conditions of Negroes in New York and the National League for the Protection of Colored Women —worked along parallel lines and in cooperation with each other for four years.

In 1910, Mrs. William H. Baldwin, Jr., then the widow of Mr. Baldwin mentioned above, called together a conference of the various organizations working in interest of Negroes in the city of New York to develop cooperation between these agencies. This conference resolved itself into the Committee on Urban Conditions Among Negroes organized: (1) to develop cooperation and coordination among these agencies; (2) to make investigations of social conditions among Negroes in cities; (3) to secure training for Negro social workers; (4) to establish new agencies for social service among Negroes when the investigation disclosed there was a need; of course, provided that there was no agency existing that could assume the responsibilities for the social needs discovered.

Later the three organizations mentioned decided for purposes of economy and efficiency to merge into one organization: The National League on Urban Conditions Among Negroes, organized for the combined purposes of all of the organizations forming the coalition. The actual consolidation took place in the spring of 1911. For the first year or two, with a combined budget of something like $8,500, the activities included a movement in New York, one in Philadelphia, Travelers Aid work in Baltimore and Norfolk and a branch in Nashville, Tennessee, where a specialty was made of training students from Fisk University for social service through field activities.

Founders Launch Journal of Negro History

A MEETING called by Dr. Woodson for the purpose of considering definite plans for the organization of a society, which should publish a magazine devoted to the study of the Negro, was held in the office of the Executive Secretary of the Wabash Avenue Department of the Chicago Y.M.C.A. Those present were C. G. Woodson, G. C. Hall, A. L. Jackson, W. B. Hartgrove, and J. E. Stamps. Dr. Hall was elected temporary chairman, J. E. Stamps, temporary secretary. The proposed constitution was read, and after alterations adopted. A permanent organization was formed, and the following officers were elected: Dr. G. C. Hall, President; J. E. Moorland, Secretary-Treasurer; C. G. Woodson, Director of Research and Editor. In addition to the above named officers the Executive Council will be J. A. Bigham, A. L. Jackson, Miss S. P. Breckinridge, and G. N. Grisham.

The editorial staff will consist of six or eight persons to be selected by the Editor and approved by the Executive Council.

A motion prevailed that in a reply to a request from Dr. Moorland we offer to cooperate with Howard University along lines satisfactory to the Executive Council.

J. E. STAMPS

September 9, 1915 Chicago

Undramatic account of beginning of Association for the Study of Negro Life and History

World War I

The 369th Infantry Regiment achieved world fame during World War I. Their proud fighting record—they never retreated and none were captured—won them France's Croix de Guerre. Members of the unit are shown in the trenches *(Upper left)*, being reviewed by General Pershing *(Below, center)*, and marching down New York's Fifth Avenue in a triumphant homecoming *(Upper right)*. All Negro troops did not enjoy such admiration. Sixty-four members of the 24th Infantry were court-martialed *(Lower left)* in Houston, Texas after 17 white persons were killed in a racial conflict growing out of the Negro soldiers' resistance to

Largest Murder Trial in the History of the United States.
Scene during Court Martial of 64 members of 24th. Infantry U.S.Q.
on trial for mutiny and murder of 17 people at Houston Tex. Aug 23, 1917
Trial Held in Gift Chapel, Ft Sam Houston.
Trial Started---Nov 1, 1917 Brig Genl George K. Hunter, Presiding.
Col S.Q Hull. Judge Advocate.   Counsel for Defense.
Maj. D V Sulphin, Asst.   Maj. Harry S. Grier.
Prisoners guarded by 19th Infantry Co. "C. Capt. Carl J Adler

violent attacks by hostile white gangs. During the War, Negro lives were as much jeopardized by home front lynch mobs as by overseas enemy troops. On July 28, 1917, 8,000 silent Negroes marched down Fifth Avenue to the beat of muffled drums *(Lower right)*. Their banners at once accused— "Your Hands are Full of Blood" —and petitioned—"Make America Safe for Democracy." In the vanguard of the marchers were NAACP leaders James Weldon Johnson and Dr. W. E. B. DuBois.

(The National Archives, Signal Corps photographs; Underwood and Underwood)

□ 233

PORTRAIT — MARCUS MANASSEH GARVEY

Marcus Garvey

Outlines Program of U.N.I.A.

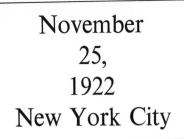

November
25,
1922
New York City

Crusade
for the redemption
of Africa justified

O VER five years ago the Universal Negro Improvement Association placed itself before the world as the movement through which the new and rising Negro would give expression of his feelings. This Association adopts an attitude not of hostility to other races and peoples of the world, but an attitude of self-respect. . . .

We represent peace, harmony, love, human sympathy, human rights and human justice, and that is why we fight. . . . Wheresoever human rights are denied to any group, wheresoever justice is denied to any group, there the U.N.I.A. finds a cause. And at this time among all the peoples of the world, the group that suffers most from injustice, the group that is denied most of those rights that belong to all humanity, is the black group. . . . Because of that injustice, because of that denial of our rights, we go forth under the leadership of the One who is always on the side of right to fight the common cause of humanity; to fight as we fought in the Revolutionary War, as we fought in the Civil War, as we fought in the Spanish-American War, and as we fought in the war between 1914–

18 on the battle plains of France and of Flanders. As we fought on the heights of Mesopotamia; even so under the leadership of the U.N.I.A., we are marshaling the 400,-000,000 Negroes of the world to fight for the emancipation of the race and of the redemption of the country of our fathers.

We represent a new line of thought among Negroes. Whether you call it advanced thought or reactionary thought, I do not care. If it is reactionary for people to seek independence in government, then we are reactionary. If it is advanced thought for people to seek liberty and freedom, then we represent the advanced school of thought among the Negroes of this country. We of the U.N.I.A. believe that what is good for the other folks is good for us. If government is something that is worth while; if government is something that is appreciable and helpful and protective to others, then we also want to experiment in government. We do not mean a government that will make us citizens without rights or subjects without consideration. We mean a kind of government that will place our race in control, even as other races are in control of their own government.

That does not suggest anything that is unreasonable. It was not unreasonable for George Washington, the great hero and father of the country, to have fought for the freedom of America giving to us this great republic and this great democracy; it was not unreasonable for the Liberals of France to have fought against the Monarchy to give to the world French Democracy and French Republicanism; it was no unrighteous cause that led Tolstoi to sound the call of liberty in Russia, which has ended in giving to the world the social democracy of Russia. . . .

. . . The U.N.I.A. is not advocating the cause of church building, because we have a sufficiently large number of churches among us to minister to the spiritual needs of the people, and we are not going to compete with those who are engaged in so splendid a work; we are not engaged in building any new social institutions, . . . because there are enough social workers engaged in those praise-worthy efforts. We are not engaged in politics because we have enough local politicians, . . . and the political situation is well taken care of. We are not engaged in domestic politics, in church building or in social uplift work, but we are engaged in nation building.

In advocating the principles of this Association we find we have been very much misunderstood and very much misrepresented by men from within our own race, as well as others from without. Any reform movement that seeks to bring about changes for the benefit of humanity is bound to be misrepresented by those who have always taken it upon themselves to administer to, and lead the unfortunate. . . . It has been so in all other movements whether social or political. . . .

I desire to remove the misunderstanding that has been created. . . .The Universal Negro Improvement Association stands for the Bigger Brotherhood; the Universal Negro Improvement Association stands for human rights, not only for Negroes, but for all races. The Universal Negro Improvement Association believes in the rights of not only the black race, but the white race, the yellow race and the brown race. The Universal Negro Improvement Association believes that the white man has as much right to be considered, the yellow man has as much right to be considered, the brown man has as much right to be considered as the black man of Africa. In view of the fact that the black man of Africa has contributed as much to the world as the white man of Europe, and the brown man and yellow man of Asia, we of the Universal Negro Improvement Association demand that the white, yellow and brown races give to the black man his place in the civilization of the world. We ask for nothing more than the rights of 400,000,000 Negroes. We are not seeking, as I said before, to destroy or disrupt the society or the government of other races, but we are determined that 400,000,000 of us shall unite ourselves to free our motherland from the grasp of the invader. We of the Universal Negro Improvement Association are determined to unite . . . Negroes for their own industrial, political, social and religious emancipation.

We of the Universal Negro Improvement Association are determined to unite the . . . Negroes of the world to give expression to their own feeling; . . . for the purpose of building a civilization of their own. And in that effort we desire to bring together the 15,000,000 of the United States, the 180,-000,000 in Asia, the West Indies and Central and South America, and the 200,000,000 in Africa. We are looking toward political freedom on the continent of Africa, the land of our fathers.

The Universal Negro Improvement Association is not seeking to build up another government within the bounds or borders of the United States of America. The Universal Negro Improvement Association is not seeking to disrupt any organized system of government, but the Association is determined to bring Negroes together for the building up of a nation of their own. And why? Because we have been forced to it. We have been forced to it throughout the world; not only in America, not only in Europe, not only in the British Empire, but wheresoever the black man happens to find himself, he has been forced to do for himself.

To talk about Government is a little more than some of our people can appreciate. . . . The average man . . . seems to say, "Why should there be need for any other government?" We are French, English or American. But we of the U.N.I.A. have studied seriously this question of nationality among Negroes—this American nationality, this British nationality, this French, Italian or Spanish nationality, and have discovered that it counts for nought when that nationality comes in conflict with the racial idealism of the group that rules. When our interests clash with those of the ruling faction, then we find that we have absolutely no rights. In times of peace, when everything is all right, Negroes have a hard time, wherever we go, wheresoever we find ourselves, getting those rights that belong to us in common with others whom we claim as fellow citizens; getting that consideration that should be ours by right of the constitution, by right of the law; but in the time of trouble they make us all partners in the cause, as happened in the last war. . . . And we were told that we must forget everything in an effort to save the nation.

We have saved many nations in this manner, and we have lost our lives doing that before. Hundreds of thousands—nay, millions of black men, lie buried under the ground due to that old-time camouflage of saving the nation. We saved the British empire; we saved the French empire; we saved this glorious country more than once; and all that we have received for our sacrifices, all that we have received for what we have done, even in giving up our lives, is just what you are receiving now, just what I am receiving now.

You and I fare no better in America, in the British empire, or any other part of the white world; we fare no better than any black man wheresoever he shows his head. And why? Because we have been satisfied to allow ourselves to be led. . . . We have allowed ourselves for the last 500 years to be a race of followers, following every race that has led, in the direction that would make them more secure.

The U.N.I.A. is reversing the old-time order of things. We refuse to be followers anymore. We are leading ourselves. That means, if any saving is to be done, . . . we are going to seek a method of saving Africa first. Why? And why Africa? Because Africa has become the grand prize of the nations. Africa has become the big game of the nation hunters. Today Africa looms as the greatest commercial, industrial and political prize in the world.

The difference between the Universal Negro Improvement Association and the other movements of this country, and probably the world, is that the Universal Negro Improvement Association seeks independence of government, while the other organizations seek to make the Negro a secondary part of existing governments. We differ from the organizations in America because they seek to subordinate the Negro as a secondary consideration in a great civilization, knowing that in America the Negro will never reach his highest ambition, knowing that the Negro in America will never get his constitutional rights. All those organizations which are fostering the improvement of Negroes in the British Empire know that the Negro in the British Empire will never reach the height of his constitutional rights. What do I mean by constitutional rights in America? If the black man is to reach the height of his ambition in this country—if the black man is to get all of his constitutional rights in America—then the black man should have the same chance in the nation as any other man to become president of the nation, or a street cleaner in New York. If the black man in the British Empire is to have all his constitutional rights it means that the Negro in the British Empire should have at least the same right to become premier of Great Britain as he has to become street cleaner in the city of London. Are they prepared to give us such political equality? You and I can live in the United States of America for 100 more years, and our generations may live for 200 years or for 5000 more

years, and so long as there is a black and white population, when the majority is on the side of the white race, you and I will never get political justice or get political equality in this country. Then why should a black man with rising ambition, after preparing himself in every possible way to give expression to that highest ambition, allow himself to be kept down by racial prejudice within a country? If I am as educated as the next man, if I am as prepared as the next man, if I have passed through the best schools and colleges and universities as the other fellow, why should I not have a fair chance to compete with the other fellow for the biggest position in the nation? . . . if America is not big enough for two presidents, if England is not big enough for two kings, then we are not going to quarrel over the matter; we will leave one president in America, we will leave one king in England, we will leave one president in France and we will have one president in Africa. Hence, the Universal Negro Improvement Association does not seek to interfere with the social and political systems . . . but by the arrangement of things to-day the U.N.I.A. refuses to recognize any political or social system in Africa except that which we are about to establish for ourselves.

We are not preaching a propaganda of hate against anybody. We love the white man; we love all humanity. . . . The white man is as necessary to the existence of the Negro as the Negro is necessary to his existence. There is a common relationship that we cannot escape. Africa has certain things that Europe wants, and Europe has certain things that Africa wants, . . . it is impossible for us to escape it. Africa has oil, diamonds, copper, gold and rubber and all the minerals that Europe wants, and there must be some kind of relationship between Africa and Europe for a fair exchange, so we cannot afford to hate anybody.

The question often asked is what does it require to redeem a race and free a country? If it takes man power, if it takes scientific intelligence, if it takes education of any kind, or if it takes blood, then the 400,000,000 Negroes of the world have it.

It took the combined power of the Allies to put down the mad determination of the Kaiser to impose German will upon the world and upon humanity. Among those who suppressed his mad ambition were two million Negroes who have not yet forgotten how to drive men across the firing line. . . . when so many white men refused to answer to the call and dodged behind all kinds of excuses, 400,000 black men were ready without a question. It was because we were told it was a war of democracy; it was a war for the liberation of the weaker peoples of the world. We heard the cry of Woodrow Wilson, not because we liked him so, but because the things he said were of such a nature that they appealed to us as men. Wheresoever the cause of humanity stands in need of assistance, there you will find the Negro ever ready to serve.

He has done it from the time of Christ up to now. When the whole world turned its back upon the Christ, the man who was said to be the Son of God, when the world cried out "Crucify Him," when the world spurned Him and spat upon Him, it was a black man, Simon, the Cyrenian, who took up the cross. Why? Because the cause of humanity appealed to him. When the black man saw the suffering Jew, struggling under the heavy cross, he was willing to go to His assistance, and he bore that cross up to the heights of Calvary. In the spirit of Simon, the Cyrenian, 1900 years ago, we answered the call of Woodrow Wilson, the call to a larger humanity, and it was for that that we willingly rushed into the war. . . .

. . . We have not forgotten the prowess of war. If we have been liberal minded enough to give our life's blood in France, in Mesopotamia and elsewhere, fighting for the white man, whom we have always assisted, surely we have not forgotten to fight for ourselves, and when the time comes that the world will again give Africa an opportunity for freedom, surely . . . black men will march out on the battle plains of Africa, under the colors of the red, the black and the green.

We shall march out, yes, as black American citizens, as black British subjects, as black French citizens, as black Italians or as black Spaniards, but we shall march out with a greater loyalty, the loyalty of race. We shall march out in answer to the cry of our fathers, who cry out to us for the redemption of our own country, our motherland, Africa.

We shall march out, not forgetting the blessings of America. We shall march out, not forgetting the blessings of civilization. We shall march out with a history of peace before and behind us, and surely that history shall be our breastplate, for how can man fight better than knowing that the cause for which he fights is righteous? . . . Glorious shall be the battle when the time comes to fight for our people and our race.

We should say to the millions who are in Africa to hold the fort, for we are coming 400,000,000 strong.

Congressman DePriest

on Equal Justice

Mr. CHAIRMAN, no race of people in the country has ever been more loyal to America than the people of my race. In every period of war this country has been engaged in they have always served the American Government, and I hope they always will. They were emancipated by the proclamation issued by the immortal Abraham Lincoln in 1863. After that the Republican Party submitted to the people of this country three amendments, the thirteenth, the fourteenth, and the fifteenth amendments to the Constitution of the United States, which gave them their liberty, made them citizens, and gave them the right to vote.

Under the guise of Ku-Kluxism my people have been intimidated and bulldozed in certain neighborhoods; people who were trying to be intelligent citizens, and standing up for their manhood rights. I have seen those night-riders in Alabama, where I was born. Of course, the Ku-Klux died out shortly after that. It was reorganized a few years ago, not only fighting the American Negro but fighting the Jews and the Catholics also. Thank God they did not last very long.

Then when the Negroes were getting more power and more control in this country the hue and cry was raised in some Southern States of Negro domination. That was only a subterfuge. The Negro in America never was in the majority in any one State in the United States except the State of Mississippi. There never was any chance for Negro domination. It was only used as a subterfuge for other people to ride into office on.

Then came those days when they were deprived of their right to vote. . . . If we had a right to exercise our franchise rights as the Constitution provides we should exercise them I would not be the only Negro on this floor. I hope to see the time come when the Federal Constitution will be actually enforced and that the Members of Congress who have sworn to support the Constitution will pass an act to enforce every section of the Constitution including the amendments to which I have referred.

But recently there has been some discussion on the floor of this Congress about Negroes getting a square deal over this country. There was a discussion here the other day when the resolution was introduced to impeach Judge Lowell, of Massachusetts, because of a decision which had nothing whatever to do with the innocence or guilt of this man Crawford. I know nothing about his guilt or innocence, but I do say one thing, that this House was misled. . . . There was not one scintilla of evidence introduced in that hearing in Massachusetts with regard to the innocence or guilt of this man charged with crime; not one. But the question was decided on its merits, on whether or not this

man had been indicted by a legally drawn grand jury. The question was raised on the issue in the State of Virginia. It was proven that those of my racial group are not included in the jury system. No Member from the State of Virginia can rise on this floor and say that any Negro has served on a jury in Virginia in the last quarter of a century, whether petit jury or grand jury. That was the ground on which that decision was rendered, that the jury was drawn unconstitutionally, because a certain group of people had been excluded from jury service, and not on the guilt of this man Crawford. I do not know anything about that. If he is guilty, he should be punished, but for God's sake indict him with a legally drawn grand jury. . . .

There was another case down in Scottsboro, Ala., quite recently, down in the State where I was born, and I have often said that if God would forgive me for being born there I would never live there again. In reading some of the evidence in that trial it was shown that there were two white girls traveling as hoboes on a freight train dressed in overalls. It happened some two years ago. I am not saying whether those boys are innocent or guilty. I could not say, for I have not read over the testimony, but I do know that one of the girls repudiated her testimony a very short time ago in the second trial of one of the defendants, and I do know that one of

the white boys who was with her substantiated her repudiation, and that is a matter of record. Everybody can read it. I do know that those boys were first convicted in the courts. The case went to the United States Supreme Court and it was reversed, and I do know that the last Negro was convicted and sentenced to the electric chair, I presume. If not, he will be; and that case will go back to the United States Supreme Court also.

I do not want a condition to arise in this country where those of my group will become discouraged and think there is no chance in America for them. I know the great rank and file of American people are on the square. I know that. . . . and I also know that the great body of Christian America and the great newspapers and periodicals of this country do not universally denounce this crime of injustice meted out to those of my particular group, especially when charged with crimes of that kind. They are convicted before they are tried. I have no brief for Negro criminals. I hold no brief for any kind of a criminal, but I do wish to say that I think the time will come when a Congress of the United States— . . . composed of American citizens—will take this question up and see that . . . rights are protected. . . .

I want particularly to discuss with you the now-famous Scottsboro case where nine youths of my race are accused of raping two white girls. The injustice imposed upon these boys in the first trial where they were convicted was such that the United States Supreme Court did not think they received a fair trial and set aside the verdict and ordered a new trial, on the ground that the fourteenth amendment to the Federal Constitution had been violated. This amendment says that no person shall be denied or deprived of life, liberty, or property without due process of law. In this connection I wish to quote as part of my remarks an editorial in the Washington Daily News of April 10, 1933, which reads as follows:

THE SCOTTSBORO VERDICT

The conviction of Haywood Patterson, first of the Negro defendants in the second trials of the Scottsboro cases, will be appealed. It should be.

Among other things prejudicial to a fair trial, the defense was able to show that the jury law apparently was administered to exclude Negroes from the panel for this case. On more than one occasion during the trial the State attorneys conducted themselves in such a way as to prevent orderly and judicious consideration of evidence by the jury.

In repudiating her testimony at the earlier trial, Ruby Bates swore that the other girl in the case, Victoria Price, had framed the Negro youths. Lester Carter, a white friend of the two girls, confirmed the testimony of Ruby Bates.

To execute boys on the discredited evidence of a woman of Victoria Price's character, and following a trial in which racial discrimination seemed to operate in the jury panel, would be unthinkable. Just as the chief justice of Alabama dissented from the first Scottsboro conviction, and just as the United States Supreme Court threw out that conviction as a violation of the fourteenth amendment of the Constitution preventing States from depriving "any person of life, liberty, or property without due process of law", so the Decatur verdict yesterday appears certain to be set aside by a higher court.

The action of courts and so-called "judicial procedure" in an atmosphere of intimidation, prejudice, and disturbance, as has happened in the Scottsboro case and as has frequently been the situation in other cases, creates disrespect of law and order and makes the Negro of America think it is impossible to get justice, especially in certain parts of the country.

May I quote again from the Washington Daily News of Tuesday, April 11, 1933, the words of Heywood Broun? He said, himself quoting—

We have no right to sit in the seats of the scornful. Nor is it the part of wisdom to think of the Scottsboro case as a local issue.

Continuing, he says:

Sunday, in Decatur, Ala., a jury of 12 white men brought in a verdict of death against Haywood Patterson. The attorney general of the great sovereign State referred to him as "that thing."

They say it was a quiet courtroom and a gentle day down in Morgan County when the jury filed in after 24 hours of deliberation. But could none of them hear the wind in the rigging of the slave ship, the creaking of her timbers, and the cries of the cargo?

Attorney General Knight could not even bring himself to admit that he was in the presence of a man on trial for his life. He had to take refuge in such a phrase as "that thing." He was afraid of the facts. He had reason to fear.

There was much panicky talk in the speeches of the men who pressed the case. "Show them that Alabama justice cannot be bought and sold with Jew money from New York!" cried Solicitor Wright at one point in the trial. And the attorney general, after deploring the injection of prejudice by his associate in the summation, went on to say: "If you acquit this Negro, put a garland of roses around his neck, give him a supper, and send him to New York City. There let Dr. Harry Fosdick dress him up in a high hat and morning coat, gray striped trousers and spats."

And that was because Dr. Fosdick had told Ruby Bates to face the danger of return and go back to confess that she lied when first she accused the Negro boys. And that was because the attorney general was afraid.

All these things have a tendency to drive into the American Negro the thought that he cannot secure justice in all parts of America and that dark-skinned people in its territorial possessions are subjected to the same prejudices. I call this to your attention, knowing full well the part colored American citizens have played in all the wars of this country where the dignity and honor of the United States have been assaulted by foes within and foes without.

No man of my racial group has ever been disloyal to our flag or to our country. I hope the time will never come when he may be goaded on to that extremity. I call your attention to dangerous possibilities lurking in a discouraged, dejected, despised, mob-ridden, and intimidated group of citizens if this condition continues to prevail. . . .

I am appealing to the Christian, law-abiding people of America through its magazines, its newspapers, its periodicals, and its pulpit; through its fraternal organizations, labor organizations, church organizations, and all manner and kind of societies, to help maintain law and order in America and abolish this blight on our American jurisprudence and to help blot out the crime known as lynching. It becomes necessary also that the provisions in the Constitution must be safeguarded, so that no man shall be deprived of life, liberty, or property without due process of law; and due process of law means a fair and impartial trial for every citizen of our country.

He who stands idly by, knowing these conditions to exist, will be guilty of contributive negligence in not routing this monster of race prejudice evidenced in many places where it cannot be controlled but occupying too serious a place in our governmental and court procedure of the land. In the interest of America—great, shining, proud symbol of freedom and of liberty and of opportunity, of which 12,000,000 men and women, boys and girls, of my racial group are an integral part—let us stand up like men and women and uphold law and order and see that every man has a fair trial, equal opportunity, and a chance under the sun to have an existence. Only by such action on the part of the American people can America free itself of this odious institution and maintain the confidence and respect of that 12,000,000 American Negroes and also of the rest of the civilized world. . . .

The Lynching of Claude Neal

The National Association for the Advancement of Colored People, 69 Fifth Avenue, New York City, presents herewith a verbatim copy of the report of the investigation of the lynching at Marianna, Florida, on October 26, 1934 of Claude Neal, charged with rape and murder. The investigator is a southern white university professor whose entire life has been spent in the South and whose family for generations has occupied high rank there. His name is not given because to do so might possibly jeopardize his life and would almost certainly lessen his future usefulness in similar cases. The N.A.A.C.P., however, vouches for his integrity, accuracy, soundness of judgment and experience in ascertaining the truth.

This report is published with the hope that its sheer sadism and abnormal cruelty may stir thoughtful Americans to action. If this report does not do so, we fear that the situation is hopeless. Claude Neal is the 5,068th person lynched in the United States since 1882; the 45th mob victim since President Franklin D. Roosevelt entered the White House. We believe that the circumstances of his lynching demolish finally all contentions that lynching can be ended by any other means than by federal legislation. Those who love America and humanity are urged to insist by telegram or letter to President Roosevelt and to the senators and congressmen from their states that the Costigan Wagner anti-lynching bill MUST be passed without delay.

WALTER WHITE,
Secretary

On October 19, 1934, Claude Neal, 23, of Greenwood, Florida was arrested by Deputy Sheriff J. P. Couliette for the murder of Lola Cannidy, 20, also of Greenwood, Florida. Neal, when arrested, was working on a peanut farm belonging to John Green. He was taken in custody with another man whom investigating officers believed to be involved in the murder to the woods and questioned. It is alleged that a confession was wrung from Neal and that he assumed entire responsibility for the crime. Sheriff W. F. Chambliss, of Jackson county, who was at the Cannidy home at the time of the arrest, was apparently aware of the lynching spirit which was beginning to rise throughout the little farming community, and ordered Neal to be taken to Chipley, Florida, for safe keeping, a distance of about 20 miles. With Neal were arrested his mother, Annie Smith and his aunt, Sallie Smith.

The Mob Chases the Law

From the moment that Neal was arrested a blood-thirsty mob relentlessly pursued him.

The Marianna *Daily Times-Courier* for October 23rd says:

> "In a determined effort to locate the three Negroes held for the murder of Lola Cannidy near Greenwood last Thursday, a relentless mob continued to search the jails of West Florida."

1934
New York City

Pamphlet
produced by NAACP
to buttress demands
for anti-lynch law

An Associated Press dispatch from Chipley, Florida, dated October 21, and appearing in *The Florida Times,* of Jacksonville, Fla., says:

"Two negro women held in connection with the slaying of Lola Cannidy, 20-year-old Greenwood girl, were removed from County jail today to Fort Barrancas, at Pensacola, after hundreds of men swarmed the streets all night threatening to destroy the jail unless the prisoners were delivered.

"Standing by, ready to protect the negro women with tear gas bombs obtained from a nearby convict camp, Sheriff John Harrell said he remained on duty all night while crowds repeatedly begged him to give up the prisoners, and finally threatened to dynamite the jail if he did not do so.

"About daybreak, the sheriff said, more men came with acetylene torches, saying the negroes were locked in the courthouse vault and they would cut through the metal to get them. Later . . . they gave up their purpose and left, telling the sheriff they would return and go through the jail and courthouse."

The angry mood of the crowd at Chipley caused the sheriff there to remove Neal to Panama City. From Panama City he was taken by boat to Pensacola. From Pensacola Neal was taken across the Florida line to Brewton, Alabama,—a distance of 61 miles. Brewton is approximately 210 miles from Marianna, county seat of Jackson county, Florida.

I am reliably informed that "a prominent business man of Marianna arranged with friends in Pensacola to notify him the moment that Neal was removed". When word of Neal's removal from Pensacola to Brewton was received several car loads of men set out for Brewton from Marianna. In my opinion, taking Neal from Pensacola to Brewton was equivalent to handing him over to the mob. It would seem that had the officers been really concerned with the safety of their prisoner that they would have either held him in Pensacola or taken him to Mobile or some other large town. Mobile is only eight miles farther away from Pensacola than Brewton.

An armed mob of approximately 100 men stormed the county jail at Brewton, Alabama, on the morning of October 26. Neal was seized after Mike Shanholster, the jailer, unlocked his cell door, and was brought screaming and crying and placed in the front car in front of the county jail. The mob had triumphed.

An Associated Press dispatch from Brewton, Alabama, dated October 26, and published in the Marianna, *Daily Times-Courier* says:

"An armed mob, estimated at 100 men, stormed the Escambia county jail between 2 and 3 o'clock a.m. today and seized Claude Neal,

23-year-old negro who allegedly confessed yesterday to the murder of Miss Lola Cannidy, 23, of Greenwood, Fla., a week ago."

"Sheriff Gus Byrne said the men came to the jail in 30 cars bearing Florida license plates.

"We are going to take him to Marianna and turn him over to the girl's father and let him do what he wants with him," leaders of the mob told Jailer Mike Shanholster . . .

"Jail attaches said the negro was placed in the first of the 30 cars and that the others trailed behind. They said no attempt was made to follow.

"We'll tear your jail up and let all the prisoners out, if you don't turn him over to us."

The Lynching of Claude Neal

According to a member of the mob with whom I talked, Claude Neal was lynched in a lonely spot about four miles from Greenwood, Florida, scene of the recent crime, and not in Alabama as it was first reported. After Neal was taken from the jail at Brewton, Alabama, he was driven approximately 200 miles over highway 231 leading into Marianna and from there to the woods near Greenwood, where he was subjected to the most brutal and savage torture imaginable.

Neal was taken from the Brewton jail between one and two o'clock Friday morning, October 26. He was in the hands of the smaller lynching group composed of approximately 100 men from then until he was left in the road in front of the Cannidy home late that same night. I was told by several people that Neal was tortured for ten or twelve hours. It is almost impossible to believe that a human being could stand such

unspeakable torture for such a long period.

Due to the great excitement sweeping the entire northern section of Florida and southeastern Alabama and to the great number of people who wanted to participate in the lynching, the original mob which secured Neal from the jail at Brewton, evidently decided that if all of the niceties of a modern Twentieth Century lynching were to be inflicted upon Neal that it would be unwise for a larger mob to handle the victim. They preferred that his last hours on earth be filled with the greatest possible humiliation and agony. However, the word was passed all over Northeastern Florida and Southeastern Alabama that there was to be a "lynching party to which all white people are invited," near the Cannidy home Friday night. It is also reported that the information was broadcast from the radio station at Dothan, Alabama. I talked to at least three persons who confirmed this statement.

A member of the lynching party with whom I talked described the lynching in all of its ghastliness, down to the minutest detail. After talking with him I went immediately to my room and tried to recall word for word all that he had told me. The story of the actual lynching as related to me and later corroborated by others is as follows:

"After taking the nigger to the woods about four miles from Greenwood, they cut off his penis. He was made to eat it. Then they cut off his testicles and made him eat them and say he liked it." (I gathered that this barbarous act consumed considerable time and that other means of torture were used from time to time on Neal).

"Then they sliced his sides and stomach with knives and every now and then somebody would cut off a finger or toe. Red hot irons were used on the nigger to burn him from top to bottom." From time to time during the torture a rope would be tied around Neal's neck and he was pulled up over a limb and held there until he almost choked to death when he would be let down and the torture begin all over again. After several hours of this unspeakable torture, "they decided just to kill him."

Neal's body was tied to a rope on the rear of an automobile and dragged over the highway to the Cannidy home. Here a mob estimated to number somewhere between 3000 and 7000 people from eleven southern states was excitedly waiting his arrival. When the car which was dragging Neal's body came in front of the Cannidy home, a man who was riding the rear bumper cut the rope.

"A woman came out of the Cannidy house and drove a butcher knife into his heart. Then the crowd came by and some kicked him and some drove their cars over him."

Men, women and children were numbered in the vast throng that came to witness the lynching. It is reported from reliable sources that the little children, some of them mere tots, who lived in the Greenwood neighborhood, waited with sharpened sticks for the return of Neal's body and that when it rolled in the dust on the road that awful night these little children drove their weapons deep into the flesh of the dead man.

The body, which by this time was horribly mutilated was taken by the mob to Marianna, a distance of ten or eleven miles, where it was hung to a tree on the northeast corner of the courthouse square. Pictures were taken of

An Artist's Conception of A Lynching.

The Lynching of Claude Neal □ 247

the mutilated form and hundreds of photographs were sold for fifty cents each. Scores of citizens viewed the body as it hung in the square. The body was perfectly nude until the early morning when someone had the decency to hang a burlap sack over the middle of the body. The body was cut down about eight-thirty Saturday morning, October 27, 1934.

Fingers and toes from Neal's body have been exhibited as souvenirs in Marianna where one man offered to divide the finger which he had with a friend as "a special favor". Another man has one of the fingers preserved in alcohol.

Press Comment

"GIRL SLAYER LYNCHED THIS A.M.

"Nude Body, Terribly Mutilated, Hanging From Tree on Court House Lawn since 3 o'clock This Morning."

"Claude Neal, Greenwood negro, was lynched last night about 10 o'clock somewhere in the county by a well organized orderly mob which waited patiently for hours to avenge the death of pretty Lola Cannidy, 18-year-old Greenwood girl.

"After slashing and shooting him into mince-meat, the mob took the negro to the home of George Cannidy, father of the slain girl, and dumped the body in the front yard. From there, another mob was organized and it brought him to Marianna at 3 o'clock this morning where it hanged him on a tree on the east side of the court house lawn. His nude body was hanging at that place at an early hour this morning. After stringing him up in the tree, the mob quickly dispersed.

"Neal's body was mutilated. Three fingers of one hand and two on the other had been amputated, besides other mutilations.

"At 1:30 this morning a mob, to be appeased, burned Neal's shack to the ground. It was just across the road from the Cannidy home.

"For hours a well organized mob of about 3,000 people, men, women and children awaited in 'ringside' seats in the field where Neal killed Lola Cannidy to witness the lynching. But it is reported the group which had the negro was fearful that someone would be injured in the melee if they brought him to the waiting crowd, consequently the lynching took place at a point on the Chipola River, as according to a Cannidy kinsman, 'the nigger was too low for anybody to be hurt on his account." *Daily Times-Courier*, October 27.

The Marianna Riot of October 27

After Neal's body had been removed from the courthouse square most of the members of the mob dispersed. Although Saturday is a "big day" in Marianna when the rural folk come to town to trade, there were not as many Negroes in the town on the day following the lynching as usual. The entire week had been one of terror and consequently all those who could remained away from the town. The feeling was very tense in Marianna between the Negroes and whites and the Negroes who came in kept pretty much to themselves.

Toward noon a white man struck a Negro who sought to defend himself and in the struggle with the white man, hurled a pop bottle at him. By this time a crowd had gathered and at the sight of a Negro resisting a white man the crowd flew into a frenzy. The Negro finally tore himself away from the mob and ran across the street and into the courthouse, where he was given protection by a friendly group of white men. The mob clamored for another victim, but they were held at bay by a machine gun. Being unable to secure their intended victim the mob began a systematic attempt to drive all Negroes from the town. I am reliably informed that this mob was led by a young man from Calhoun county, who has money and comes from a *good* family. The mob apparently started from the west side of the Plaza and began driving Negroes from the streets and stores where some were engaged in buying and selling and working for white employers. An observer stated that, "the mob attacked men, women and children and that several blind persons were ruthlessly beaten." Another observer said: "They (The Negroes) came from the town in droves, some driving, some running, some crying, all scared to death."

In several instances the mob met resistance on the part of white employers of Negro labor. A Negro porter was serving a white customer in front of his employer's store. Before he knew what was happening the mob was upon him. With a knife he slashed his way through the mob and gained the front door of the store. His employer locked him in a room and kept the mob away with a shot gun. A woman who was caught downtown with her maid almost single handedly drove the mob away from their intended victim. After emptying the streets, stores, places of business, hotels, etc., of Negroes the mob started into the residential section to drive out the Negro maids. Some women sent their maids home, others hid them in closets. One man whose wife shielded her maid from the mob said, "Saturday was a day of terror and madness, never to be forgotten by anyone."

Lack of Police Protection

During the rioting the city of Marianna was completely without police protection. I was told that members of the mob searched the town for members of the police force and threatened to beat them up if they were found. One observer said, "The United States army couldn't have stopped that crowd Saturday morning." When Mayor Burton realized what was going on and that the city was at the mercy of the mob, he tried to locate the policemen but was unable to do so. He then tried personally to deputize some special officers, but was unable to find anyone to serve. He later sent a friend out to find some men who would serve. This man finally returned and said he could not find anyone who would serve.

National Guards Called

At this juncture the Mayor called Governor Sholtz in Tallahassee. In response to the mayor's request a detachment of National Guards arrived from Apalachicola about 4:30 Saturday afternoon and gradually dispersed the mob. The guards patrolled the streets of the town and particularly the Negro section. The mob retreated before the guards but left the parting warning that they would "be back Saturday to finish up what we started."

On the following Saturday the police force was increased by about twenty men. Several Negroes were attacked early Saturday morning by white men who were arrested and placed in jail. A drizzling rain began about 9 A.M. followed by a downpour about 11 A.M. which probably prevented another "day of terror and madness" in Marianna.

Lola Cannidy

On the afternoon of October 18, 1934, Lola

All of America Knew of Lynching in Advance.
(From the Original Document)

Cannidy, 20, daughter of Mr. and Mrs. George Cannidy, farmers, near Greenwood, Florida, disappeared from home. It is alleged that Lola Cannidy told her parents that she was going to "water the pigs" and attend to some other chores about the farm. The family took no particular notice of her absence when she failed to return in the late afternoon. She had been seen by her brother, who was working in a nearby field, talking to someone on the farm. When she failed to return in the evening her parents called her sister in Tallahassee to find out if Lola was there. When they were unable to locate her in Tallahassee and she did not return home, a search was begun for her in the community. Early on the morning of October 19, her body, fully clothed, was discovered by an uncle, John

King, a short distance from the Cannidy home, badly mutilated about the head and arms and partially covered with brush-wood and pine logs.

Sheriff W. F. Chambliss of Jackson County was called to the Cannidy home and an investigation was begun immediately. A watch, ring, a piece of clothing and a hammer were among the things discovered near the place where Lola Cannidy came to her death. Among the first homes in the community to be searched was that of Annie Smith, mother of Claude Neal, who lived just across the road from the Cannidy home. The officers investigating the case claim to have found some bloody garments in the home.

Several boys claimed that they saw Claude Neal near the scene of the crime that afternoon and that he had some wounds on his hand which he said that he received while repairing a fence.

Claude Neal Arrested

A search was immediately begun for Claude Neal. He was arrested on the peanut farm belonging to John Green. When Neal was arrested he told officers that another man, Herbert Smith, was associated with him in the crime. Smith was later arrested and he and Neal were taken to the nearby woods and questioned. I am reliably informed that Neal had been in a fight with Herbert Smith on the Saturday previous and that in the fight "Herbert had whipped him." In order to "get even" with Smith, Neal sought to involve him in the case. Smith later related the entire incident to an informant who described Smith as being literally scared to death. Neal finally admitted that Smith had nothing to do with the crime and that he alone was involved. Smith was subsequently released by the officers.

Claude Neal and Lola Cannidy

Claude Neal and Lola Cannidy had always lived in the same neighborhood. Mrs. Smith's home (Neal's mother) was just across the road from the Cannidy home. Neal had played with the Cannidy children and when he was large enough to work, worked on the Cannidy farm. For some months, and possibly for a period of years, Claude Neal and Lola Cannidy had been having intimate relations with each other. The nature of their relationship was common knowledge in the Negro community. Some of his friends advised him of the danger of the relationship and had asked him not to continue it. Miss Cannidy, it seems, desired to break the relationship existing between herself and Neal and the fatal meeting was prearranged for the purpose of arriving at some understanding. At the meeting in the woods Miss Cannidy told Neal that she did not want him to speak to her again and that if he did so she would tell the white men in the community on him. (Should Miss Cannidy have "told on him" it would have meant certain death.) When she told Neal that she wanted to "quit" and further threatened to "tell on him," he "got mad and killed her." Neal later told a friend what had happened. Neal is reported to have told the friend, "When she said she didn't want me to speak to her and then told me that she'd tell the white men on me, I just got mad and killed her."

Was Claude Neal Guilty?

When I first arrived in Marianna I heard that there was serious doubt as to Neal's guilt. The rumor was that a white man had murdered Lola Cannidy, had taken the bloody garments to Neal's home to have them washed and had later laid the murder on Neal. Knowing how often innocent Negroes are framed by guilty white men I gave particular attention to the theory. I was unable to find any substantial support for this theory among the Negroes in the Greenwood community. It is entirely possible that due to the great terror under which Negroes all over this section of Florida are living that they were too frightened to say or do anything which might cause them to become the victims of another mob as had so recently descended upon them. Feeling was running so high during the period of investigation that it was not safe for a citizen to ask too many questions about the lynching. Naturally it was difficult for an outsider to carry out a thorough investigation of every particular. The account of the murder came to me from the most reliable sources including white and Negro informers. I still have some doubts in my mind but I accept the story as told as the most plausible and reliable account which I received.

State of Public Opinion as Revealed in the Local Press

(1) Statement from George Cannidy in Marianna *Daily Times-Courier*.

Headline: YOU CAN'T KNOW HOW IT HURTS UNLESS THIS HAPPENS TO YOU, STATES FATHER OF YOUNG GIRL.

> "Lord, but you can't know how it hurts unless you had something like this happen to someone you loved . . . *The bunch have promised me that they will give me first chance at him when they bring him back and I'm ready.* We'll put those two logs on him and ease him off by degrees. I can't get the picture of Lola out of my mind when we found her. Her

throat was bruised and scratched where he had choked her so she couldn't cry out. My son was in the field about a quarter of a mile away when he saw someone talking with her at the pump, but he thought it was just one of the local boys and didn't pay much attention. He was right there in the field when she was being killed. Her head was beat in and she had been choked so hard her eyes were coming out of their sockets, her arms were broken and she was all beat up. *When I get my hands on that nigger, there isn't any telling what I'll do.*"
(*All italics mine*)

(2) Statement from Lola Cannidy's sister in Marianna *Daily Times-Courier*.

Headline: I WISH EVERY RESIDENT OF JACK-SON COUNTY COULD SEE THE BODY OF LOLA, SAYS SISTER OF SLAIN GIRL.

"When I viewed the body of my sister I was horrified. Whoever killed her—*well I don't believe any form of punishment could fit the crime.* I can hardly believe that such a horrible thing could happen to my sister. If I have to be killed I hope it won't be in the manner she met death. I know that there has never been anything in Jackson county that was as brutal. I'd just like to see the man who did this just once. I can't understand what the motive was for this brutal deed. To think that Claude Neal, who has been raised with my sister and me and worked for us all his life, could do such a thing—it is unbelievable. *I only wish that every resident of*

Jackson county could view the body of my sister. If they could, they wouldn't rest until the murderer was caught and justice meted out." *Daily Times-Courier*, October 20, 1934.

(3) *Letter from Negro Citizen of Marianna in Daily Times-Courier.*

Headline: COLORED MAN WRITES ANENT RE-CENT CRIME. MAKES PLEA THAT GOOD COL-ORED PEOPLE NOT BE BLAMED FOR ACT OF CLAUDE NEAL.

"Marianna, Florida
October 22, 1934
"To the White Citizens of Jackson County:

"Just a few lines to let you all know that we good colored citizens of Jackson County don't feel no sympathy toward the nigger that . . . the white lady and killed her. No! we haven't felt that he did right because he should stay in his place, and since he did such as he did, we are not feeling that we have a right to plead to you all for mercy.

"It makes us chagrined and feel that he has ruined the good colored people that try to behave themselves and work for an honest living.

"I feel very bad over it myself to see that we have such a fellow in the Race and I am among the good col-ored people that feel just like I do toward him. I talked with them, and they can't see how they can have any sympathy for him.

"But I am writing to let you know that we leave it to you all to do what you all see fit to do to him. But still asking you all not to be hard on your good servants that have been honest and faithful for the time that we have been working with you for the other fellow. Because we good colored people want to thank you all for the favors and the chance that you will have given us to let us have schools for our children and teachers to teach them and jobs for us to work and to get bread for them that they can have a chance. Also we thank you all for making it easy.

"Because if it wasn't for the good white citizens, we realize that many of our girls and boys could have been mobbed for nothing they done, but for the brutal act that was done. I also thank the sheriff for working so faithfully to get the right man.

Your faithful servant

John Curry

still pleading for a chance for the better class of colored people and not to punish us for him, because if he do wrong he is wrong, and we have no sympathy for him!"

(4) Letter from Negro Citizens in the Marianna *Times-Courier*.

Headline: COLORED CITIZENS DISAPPROVE CRIME.

"Marianna, Florida
October 23, 1934

"WHEREAS, it has come to our attention that one of the most brutal crimes is supposed to have been committed by one of our race; and

"WHEREAS, that friendly and mutual relationships that have so long existed among the white and colored citizens of our fair county has been interrupted by such a brutal act;

"BE IT RESOLVED, That we, the colored citizens of Jackson county, Florida, do here and now place our stamp of disapproval on such an atrocious act, and assure the family that they have our deepest sympathy and the law our unstinted support in bringing the guilty to speedy justice.

"We do not condone crime in any form. We believe in, teach our race to be law abiding citizens. We trust that the brutal act will not break that friendly and mutual relationship that exists among the white and colored people of this, our good country. We have the utmost confidence in the white citizens of this county, and trust that you have the same in us. We shall ever strive and teach our race never to betray that trust. We pray that the guilty may be apprehended and punished and that the innocent will be protected."

Your humble citizens

R. W. Whitehurst

E. Harley

M. Robinson

W. R. Robinson

H. H. Fagan

D. P. Preston

M. L. Clay

R. T. Gilmore."

(5) *News Item in the Marianna Times-Courier*, October 26, by Emmet G. Shepherd. (Associate Editor.)

Headline: KU KLUX MAY RIDE AGAIN.

"Jackson County Citizens May Rally to Fiery Cross to Protect Womanhood."

"Taking a determined stand to

protect the honor of womanhood and to champion the oppressed in Jackson county, a group of sober-minded, straight forward men will probably organize a local Ku Klux Klan, it was revealed to the writer the other day by a prominent Marianna citizen.

"The purpose of the Klan is to take over where the law fails, or where the law has no jurisdiction. It will defend and protect the constitution and the flag of the United States and make this section safe for 'life, liberty and the pursuit of happiness.' "

(6) *Editorial in the Jackson County Floridan, October 26, 1934.*

"Although many have strongly favored the court of Judge Lynch for the brutal slaying of a Jackson county girl this week, local officers have spared no effort to uphold their oath of office and to protect their prisoner. *In many instances this action has been contrary to the wishes of citizens,* but the concensus of opinion is that one crime in a week is enough."

(7) *News Item in Marianna Daily Times-Courier, October 27, 1934.*

Headline: MOB NOT TO BE BOTHERED OPINES S. PAUL GREENE.

"S. P. Greene, deputy sheriff of Jackson county, told a *Times-Courier* reporter late yesterday afternoon that, 'in my opinion, *the mob will not be bothered, either before or after the lynching'."*

Note: On November 1, The *Times-Courier* of Marianna carried a front page announcement that S. P. Greene would run for sheriff of Jackson county in 1936.

The Women in the Case

Claude Neal's mother, Annie Smith, and his aunt, Sallie Smith, with whom Neal lived, were arrested as accomplices in the crime with Neal. Mrs. Smith lived on a small farm opposite the Cannidy home and worked for the Cannidys and other white people in the community. The two women apparently had nothing whatsoever to do with the crime but in the mad excitement of the hour became the victims of the mob's desire to wreak its vengeance upon all and sundry who had the slightest connection with Claude Neal. Mrs. Smith and her sister were taken to Chipley and lodged in the jail there. A large mob stormed the jail in search of the women and Neal and threatened to dynamite the jail and to employ acetylene torches to secure the prisoners. It is probable that had the two women accompanied Neal on his fateful ride from Pensacola to Brewton that they too would have suffered the same fate as he did. On Saturday morning shortly after Neal's body had been brought to the Cannidy home, the mob descended upon the Smith home and burned it with several out-buildings to the ground. When last heard of the two women were at Fort Barrancas near Pensacola.

Local History

Jackson county, in which the lynching of Claude Neal and the rioting in Marianna occurred, is one of the four original counties of Florida. It has a population of approximately thirty thousand inhabitants of whom some two-thirds live on farms. Agriculture is the principal industry of the county. Cotton is the chief product, while tobacco, peanuts, lumbering and lime stone products are produced in considerable quantities.

Prior to 1900 the Negro population greatly outnumbered the white but since that time it has steadily declined. It is estimated that between 40% and 45% of the population of Jackson county is at present Negro. Most of the old plantations have either been broken up or have been taken over by syndicates which work them now.

The county has the highest illiteracy rate of any in the state in proportion to the number of schools. There are no public libraries in the county. Negro teachers in the public schools receive from $25.00 to $35.00 per month. A recent survey of the county shows that between 75% and 80% of the citizens of Jackson county belong to either the Methodist or Baptist church. Revivals are always eagerly and well attended.

Marianna, the county seat of Jackson county, has a population of about 3,300. The Negro population is between 35% and 40%. The town is on the main highway between Tallahassee and Mobile and is in line for considerable tourist trade.

It is a typical southern town with the general run of stores and a town square, except in Marianna the square is called, "the Plaza." The drug stores carry a large line of cheap detective, "wild west," and mystery magazines. *Time, The American Magazine, Cosmopolitan, Literary Digest, Red Book* represent about the best available reading material to be purchased in the town.

Compete for Jobs

Severe competition exists between the Negroes and whites for what few jobs there are in Marianna and the surrounding territory. For some time past there has been a constant agitation going on among the poor and disinherited whites for the jobs of the equally poor and exploited Negroes. Employers who give work to Negroes when white men could do the work are frowned upon. Frequently they are boycotted and threatened. Many occupations which Negroes formerly occupied to the exclusion of whites are now completely occupied by whites. The Negroes have been gradually forced deeper and deeper into economic misery and insecurity. With them have gone large numbers of the white population and as the present economic crisis deepens the struggle for survival grows in intensity and severity.

Some Wage Scales

Porters who work in drug stores, grocery stores, etc., receive from $4.00 to $6.00 per week. $2.25 per week is considered very good pay for domestic servants. $2.50 is considered extraordinarily good. Cooks in boarding houses during the tourist season receive around $3.00 per week. The bell boys in the Chipola Hotel receive $1.50 per week for twelve hours. Maids in the same hotel receive $4.00 per week for seven days work. Each maid has the care of an entire floor of nineteen rooms. The white waitresses in the dining room receive $4.00 per week plus tips. They work from 5:30 A.M. until 9 P.M with time off between the main meals.

Relief Cut Off

It is claimed that a large number of those who participated in the rioting in Marianna on Saturday, October 27, had been on the county relief rolls for some time. Relief had been cut off about two weeks before the lynching occurred. There has been considerable discontent over the way relief in the county has been handled. An organization known as the Jackson county FERA Purification League headed by W. Pooser led a demonstration through the streets of Marianna on the Saturday preceding the lynching. From what I was able to learn, Pooser's League is a semi-Fascist organization combining some of Huey Long's ideas of "share the wealth" with a deep seated and violent race prejudice. Pooser disclaimed any part in the Marianna riot of the 27th.

Basic Cause of Lynching

While the feeling against Claude Neal was certainly very great because of the crime which he was alleged to have committed, the lynching was to a large extent a surface eruption. Beneath this volcanic eruption lay the pressing problem of jobs and bread and economic security. A very competent observer said to me: "This lynching was a surface eruption. The basic cause of the lynching was economic. Here you put your finger on the sore spot. The lynching had two objects, first, to intimidate and threaten the white employers of Negro labor and secondly to scare and terrorize the Negroes so that they would leave the county and their jobs could be taken over by white men." A white man with whom I talked observed: "There are too many niggers and too many white people looking for the same job." A clerk in a store said, "A nigger hasn't got no right to have a job when there are white men who can do the work and are out of work."

Attitudes Toward the Lynching

It is a well known fact that some of Marianna's "prominent business men and citizens" participated in the mob which lynched Claude Neal. There were some people with whom I talked who were horrified over the lynching and who wanted to raise their voices in protest but felt it to be useless to do so at the time. I felt that on the whole the lynching was accepted by the citizens of Marianna as a righteous act. When buying a magazine in a drug store for which I had no earthly use, I said to the clerk who waited on me, "That was a pretty bad lynching you had here the other night, wasn't it?" He replied, "No! the lynching wasn't bad, it was all right. What happened to business when the mob came in and drove the niggers out of town was the only bad thing about it." There seemed to be a general acceptance by the people of Judge Lynch. They seemed to believe that lynch law was really the only way they could "keep the nigger in his place." The chain gang, prison and the electric chair are not enough. To have a Negro suddenly disappear never to return to his people seemed to them to be the best method of "handlin' the niggers."

Conclusions

It is evident from these findings that:

(1) The mob intended to lynch Claude Neal from the beginning,
(2) That the nature of the press reports confirmed their intention,
(3) That the statements occurring in the local press incited to lynching,
(4) That the local officials and the Governor of the state must have been aware of the probability of lynching, and
(5) That insufficient protection was given to the prisoner.

Issued November 30, 1934

EXECUTIVE ORDER 8802

FAIR EMPLOYMENT PRACTICE IN DEFENSE INDUSTRIES

. . . . . . I do hereby reaffirm the policy of the United States that there shall be no discrimination in the employment of workers in defense industries or Government because of race, creed, color, or national origin, and I do hereby declare that it is the duty of employers and of labor organizations, in furtherance of said policy and of this order, to provide for the full and equitable participation of all workers in defense industries, without discrimination because of race, creed, color, or national origin . . . . . .*

Franklin D. Roosevelt

THE PRESIDENT OF THE UNITED STATES OF AMERICA

THE WHITE HOUSE
June 25, 1941

*Excerpt from Executive Order 8802

In this century's second war in the name of democracy, Negroes played many roles in many places. Throughout the Pacific Theatre of Operations, infantrymen like First Sergeant Rance Richardson *(Upper left)* saw action; in England, members of the Women's Army Corps, here being inspected by Major Charity E. Adams *(Lower left)*, relieved male enlisted personnel for active front-line duty; at Pearl Harbor aboard the USS *Arizona*, messman Dorie Miller *(Above, left)* became one of the first heroes of the war by shooting down four enemy aircraft; in France the war's highest ranking Negro officer, Brigadier General Benjamin O. Davis, Sr. *(Above, right)*, inspected American military installations; and in Italy, Captain Andrew O. Turner, shown here in the cockpit of his Mustang P-51 *(Below)*, commanded an all-Negro squadron of the 332nd Fighter Group, attached to the 15th Air Force. However, the armed services remained segregated until a few years after the war ended.

(U.S. Army; National Archives, Navy Department; U.S. Air Force)

PILOT-Capt. A. Turner.
C/CHIEF-S/Sgt. U. Cochran.
Asst- Sgt. C. Bentley.
NT C/ARM-Cpl. H. Beguesse.

President Truman

Ends Segregation

in the

Armed Services

July 26, 1948

Committee created
to integrate the
military establishment

WHEREAS it is essential that there be maintained in the armed services of the United States the highest standards of democracy, with equality of treatment and opportunity for all those who serve in our country's defense:

NOW, THEREFORE, by virtue of the authority vested in me as President of the United States, by the Constitution and the statutes of the United States, and as Commander in Chief of the armed services, it is hereby ordered as follows:

1. It is hereby declared to be the policy of the President that there shall be equality of treatment and opportunity for all persons in the armed services without regard to race, color, religion or national origin. This policy shall be put into effect as rapidly as possible, having due regard to the time required to effectuate any necessary changes without impairing efficiency or morals.

2. There shall be created in the National Military Establishment an advisory committee to be known as the President's Committee on Equality of Treatment and Opportunity in the Armed Services, which shall be composed of seven members to be designated by the President.

3. The Committee is authorized on behalf of the President to examine into the rules, procedures and practices of the armed services in order to determine in what respect such rules, procedures and practices may be altered or improved with a view to carrying out the policy of this order. The Committee shall confer and advise with the Secretary of Defense, the Secretary of the Army, the Secretary of the Navy, and the Secretary of the Air Force, and shall make such recommendations to the President and to said Secretaries as in the judgment of the Committee will effectuate the policy hereof.

4. All executive departments and agencies of the Federal Government are authorized and directed to cooperate with the Committee in its work, and to furnish the Committee such information or the services of such persons as the Committee may require in the performance of its duties.

5. When requested by the Committee to do so, persons in the armed services or in any of the executive departments and agencies of the Federal Government shall testify before the Committee and shall make available for the use of the Committee such documents and other information as the Committee may require.

6. The Committee shall continue to exist until such time as the President shall terminate its existence by Executive order.

HARRY S. TRUMAN

THE WHITE HOUSE
July 26, 1948.

Brown vs. Board of Education

[MR. CHIEF JUSTICE WARREN delivered the opinion of the Court.]

THESE cases come to us from the States of Kansas, South Carolina, Virginia, and Delaware. They are premised on different facts and different local conditions, but a common legal question justifies their consideration together in this consolidated opinion.

In each of the cases, minors of the Negro race, through their legal representatives, seek the aid of the courts in obtaining admission to the public schools of their community on a nonsegregated basis. In each instance, they had been denied admission to schools attended by white children under laws requiring or permitting segregation according to race. This segregation was alleged to deprive the plaintiffs of the equal protection of the laws under the Fourteenth Amendment. In each of the cases other than the Delaware case, a three-judge federal district court denied relief to the plaintiffs on the so-called "separate but equal" doctrine announced by this Court in *Plessy v. Ferguson,* 163 U.S.537. Under that doctrine, equality of treatment is accorded when the races are provided substantially equal facilities, even though these facilities be separate. In the Delaware case, the Supreme Court of Delaware adhered to that doctrine, but ordered that the plaintiffs be admitted to the white schools because of their superiority to the Negro schools.

The plaintiffs contend that segregated public schools are not "equal" and cannot be made "equal," and that hence they are deprived of the equal protection of the laws. Because of the obvious importance of the question presented, the Court took jurisdiction. . . .

In the first cases in this Court construing the Fourteenth Amendment, decided shortly after its adoption, the Court interpreted it as proscribing all state-imposed discriminations against the Negro race. The doctrine of "separate but equal" did not make its appearance in this Court until 1896 in the case of *Plessy v. Ferguson, supra,* involving not education but transportation. American courts have since labored with the doctrine for over half a century. In this Court, there have been six cases involving the "separate but equal" doctrine in the field of public education. . . .

In approaching this problem, we cannot turn the clock back to 1868 when the Amendment was adopted, or even to 1896 when *Plessy v. Ferguson* was written. We must consider public education in the light of its full development and its present place in American life throughout the Nation. Only in this way can it be determined if segregation in public schools deprives these plaintiffs of the equal protection of the laws.

Today, education is perhaps the most important function of state and local govern-

ments. Compulsory school attendance laws and the great expenditures for education both demonstrate our recognition of the importance of education to our democratic society. It is required in the performance of our most basic public responsibilities, even service in the armed forces. It is the very foundation of good citizenship. Today it is a principal instrument in awakening the child to cultural values, in preparing him for later professional training, and in helping him to adjust normally to his environment. In these days, it is doubtful that any child may reasonably be expected to succeed in life if he is denied the opportunity of an education. Such an opportunity, where the state has undertaken to provide it, is a right which must be made available to all on equal terms.

We come then to the question presented: Does segregation of children in public schools solely on the basis of race, even though the physical facilities and other "tangible" factors may be equal, deprive the children of the minority group of equal educational opportunities? We believe that it does.

In *Sweatt v. Painter, supra,* in finding that a segregated law school for Negroes could not provide them equal educational opportunities, this Court relied in large part on "those qualities which are incapable of objective measurement but which make for greatness in a law school." In *McLaurin v. Oklahoma State Regents, supra,* the Court, in requiring that a Negro admitted to a white graduate school be treated like all other students, again resorted to intangible considerations: ". . . his ability to study, to engage in discussions and exchange views with other students, and, in general, to learn his profession." Such considerations apply with added force to children in grade and high schools. To separate them from others of similar age and qualifications solely because of their race generates a feeling of inferiority as to their status in the community that may affect their hearts and minds in a way unlikely ever to be undone. The effect of this separation on their educational opportunities was well stated by a finding in the Kansas case by a court which nevertheless felt compelled to rule against the Negro plaintiffs:

> "Segregation of white and colored children in public schools has a detrimental effect upon the colored children. The impact is greater when it has the sanction of the law; for the policy of separating the races is usually interpreted as denoting the inferiority of the negro group. A sense of inferiority affects the motivation of a child to learn. Segregation with the sanction of law, therefore, has a tendency to [retard] the educational and mental development of negro children and to deprive them of some of the benefits they would receive in a

AUTHORS OF A NEW DIRECTION IN AMERICAN EDUCATION *Members of the United States Supreme Court who handed down the historic decision in* Brown v. Board of Education *which overthrew the doctrine of "Separate but equal."*

Left to right (seated) Associate Justices Felix Frankfurter and Hugo L. Black, Chief Justice Earl Warren, Associate Justices Stanley F. Reed and William O. Douglas: (standing) Associate Justices Tom C. Clark, Robert H. Jackson, Harold H. Burton and Sherman Minton.   (Wide World Photo)

racial [ly] integrated school system."

Whatever may have been the extent of psychological knowledge at the time of *Plessy v. Ferguson,* this finding is amply supported by modern authority. Any language in *Plessy v. Ferguson* contrary to this finding is rejected.

We conclude that in the field of public education the doctrine of "separate but equal" has no place. Separate educational facilities are inherently unequal. Therefore, we hold that the plaintiffs and others similarly situated for whom the actions have been brought are, by reason of the segregation complained of, deprived of the equal protection of the laws guaranteed by the Fourteenth Amendment. This disposition makes unnecessary any discussion whether such segregation also violates the Due Process Clause of the Fourteenth Amendment.

Because these are class actions, because of the wide applicability of this decision, and because of the great variety of local conditions, the formulation of decrees in these cases presents problems of considerable complexity. On reargument, the consideration of appropriate relief was necessarily subordinated to the primary question—the constitutionality of segregation in public education. We have now announced that such segregation is a denial of the equal protection of the laws. In order that we may have the full assistance of the parties in formulating decrees, the cases will be restored to the docket, and the parties are requested to present further argument on Questions 4 and 5 previously propounded by the Court for the reargument this Term. The Attorney General of the United States is again invited to participate. The Attorneys General of the states requiring or permitting segregation in public education will also be permitted to appear as *amici curiae* upon request to do so by September 15, 1954, and submission of briefs by October 1, 1954.

It is so ordered.

Ninety-Six Southern Congressmen

Denounce the Supreme Court

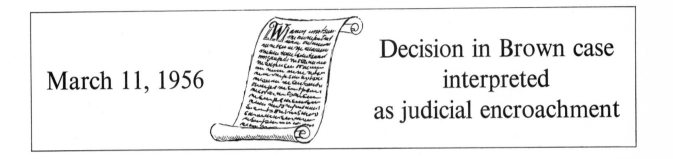

March 11, 1956

Decision in Brown case
interpreted
as judicial encroachment

W<small>E</small> regard the decision of the Supreme Court in the school cases as clear abuse of judicial power. It climaxes a trend in the Federal judiciary undertaking to legislate, in derogation of the authority of Congress, and to encroach upon the reserved rights of the states and the people.

The original Constitution does not mention education. Neither does the Fourteenth Amendment nor any other amendment. . . .

The very Congress which proposed the [14th] amendment subsequently provided for segregated schools in the District of Columbia. . . .

As admitted by the Supreme Court in the public school case [Brown v. Board of Education], the doctrine of separate but equal schools "apparently originated in Roberts v. City of Boston (1849), upholding school segregation against attack as being violative of a state constitutional guarantee of equality." This constitutional doctrine began in the North—not in the South—and it was followed not only in Massachusetts but in Connecticut, New York, Illinois, Indiana, Michigan, Minnesota, New Jersey, Ohio, Pennsylvania and other northern states until they, exercising their rights as states through the constitutional processes of local self-government, changed their school systems.

In the case of Plessy v. Ferguson in 1896 the Supreme Court expressly declared that under the Fourteenth Amendment no person was denied any of his rights if the states provided separate but equal public facilities. . . .

This interpretation, restated time and again, became a part of the life of the people of many of the states and confirmed their habits, customs, traditions and way of life. It is founded on elemental humanity and common sense, for parents should not be deprived by Government of the right to direct the lives and education of their own children.

Though there has been no constitutional amendment or act of Congress changing this established legal principle almost a century old, the Supreme Court of the United States, with no legal basis for such action, undertook to exercise their naked judicial power and substituted their personal political and social ideas for the established law of the land.

This unwarranted exercise of power by the court, contrary to the Constitution, is creating chaos and confusion in the states principally affected. It is destroying the amicable relations between the white and Negro races that have been created through ninety years of patient effort by the good people of both races. It has planted hatred and suspicion where there has been heretofore friendship and understanding.

Without regard to the consent of the governed, outside agitators are threatening immediate and revolutionary changes in our public school systems. If done, this is certain to destroy the system of public education in some of the states.

With the gravest concern for the explosive and dangerous condition created by this decision and inflamed by outside meddlers:

We reaffirm our reliance on the Constitution as the fundamental law of the land.

We decry the Supreme Court's encroachments on rights reserved to the states and to the people, contrary to established law and to the Constitution.

We commend the motives of those states which have declared the intention to resist forced integration by any lawful means.

We appeal to the states and people who are not directly affected by these decisions to consider the constitutional principles involved against the time when they too, on issues vital to them, may be the victims of judicial encroachment.

Even though we constitute a minority in the present Congress, we have full faith that a majority of the American people believe in the dual system of government which has enabled us to achieve our greatness and will in time demand that the reserved rights of the states and of the people be made secure against judicial usurpation.

We pledge ourselves to use all lawful means to bring about a reversal of this decision which is contrary to the Constitution and to prevent the use of force in its implementation.

In this trying period, as we all seek to right this wrong, we appeal to our people not to be provoked by the agitators and troublemakers invading our states and to scrupulously refrain from disorder and lawless acts.

President Eisenhower's

Little Rock Intervention

September 24, 1957

Troops dispatched to secure compliance with Court-ordered integration

WHEREAS on September 23, 1957, I issued Proclamation No. 3204 reading in part as follows:

"WHEREAS certain persons in the State of Arkansas, individually and in unlawful assemblages, combinations, and conspiracies, have wilfully obstructed the enforcement of orders of the United States District Court for the Eastern District of Arkansas with respect to matters relating to enrollment and attendance at public schools, particularly at Central High School, located in Little Rock School District, Little Rock, Arkansas; and

"WHEREAS such wilful obstruction of justice hinders the execution of the laws of that State and of the United States, and makes it impracticable to enforce such laws by the ordinary course of judicial proceedings; and

"WHEREAS such obstructions of justice constitutes a denial of the equal protection of the laws secured by the Constitution of the United States and impedes the course of justice under those laws:

"Now, THEREFORE, I, DWIGHT D. EISENHOWER, President of the United States, under and by virtue of the authority vested in me by the Constitution and Statutes of the United States, including Chapter 15 of Title 10 of the United States Code, particularly sections 332, 333 and 334 thereof, do command all persons engaged in such obstruction of justice to cease and desist therefrom, and to disperse forthwith;" and

WHEREAS the command contained in that Proclamation has not been obeyed and wilful obstruction of enforcement of said court orders still exists and threatens to continue:

NOW, THEREFORE, by virtue of the authority vested in me by the Constitution and Statutes of the United States, including

NINE BRAVE YOUNG PEOPLE DEFY LITTLE ROCK MOB TO ATTEND SCHOOL *Wednesday, September 24, 1957: "At 9:22 A.M. the nine Negro pupils marched solemnly through the doors of Central High School, surrounded by twenty-two soldiers . . . within minutes a world that had been holding its breath learned that the nine -pupils, protected by the might of the United States Military, had finally entered the 'never-never land.'"* [*Quoted from* The Long Shadow of Little Rock, *A Memoir by Daisy Bates.*]   (United Press International Photo taken on October 14, 1957)

Chapter 15 of Title 10, particularly sections 332, 333 and 334 thereof, and section 301 of Title 3 of the United States Code, it is hereby ordered as follows:

SECTION 1. I hereby authorize and direct the Secretary of Defense to order into the active military service of the United States as he may deem appropriate to carry out the purposes of this Order, any or all of the units of the National Guard of the United States and of the Air National Guard of the United States within the State of Arkansas to serve in the active military service of the United States for an indefinite period and until relieved by appropriate orders.

SEC. 2. The Secretary of Defense is authorized and directed to take all appropriate steps to enforce any orders of the United States District Court for the Eastern District of Arkansas for the removal of obstruction of justice in the State of Arkansas with respect to matters relating to enrollment and attendance at public schools in the Little Rock School District, Little Rock, Arkansas. In carrying out the provisions of this section, the Secretary of Defense is authorized to use the units, and members thereof, ordered into the active military service of the United States pursuant to Section 1 of this Order.

SEC. 3. In furtherance of the enforcement of the aforementioned orders of the United States District Court for the Eastern District of Arkansas, the Secretary of Defense is authorized to use such of the armed forces of the United States as he may deem necessary.

SEC. 4. The Secretary of Defense is authorized to delegate to the Secretary of the Army or the Secretary of the Air Force, or both, any of the authority conferred upon him by this Order.

DWIGHT D. EISENHOWER

THE WHITE HOUSE
September 24, 1957.

President Kennedy Authorizes

Troops to End Segregation

at University of Mississippi

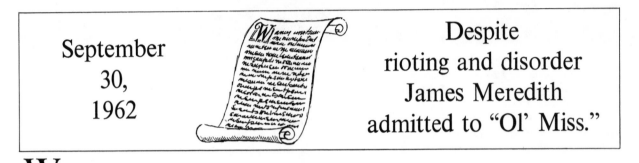

September
30,
1962

Despite
rioting and disorder
James Meredith
admitted to "Ol' Miss."

WHEREAS on September 30, 1962, I issued Proclamation No. 3497 reading in part as follows:

"WHEREAS the Governor of the State of Mississippi and certain law enforcement officers and other officials of that State, and other persons, individually and in unlawful opposing and obstructing the enforcement of orders entered by the United States District Court for the Southern District of Mississippi and the United States Court of Appeals for the Fifth Circuit; and

"WHEREAS such unlawful assemblies, combinations, and conspiracies oppose and obstruct the execution of the laws of the United States, impede the course of justice under those laws and make it impracticable to enforce those laws in the State of Mississippi by the ordinary course of judicial proceedings; and

"WHEREAS I have expressly called the attention of the Governor of Mississippi to the perilous situation that exists and to his duties in the premises, and have requested but have not received from him adequate assurances that the orders of the courts of the United States will be obeyed and that law and order will be maintained:

"Now, THEREFORE, I, JOHN F. KENNEDY, President of the United States, under and by virtue of the authority vested in me by the Constitution and laws of the United States, including Chapter 15 of Title 10 of the United States Code, particularly sections 332, 333 and 334 thereof, do command all persons engaged in such obstructions of justice to cease and desist therefrom and to disperse and retire peaceably forthwith;" and

WHEREAS the commands contained in that proclamation have not been obeyed and obstruction of enforcement of those court orders still exists and threatens to continue:

Now, THEREFORE, by virtue of the authority vested in me by the Constitution and laws of the United States, including Chapter 15 of Title 10, particularly Sections 332, 333 and

THE END OF A BATTLE   *Sunday, August 18, 1963: 322 days after entering "Ole Miss" protected by federal troops, James Meredith tastes the bitter-sweet fruit of courage as he receives Bachelor of Arts degree from University Chancellor J. D. Williams.*

News photographers recorded the event without incident, a marked contrast to the violence reporters and cameramen experienced when Meredith first came to the campus.   (United Press International Photo)

334 thereof, and Section 301 of Title 3 of the United States Code, it is hereby ordered as follows:

SECTION 1. The Secretary of Defense is authorized and directed to take all appropriate steps to enforce all orders of the United States District Court for the Southern District of Mississippi and the United States Court of Appeals for the Fifth Circuit and to remove all obstructions of justice in the State of Mississippi.

SEC. 2. In furtherance of the enforcement of the aforementioned orders of the United States District Court for the Southern District of Mississippi and the United States Court of Appeals for the Fifth Circuit, the Secretary of Defense is authorized to use such of the armed forces of the United States as he may deem necessary.

SEC. 3. I hereby authorize the Secretary of Defense to call into the active military service of the United States, as he may deem appropriate to carry out the purposes of this order, any or all of the units of the Army National Guard and of the Air National Guard of the State of Mississippi to serve in the active military service of the United States for an indefinite period and until relieved by appropriate orders. In carrying out the provisions of Section 1, the Secretary of Defense is authorized to use the units, and members thereof, ordered into the active military service of the United States pursuant to this section.

SEC. 4. The Secretary of Defense is authorized to delegate to the Secretary of the Army or the Secretary of the Air Force, or both, any of the authority conferred upon him by this order.

JOHN F. KENNEDY

THE WHITE HOUSE
September 30, 1962

Governor Wallace

Defies the Supreme Court

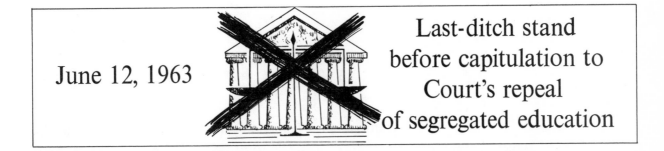

June 12, 1963

Last-ditch stand
before capitulation to
Court's repeal
of segregated education

. . . as Governor of the State of Alabama, I do hereby make the following solemn proclamation:

Whereas, the Constitution of Alabama vests the supreme executive powers of the state in the Governor as the chief magistrate, and said Constitution requires of the Governor that he take care that the laws be faithfully executed; and,

Whereas, the Constitution of the United States, Amendment 10, reserves to the states respectively or to the people, those powers not delegated to the United States, nor prohibited to the states; and,

Whereas, the operation of the public school system is a power reserved to the State of Alabama under the Constitution of the United States and Amendment 10 thereof; and,

Whereas, it is the duty of the Governor of the State of Alabama to preserve the peace under the circumstances now existing, which power is one reserved to the State of Alabama and the people thereof under the Constitution of the United States and Amendment 10 thereof;

Now, therefore, I, George C. Wallace, as Governor of the State of Alabama, have by my action raised issues between the Central Government and the sovereign State of Alabama, which said issues should be adjudicated in the manner prescribed by the Constitution of the United States; and now being mindful of my duties and responsibilities under the Constitution of the United States, the Constitution of the State of Alabama, and seeking to preserve and maintain the peace and dignity of this state, and the individual freedoms of the citizens thereof, do hereby denounce and forbid this illegal and unwarranted action by the Central Government.

GEORGE C. WALLACE
Governor of Alabama

President Kennedy

Calls for Action

to End Segregation

THIS afternoon, following a series of threats and defiant statements, the presence of Alabama National Guardsmen was required on the University of Alabama to carry out the final and unequivocal order of the United States District Court of the Northern District of Alabama.

That order called for the admission of two clearly qualified young Alabama residents who happened to have been born Negro.

That they were admitted peacefully on the campus is due in good measure to the conduct of the students of the University of Alabama who met their responsibilities in a constructive way.

I hope that every American, regardless of where he lives, will stop and examine his conscience about this and other related incidents.

This nation was founded by men of many nations and backgrounds. It was founded on the principle that all men are created equal, and that the rights of every man are diminished when the rights of one man are threatened.

Today we are committed to a worldwide struggle to promote and protect the rights of all who wish to be free. And when Americans are sent to Vietnam or West Berlin we do not ask for whites only.

It ought to be possible, therefore, for American students of any color to attend any public institution they select without having to be backed up by troops. It ought to be possible for American consumers of any color to receive equal service in places of public accommodation, such as hotels and restaurants, and theaters and retail stores without being forced to resort to demonstrations in the street.

And it ought to be possible for American citizens of any color to register and to vote in a free election without interference or fear of reprisal.

It ought to be possible . . . for every American to enjoy the privileges of being American without regard to his race or his color.

In short, every American ought to have the right to be treated as he would wish to

June 12, 1963

Historic declaration
that segregation
is a moral issue

be treated, as one would wish his children to be treated. But this is not the case.

The Negro baby born in America today, regardless of the section or the state in which he is born, has about one-half as much chance of completing a high school as a white baby, born in the same place, on the same day; one-third as much chance of completing college; one-third as much chance of becoming a professional man; twice as much chance of becoming unemployed; about one-seventh as much chance of earning $10,000 a year; a life expectancy which is seven years shorter and the prospects of earning only half as much.

This is not a sectional issue. Difficulties over segregation and discrimination exist in every city, in every state of the Union, producing in many cities a rising tide of discontent that threatens the public safety.

Nor is this a partisan issue. In a time of domestic crisis, men of goodwill and generosity should be able to unite regardless of party or politics.

This is not even a legal or legislative issue alone. It is better to settle these matters in the courts than on the streets, and new laws are needed at every level. But law alone cannot make men see right.

We are confronted primarily with a moral issue. It is as old as the Scriptures and is as clear as the American Constitution. The heart of the question is whether all Americans are to be afforded equal rights and equal opportunities; whether we are going to treat our fellow Americans as we want to be treated.

If an American, because his skin is dark, cannot eat lunch in a restaurant open to the public; if he cannot send his children to the best public school available; if he cannot vote for the public officials who represent him; if, in short, he cannot enjoy the full and free life which all of us want, then who among us would be content to have the color of his skin changed and stand in his place?

Who among us would then be content with the counsels of patience and delay. One hundred years of delay have passed since President Lincoln freed the slaves, yet their heirs, their grandsons, are not fully free. They are not yet freed from the bonds of injustice; they are not yet freed from social and economic oppression.

And this nation, for all its hopes and all its boasts, will not be fully free until all its citizens are free.

We preach freedom around the world, and we mean it. And we cherish our freedom here at home. But are we to say to the world —and much more importantly to each other —that this is the land of the free, except for the Negroes; that we have no second-class citizens, except Negroes; that we have no class or caste system, no ghettos, no master race, except with respect to Negroes.

Now the time has come for this nation to fulfill its promise. . . .

The fires of frustration and discord are burning in every city, North and South. Where legal remedies are not at hand, redress is sought in the streets in demonstrations, parades and protests, which create tensions and threaten violence—and threaten lives.

We face, therefore, a moral crisis as a country and a people. It cannot be met by repressive police action. It cannot be left to increased demonstrations in the streets. It cannot be quieted by token moves or talk. It is a time to act in the Congress, in your state and local legislative body, and, above all, in all of our daily lives.

It is not enough to pin the blame on others, to say this is a problem of one section of the country, or another, or deplore the facts that we face. A great change is at hand, and our . . . obligation is to make that revolution, that change peaceful and constructive for all.

Those who do nothing are inviting shame as well as violence. Those who act boldly are recognizing right as well as reality.

Next week I shall ask the Congress of the United States to act, to make a commitment it has not fully made in this century to the proposition that race has no place in American life or law.

The Federal judiciary has upheld that proposition in a series of forthright cases. The Executive Branch has adopted that proposition in the conduct of its affairs, including the employment of Federal personnel, and, the use of Federal facilities, and the sale of Federally financed housing.

But there are other necessary measures which only the Congress can provide, and they must be provided at this session.

The old code of equity law under which we live commands for every wrong a remedy. But in too many communities, in too many parts of the country wrongs are inflicted on Negro citizens and there are no remedies in law.

Unless the Congress acts their only remedy is the street.

I am, therefore, asking the Congress to enact legislation giving all Americans the right to be served in facilities which are open to the public—hotels, restaurants and theaters, retail stores and similar establishments. This seems to me to be an elementary right.

Its denial is an arbitrary indignity that no American in 1963 should have to endure, but many do. . . .

But many are unwilling to act alone. And for this reason nationwide legislation is needed, if we are to move this problem from the streets to the courts.

I'm also asking Congress to authorize the Federal Government to participate more fully in lawsuits designed to end segregation in public education. We have succeeded in persuading many districts to desegregate voluntarily. Dozens have admitted Negroes without violence.

Today a Negro is attending a state-supported institution in every one of our 50 states. But the pace is very slow.

Too many Negro children entering segregated grade schools at the time of the Supreme Court's decision nine years ago, will enter segregated high schools this fall, having suffered a loss which can never be restored.

The lack of an adequate education denies the Negro a chance to get a decent job. The orderly implementation of the Supreme Court decision therefore, cannot be left solely to those who may not have the economic resources to carry their legal action or who may be subject to harassment.

Other features will be also requested, including greater protection for the right to vote.

But legislation, I repeat, cannot solve this problem alone. It must be solved in the homes of every American in every community across our country.

In this respect, I want to pay tribute to those citizens, North and South, who've been working in their communities to make life better for all.

They are acting not out of a sense of legal duty but out of a sense of human decency. Like our soldiers and sailors in all parts of the world, they are meeting freedom's challenge on the firing line and I salute them for their honor—their courage.

My fellow Americans, this is a problem which faces us all, in every city of the North as well as the South.

Today there are Negroes unemployed—two or three times as many compared to whites—inadequate education; moving into the large cities, unable to find work; young people particularly out of work, without hope, denied equal rights, denied the opportunity to eat at a restaurant or a lunch counter, or go to a movie theater; denied the right to a decent education; denied, almost today, the right to attend a state university even though qualified.

It seems to me that these are matters which concern us all—not merely Presidents, or Congressmen, or Governors, but every citizen of the United States.

This is one country. It has become one country because all of us and all the people who came here had an equal chance to develop their talents.

We cannot say to 10 percent of the population that "you can't have that right. Your children can't have the chance to develop whatever talents they have, that the only way that they're going to get their rights is to go in the street and demonstrate."

I think we owe them and we owe ourselves a better country than that.

Therefore, I'm asking for your help in making it easier for us to move ahead and provide the kind of equality of treatment which we would want ourselves—to give a chance for every child to be educated to the limit of his talent. . . .

We have a right to expect that the Negro community will be responsible, will uphold the law. But they have a right to expect the law will be fair, that the Constitution will be color blind, as Justice Harlan said at the turn of the century.

This is what we're talking about. This is a matter which concerns this country and what it stands for. . . .

Birmingham Manifesto

THE patience of an oppressed people cannot endure forever. The Negro citizens of Birmingham for the last several years have hoped in vain for some . . . resolution of our just grievances.

Birmingham is part of the United States and we are bona fide citizens. Yet the history of Birmingham reveals that very little of the democratic process touches the life of the Negro in Birmingham. We have been segregated racially, exploited economically, and dominated politically. Under the leadership of the Alabama Christian Movement for Human Rights, we sought . . . repeal of city ordinances requiring segregation and the institution of a merit hiring policy in city employment. We were rebuffed. We then turned to the system of the courts. We weathered set-back after set-back, with all of its costliness, finally winning the terminal, bus, parks and airport cases. The bus decision has been implemented begrudgingly and the parks decision prompted the closing of all municipally-owned recreational facilities with the exception of the zoo and Legion Field. The airport case has been a slightly better experience with the exception of hotel ac-

1963
Birmingham

The Alabama
Christian Movement
for Human Rights
nears end of patience

commodations and the subtle discrimination that continues in the limousine service.

We have always been a peaceful people, bearing our oppression with super-human effort. Yet we have been the victims of repeated violence, not only that inflicted by the hoodlum element but also that inflicted by the blatant misuse of police power. Our memories are seared with painful mob experience. . . . For years, while our homes and churches were being bombed, we heard nothing but the rantings and ravings of racist city officials.

The Negro protest for equality and justice has been a voice crying in the wilderness. Most of Birmingham has remained silent, probably out of fear. . . . meanwhile, our city has acquired the dubious reputation of being the worst big city in race relations in the United States. Last Fall, for a flickering moment, it appeared that sincere community leaders from religion, business and industry discerned the inevitable confrontation in race relations approaching. Their concern for the city's image and commonweal of all its citizens did not run deep enough. Solemn promises were made, pending a postponement

of direct action, that we would be joined in a suit seeking the relief of segregation ordinances. Some merchants agreed to desegregate their rest-rooms as a good faith start, some actually complying, only to retreat shortly thereafter. We hold in our hands now, broken faith and broken promises. . . .

Twice since September we have deferred our direct action thrust in order that a change in city government would not be made in the hysteria of a community crisis. We act today in full concert with our Hebraic-Christian tradition, the law of morality and the Constitution of our nation. The absence of justice and progress in Birmingham demands that we make a moral witness to give our community a chance to survive. We demonstrate our faith that we believe that the beloved community can come to Birmingham. We appeal to the citizenry of Birmingham, Negro and white, to join us in this witness for decency, morality, self-respect and human dignity. Your individual and corporate support can hasten the day of "liberty and justice for all." This is Birmingham's moment of truth. . . .

F. L. SHUTTLESWORTH, *President*
N. H. SMITH, *Secretary*

Episcopal Bishop's

Message at Whitsuntide

RECENT events in a number of American communities . . . underscore the fact that countless citizens have lost patience with the slow pace of response to their legitimate cry for human rights. Pleas of moderation or caution about timing on the part of white leaders are seen increasingly as an unwillingness to face the truth about the appalling injustice which more than a tenth of our citizens suffer daily. While we are thankful for the progress that has been made, this is not enough.

Our Church's position on racial inclusiveness within its own body and its responsibility for racial justice in society has been made clear on many occasions by the General Convention. But there is urgent need to demonstrate by specific actions what God has laid upon us. Such actions must move beyond expressions of corporate penitence for our failures to an unmistakable identification of the Church, at all levels of its life, with those who are victims of oppression.

I think of the words we sing as we hail the ascended Christ, "Lord and the ruler of all men," and of our prayers at Whitsuntide as we ask God to work His will in us through His Holy Spirit. And then in contrast to our praises and our prayers our failure to put ourselves at the disposal of the Holy Spirit becomes painfully clear. Only as we take every step possible to join with each other across lines of racial separation in a common strug-

1963
New York City

Bishop Lichtenberger
calls for
increased action to
remove racial injustice

gle for justice will our unity in the Spirit become a present reality.

It is not enough for the Church to exhort men to be good. Men, women and children are today risking their livelihood and their lives in protesting for their rights. We must support and strengthen their protest in every way possible, rather than give support to the forces of resistance by our silence. It should be a cause of rejoicing to the Christian community that Negro Americans and oppressed peoples everywhere are displaying a heightened sense of human dignity in their refusal to accept second-class citizenship any longer.

. . . It is our shame that demonstrations must be carried out to win them. These constitutional rights *belong* to the Negro as to the white, because we are all men and we are all citizens. The white man needs to recognize this if he is to preserve his own humanity. It is a mark of the inversion of values in our society that those who today struggle to make the American experiment a reality through their protest are accused of disturbing the peace—and that more often than not the Church remains silent on this, our greatest domestic moral crisis.

I commend these specific measures to your attention:

1) I would ask you to involve yourselves. . . . It is the duty of every Christian citizen to know fully what is happening in his own community, and actively to support efforts to meet the problems he encounters.

2) I would also ask you to give money as an expression of our unity and as a sign of our support for the end of racial injustice in this land. . . .

3) I would ask you to take action. Discrimination within the Body of the Church itself is an intolerable scandal. Every congregation has a continuing need to examine its own life and to renew those efforts necessary to insure its inclusiveness fully. Diocesan and church-related agencies, schools, and other institutions also have a considerable distance to go in bringing their practices up to the standard of the clear position of the Church on race. . . . the firm action of the recent Convention of the Diocese of Washington . . . directed all diocesan-related institutions to eliminate any discriminatory practices within six months. It further requested the Bishop and Executive Council to take steps necessary to disassociate such diocesan and parish-related institutions from moral or financial support if these practices are not eliminated in the specified time. I believe we must make known where we stand unmistakably.

So I write with a deep sense of the urgency of the racial crisis in our country and the necessity for the Church to act. Present events reveal the possible imminence of catastrophe. The entire Christian community must pray and act.

The Cardinal's Message

to New York Catholics

WHEN we speak of all races, creeds and colors we touch upon something which is on everyone's mind today, and about which it is impossible to remain silent . . . that is the crying need for full justice and equality for our fellow American citizens who are Negroes. The inequities inflicted upon them have been a festering problem in our society for many decades. There is simply no reason —there never was and there never can be— why the color of a man's skin should limit his opportunities in a society that boasts of freedom.

The Negro is asked to give as much as any other man for his country. He has a right to receive back from his country in equal measure. On my trips over many years to visit our soldier-sons all over the world, I have seen White and Negro soldiers serving our country, suffering the same hardships and confronting the same hazards of war. Yet contrary to every Christian principle and in downright defiance of the American ideal of equal justice for all, some of those same Americans who risked their lives for America—for you and for me—are denied the right to vote, the right to receive an adequate education, the right to live where they desire . . . and to receive the normal courtesies befitting their dignity as human beings.

They are denied these rights for only one reason—the color of their skin. How lamentable that some Americans who would die together today, will not eat together, will not travel together, will not live together! This is an outrage which America cannot tolerate. . . .

People today are restless and impatient with the painfully slow progress that has been made in solving this problem of racism. The tradition of America is to get things done promptly and efficiently. Her tradition is also to get them done peacefully. . . . We must accomplish what has to be done by working together, as one people with a common ideal, working calmly but with determination to progress and to succeed in making our ideals a reality.

These ideals could be effectively realized if all Americans regardless of religion would drop the barriers of discrimination. . . .

In the field of housing, . . . laws against discrimination . . . must be supplemented by the active interest and vigilant efforts of all our citizens. Different races can live side by side harmoniously. . . .

Pope John XXIII—in . . . his encyclical, "Peace on Earth," . . . states: ". . . even

1963
New York City

Statement by Cardinal
Spellman read one Sunday
at all masses
in the Archdiocese

though human beings differ from one another by virtue of their ethnic qualities, they all possess certain essential common elements and are inclined by nature to meet each other in the world of spiritual values, whose progressive assimilation opens to them the possibility of perfection without limits. They have the right and duty, therefore, to live in communion with one another."

The American Catholic Bishops declared in 1958 that "the heart of the race question is moral and religious. It concerns the rights of man and our attitude toward our fellowman." Only last week when President Kennedy visited our new Holy Father, Pope Paul VI, His Holiness said, "We are ever mindful in our prayers of your efforts to insure all your citizens the equal benefits of citizenship which have as their foundation the equality of all men because of their dignity as persons and children of God."

On the occasion of the 40th Anniversary of the National Association for the Advancement of Colored People, of which I have the honor of being a life member, I sent my congratulations and good wishes. I said then, and now I repeat: "The Catholic Church repudiates as abhorrent to her very nature the pernicious doctrine that men are born with the stamp upon them of essential racial superiority or inferiority. She recognizes no master race, but proclaims the God-given equality before God of all souls, for whose salvation our Blessed Redeemer suffered and sacrificed."

Our own Catholic Interracial Council has done much to turn the attention of people to the problems of racial injustice. Many of our parishes have conducted workshops and study programs in an effort to further integrated living and equal educational opportunity for all and to end discrimination in employment and in union membership.

But much—ever so much—remains to be done. The great Christian and American principle of equality must be reduced to action in local circumstances and in specific ways. We need civil rights measures enacted into law; but we also need the attitudes of justice and charity to be applied by every person in our society to the concrete problems of housing, employment and education. This is the challenge which 1963 has set squarely before us and it must at all costs be faced and solved.

Our Negro brother wants more than a house in America. He wants a home in America. . . ."

Reform Judaism's Call to Racial Justice

*P*REAMBLE—"Have we not all one father? Hath not one God created us? Why do we deal treacherously, every man against his brother, profaning the covenant of our fathers?" (Malachi 2:10)

Two and one-half millenia since the utterance of these words declaring the brotherhood of all men, one hundred years since the Emancipation Proclamation freeing the slaves, and nine years since the Supreme Court decision declaring segregated schools unconstitutional, millions of our fellow Americans are still living as second class citizens.

We who strive to fulfill the covenants of our Jewish and democratic heritages have always considered one of our primary duties to be the eradication of every semblance of discrimination. Today, however, we are confronted by a new urgency. The eternal struggle to redeem the enslaved, first waged successfully in ancient Egypt, is again reaching an inexorable climax in our time and in our nation.

The resolution of America's race problem is not the exclusive responsibility of any single group, of Negroes or Whites, of Christians or Jews, but rather it is the collective responsibility of all Americans. However, we who every Passover still relive the lash of the taskmaster and who still recall that the ghetto was first invented to segregate Jews, have a special commitment. Jews are committed by faith and fate, by theology and history, to eradicate every trace of racism. The synagogue, the institutionalization of Jewish ideals, must not be a passive participant in the struggle, but must take initiatives and assume positions of leadership, true to the essence of Judaism that "not the word, but the deed is primary."

In order to fulfill our moral responsibilities, we herewith endorse the following policies:

I. RACIAL JUSTICE IN OUR CONGREGATION'S ADMINISTRATIVE POLICIES

1. Our congregation and all its affiliate groups will not patronize or sponsor any activity at a place of public accommodation which discriminates against anyone because of race, religion or ethnic origin.
2. Our congregation will pursue a policy of non-discrimination in all relationships with our employees.
3. Our congregation will require a non-discrimination employment clause in any contract to build or improve our physical facilities.
4. Our congregation, in connection with investments and loans, will seek out financial institutions which have non-discriminatory lending, borrowing, and employment practices.
5. Our congregation will not be party to any restrictive covenant or gentleman's agreement in the purchase, sale, rental or use of property.
6. Our congregation will not purchase any equipment or supplies from purveyors who are known to have discriminatory hiring policies.
7. Our congregation will welcome as members all Jews, regardless of their racial origins.

1963
New York City

A proposed program for
Reform congregations
implementing covenants
of Jewish Heritage

II. RACIAL JUSTICE IN OUR CONGREGATION'S EDUCATIONAL CULTURAL AND WORSHIP PROGRAMS

1. We are pleased that our worship services reflect in prayer, sermon and educational content our efforts to achieve racial justice.
2. We urge those responsible to see that our religious school curriculum and program incorporates the most recent developments and the most progressive techniques for inculcation of respect for all races and creeds.
3. Our congregation should devote sessions to the subject of racial equality in our educational programs for youth and adults.
4. We urge our congregation and affiliate groups—youth, men's club and sisterhood —to sponsor programs at home, in our temple and in other religious institutions with Negro groups and individuals in an effort to establish positive and meaningful interpersonal relationships.

III. RACIAL JUSTICE IN OUR CONGREGATION'S COOPERATIVE RELATIONSHIPS WITH OTHER INSTITUTIONS

1. Our congregation will cooperate with organizations working for racial justice and will encourage the active participation of our members in their programs. Appropriate evaluation will be made of the purpose, character and tactics of such direct action programs to assure their consonance with our objectives and with consideration for the rights of all.
2. Our congregation will support the freedom of our rabbi and board to join with others in issuing public statements to further the cause of equal opportunity.
3. Our congregation will take initiatives to urge the formulation and implementation of policies on racial justice similar to the one herein approved in other institutions, agencies and associations within the Jewish community.

IV. RACIAL JUSTICE IN THE LIVES OF OUR INDIVIDUAL CONGREGANTS

Because the ultimate objective of the synagogue is to have an impact on the lives and characters of our individual members, we deem it our duty now and in the future to direct the attention of our members to discriminatory practices in their own businesses, occupations and neighborhoods. . . .

The March on Washington August 28, 1963

THE MARCHERS:

They were a quarter of a million souls intent on "Freedom Now."
They marched through the streets of the Capital, then gathered
on the steps and in the shadows of the Lincoln Memorial to lis-
ten to the leaders of the March as they gave voice to their collective hopes, fears, dreams and demands. That night they went
back to their far-flung homes. They departed feeling a strange
awareness that somehow the impact of this extraordinary demonstration would be an instrument for democracy's growth in
America.   (Bert Miles)

THE LEADERS:

(Standing, left to right)

Matthew Ahman, National Catholic Conference for Interracial Justice; Rabbi Joachim Prinz, American Jewish Congress; John Lewis, Student Nonviolent Coordinating Committee; Eugene Carson Blake, United Presbyterian Church; Floyd H. McKissick, Congress of Racial Equality; Walter Reuther, United Auto Workers.

(Seated, left to right)

Whitney Young, Jr., National Urban League; Cleveland Robinson, Administrative Chairman of the March; A. Philip Randolph, Brotherhood of Sleeping Car Porters and Father of the March; Martin Luther King, Jr., Southern Christian Leadership Conference; and Roy Wilkins, National Association for the Advancement of Colored People.   *(Bert Miles)*

The Civil Rights Act

AN ACT

To enforce the constitutional right to vote, to confer jurisdiction upon the district courts of the United States to provide injunctive relief against discrimination in public accommodations, to authorize the Attorney General to institute suits to protect constitutional rights in public facilities and public education, to extend the Commission on Civil Rights, to prevent discrimination in federally assisted programs, to establish a Commission on Equal Employment Opportunity, and for other purposes.

1964  The law of the land removes major obstacles to Negro enjoyment of full citizenship

Be it enacted by the Senate and House of Representatives of the United States of America in Congress assembled, That this Act may be cited as the "Civil Rights Act of 1964".

TITLE I—VOTING RIGHTS

SEC. 101. Section 2004 of the Revised Statutes (42 U.S.C. 1971), as amended by section 131 of the Civil Rights Act of 1957 (71 Stat. 637), and as further amended by section 601 of the Civil Rights Act of 1960 (74 Stat. 90), is further amended as follows:

(a) Insert "1" after "(a)" in subsection (a) and add at the end of subsection (a) the following new paragraphs:

"(2) No person acting under color of law shall—

"(A) in determining whether any individual is qualified under State law or laws to vote in any Federal election, apply any standard, practice, or procedure different from the standards, practices, or procedures applied under such law or laws to other individuals within the same county, parish, or similar political subdivision who have been found by State officials to be qualified to vote;

"(B) deny the right of any individual to vote in any Federal election because of an error or omission on any record or paper relating to any application, registration, or other act requisite to voting, if such error or omission is not material in determining whether such individual is qualified under State law to vote in such election; or

"(C) employ any literacy test as a qualification for voting in any Federal election unless (i) such test is administered to each individual and is conducted wholly in writing, and (ii) a certified copy of the test and of the answers given by the individual is furnished to him within twenty-five days of the submission of his request made within the period of time during which records and papers are required to be retained and preserved pursuant to title III of the Civil Rights Act of 1960 (42 U.S.C. 1974– 74e; 74 Stat. 88): *Provided, however,* That the Attorney General may enter into agreements with appropriate State or local authorities that preparation, conduct, and maintenance of such tests in accordance with the provisions of applicable State or local law, including such special provisions as are necessary in the preparation, conduct, and maintenance of such tests for persons who are blind or otherwise physically handicapped, meet the purposes of this subparagraph and constitute compliance therewith.

"(3) For purposes of this subsection—

"(A) the term 'vote' shall have the same meaning as in subsection (e) of this section;

"(B) the phrase 'literacy test' includes any test of the ability to read, write, understand, or interpret any matter."

(b) Insert immediately following the period at the end of the first sentence of subsection (c) the following new sentence: "If in any such proceeding literacy is a relevant fact there shall be a rebuttable presumption that any person who has not been adjudged an incompetent and who has completed the sixth grade in a public school in, or a private school accredited by, any State or territory, the District of Columbia, or the Commonwealth of Puerto Rico where instruction is carried on predominantly in the English language, possesses sufficient literacy, comprehension, and intelligence to vote in any Federal election."

(c) Add the following subsection "(f)" and designate the present subsection "(f)" as subsection "(g)":

"(f) When used in subsection (a) or (c) of this section, the words 'Federal election' shall mean any general, special, or primary election held solely or in part for the purpose of electing or selecting any candidate for the office of President, Vice President, presidential elector, Member of the Senate, or Member of the House of Representatives."

(d) Add the following subsection "(h)":

"(h) In any proceeding instituted by the United States in any district court of the United States under this section in which the Attorney General requests a finding of a pattern or practice of discrimination pursuant to subsection (e) of this section the Attorney General, at the time he files the complaint, or any defendant in the proceeding, within twenty days after service upon him of the complaint, may file with the clerk of such court a request that a court of three judges be convened to hear and determine the entire case. A copy of the request for a three-judge court shall be immediately furnished by such clerk to the chief judge of the circuit (or in his absence, the presiding circuit judge of the circuit) in which the case is pending. Upon receipt of the copy of such request it shall be the duty of the chief judge of the circuit or the presiding circuit judge, as the case may be, to designate immediately three judges in such circuit, of whom at least one shall be a circuit judge and another of whom shall be a district judge of the court in which the proceeding was instituted, to hear and determine such case, and it shall be the duty of the judges so designated to assign the case for hearing at the earliest practicable date, to participate in the hearing and determination thereof, and to cause the case to be in every way expedited. An appeal from the final judgment of such court will lie to the Supreme Court.

"In any proceeding brought under subsection (c) of this section to enforce subsection (b) of this section, or in the event neither the Attorney General nor any defendant files a request for a three-judge court in any proceeding authorized by this subsection, it shall be the duty of the chief judge of the district (or in his absence, the acting chief judge) in which the case is pending immediately to designate a judge in such district to hear and determine the case. In the event that no judge in the district is available to hear and determine the case, the chief judge of the district, or the acting chief judge, as the case may be, shall certify this fact to the chief judge of the circuit (or, in his absence, the acting chief judge) who shall then designate a district or circuit judge of the circuit to hear and determine the case.

"It shall be the duty of the judge designated pursuant to this section to assign the case for hearing at the earliest practicable date and to cause the case to be in every way expedited."

TITLE II—INJUNCTIVE RELIEF AGAINST DISCRIMINATION IN PLACES OF PUBLIC ACCOMMODATION

SEC. 201. (a) All persons shall be entitled to the full and equal enjoyment of the goods, services, facilities, privileges, advantages, and accommodations of any place of public accommodation, as defined in this section, without discrimination or segregation on the ground of race, color, religion, or national origin.

(b) Each of the following establishments which serves the public is a place of public accommodation within the meaning of this title if its operations affect commerce, or if discrimination or segregation by it is supported by State action:

(1) any inn, hotel, motel, or other establishment which provides lodging to transient guests, other than an establishment located within a building which contains not more than five rooms for rent or hire and which is actually occupied by the proprietor of such establishment as his residence;

(2) any restaurant, cafeteria, lunchroom, lunch counter, soda fountain, or other facility principally engaged in selling food for consumption on the premises, including, but not limited to, any such facility located on the premises of any retail establishment; or any gasoline station;

(3) any motion picture house, theater, concert hall, sports arena, stadium or other place of exhibition or entertainment; and

(4) any establishment (A)(i) which is physically located within the premises of any establishment otherwise covered by

this subsection, or (ii) within the premises of which is physically located any such covered establishment, and (B) which holds itself out as serving patrons of such covered establishment.

Operations affecting commerce criteria.

(c) The operations of an establishment affect commerce within the meaning of this title if (1) it is one of the establishments described in paragraph (1) of subsection (b); (2) in the case of an establishment described in paragraph (2) of subsection (b), it serves or offers to serve interstate travelers or a substantial portion of the food which it serves, or gasoline or other products which it sells, has moved in commerce; (3) in the case of an establishment described in paragraph (3) of subsection (b), it customarily presents films, performances, athletic teams, exhibitions, or other sources of entertainment which move in commerce; and (4) in the case of an establishment described in paragraph (4) of subsection (b), it is physically located within the premises of, or there is physically located within its premises, an establishment the operations of which affect commerce within the meaning of this subsection. For purposes of this section, "commerce" means travel, trade, traffic, commerce, transportation, or communication among the several States, or between the District of Columbia and any State, or between any foreign country or any territory or possession and any State or the District of Columbia, or between points in the same State but through any other State or the District of Columbia or a foreign country.

"Commerce."

(d) Discrimination or segregation by an establishment is supported by State action within the meaning of this title if such discrimination or segregation (1) is carried on under color of any law, statute, ordinance, or regulation; or (2) is carried on under color of any custom or usage required or enforced by officials of the State or political subdivision thereof; or (3) is required by action of the State or political subdivision thereof.

Support by State action.

(e) The provisions of this title shall not apply to a private club or other establishment not in fact open to the public, except to the extent that the facilities of such establishment are made available to the customers or patrons of an establishment within the scope of subsection (b).

Private establishments.

Sec. 202. All persons shall be entitled to be free, at any establishment or place, from discrimination or segregation of any kind on the ground of race, color, religion, or national origin, if such discrimination or segregation is or purports to be required by any law, statute, ordinance, regulation, rule, or order of a State or any agency or political subdivision thereof.

Entitlement.

Sec. 203. No person shall (a) withhold, deny, or attempt to withhold or deny, or deprive or attempt to deprive, any person of any right or privilege secured by section 201 or 202, or (b) intimidate,

Interference.

threaten, or coerce, or attempt to intimidate, threaten, or coerce any person with the purpose of interfering with any right or privilege secured by section 201 or 202, or (c) punish or attempt to punish any person for exercising or attempting to exercise any right or privilege secured by section 201 or 202.

SEC. 204. (a) Whenever any person has engaged or there are reasonable grounds to believe that any person is about to engage in any act or practice prohibited by section 203, a civil action for preventive relief, including an application for a permanent or temporary injunction, restraining order, or other order, may be instituted by the person aggrieved and, upon timely application, the court may, in its discretion, permit the Attorney General to intervene in such civil action if he certifies that the case is of general public importance. Upon application by the complainant and in such circumstances as the court may deem just, the court may appoint an attorney for such complainant and may authorize the commencement of the civil action without the payment of fees, costs, or security. Restraining orders, etc.

(b) In any action commenced pursuant to this title, the court, in its discretion, may allow the prevailing party, other than the United States, a reasonable attorney's fee as part of the costs, and the United States shall be liable for costs the same as a private person. Attorneys' fees.

(c) In the case of an alleged act or practice prohibited by this title which occurs in a State, or political subdivision of a State, which has a State or local law prohibiting such act or practice and establishing or authorizing a State or local authority to grant or seek relief from such practice or to institute criminal proceedings with respect thereto upon receiving notice thereof, no civil action may be brought under subsection (a) before the expiration of thirty days after written notice of such alleged act or practice has been given to the appropriate State or local authority by registered mail or in person, provided that the court may stay proceedings in such civil action pending the termination of State or local enforcement proceedings. Notification of State.

(d) In the case of an alleged act or practice prohibited by this title which occurs in a State, or political subdivision of a State, which has no State or local law prohibiting such act or practice, a civil action may be brought under subsection (a): *Provided,* That the court may refer the matter to the Community Relations Service established by title X of this Act for as long as the court believes there is a reasonable possibility of obtaining voluntary compliance, but for not more than sixty days: *Provided further,* That upon expiration of such sixty-day period, the court may extend such period for an additional period, not to exceed a cumulative total of one hundred and twenty days, if it believes there then exists a reasonable possibility of securing voluntary compliance. Community Relations Service.

SEC. 205. The Service is authorized to make a full investigation of any complaint referred to it by the court under section 204(d) and may hold such hearings with respect thereto as may be necessary. The Service shall conduct any hearings with respect to any such complaint in executive session, and shall not release any testimony given therein except by agreement of all parties involved in the complaint with the permission of the court, and the Service shall endeavor to bring about a voluntary settlement between the parties.

Suits by
Attorney General.

SEC. 206. (a) Whenever the Attorney General has reasonable cause to believe that any person or group of persons is engaged in a pattern or practice of resistance to the full enjoyment of any of the rights secured by this title, and that the pattern or practice is of such a nature and is intended to deny the full exercise of the rights herein described, the Attorney General may bring a civil action in the appropriate district court of the United States by filing with it a complaint (1) signed by him (or in his absence the Acting Attorney General), (2) setting forth facts pertaining to such pattern or practice, and (3) requesting such preventive relief, including an application for a permanent or temporary injunction, restraining order or other order against the person or persons responsible for such pattern or practice, as he deems necessary to insure the full enjoyment of the rights herein described.

(b) In any such proceeding the Attorney General may file with the clerk of such court a request that a court of three judges be convened to hear and determine the case. Such request by the Attorney General shall be accompanied by a certificate that, in his opinion, the case is of general public importance. A copy of the certificate and request for a three-judge court shall be immediately furnished by such clerk to the chief judge of the circuit (or in his absence, the presiding circuit judge of the circuit) in which the case is pending.

Designation of
judges.

Upon receipt of the copy of such request it shall be the duty of the chief judge of the circuit or the presiding circuit judge, as the case may be, to designate immediately three judges in such circuit, of whom at least one shall be a circuit judge and another of whom shall be a district judge of the court in which the proceeding was instituted, to hear and determine such case, and it shall be the duty of the judges so designated to assign the case for hearing at the earliest practicable date, to participate in the hearing and determination thereof, and to cause the case to be in every way expedited. An

Appeals.

appeal from the final judgment of such court will lie to the Supreme Court.

In the event the Attorney General fails to file such a request in any such proceeding, it shall be the duty of the chief judge of the district (or in his absence, the acting chief judge) in which the case is pending immediately to designate a judge in such district to hear and determine the case. In the event that no judge in the district is available to hear and determine the case, the chief judge of the district, or the acting chief judge, as the case may be, shall certify this fact to the chief judge of the circuit (or in his absence, the acting chief judge) who shall then designate a district or circuit judge of the circuit to hear and determine the case.

It shall be the duty of the judge designated pursuant to this section to assign the case for hearing at the earliest practicable date and to cause the case to be in every way expedited.

SEC. 207. (a) The district courts of the United States shall have jurisdiction of proceedings instituted pursuant to this title and shall exercise the same without regard to whether the aggrieved party shall have exhausted any administrative or other remedies that may be provided by law.

District courts, jurisdiction.

(b) The remedies provided in this title shall be the exclusive means of enforcing the rights based on this title, but nothing in this title shall preclude any individual or any State or local agency from asserting any right based on any other Federal or State law not inconsistent with this title, including any statute or ordinance requiring nondiscrimination in public establishments or accommodations, or from pursuing any remedy, civil or criminal, which may be available for the vindication or enforcement of such right.

Enforcement.

TITLE III—DESEGREGATION OF PUBLIC FACILITIES

SEC. 301. (a) Whenever the Attorney General receives a complaint in writing signed by an individual to the effect that he is being deprived of or threatened with the loss of his right to the equal protection of the laws, on account of his race, color, religion, or national origin, by being denied equal utilization of any public facility which is owned, operated, or managed by or on behalf of any State or subdivision thereof, other than a public school or public college as defined in section 401 of title IV hereof, and the Attorney General believes the complaint is meritorious and certifies that the signer or signers of such complaint are unable, in his judgment, to initiate and maintain appropriate legal proceedings for relief and that the institution of an action will materially further the orderly progress of desegregation in public facilities, the Attorney General is authorized to institute for or in the name of the United States a civil action in any appropriate district court of the United States against such parties and for such relief as may be appropriate, and such court shall have and shall exercise jurisdiction of proceedings instituted pursuant to this section. The Attorney General may implead as

Suits by Attorney General.

defendants such additional parties as are or become necessary to the grant of effective relief hereunder.

(b) The Attorney General may deem a person or persons unable to initiate and maintain appropriate legal proceedings within the meaning of subsection (a) of this section when such person or persons are unable, either directly or through other interested persons or organizations, to bear the expense of the litigation or to obtain effective legal representation; or whenever he is satisfied that the institution of such litigation would jeopardize the personal safety, employment, or economic standing of such person or persons, their families, or their property.

Costs, fees.

SEC. 302. In any action or proceeding under this title the United States shall be liable for costs, including a reasonable attorney's fee, the same as a private person.

SEC. 303. Nothing in this title shall affect adversely the right of any person to sue for or obtain relief in any court against discrimination in any facility covered by this title.

62 Stat. 749.

SEC. 304. A complaint as used in this title is a writing or document within the meaning of section 1001, title 18, United States Code.

TITLE IV—DESEGREGATION OF PUBLIC EDUCATION

DEFINITIONS

SEC. 401. As used in this title—

"Commissioner."

(a) "Commissioner" means the Commissioner of Education.

"Desegregation."

(b) "Desegregation" means the assignment of students to public schools and within such schools without regard to their race, color, religion, or national origin, but "desegregation" shall not mean the assignment of students to public schools in order to overcome racial imbalance.

"Public school."

(c) "Public school" means any elementary or secondary educational institution, and "public college" means any institution of higher education or any technical or vocational school above the secondary school level, provided that such public school or public college is operated by a State, subdivision of a State, or governmental agency within a State, or operated wholly or predominantly from or through the use of governmental funds or property, or funds or property derived from a governmental source.

"School board."

(d) "School board" means any agency or agencies which administer a system of one or more public schools and any other agency which is responsible for the assignment of students to or within such system.

SEC. 402. The Commissioner shall conduct a survey and make a report to the President and the Congress, within two years of the enactment of this title, concerning the lack of availability of equal educational opportunities for individuals by reason of race, color, religion, or national origin in public educational institutions at all levels in the United States, its territories and possessions, and the District of Columbia.

Report to President and Congress.

TECHNICAL ASSISTANCE

SEC. 403. The Commissioner is authorized, upon the application of any school board, State, municipality, school district, or other governmental unit legally responsible for operating a public school or schools, to render technical assistance to such applicant in the preparation, adoption, and implementation of plans for the desegregation of public schools. Such technical assistance may, among other activities, include making available to such agencies information regarding effective methods of coping with special educational problems occasioned by desegregation, and making available to such agencies personnel of the Office of Education or other persons specially equipped to advise and assist them in coping with such problems.

TRAINING INSTITUTES

SEC. 404. The Commissioner is authorized to arrange, through grants or contracts, with institutions of higher education for the operation of short-term or regular session institutes for special training designed to improve the ability of teachers, supervisors, counselors, and other elementary or secondary school personnel to deal effectively with special educational problems occasioned by desegregation. Individuals who attend such an institute on a full-time basis may be paid stipends for the period of their attendance at such institute in amounts specified by the Commissioner in regulations, including allowances for travel to attend such institute.

Stipends, etc.

GRANTS

SEC. 405. (a) The Commissioner is authorized, upon application of a school board, to make grants to such board to pay, in whole or in part, the cost of—

> (1) giving to teachers and other school personnel inservice training in dealing with problems incident to desegregation, and

(2) employing specialists to advise in problems incident to desegregation.

(b) In determining whether to make a grant, and in fixing the amount thereof and the terms and conditions on which it will be made, the Commissioner shall take into consideration the amount available for grants under this section and the other applications which are pending before him; the financial condition of the applicant and the other resources available to it; the nature, extent, and gravity of its problems incident to desegregation; and such other factors as he finds relevant.

PAYMENTS

SEC. 406. Payments pursuant to a grant or contract under this title may be made (after necessary adjustments on account of previously made overpayments or underpayments) in advance or by way of reimbursement, and in such installments, as the Commissioner may determine.

SUITS BY THE ATTORNEY GENERAL

SEC. 407. (a) Whenever the Attorney General receives a complaint in writing—

(1) signed by a parent or group of parents to the effect that his or their minor children, as members of a class of persons similarly situated, are being deprived by a school board of the equal protection of the laws, or

(2) signed by an individual, or his parent, to the effect that he has been denied admission to or not permitted to continue in attendance at a public college by reason of race, color, religion, or national origin,

and the Attorney General believes the complaint is meritorious and certifies that the signer or signers of such complaint are unable, in his judgment, to initiate and maintain appropriate legal proceedings for relief and that the institution of an action will materially further the orderly achievement of desegregation in public education, the Attorney General is authorized, after giving notice of such complaint to the appropriate school board or college authority and after certifying that he is satisfied that such board or authority has had a reasonable time to adjust the conditions alleged in such complaint, to institute for or in the name of the United States a civil action in any appropriate district court of the United States against such parties and for such relief as may be appropriate, and such court shall have and shall exercise jurisdiction of proceedings instituted pursuant to this section, provided that nothing herein shall empower any official or court of the United States to issue any order seeking to achieve a racial balance in any school by requiring the transportation of pupils or students from one school to another or one school district to another in order to achieve such racial balance, or otherwise enlarge the existing power of the court to insure compliance with constitutional standards. The Attorney General may implead as defendants such additional parties as are or become necessary to the grant of effective relief hereunder.

(b) The Attorney General may deem a person or persons unable to initiate and maintain appropriate legal proceedings within the meaning of subsection (a) of this section when such person or persons are unable, either directly or through other interested persons or organizations, to bear the expense of the litigation or to obtain effective legal representation; or whenever he is satisfied that the institution of such litigation would jeopardize the personal safety, employment, or economic standing of such person or persons, their families, or their property. Persons unable to initiate suits.

(c) The term "parent" as used in this section includes any person standing in loco parentis. A "complaint" as used in this section is a writing or document within the meaning of section 1001, title 18, United States Code. "Parent." "Complaint." 62 Stat. 749.

Sec. 408. In any action or proceeding under this title the United States shall be liable for costs the same as a private person.

Sec. 409. Nothing in this title shall affect adversely the right of any person to sue for or obtain relief in any court against discrimination in public education.

Sec. 410. Nothing in this title shall prohibit classification and assignment for reasons other than race, color, religion, or national origin.

TITLE V—COMMISSION ON CIVIL RIGHTS

Sec. 501. Section 102 of the Civil Rights Act of 1957 (42 U.S.C. 1975a; 71 Stat. 634) is amended to read as follows:

"RULES OF PROCEDURE OF THE COMMISSION HEARINGS

"Sec. 102. (a) At least thirty days prior to the commencement of any hearing, the Commission shall cause to be published in the Federal Register notice of the date on which such hearing is to commence, the place at which it is to be held and the subject of the hearing. The Chairman, or one designated by him to act as Chairman at a hearing of the Commission, shall announce in an opening statement the subject of the hearing. Publication in Federal Register.

"(b) A copy of the Commission's rules shall be made available to any witness before the Commission, and a witness compelled to appear before the Commission or required to produce written or other matter shall be served with a copy of the Commission's rules at the time of service of the subpena.

Right of counsel.

"(c) Any person compelled to appear in person before the Commission shall be accorded the right to be accompanied and advised by counsel, who shall have the right to subject his client to reasonable examination, and to make objections on the record and to argue briefly the basis for such objections. The Commission shall proceed with reasonable dispatch to conclude any hearing in which it is engaged. Due regard shall be had for the convenience and necessity of witnesses.

"(d) The Chairman or Acting Chairman may punish breaches of order and decorum by censure and exclusion from the hearings.

Executive sessions.

"(e) If the Commission determines that evidence or testimony at any hearing may tend to defame, degrade, or incriminate any person, it shall receive such evidence or testimony or summary of such evidence or testimony in executive session. The Commission shall afford any person defamed, degraded, or incriminated by such evidence or testimony an opportunity to appear and be heard in executive session, with a reasonable number of additional witnesses requested by him, before deciding to use such evidence or testimony. In the event the Commission determines to release or use such evidence or testimony in such manner as to reveal publicly the identity of the person defamed, degraded, or incriminated, such evidence or testimony, prior to such public release or use, shall be given at a public session, and the Commission shall afford such person an opportunity to appear as a voluntary witness or to file a sworn statement in his behalf and to submit brief and pertinent sworn statements of others. The Commission shall receive and dispose of requests from such person to subpena additional witnesses.

"(f) Except as provided in sections 102 and 105(f) of this Act, the Chairman shall receive and the Commission shall dispose of requests to subpena additional witnesses.

Testimony, release restrictions.

"(g) No evidence or testimony or summary of evidence or testimony taken in executive session may be released or used in public sessions without the consent of the Commission. Whoever releases or uses in public without the consent of the Commission such evidence or testimony taken in executive session shall be fined not more than $1,000, or imprisoned for not more than one year.

"(h) In the discretion of the Commission, witnesses may submit brief and pertinent sworn statements in writing for inclusion in the record. The Commission shall determine the pertinency of testimony and evidence adduced at its hearings.

Transcript copies.

"(i) Every person who submits data or evidence shall be entitled to retain or, on payment of lawfully prescribed costs, procure a copy or transcript thereof, except that a witness in a hearing held in executive session may for good cause be limited to inspection of the official transcript of his testimony. Transcript copies of public sessions may be obtained by the public upon the payment of the cost thereof. An accurate transcript shall be made of the testimony of all witnesses at all hearings, either public or executive sessions, of the Commission or of any subcommittee thereof.

"(j) A witness attending any session of the Commission shall receive $6 for each day's attendance and for the time necessarily occupied in going to and returning from the same, and 10 cents per mile for going from and returning to his place of residence. Witnesses who attend at points so far removed from their respective residences as to prohibit return thereto from day to day shall be entitled to an additional allowance of $10 per day for expenses of subsistence, including the time necessarily occupied in going to and returning from the place of attendance. Mileage payments shall be tendered to the witness upon service of a subpena issued on behalf of the Commission or any subcommittee thereof.

Witness fees.

"(k) The Commission shall not issue any subpena for the attendance and testimony of witnesses or for the production of written or other matter which would require the presence of the party subpenaed at a hearing to be held outside of the State wherein the witness is found or resides or is domiciled or transacts business, or has appointed an agent for receipt of service of process except that, in any event, the Commission may issue subpenas for the attendance and testimony of witnesses and the production of written or other matter at a hearing held within fifty miles of the place where the witness is found or resides or is domiciled or transacts business or has appointed an agent for receipt of service of process.

Subpena of witnesses.

"(1) The Commission shall separately state and currently publish in the Federal Register (1) descriptions of its central and field organization including the established places at which, and methods whereby, the public may secure information or make requests; (2) statements of the general course and method by which its functions are channeled and determined, and (3) rules adopted as authorized by law. No person shall in any manner be subject to or required to resort to rules, organization, or procedure not so published."

Organization statement, etc. Publication in Federal Register.

SEC. 502. Section 103(a) of the Civil Rights Act of 1957 (42 U.S.C. 1975b(a); 71 Stat. 634) is amended to read as follows:

"SEC. 103. (a) Each member of the Commission who is not otherwise in the service of the Government of the United States shall receive the sum of $75 per day for each day spent in the work of the Commission, shall be paid actual travel expenses, and per diem in lieu of subsistence expenses when away from his usual place of residence, in accordance with section 5 of the Administrative Expenses Act of 1946,

Payments to members.

as amended (5 U.S.C. 73b–2; 60 Stat. 808)."

SEC. 503. Section 103(b) of the Civil Rights Act of 1957 (42 U.S.C. 1975b(b); 71 Stat. 634) is amended to read as follows:

"(b) Each member of the Commission who is otherwise in the service of the Government of the United States shall serve without compensation in addition to that received for such other service, but while engaged in the work of the Commission shall be paid actual travel expenses, and per diem in lieu of subsistence expenses when away from his usual place of residence, in accordance with the provisions of the Travel Expenses Act of 1949, as amended (5 U.S.C. 835–42; 63 Stat. 166)."

SEC. 504. (a) Section 104(a) of the Civil Rights Act of 1957 (42 U.S.C. 1975c(a); 71 Stat. 635), as amended, is further amended to read as follows:

"DUTIES OF THE COMMISSION

"SEC. 104. (a) The Commission shall—

"(1) investigate allegations in writing under oath or affirmation that certain citizens of the United States are being deprived of their right to vote and have that vote counted by reason of their color, race, religion, or national origin; which writing, under oath or affirmation, shall set forth the facts upon which such belief or beliefs are based;

"(2) study and collect information concerning legal developments constituting a denial of equal protection of the laws under the Constitution because of race, color, religion or national origin or in the administration of justice;

"(3) appraise the laws and policies of the Federal Government with respect to denials of equal protection of the laws under the Constitution because of race, color, religion or national origin or in the administration of justice;

"(4) serve as a national clearinghouse for information in respect to denials of equal protection of the laws because of race, color, religion or national origin, including but not limited to the fields of voting, education, housing, employment, the use of public facilities, and transportation, or in the administration of justice;

"(5) investigate allegations, made in writing and under oath or affirmation, that citizens of the United States are unlawfully being accorded or denied the right to vote, or to have their votes properly counted, in any election of presidential electors, Members of the United States Senate, or of the House of Representatives, as a result of any patterns or practice of fraud or discrimination in the conduct of such election; and

"(6) Nothing in this or any other Act shall be construed as authorizing the Commission, its Advisory Committees, or any person under its supervision or control to inquire into or investigate any membership practices or internal operations of any fraternal organization, any college or university fraternity or sorority, any private club or any religious organization."

(b) Section 104(b) of the Civil Rights Act of 1957 (42 U.S.C. 1975c(b); 71 Stat. 635), as amended, is further amended by striking out the present subsection "(b)" and by substituting therefor:

77 Stat. 271.

Reports to the President and Congress.

"(b) The Commission shall submit interim reports to the President and to the Congress at such times as the Commission, the Congress or the President shall deem desirable, and shall submit to the President and to the Congress a final report of its activities, findings, and recommendations not later than January 31, 1968."

SEC. 505. Section 105(a) of the Civil Rights Act of 1957 (42 U.S.C. 1975d(a); 71 Stat. 636) is amended by striking out in the last sentence thereof "$50 per diem" and inserting in lieu thereof "$75 per diem."

SEC. 506. Section 105(f) and section 105(g) of the Civil Rights Act of 1957 (42 U.S.C. 1975d (f) and (g); 71 Stat. 636) are amended to read as follows:

Powers.

"(f) The Commission, or on the authorization of the Commission any subcommittee of two or more members, at least one of whom shall be of each major political party, may, for the purpose of carrying out the provisions of this Act, hold such hearings and act at such times and places as the Commission or such authorized subcommittee may deem advisable. Subpenas for the attendance and testimony of witnesses or the production of written or other matter may be issued in accordance with the rules of the Commission as contained in section 102 (j) and (k) of this Act, over the signature of the Chairman of the Commission or of such subcommittee, and may be served by any person designated by such Chairman. The holding of hearings by the Commission, or the appointment of a subcommittee to hold hearings pursuant to this subparagraph, must be approved by a majority of the Commission, or by a majority of the members present at a meeting at which at least a quorum of four members is present.

Ante, p. 250.

"(g) In case of contumacy or refusal to obey a subpena, any district court of the United States or the United States court of any territory or possession, or the District Court of the United States for the District of Columbia, within the jurisdiction of which the inquiry is carried on or within the jurisdiction of which said person guilty of contumacy or refusal to obey is found or resides or is domiciled or transacts business, or has appointed an agent for receipt of service of process, upon application by the Attorney General of the United States shall have jurisdiction to issue to such person an order requiring such person to appear before the Commission or a subcommittee thereof, there to produce pertinent, relevant and nonprivileged evidence if so ordered, or there to give testimony touching the matter under investigation; and any failure to obey such order of the court may be punished by said court as a contempt thereof."

SEC. 507. Section 105 of the Civil Rights Act of 1957 (42 U.S.C. 1975d; 71 Stat. 636), as amended by section 401 of the Civil Rights Act of 1960 (42 U.S.C. 1975d(h); 74 Stat. 89), is further amended by adding a new subsection at the end to read as follows:

"(i) The Commission shall have the power to make such rules and regulations as are necessary to carry out the purposes of this Act."

TITLE VI—NONDISCRIMINATION IN FEDERALLY ASSISTED PROGRAMS

SEC. 601. No person in the United States shall, on the ground of race, color, or national origin, be excluded from participation in, be denied the benefits of, or be subjected to discrimination under any program or activity receiving Federal financial assistance.

Rules governing grants, loans, and contracts.

SEC. 602. Each Federal department and agency which is empowered to extend Federal financial assistance to any program or activity, by way of grant, loan, or contract other than a contract of insurance or guaranty, is authorized and directed to effectuate the provisions of section 601 with respect to such program or activity by issuing rules, regulations, or orders of general applicability which shall be consistent with achievement of the objectives of the statute authorizing the financial assistance in connection with which the action is taken.

Approval by President.

No such rule, regulation, or order shall become effective unless and until approved by the President. Compliance with any requirement adopted pursuant to this section may be effected (1) by the termination of or refusal to grant or to continue assistance under such program or activity to any recipient as to whom there has been an express finding on the record, after opportunity for hearing, of a failure to comply with such requirement, but such termination or refusal shall be limited to the particular political entity, or part thereof, or other recipient as to whom such a finding has been made and, shall be limited in its effect to the particular program, or part thereof, in which such noncompliance has been so found, or (2) by any other means authorized by law: *Provided, however,* That no such action shall be taken until the department or agency concerned has advised the appropriate person or persons of the failure to comply with the requirement and has determined that compliance cannot be secured by voluntary means.

Termination.

In the case of any action terminating, or refusing to grant or continue, assistance because of failure to comply with a requirement imposed pursuant to this section, the head of the Federal department or agency shall file with the committees of the House and Senate having legislative jurisdiction over the program or activity involved a full written report of the circumstances and the grounds for such action. No such action shall become effective until thirty days have elapsed after the filing of such report.

Judicial review.

SEC. 603. Any department or agency action taken pursuant to section 602 shall be subject to such judicial review as may otherwise be provided by law for similar action taken by such department or agency on other grounds. In the case of action, not otherwise subject to judicial review, terminating or refusing to grant or to continue financial assistance upon a finding of failure to comply with any requirement imposed pursuant to section 602, any person aggrieved (including any State or political subdivision thereof and any agency of either) may obtain judicial review of such action in accordance with section 10 of the Administrative Procedure Act, and such action shall not be deemed committed to unreviewable agency discretion within the meaning of that section.

60 Stat. 243.
5 USC 1009.

SEC. 604. Nothing contained in this title shall be construed to authorize action under this title by any department or agency with respect to any employment practice of any employer, employment agency, or labor organization except where a primary objective of the Federal financial assistance is to provide employment.

SEC. 605. Nothing in this title shall add to or detract from any existing authority with respect to any program or activity under which Federal financial assistance is extended by way of a contract of insurance or guaranty.

TITLE VII—EQUAL EMPLOYMENT OPPORTUNITY

DEFINITIONS

SEC. 701. For the purposes of this title—

(a) The term "person" includes one or more individuals, labor unions, partnerships, associations, corporations, legal representatives, mutual companies, joint-stock companies, trusts, unincorporated organizations, trustees, trustees in bankruptcy, or receivers.

"Person."

(b) The term "employer" means a person engaged in an industry affecting commerce who has twenty-five or more employees for each working day in each of twenty or more calendar weeks in the current or preceding calendar year, and any agent of such a person, but such term does not include (1) the United States, a corporation wholly owned by the Government of the United States, an Indian tribe, or a State or political subdivision thereof, (2) a bona fide private membership club (other than a labor organization) which is exempt from

"Employer."

68A Stat. 163;
74 Stat. 534.
26 USC 501.

taxation under section 501(c) of the Internal Revenue Code of 1954: *Provided,* That during the first year after the effective date prescribed in subsection (a) of section 716, persons having fewer than one hundred employees (and their agents) shall not be considered employers, and, during the second year after such date, persons having fewer than seventy-five employees (and their agents) shall not be considered employers, and, during the third year after such date, persons having fewer than fifty employees (and their agents) shall not be considered employers: *Provided further,* That it shall be the policy of the United States to insure equal employment opportunities for Federal employees without discrimination because of race, color, religion, sex or national origin and the President shall utilize his existing authority to effectuate this policy.

"Employment
agency."

(c) The term "employment agency" means any person regularly undertaking with or without compensation to procure employees for an employer or to procure for employees opportunities to work for an employer and includes an agent of such a person; but shall not include an agency of the United States, or an agency of a State or political subdivision of a State, except that such term shall include the United States Employment Service and the system of State and local employment services receiving Federal assistance.

"Labor
organization."

(d) The term "labor organization" means a labor organization engaged in an industry affecting commerce, and any agent of such an organization, and includes any organization of any kind, any agency, or employee representation committee, group, association, or plan so engaged in which employees participate and which exists for the purpose, in whole or in part, of dealing with employers concerning grievances, labor disputes, wages, rates of pay, hours, or other terms or conditions of employment, and any conference, general committee, joint or system board, or joint council so engaged which is subordinate to a national or international labor organization.

(e) A labor organization shall be deemed to be engaged in an industry affecting commerce if (1) it maintains or operates a hiring hall or hiring office which procures employees for an employer or procures for employees opportunities to work for an employer, or (2) the number of its members (or, where it is a labor organization composed of other labor organizations or their representatives, if the aggregate number of the members of such other labor organization) is (A) one hundred or more during the first year after the effective date prescribed in subsection (a) of section 716, (B) seventy-five or more during the second year after such date or fifty or more during the third year, or (C) twenty-five or more thereafter, and such labor organization—

(1) is the certified representative of employees under the provisions of the National Labor Relations Act, as amended, or the Railway Labor Act, as amended;

61 Stat. 136.
29 USC 167.
44 Stat. 577;
49 Stat. 1189.
45 USC 151.

(2) although not certified, is a national or international labor organization or a local labor organization recognized or acting as the representative of employees of an employer or employers engaged in an industry affecting commerce; or

(3) has chartered a local labor organization or subsidiary body which is representing or actively seeking to represent employees of employers within the meaning of paragraph (1) or (2); or

(4) has been chartered by a labor organization representing or actively seeking to represent employees within the meaning of paragraph (1) or (2) as the local or subordinate body through which such employees may enjoy membership or become affiliated with such labor organization; or

(5) is a conference, general committee, joint or system board, or joint council subordinate to a national or international labor organization, which includes a labor organization engaged in an industry affecting commerce within the meaning of any of the preceding paragraphs of this subsection.

(f) The term "employee" means an individual employed by an employer.

"Employee."

(g) The term "commerce" means trade, traffic, commerce, transportation, transmission, or communication among the several States; or between a State and any place outside thereof; or within the District of Columbia, or a possession of the United States; or between points in the same State but through a point outside thereof.

"Commerce."

(h) The term "industry affecting commerce" means any activity, business, or industry in commerce or in which a labor dispute would hinder or obstruct commerce or the free flow of commerce and includes any activity or industry "affecting commerce" within the meaning of the Labor-Management Reporting and Disclosure Act of 1959.

"Industry affecting commerce."

73 Stat. 519.
29 USC 401 note.

(i) The term "State" includes a State of the United States, the District of Columbia, Puerto Rico, the Virgin Islands, American Samoa, Guam, Wake Island, the Canal Zone, and Outer Continental Shelf lands defined in the Outer Continental Shelf Lands Act.

"State."

67 Stat. 462.
43 USC 1331 note.

EXEMPTION

SEC. 702. This title shall not apply to an employer with respect to the employment of aliens outside any State, or to a religious corporation, association, or society with respect to the employment of indi-

Religious organizations, etc.

viduals of a particular religion to perform work connected with the carrying on by such corporation, association, or society of its religious activities or to an educational institution with respect to the employment of individuals to perform work connected with the educational activities of such institution.

DISCRIMINATION BECAUSE OF RACE, COLOR, RELIGION, SEX, OR NATIONAL ORIGIN

Unlawful practices. Employers.

SEC. 703. (a) It shall be an unlawful employment practice for an employer—

(1) to fail or refuse to hire or to discharge any individual, or otherwise to discriminate against any individual with respect to his compensation, terms, conditions, or privileges of employment, because of such individual's race, color, religion, sex, or national origin; or

(2) to limit, segregate, or classify his employees in any way which would deprive or tend to deprive any individual of employment opportunities or otherwise adversely affect his status as an employee, because of such individual's race, color, religion, sex, or national origin.

Employment agency.

(b) It shall be an unlawful employment practice for an employment agency to fail or refuse to refer for employment, or otherwise to discriminate against, any individual because of his race, color, religion, sex, or national origin, or to classify or refer for employment any individual on the basis of his race, color, religion, sex, or national origin.

Labor organization.

(c) It shall be an unlawful employment practice for a labor organization—

(1) to exclude or to expel from its membership, or otherwise to discriminate against, any individual because of his race, color, religion, sex, or national origin;

(2) to limit, segregate, or classify its membership, or to classify or fail or refuse to refer for employment any individual, in any way which would deprive or tend to deprive any individual of employment opportunities, or would limit such employment opportunities or otherwise adversely affect his status as an employee or as an applicant for employment, because of such individual's race, color, religion, sex, or national origin; or

(3) to cause or attempt to cause an employer to discriminate against an individual in violation of this section.

Training programs.

(d) It shall be an unlawful employment practice for any employer, labor organization, or joint labor-management committee controlling apprenticeship or other training or retraining, including on-the-job training programs to discriminate against any individual because of his race, color, religion, sex, or national origin in admission to, or employment in, any program established to provide apprenticeship or other training.

(e) Notwithstanding any other provision of this title, (1) it shall not be an unlawful employment practice for an employer to hire and employ employees, for an employment agency to classify, or refer for employment any individual, for a labor organization to classify its membership or to classify or refer for employment any individual, or for an employer, labor organization, or joint labor-management committee controlling apprenticeship or other training or retraining programs to admit or employ any individual in any such program, on the basis of his religion, sex, or national origin in those certain instances where religion, sex, or national origin is a bona fide occupational qualification reasonably necessary to the normal operation of that particular business or enterprise, and (2) it shall not be an unlawful employment practice for a school, college, university, or other educational institution or institution of learning to hire and employ employees of a particular religion if such school, college, university, or other educational institution or institution of learning is, in whole or in substantial part, owned, supported, controlled, or managed by a particular religion or by a particular religious corporation, association, or society, or if the curriculum of such school, college, university, or other educational institution or institution of learning is directed toward the propagation of a particular religion.

(f) As used in this title, the phrase "unlawful employment practice" shall not be deemed to include any action or measure taken by an employer, labor organization, joint labor-management committee, or employment agency with respect to an individual who is a member of the Communist Party of the United States or of any other organization required to register as a Communist-action or Communist-front organization by final order of the Subversive Activities Control Board pursuant to the Subversive Activities Control Act of 1950.

(g) Notwithstanding any other provision of this title, it shall not be an unlawful employment practice for an employer to fail or refuse to hire and employ any individual for any position, for an employer to discharge any individual from any position, or for an employment agency to fail or refuse to refer any individual for employment in any position, or for a labor organization to fail or refuse to refer any individual for employment in any position, if—

(1) the occupancy of such position, or access to the premises in or upon which any part of the duties of such position is performed or is to be performed, is subject to any requirement imposed in the interest of the national security of the United States under any security program in effect pursuant to or administered under any statute of the United States or any Executive

order of the President; and

(2) such individual has not fulfilled or has ceased to fulfill that requirement.

(h) Notwithstanding any other provision of this title, it shall not be an unlawful employment practice for an employer to apply different standards of compensation, or different terms, conditions, or privileges of employment pursuant to a bona fide seniority or merit system, or a system which measures earnings by quantity or quality of production or to employees who work in different locations, provided that such differences are not the result of an intention to discriminate because of race, color, religion, sex, or national origin, nor shall it be an unlawful employment practice for an employer to give and to act upon the results of any professionally developed ability test provided that such test, its administration or action upon the results is not designed, intended or used to discriminate because of race, color, religion, sex or national origin. It shall not be an unlawful employment practice under this title for any employer to differentiate upon the basis of sex in determining the amount of the wages or compensation paid or to be paid to employees of such employer if such differentiation is authorized by the provisions of section 6(d) of the Fair Labor Standards Act of 1938, as amended (29 U.S.C. 206(d)).

(i) Nothing contained in this title shall apply to any business or enterprise on or near an Indian reservation with respect to any publicly announced employment practice of such business or enterprise under which a preferential treatment is given to any individual because he is an Indian living on or near a reservation.

(j) Nothing contained in this title shall be interpreted to require any employer, employment agency, labor organization, or joint labor-management committee subject to this title to grant preferential treatment to any individual or to any group because of the race, color, religion, sex, or national origin of such individual or group on account of an imbalance which may exist with respect to the total number or percentage of persons of any race, color, religion, sex, or national origin employed by any employer, referred or classified for employment by any employment agency or labor organization, admitted to membership or classified by any labor organization, or admitted to, or employed in, any apprenticeship or other training program, in comparison with the total number or percentage of persons of such race, color, religion, sex, or national origin in any community, State, section, or other area, or in the available work force in any community, State, section, or other area.

OTHER UNLAWFUL EMPLOYMENT PRACTICES

SEC. 704. (a) It shall be an unlawful employment practice for an employer to discriminate against any of his employees or applicants for employment, for an employment agency to discriminate against any individual, or for a labor organization to discriminate against any member thereof or applicant for membership, because he has opposed any practice made an unlawful employment practice by this title, or because he has made a charge, testified, assisted, or participated in any manner in an investigation, proceeding, or hearing under this title.

(b) It shall be an unlawful employment practice for an employer, labor organization, or employment agency to print or publish or cause to be printed or published any notice or advertisement relating to employment by such an employer or membership in or any classification or referral for employment by such a labor organization, or relating to any classification or referral for employment by such an employment agency, indicating any preference, limitation, specification, or discrimination, based on race, color, religion, sex, or national origin, except that such a notice or advertisement may indicate a preference, limitation, specification, or discrimination based on religion, sex, or national origin when religion, sex, or national origin is a bona fide occupational qualification for employment.

EQUAL EMPLOYMENT OPPORTUNITY COMMISSION

SEC. 705. (a) There is hereby created a Commission to be known as the Equal Employment Opportunity Commission, which shall be composed of five members, not more than three of whom shall be members of the same political party, who shall be appointed by the President by and with the advice and consent of the Senate. One of the original members shall be appointed for a term of one year, one for a term of two years, one for a term of three years, one for a term of four years, and one for a term of five years, beginning from the date of enactment of this title, but their successors shall be appointed for terms of five years each, except that any individual chosen to fill a vacancy shall be appointed only for the unexpired term of the member whom he shall succeed. The President shall designate one member to serve as Chairman of the Commission, and one member to serve as Vice Chairman. The Chairman shall be responsible on behalf of the Commission for the administrative operations of the Commission, and shall appoint, in accordance with the civil service laws, such officers, agents, attorneys, and employees as it deems necessary to assist it in the performance of its functions and to fix their compensation in accordance with the Classification Act of 1949, as amended. The Vice Chairman shall act as Chairman in the absence or disability of the Chairman or in the event of a vacancy in that office.

(b) A vacancy in the Commission shall not impair the right of the remaining members to exercise all the powers of the Commission and

Establishment.

Term of office.

63 Stat. 954;
76 Stat. 843.
5 USC 1071 note.

three members thereof shall constitute a quorum.

(c) The Commission shall have an official seal which shall be judicially noticed.

Reports to the President and Congress.

(d) The Commission shall at the close of each fiscal year report to the Congress and to the President concerning the action it has taken; the names, salaries, and duties of all individuals in its employ and the moneys it has disbursed; and shall make such further reports on the cause of and means of eliminating discrimination and such recommendations for further legislation as may appear desirable.

(e) The Federal Executive Pay Act of 1956, as amended (5 U.S.C. 2201–2209), is further amended—

70 Stat. 736.
5 USC 2201 note.

(1) by adding to section 105 thereof (5 U.S.C. 2204) the following clause:

"(32) Chairman, Equal Employment Opportunity Commission"; and

(2) by adding to clause (45) of section 106(a) thereof (5 U.S.C. 2205(a)) the following: "Equal Employment Opportunity Commission (4)."

70 Stat. 737.
5 USC 2205.

(f) The principal office of the Commission shall be in or near the District of Columbia, but it may meet or exercise any or all its powers at any other place. The Commission may establish such regional or State offices as it deems necessary to accomplish the purpose of this title.

Powers.

(g) The Commission shall have power—

(1) to cooperate with and, with their consent, utilize regional, State, local, and other agencies, both public and private, and individuals;

(2) to pay to witnesses whose depositions are taken or who are summoned before the Commission or any of its agents the same witness and mileage fees as are paid to witnesses in the courts of the United States;

(3) to furnish to persons subject to this title such technical assistance as they may request to further their compliance with this title or an order issued thereunder;

(4) upon the request of (i) any employer, whose employees or some of them, or (ii) any labor organization, whose members or some of them, refuse or threaten to refuse to cooperate in effectuating the provisions of this title, to assist in such effectuation by conciliation or such other remedial action as is provided by this title;

(5) to make such technical studies as are appropriate to effectuate the purposes and policies of this title and to make the results of such studies available to the public;

(6) to refer matters to the Attorney General with recommendations for intervention in a civil action brought by an aggrieved

party under section 706, or for the institution of a civil action by the Attorney General under section 707, and to advise, consult, and assist the Attorney General on such matters.

(h) Attorneys appointed under this section may, at the direction of the Commission, appear for and represent the Commission in any case in court.

(i) The Commission shall, in any of its educational or promotional activities, cooperate with other departments and agencies in the performance of such educational and promotional activities.

(j) All officers, agents, attorneys, and employees of the Commission shall be subject to the provisions of section 9 of the Act of August 2, 1939, as amended (the Hatch Act), notwithstanding any exemption contained in such section.

53 Stat. 1148;
64 Stat. 475.
5 USC 118i.

PREVENTION OF UNLAWFUL EMPLOYMENT PRACTICES

Sec. 706. (a) Whenever it is charged in writing under oath by a person claiming to be aggrieved, or a written charge has been filed by a member of the Commission where he has reasonable cause to believe a violation of this title has occurred (and such charge sets forth the facts upon which it is based) that an employer, employment agency, or labor organization has engaged in an unlawful employment practice, the Commission shall furnish such employer, employment agency, or labor organization (hereinafter referred to as the "respondent") with a copy of such charge and shall make an investigation of such charge, provided that such charge shall not be made public by the Commission. If the Commission shall determine, after such investigation, that there is reasonable cause to believe that the charge is true, the Commission shall endeavor to eliminate any such alleged unlawful employment practice by informal methods of conference, conciliation, and persuasion. Nothing said or done during and as a part of such endeavors may be made public by the Commission without the written consent of the parties, or used as evidence in a subsequent proceeding. Any officer or employee of the Commission, who shall make public in any manner whatever any information in violation of this subsection shall be deemed guilty of a misdemeanor and upon conviction thereof shall be fined not more than $1,000 or imprisoned not more than one year.

(b) In the case of an alleged unlawful employment practice occurring in a State, or political subdivision of a State, which has a State or local law prohibiting the unlawful employment practice alleged and establishing or authorizing a State or local authority to grant or seek relief from such practice or to institute criminal proceedings with respect thereto upon receiving notice thereof, no charge may be filed under subsection (a) by the person aggrieved before the expira-

Legal proceedings.

The Civil Rights Act □ 311

tion of sixty days after proceedings have been commenced under the State or local law, unless such proceedings have been earlier terminated, provided that such sixty-day period shall be extended to one hundred and twenty days during the first year after the effective date of such State or local law. If any requirement for the commencement of such proceedings is imposed by a State or local authority other than a requirement of the filing of a written and signed statement of the facts upon which the proceeding is based, the proceeding shall be deemed to have been commenced for the purposes of this subsection at the time such statement is sent by registered mail to the appropriate State or local authority.

Time requirements.

(c) In the case of any charge filed by a member of the Commission alleging an unlawful employment practice occurring in a State or political subdivision of a State, which has a State or local law prohibiting the practice alleged and establishing or authorizing a State or local authority to grant or seek relief from such practice or to institute criminal proceedings with respect thereto upon receiving notice thereof, the Commission shall, before taking any action with respect to such charge, notify the appropriate State or local officials and, upon request, afford them a reasonable time, but not less than sixty days (provided that such sixty-day period shall be extended to one hundred and twenty days during the first year after the effective day of such State or local law), unless a shorter period is requested, to act under such State or local law to remedy the practice alleged.

(d) A charge under subsection (a) shall be filed within ninety days after the alleged unlawful employment practice occurred, except that in the case of an unlawful employment practice with respect to which the person aggrieved has followed the procedure set out in subsection (b), such charge shall be filed by the person aggrieved within two hundred and ten days after the alleged unlawful employment practice occurred, or within thirty days after receiving notice that the State or local agency has terminated the proceedings under the State or local law, whichever is earlier, and a copy of such charge shall be filed by the Commission with the State or local agency.

(e) If within thirty days after a charge is filed with the Commission or within thirty days after expiration of any period of reference under subsection (c) (except that in either case such period may be extended to not more than sixty days upon a determination by the Commission that further efforts to secure voluntary compliance are warranted), the Commission has been unable to obtain voluntary compliance with this title, the Commission shall so notify the person aggrieved and a civil action may, within thirty days thereafter, be brought against the respondent named in the charge (1) by the person claiming to be aggrieved, or (2) if such charge was filed by a member of the Commission, by any person whom the charge alleges was aggrieved by the alleged unlawful employment practice. Upon application by the complainant and in such circumstances as the court may deem just, the court may appoint an attorney for such complainant and may authorize the commencement of the action without the payment of fees, costs, or security. Upon timely application, the court may, in its discretion, permit the Attorney General to intervene in such civil action if he certifies that the case is of general public importance. Upon request, the court may, in its discretion, stay further proceedings for not more than sixty days pending the termination of State or local proceedings described in subsection (b) or the efforts of the Commission to obtain voluntary compliance.

(f) Each United States district court and each United States court of a place subject to the jurisdiction of the United States shall have jurisdiction of actions brought under this title. Such an action may be brought in any judicial district in the State in which the unlawful employment practice is alleged to have been committed, in the judicial district in which the employment records relevant to such practice are maintained and administered, or in the judicial district in which the plaintiff would have worked but for the alleged unlawful employment practice, but if the respondent is not found within any such district, such an action may be brought within the judicial district in which the respondent has his principal office. For purposes of sections 1404 and 1406 of title 28 of the United States Code, the judicial district in which the respondent has his principal office shall in all cases be considered a district in which the action might have been brought.

(g) If the court finds that the respondent has intentionally engaged in or is intentionally engaging in an unlawful employment practice charged in the complaint, the court may enjoin the respondent from engaging in such unlawful employment practice, and order such affirmative action as may be appropriate, which may include reinstatement or hiring of employees, with or without back pay (payable by the employer, employment agency, or labor organization, as the case may be, responsible for the unlawful employment practice). Interim earnings or amounts earnable with reasonable diligence by the person or persons discriminated against shall operate to reduce the back pay otherwise allowable. No order of the court shall require the admission or reinstatement of an individual as a member of a union or the hiring, reinstatement, or promotion of an individual as an employee, or the payment to him of any back pay, if such individual was refused admission, suspended, or expelled or was refused employment or advancement or was suspended or discharged for any reason other than discrimination on account of race, color, religion, sex or national origin or in violation of section 704 (a).

Courts.
Jurisdiction.

62 Stat. 937.
74 Stat. 912;
76A Stat. 699.

(h) The provisions of the Act entitled "An Act to amend the Judicial Code and to define and limit the jurisdiction of courts sitting in equity, and for other purposes," approved March 23, 1932 (29 U.S.C. 101–115), shall not apply with respect to civil actions brought under this section.

(i) In any case in which an employer, employment agency, or labor organization fails to comply with an order of a court issued in a civil action brought under subsection (e), the Commission may commence proceedings to compel compliance with such order.

(j) Any civil action brought under subsection (e) and any proceedings brought under subsection (i) shall be subject to appeal as provided in sections 1291 and 1292, title 28, United States Code.

(k) In any action or proceeding under this title the court, in its discretion, may allow the prevailing party, other than the Commission or the United States, a reasonable attorney's fee as part of the costs, and the Commission and the United States shall be liable for costs the same as a private person.

SEC. 707. (a) Whenever the Attorney General has reasonable cause to believe that any person or group of persons is engaged in a pattern or practice of resistance to the full enjoyment of any of the rights secured by this title, and that the pattern or practice is of such a nature and is intended to deny the full exercise of the rights herein described, the Attorney General may bring a civil action in the appropriate district court of the United States by filing with it a complaint (1) signed by him (or in his absence the Acting Attorney General), (2) setting forth facts pertaining to such pattern or practice, and (3) requesting such relief, including an application for a permanent or temporary injunction, restraining order or other order against the person or persons responsible for such pattern or practice, as he deems necessary to insure the full enjoyment of the rights herein described.

(b) The district courts of the United States shall have and shall exercise jurisdiction of proceedings instituted pursuant to this section, and in any such proceeding the Attorney General may file with the clerk of such court a request that a court of three judges be convened to hear and determine the case. Such request by the Attorney General shall be accompanied by a certificate that, in his opinion, the case is of general public importance. A copy of the certificate and request for a three-judge court shall be immediately furnished by such clerk to the chief judge of the circuit (or in his absence, the presiding circuit judge of the circuit) in which the case is pending. Upon receipt of such request it shall be the duty of the chief judge of the circuit or the presiding circuit judge, as the case may be, to designate immediately three judges in such circuit, of whom at least one shall be a circuit judge and another of whom shall be a district judge of the court in which the proceeding was instituted, to hear and determine such case, and it shall be the duty of the judges so designated to assign the case for hearing at the earliest practicable date, to participate in the hearing and determination thereof, and to cause the case to be in every way expedited. An appeal from the final judgment of such court will lie to the Supreme Court.

In the event the Attorney General fails to file such a request in any such proceeding, it shall be the duty of the chief judge of the district (or in his absence, the acting chief judge) in which the case is pending immediately to designate a judge in such district to hear and determine the case. In the event that no judge in the district is available to hear and determine the case, the chief judge of the district, or the acting chief judge, as the case may be, shall certify this fact to the chief judge of the circuit (or in his absence, the acting chief judge) who shall then designate a district or circuit judge of the circuit to hear and determine the case.

It shall be the duty of the judge designated pursuant to this section to assign the case for hearing at the earliest practicable date and to cause the case to be in every way expedited.

EFFECT ON STATE LAWS

SEC. 708. Nothing in this title shall be deemed to exempt or relieve any person from any liability, duty, penalty, or punishment provided by any present or future law of any State or political subdivision of a State, other than any such law which purports to require or permit the doing of any act which would be an unlawful employment practice under this title.

INVESTIGATIONS, INSPECTIONS, RECORDS, STATE AGENCIES

SEC. 709. (a) In connection with any investigation of a charge filed under section 706, the Commission or its designated representative shall at all reasonable times have access to, for the purposes of examination, and the right to copy any evidence of any person being investigated or proceeded against that relates to unlawful employment practices covered by this title and is relevant to the charge under investigation.

(b) The Commission may cooperate with State and local agencies charged with the administration of State fair employment practices laws and, with the consent of such agencies, may for the purpose of carrying out its functions and duties under this title and within the limitation of funds appropriated specifically for such purpose, utilize the services of such agencies and their employees and, notwithstanding any other provision of law, may reimburse such agencies and their employees for services rendered to assist the Commission in carrying

Agreements, State and local agencies.

out this title. In furtherance of such cooperative efforts, the Commission may enter into written agreements with such State or local agencies and such agreements may include provisions under which the Commission shall refrain from processing a charge in any cases or class of cases specified in such agreements and under which no person may bring a civil action under section 706 in any cases or class of cases so specified, or under which the Commission shall relieve any person or class of persons in such State or locality from requirements imposed under this section. The Commission shall rescind any such agreement whenever it determines that the agreement no longer serves the interest of effective enforcement of this title.

Records.

(c) Except as provided in subsection (d), every employer, employment agency, and labor organization subject to this title shall (1) make and keep such records relevant to the determinations of whether unlawful employment practices have been or are being committed, (2) preserve such records for such periods, and (3) make such reports therefrom, as the Commission shall prescribe by regulation or order, after public hearing, as reasonable, necessary, or appropriate for the enforcement of this title or the regulations or orders thereunder. The Commission shall, by regulation, require each employer, labor organization, and joint labor-management committee subject to this title which controls an apprenticeship or other training program to maintain such records as are reasonably necessary to carry out the purpose of this title, including, but not limited to, a list of applicants who wish to participate in such program, including the chronological order in which such applications were received, and shall furnish to the Commission, upon request, a detailed description of the manner in which persons are selected to participate in the apprenticeship or other training program. Any employer, employment agency, labor organization, or joint labor-management committee which believes that the application to it of any regulation or order issued under this section would result in undue hardship may (1) apply to the Commission for an exemption from the application of such regulation or order, or (2) bring a civil action in the United States district court for the district where such records are kept. If the Commission or the court, as the case may be, finds that the application of the regulation or order to the employer, employment agency, or labor organization in question would impose an undue hardship, the Commission or the court, as the case may be, may grant appropriate relief.

Exceptions.

(d) The provisions of subsection (c) shall not apply to any employer, employment agency, labor organization, or joint labor-management committee with respect to matters occurring in any State or political subdivision thereof which has a fair employment practice law during any period in which such employer, employment agency, labor organization, or joint labor-management committee is subject to such law, except that the Commission may require such notations on records which such employer, employment agency, labor organization, or joint labor-management committee keeps or is required to keep as are necessary because of differences in coverage or methods of enforcement between the State or local law and the provisions of this title. Where an employer is required by Executive Order 10925, issued March 6, 1961, or by any other Executive order prescribing fair employment practices for Government contractors and subcontractors, or by rules or regulations issued thereunder, to file reports relating to his employment practices with any Federal agency or committee, and he is substantially in compliance with such requirements, the Commission shall not require him to file additional reports pursuant to subsection (c) of this section.

3 CFR, 1961 Supp., p. 86. 5 USC 631 note.

(e) It shall be unlawful for any officer or employee of the Commission to make public in any manner whatever any information obtained by the Commission pursuant to its authority under this section prior to the institution of any proceeding under this title involving such information. Any officer or employee of the Commission who shall make public in any manner whatever any information in violation of this subsection shall be guilty of a misdemeanor and upon conviction thereof, shall be fined not more than $1,000, or imprisoned not more than one year.

Prohibited disclosures.

INVESTIGATORY POWERS

SEC. 710. (a) For the purposes of any investigation of a charge filed under the authority contained in section 706, the Commission shall have authority to examine witnesses under oath and to require the production of documentary evidence relevant or material to the charge under investigation.

(b) If the respondent named in a charge filed under section 706 fails or refuses to comply with a demand of the Commission for permission to examine or to copy evidence in conformity with the peovisions of section 709 (a), or if any person required to comply with the provisions of section 709 (c) or (d) fails or refuses to do so, or if any person fails or refuses to comply with a demand by the Commission to give testimony under oath, the United States district court for the district in which such person is found, resides, or transacts business, shall, upon application of the Commission, have jurisdiction to issue to such person an order requiring him to comply with the provisions of section 709 (c) or (d) or to comply with the demand of the Commission, but the attendance of a witness may not be required outside the State where he is found, resides, or transacts business and the production of evidence may not be required outside the State where such evidence is kept.

(c) Within twenty days after the service upon any person charged under section 706 of a demand by the Commission for the production of documentary evidence or for permission to examine or to copy evidence in conformity with the provisions of section 709(a), such person may file in the district court of the United States for the judicial district in which he resides, is found, or transacts business, and serve upon the Commission a petition for an order of such court modifying or setting aside such demand. The time allowed for compliance with the demand in whole or in part as deemed proper and ordered by the court shall not run during the pendency of such petition in the court. Such petition shall specify each ground upon which the petitioner relies in seeking such relief, and may be based upon any failure of such demand to comply with the provisions of this title or with the limitations generally applicable to compulsory process or upon any constitutional or other legal right or privilege of such person. No objection which is not raised by such a petition may be urged in the defense to a proceeding initiated by the Commission under subsection (b) for enforcement of such a demand unless such proceeding is commenced by the Commission prior to the expiration of the twenty-day period, or unless the court determines that the defendant could not reasonably have been aware of the availability of such ground of objection.

(d) In any proceeding brought by the Commission under subsection (b), except as provided in subsection (c) of this section, the defendant may petition the court for an order modifying or setting aside the demand of the Commission.

NOTICES TO BE POSTED

SEC. 711. (a) Every employer, employment agency, and labor organization, as the case may be, shall post and keep posted in conspicuous places upon its premises where notices to employees, applicants for employment, and members are customarily posted a notice to be prepared or approved by the Commission setting forth excerpts from or, summaries of, the pertinent provisions of this title and information pertinent to the filing of a complaint.

(b) A willful violation of this section shall be punishable by a fine of not more than $100 for each separate offense.

VETERANS' PREFERENCE

SEC. 712. Nothing contained in this title shall be construed to repeal or modify any Federal, State, territorial, or local law creating special rights or preference for veterans.

SEC. 713. (a) The Commission shall have authority from time to time to issue, amend, or rescind suitable procedural regulations to carry out the provisions of this title. Regulations issued under this section shall be in conformity with the standards and limitations of the Administrative Procedure Act.

60 Stat. 237.
5 USC 1001
note.

(b) In any action or proceeding based on any alleged unlawful employment practice, no person shall be subject to any liability or punishment for or on account of (1) the commission by such person of an unlawful employment practice if he pleads and proves that the act or omission complained of was in good faith, in conformity with, and in reliance on any written interpretation or opinion of the Commission, or (2) the failure of such person to publish and file any information required by any provision of this title if he pleads and proves that he failed to publish and file such information in good faith, in conformity with the instructions of the Commission issued under this title regarding the filing of such information. Such a defense, if established, shall be a bar to the action or proceeding, notwithstanding that (A) after such act or omission, such interpretation or opinion is modified or rescinded or is determined by judicial authority to be invalid or of no legal effect, or (B) after publishing or filing the description and annual reports, such publication or filing is determined by judicial authority not to be in conformity with the requirements of this title.

FORCIBLY RESISTING THE COMMISSION OR ITS REPRESENTATIVES

SEC. 714. The provisions of section 111, title 18, United States Code, shall apply to officers, agents, and employees of the Commission in the performance of their official duties.

62 Stat. 688.

SPECIAL STUDY BY SECRETARY OF LABOR

SEC. 715. The Secretary of Labor shall make a full and complete study of the factors which might tend to result in discrimination in employment because of age and of the consequences of such discrimination on the economy and individuals affected. The Secretary of Labor shall make a report to the Congress not later than June 30, 1965, containing the results of such study and shall include in such report such recommendations for legislation to prevent arbitrary discrimination in employment because of age as he determines advisable.

Report to
Congress.

SEC. 716. (a) This title shall become effective one year after the date of its enactment.

(b) Notwithstanding subsection (a), sections of this title other than sections 703, 704, 706, and 707 shall become effective immediately·

Presidential conferences.

(c) The President shall, as soon as feasible after the enactment of this title, convene one or more conferences for the purpose of enabling the leaders of groups whose members will be affected by this title to become familiar with the rights afforded and obligations imposed by its provisions, and for the purpose of making plans which will result in the fair and effective administration of this title when all of its provisions become effective. The President shall invite the participa-

Membership.

tion in such conference or conferences of (1) the members of the President's Committee on Equal Employment Opportunity, (2) the members of the Commission on Civil Rights, (3) representatives of State and local agencies engaged in furthering equal employment opportunity, (4) representatives of private agencies engaged in furthering equal employment opportunity, and (5) representatives of employers, labor organizations, and employment agencies who will be subject to this title.

TITLE VIII—REGISTRATION AND VOTING STATISTICS

Survey.

SEC. 801. The Secretary of Commerce shall promptly conduct a survey to compile registration and voting statistics in such geographic areas as may be recommended by the Commission on Civil Rights. Such a survey and compilation shall, to the extent recommended by the Commission on Civil Rights, only include a count of persons of voting age by race, color, and national origin, and determination of the extent to which such persons are registered to vote, and have voted in any statewide primary or general election in which the Members of the United States House of Representatives are nominated or elected, since January 1, 1960. Such information shall also be collected and compiled in connection with the Nineteenth Decennial Census, and at such other times as the Congress may prescribe. The

68 Stat. 1013, 1022.
76 Stat. 922.
13 USC 9, 211-241.

provisions of section 9 and chapter 7 of title 13, United States Code, shall apply to any survey, collection, or compilation of registration and voting statistics carried out under this title: *Provided, however,* That no person shall be compelled to disclose his race, color, national origin, or questioned about his political party affiliation, how he voted, or the reasons therefore, nor shall any penalty be imposed for his failure or refusal to make such disclosure. Every person interrogated orally, by written survey or questionnaire or by any other means with respect to such information shall be fully advised with respect to his right to fail or refuse to furnish such information.

TITLE IX—INTERVENTION AND PROCEDURE AFTER REMOVAL IN CIVIL RIGHTS CASES

SEC. 901. Title 28 of the United States Code, section 1447 (d), is amended to read as follows:

63 Stat. 102.

"An order remanding a case to the State court from which it was removed is not reviewable on appeal or otherwise, except that an order remanding a case to the State court from which it was removed pursuant to section 1443 of this title shall be reviewable by appeal or otherwise."

62 Stat. 938.

SEC. 902. Whenever an action has been commenced in any court of the United States seeking relief from the denial of equal protection of the laws under the fourteenth amendment to the Constitution on account of race, color, religion, or national origin, the Attorney General for or in the name of the United States may intervene in such action upon timely application if the Attorney General certifies that the case is of general public importance. In such action the United States shall be entitled to the same relief as if it had instituted the action.

TITLE X—ESTABLISHMENT OF COMMUNITY RELATIONS SERVICE

SEC. 1001. (a) There is hereby established in and as a part of the Department of Commerce a Community Relations Service (hereinafter referred to as the "Service"), which shall be headed by a Director who shall be appointed by the President with the advice and consent of the Senate for a term of four years. The Director is authorized to appoint, subject to the civil service laws and regulations, such other personnel as may be necessary to enable the Service to carry out its functions and duties, and to fix their compensation in accordance with the Classification Act of 1949, as amended. The Director is further authorized to procure services as authorized by section 15 of the Act of August 2, 1946 (60 Stat. 810; 5 U.S.C. 55 (a)), but at rates for individuals not in excess of $75 per diem.

63 Stat. 954;
76 Stat. 843.
5 USC 1071
note.

(b) Section 106(a) of the Federal Executive Pay Act of 1956, as amended (5 U.S.C. 2205(a)), is further amended by adding the following clause thereto:

70 Stat. 737.

"(52) Director, Community Relations Service."

SEC. 1002. It shall be the function of the Service to provide assistance to communities and persons therein in resolving disputes, disagreements, or difficulties relating to discriminatory practices based on race,

Functions.

color, or national origin which impair the rights of persons in such communities under the Constitution or laws of the United States or which affect or may affect interstate commerce. The Service may offer its services in cases of such disputes, disagreements, or difficulties whenever, in its judgment, peaceful relations among the citizens of the community involved are threatened thereby, and it may offer its services either upon its own motion or upon the request of an appropriate State or local official or other interested person.

SEC. 1003. (a) The Service shall, whenever possible, in performing its functions, seek and utilize the cooperation of appropriate State or local, public, or private agencies.

(b) The activities of all officers and employees of the Service in providing conciliation assistance shall be conducted in confidence and without publicity, and the Service shall hold confidential any information acquired in the regular performance of its duties upon the understanding that it would be so held. No officer or employee of the Service shall engage in the performance of investigative or prosecuting functions of any department or agency in any litigation arising out of a dispute in which he acted on behalf of the Service. Any officer or other employee of the Service, who shall make public in any manner whatever any information in violation of this subsection, shail be deemed guilty of a misdemeanor and, upon conviction thereof, shall be fined not more than $1,000 or imprisoned not more than one year.

Report to
Congress. SEC. 1004. Subject to the provisions of sections 205 and 1003(b), the Director shall, on or before January 31 of each year, submit to the Congress a report of the activities of the Service during the preceding fiscal year.

TITLE XI—MISCELLANEOUS

Trial by jury. SEC. 1101. In any proceeding for criminal contempt arising under title II, III, IV, V, VI, or VII of this Act, the accused, upon demand therefor, shall be entitled to a trial by jury, which shall conform as near as may be to the practice in criminal cases. Upon conviction, the accused shall not be fined more than $1,000 or imprisoned for more than six months.

Exceptions. This section shall not apply to contempts committed in the presence of the court, or so near thereto as to obstruct the administration of justice, nor to the misbehavior, misconduct, or disobedience of any officer of the court in respect to writs, orders, or process of the court. No person shall be convicted of criminal contempt hereunder unless the act or omission constituting such contempt shall have been intentional, as required in other cases of criminal contempt.

Nor shall anything herein be construed to deprive courts of their power, by civil contempt proceedings, without a jury, to secure compliance with or to prevent obstruction of, as distinguished from punishment for violations of, any lawful writ, process, order, rule, decree, or command of the court in accordance with the prevailing usages of law and equity, including the power of detention.

SEC. 1102. No person should be put twice in jeopardy under the laws of the United States for the same act or omission. For this reason, an acquittal or conviction in a prosecution for a specific crime under the laws of the United States shall bar a proceeding for criminal contempt, which is based upon the same act-or omission and which arises under the provisions of this Act; and an acquittal or conviction in a proceeding for criminal contempt, which arises under the provisions of this Act, shall bar a prosecution for a specific crime under the laws of the United States based upon the same act or omission. **Double jeopardy.**

SEC. 1103. Nothing in this Act shall be construed to deny, impair, or otherwise affect any right or authority of the Attorney General or of the United States or any agency or officer thereof under existing law to institute or intervene in any action or proceeding. **Attorney General, etc., authority.**

SEC. 1104. Nothing contained in any title of this Act shall be construed as indicating an intent on the part of Congress to occupy the field in which any such title operates to the exclusion of State laws on the same subject matter, nor shall any provision of this Act be construed as invalidating any provision of State law unless such provision is inconsistent with any of the purposes of this Act, or any provision thereof. **States' authority.**

SEC. 1105. There are hereby authorized to be appropriated such sums as are necessary to carry out the provisions of this Act. **Appropriation.**

SEC. 1106. If any provision of this Act or the application thereof to any person or circumstances is held invalid, the remainder of the Act and the application of the provision to other persons not similarly situated or to other circumstances shall not be affected thereby. **Separability clause.**

Approved July 2, 1964.

DIGEST OF PRINCIPAL PROVISIONS

TITLE I—VOTING

Prohibits: Registrars' use of different standards for Negro and white voting applicants.

Registrars' disqualification of applicants because of unimportant mistakes on application forms.

Requires: Written literacy tests (except special arrangements may be made for the blind). An applicant may be given upon request a copy of the questions and his answers. A sixth-grade education is made a rebuttable presumption of literacy.

Permits: Either the Attorney General or State officials accused of violation of this title to request trial by a panel of three judges in a Federal Court.

TITLE II—PUBLIC ACCOMMODATIONS

Prohibits: Discrimination or refusal of services on the basis of race in hotels, motels, restaurants, gasoline stations, and places of amusement whose operations are in interstate commerce or whose discrimination "is supported by state action."

Permits: The Attorney General to bring suit in Federal Courts against persons or groups of persons found resisting the rights secured by this title.

TITLE III—PUBLIC FACILITIES

Requires: Negroes to be accorded equal access to, and treatment in, public-owned or operated facilities such as parks, stadiums and swimming pools.

Authorizes: The Attorney General to bring suit for enforcement of this title if private citizens are unable to sue effectively.

TITLE IV—PUBLIC SCHOOLS

Authorizes: Technical and financial aid to school districts to assist in desegregation.

Empowers: The Attorney General to sue for school desegregation if private citizens are themselves unable to sue effectively.

TITLE V—CIVIL RIGHTS COMMISSION

Extends: The Civil Rights Commission's tenure until January 31, 1968.

TITLE VI—FEDERAL AID

Provides: No person shall be subject to racial discrimination in any program receiving Federal aid.

Directs: Federal agencies to take steps against discrimination. State or local agencies resisting this title may—after hearings—be denied Federal funds.

IN CIVIL RIGHTS ACT

TITLE VII—EMPLOYMENT

Prohibits: Discrimination by employers or unions with 100 or more employees or members during the Act's first year. Within a four-year period the number is to be reduced to 25 or more employees or members.

Establishes: A Commission to investigate and mediate charges of discrimination in employment or employee organizations.

Empowers: The Attorney General to sue in instances where a "pattern or practice" of resistance to the provisions of this title has been found. The Attorney General may request that such suits be heard by a three-judge Federal court.

TITLE VIII—STATISTICS

Directs: The Census Bureau to compile statistics of registration and voting by race in areas of the country which the Civil Rights Commission designates. (This may be a means of enforcing the section of the 14th Amendment which provides that states discriminating in voting shall lose seats in the House of Representatives.)

TITLE IX—COURTS

Establishes: Right to appeal decisions of Federal District Courts which have sent cases back to State Courts although defendants have asked removal on the grounds that their civil rights would be jeopardized in the lower Courts. (Formerly, once a case was returned to a State Court the decision could not be appealed.)

Permits: Intervention by the Attorney General in suits filed by private persons who complain that they have been denied equal protection of the laws.

TITLE X—CONCILIATORY SERVICES

Establishes: A Community Relations Service in the Commerce Department. The Service will mediate racial disputes, and it may enter a troubled situation on invitation from local authorities or on its own motion.

TITLE XI—MISCELLANEOUS

Guarantees: Jury trial in criminal contempt cases growing out of any part of the Act except Title I.

Provides: That where state laws exist which afford protections similar to those in this Act they will remain in force. Existing powers of Federal officials will not be imposed.

Secures: The effectiveness of remaining sections of the Act in the event any specific portion is ruled invalid.

PRESIDENT LYNDON B. JOHNSON

JULY 2, 1964

(The President's televised address to the nation at the signing of the Civil Rights Bill of 1964)

THE SUMMATION

My fellow Americans:

I am about to sign into law the Civil Rights Act of 1964. I want to take this occasion to talk to you about what that law means to every American.

One hundred and eighty-eight years ago this week a small band of valiant men began a long struggle for freedom.

They pledged their lives, their fortunes and their sacred honor not only to found a nation but to forge an ideal of freedom, not only for political independence but for personal liberty, not only to eliminate foreign rule but to establish the rule of justice in the affairs of men.

That struggle was a turning point in our history.

Today in far corners of distant continents the ideals of those American patriots still shape the struggles of men who hunger for freedom.

This is a proud triumph. Yet those who founded our country knew that freedom would be secure only if each generation thought to renew and enlarge its meaning.

From the Minutemen at Concord to the soldiers in Vietnam, each generation has been equal to that trust.

Americans of every race and color have worked to build a nation of widening opportunities.

Now, our generation of Americans, has been called on to continue the unending search for justice within our own borders.

We believe that all men are created equal —yet many are denied equal treatment.

We believe that all men have certain un-alienable rights—yet many Americans do not enjoy those rights.

We believe that all men are entitled to the blessings of liberty—yet millions are being deprived of those blessings, not because of their own failures, but because of the color of their skin.

The reasons are deeply imbedded in history and tradition and the nature of man. We can understand without rancor or hatred how this all happened. But it cannot continue.

Our Constitution, the foundation of our Republic forbids it. The principles of our freedom forbid it. Morality forbids it. And the law I will sign . . . forbids it. That law is the product of months of the most careful debate and discussion. It was proposed more than one year ago by our late and beloved President, John F. Kennedy. It received the bipartisan support of more than two-thirds of the members of both the House and the Senate. An overwhelming majority of Republicans as well as Democrats voted for it.

It has received the thoughtful support of tens of thousands of civic and religious leaders in all parts of this nation, and it is supported by the great majority of the American people.

The purpose of this law is simple. It does not restrict the freedom of any American so long as he respects the rights of others. It does not give special treatment to any citizen. It does say the only limit to a man's hope for happiness and for the future of his children shall be his own ability.

It does say that those who are equal before God shall now also be equal in the polling booths, in the classrooms, in the factories and in hotels and restaurants, and movie theatres, and other places that provide service to the public.

I'm taking steps to implement the law under my constitutional obligation to take care that the laws are faithfully executed. . . .

. . . already today in a meeting of my Cabinet this afternoon I directed the agencies of this Government to fully discharge the new responsibilities imposed upon them by the law and to do it without delay and to keep me personally informed of their progress.

. . . I am asking appropriate officials to meet with representative groups to promote greater understanding of the law and to achieve a spirit of compliance.

We must not approach the observance and enforcement of this law in a vengeful spirit. Its purpose is not to punish. Its purpose is not to divide but to end divisions, divisions which have lasted all too long.

Its purpose is national not regional. Its purpose is to promote a more abiding commitment to freedom, a more constant pursuit of justice and a deeper respect for human dignity.

We will achieve these goals because most Americans are law-abiding citizens who want to do what is right. This is why the Civil Rights Act relies first on voluntary compliance, then on the efforts of local communities and states to secure the rights of citizens.

It provides for the national authority to step in only when others cannot or will not do the job.

This Civil Rights Act is a challenge to all of us to go to work in our communities and our states, in our homes and in our hearts to eliminate the last vestiges of injustice in our beloved country.

So, . . . I urge every public official, every religious leader, every business and professional man, every working man, every housewife—I urge every American to join in this effort to bring justice and hope to all our people and to bring peace to our land.

My fellow citizens, we have come now to a time of testing. We must not fail. . . .

...we have come now to a time of testing.

We must not fail...

AN APPRECIATORY NOTE

NAACP Legal Defense and Educational Fund Friend of the Court and Justice

The NAACP Legal Defense and Educational Fund was established on October 11, 1939, under the laws of New York State, as a membership corporation eligible to receive tax-deductible contributions from supporters. Though autonomous, strong emotional ties join it to the parent organization, the National Association for the Advancement of Colored People.

Over the years, it has been characterized as both the "world's biggest law firm" and as the "legal arm of the entire civil rights movement." It is a stalwart champion of civil liberties, ever alert against encroachments on the rule of law in America. Its corps of respected lawyers has combined legal wisdom with human resources to validate and invigorate democracy's promise of equal justice under law—justice that is truly blind to extraneous factors of color, creed or national origin. Through its efforts many vestiges of segregation have been stripped of legal sanction, and legal barriers to the Negro's enjoyment of first-class citizenship have been relentlessly assaulted.

Neither success in the courts nor popular acclaim has tempted the Legal Defense Fund to become complacent. Rather, each new victory has posed new and greater challenges. The Fund's 1963 Annual Report noted that:

> ". . . progress is always relative: victories one year become the basis for meeting even more urgent needs the next. The more we accomplish, the more crucial it becomes to expand our facilities; to extend our services . . . ; to open, as we have in the past, new frontiers in civil rights law."

The strategic battleground of civil rights has been the United States Supreme Court. According to Joseph O'Meara, Dean of the Notre Dame University Law School:

SUPPLEMENT

> "... the chief protector of liberty is the *will* of the people to be free. But the Supreme Court can encourage and strengthen that will, as in fact it has. The Court is the greatest institutional safeguard we possess."
>
> (from the Introduction to *The Supreme Court and Civil Liberties,* Osmond H. Fraenkel, second edition)

But the *will* of the people must be determined and presented to the Court. This is achieved by attorneys who either represent opposing parties in litigations or submit briefs *amici curiae*—friends of the Court. In cases involving fundamental rights of citizens, Negro Americans have no more effective voice than the NAACP Legal Defense Fund.

In its advocacy of Negro freedom and equality the NAACP Legal Defense and Educational Fund has emerged as a true friend of the Court and American justice as well.

The cases in this supplement—though not all were brought to the Supreme Court by the NAACP Legal Defense and Educational Fund—suggest that equal justice under law may someday be realized.

Resolute in its faith in American democracy and fearless in the face of adversity, the NAACP Legal Defense and Educational Fund has hastened the dawn of that new and better day.

A Digest of Significant Supreme Court Cases

1915 Guinn *v.* United States	1948 Sipuel *v.* University of Oklahoma
1917 Buchanan *v.* Warley	1948 Bob-Lo *v.* Michigan
1923 Moore *v.* Dempsey	1948 Lee *v.* Mississippi
1927 Nixon *v.* Herndon	1948 Hurd *v.* Hodge
1932 Powell *v.* Alabama	1948 Shelley *v.* Kraemer
1935 Norris *v.* Alabama	1950 Cassell *v.* Texas
1936 Brown *v.* Mississippi	1950 McLaurin *v.* Oklahoma State Regents
1938 Hale *v.* Kentucky	1950 Sweatt *v.* Painter
1938 Gaines *v.* Canada	1950 Henderson *v.* United States
1939 Lane *v.* Wilson	1954 Brown *v.* Board of Education
1940 Chambers *v.* Florida	1955 Reece *v.* Georgia
1944 Smith *v.* Allwright	1959 Fikes *v.* Alabama
1946 Morgan *v.* Virginia	1964 Heart of Atlanta *v.* United States
1947 Patton *v.* Mississippi	1964 Katzenbach *v.* McClung

Guinn v. United States

FRANK GUINN and J. J. Beal

v.

UNITED STATES

238 U.S. 347   Decided June 15, 1915

**Chief Justice White
delivered the opinion of the Court.**

Attorney Joseph W. Bailey
represented Frank Guinn and J. J. Beal.

Solicitor General John W. Davis
represented the United States.

THE ISSUE:
Registering to vote

SUMMARY OF THE FACTS:
In 1910 the Constitution of Oklahoma was amended, restricting the franchise by a *"Grandfather Clause"* which provided that no person could be registered unless he was able to read and write. However, the clause also granted exemption for an illiterate provided he had lived in some foreign country prior to January 1, 1866, or had been eligible to register prior to that date, or if his lineal ancestor was eligible as of that date. Prior to 1866, Negroes were not eligible to vote, so the law actually disfranchised Negroes.

State election officials were indicted for refusing Negroes the right to vote.

THE QUESTIONS:
"(1) Was the amendment to the Constitution of Oklahoma . . . valid?
"(2) Was that amendment void in so far as it attempted to debar from the right or privilege of voting for a qualified candidate for a member of Congress in Oklahoma unless they were able to read and write any section of the Constitution of Oklahoma, negro (*sic*) citizens of the United States who were otherwise qualified to vote . . . but who were not, and none of whose lineal ancestors was, entitled to vote under any form of government on January 1, 1866, or at any time prior thereto, because they were then slaves?"

THE FINDINGS:
"With these principles before us how can there be room for any serious dispute concerning the repugnancy of the standard based upon January 1, 1866 (a date which preceded the adoption of the 15th Amendment), if the suffrage provision fixing that standard is susceptible of the significance which the government attributes to it? Indeed, there seems no escape from the conclusion that to hold that there was even possibility for dispute on the subject would be but to declare that the 15th Amendment not only had not the self-executing power which it has been recognized to have from the beginning, but that its provisions were wholly inoperative because susceptible of being rendered inapplicable by mere forms of expression embodying no exercise of judgment and resting upon no discernible reason other than the purpose to disregard the prohibitions of the Amendment by creating a standard of voting which, on its face, was in substance but a revitalization of conditions which, when they prevailed in the past, had been destroyed by the self-operative force of the Amendment."

THE DECISION:
"We answer the first question, No, and the second question, Yes."

Buchanan v. Warley

CHARLES H. BUCHANAN, Plaintiff in Error

v.

WILLIAM WARLEY, Defendant in Error

245 U.S. 60   Decided November 5, 1917

Mr. Justice Day delivered the opinion of the Court.

Attorneys Clayton B. Blakey and Moorfield Storey represented Charles H. Buchanan.

Attorneys Pendleton Beckley and Stuart Chevalier represented William Warley.

THE ISSUE:

Infringement of property rights (Segregation Ordinances)

SUMMARY OF THE FACTS:

Buchanan, the white plaintiff in error, brought an action in the chancery branch of Jefferson circuit court of Kentucky for the specific performance of a contract for the sale of certain real estate in the city of Louisville. The purchaser, Warley, a Negro, was unable to occupy said real estate property as a residence since such occupancy violated an ordinance of the city of Louisville, approved May 11, 1914, prohibiting occupancy by a Negro of a residence in a white neighborhood. The ordinance thus made fulfillment of the contract impossible.

Buchanan then asserted that the Louisville ordinance was in conflict with the 14th Amendment of the United States, which provides equal protection of the laws, regardless of race, and that said ordinance was thus constitutionally invalid.

THE QUESTIONS:

(1) Was the Louisville ordinance prohibiting whites from living in Negro districts or Negroes from living in white districts valid?

(2) May the occupancy, and, necessarily, the purchase and sale of property of which occupancy is an incident, be inhibited by the states, or by one of its municipalities, solely because of the color of the proposed occupant of the premises?

(3) Can a white man be denied, consistently with due process of law, the right to dispose of his property to a purchaser by prohibiting the occupation of it for the sole reason that the purchaser is a person of color, intending to occupy the premises as a place of residence?

THE FINDINGS:

"The property here involved was sold by the plaintiff in error, a white man . . . to a colored man; . . . in the court below . . . plaintiff's right to have the contract enforced was denied solely because of the effect of the ordinance making it illegal for a colored person to occupy the lot sold. But for the ordinance the state courts would have enforced the contract, and the defendant would have been compelled to pay the purchase price and take a conveyance of the premises. . . .

"All persons within the jurisdiction of the United States shall have the same right in every state and territory to make and enforce contracts, to sue, be parties, give evidence, and to the full and equal benefit of all laws and proceedings for the security of persons and property as is enjoyed by white citizens, and shall be subject to like punishment, pains, penalties, taxes, licences and exactions of every kind. . . ."

THE DECISION:

"The right which the ordinance annulled was the civil right of a white man to dispose of his property if he saw fit to do so to a person of color, and of a colored person to make such a disposition to a white person. . . . We think that this attempt to prevent the alienation of the property in question to a person of color was not a legitimate exercise of the police power of the state, and is in direct violation of the fundamental law enacted in the 14th Amendment of the Constitution preventing state interference with the property rights except by due process of law. That being the case, the ordinance cannot stand. . . ."

Judgment of the Kentucky Court of Appeals reversed

Moore v. Dempsey

FRANK MOORE,
Ed. Hicks, J. E. Knox, et al., Appellants

v.

E. H. DEMPSEY,
Keeper of the Arkansas State Penitentiary, Appellee.

261 U.S. 86   Decided February 19, 1923

Mr. Justice Holmes
delivered the opinion of the Court.

Attorneys U. S. Bratton and Moorfield Storey
represented Moore et al.

Attorney Elbert Godwin represented Dempsey.

THE ISSUE:
Due Process of Law

SUMMARY OF THE FACTS:
On the night of September 30, 1919, a group of colored persons assembled in their church, were fired upon by a body of white men. In the ensuing melee, one white man was killed. As a result, many Negroes were hunted down and shot. In the following month, on October 1, 1919, one Clinton Lee, a white man was killed, for whose murder, five Negroes were convicted of murder in the first degree and sentenced to death by the court of the State of Arkansas. Petitioners denied any responsibility for, or involvement in, the circumstances leading to Clinton's death.

The case went to the docket. Negro witnesses used in the trial were whipped until they agreed to testify against the men.

The defendants were tried by a jury of white men in the presence of a mob which threatened lynching and mob violence if there were no convictions. Court-appointed counsel did not ask for a change of venue, called no witnesses and did not put the defendants on the stand. The entire trial of all the men

lasted three-quarters of an hour and in less than five minutes the jury brought in a verdict of guilty in the first degree.

THE QUESTION:
". . . that the proceedings in the state court, although a trial in form, were only a form, and that the appellants were hurried to conviction under the pressure of a mob, without any regard for their rights, and without according to them due process of law."

THE FINDINGS:
"**. . . if the case is that the whole proceeding is a mask, —that counsel, jury and judge were swept to the fatal end by an irresistible wave of public passion . . . neither perfection in the machinery for correction nor the possibility that the trial court and counsel saw no other way of avoiding an immediate outbreak of the mob can prevent this Court from securing to the petitioners their constitutional rights.**"

THE DECISION:
Order of the District Court of the United States for the Eastern District of Arkansas, reversed

Nixon v. Herndon

L. A. Nixon, Plaintiff in Error,

v.

C. C. HERNDON and Charles Porras,
Defendants in Error.

273 U.S. 536   Decided March 7, 1927

Mr. Justice Holmes delivered the opinion of the Court.

Attorneys Fred C. Knollenberg and
Arthur B. Spingarn represented Nixon.

Texas Attorney General Claude Pollard and
D. A. Simmons represented Herndon and Porras.

THE ISSUE:
The right to vote in primary elections

SUMMARY OF THE FACTS:
"This is an action against the judges of elections for refusing to permit the plaintiff to vote at a primary election in Texas. . . . The petition alleges that the plaintiff is a negro (*sic*), a citizen of the United States and of Texas and a resident of El Paso, and in every way qualified to vote . . . except that the statute . . . interferes with his right; that on July 26, 1924, a primary election was held at El Paso for the nomination of candidates for a senator and representatives in Congress and state and other officers, upon the Democratic ticket; that the plaintiff, being a member of the Democratic party, sought to vote, but was denied the right by defendants; that the denial was based upon a statute of Texas enacted in May, 1923, and designated article 3093a, by the words of which 'in no event shall a negro (*sic*) be eligible to participate in a Democratic party primary election held in the state of Texas. . . .' "

THE QUESTION:
Is the Texas statute denying Negroes the right to vote in primary elections valid?

THE FINDINGS:
". . . it seems to us hard to imagine a more direct and obvious infringement of the 14th [Amendment]. That Amendment, while it applies to all, was passed, as we know, with a special intent to protect the blacks from discrimination against them . . . the law in the states shall be the same for the black as for the white; that all persons, whether colored or white, shall stand equal before the laws of the states, and, in regard to the colored race, for whose protection the Amendment was primarily designed, that no discrimination shall be made against them by law because of their color. . . .

"The statute of Texas, in the teeth of the prohibitions referred to, assumes to forbid negroes (sic) to take part in a primary election the importance of which we have indicated, discriminating against them by distinction of color alone. States may do a good deal of classifying that it is difficult to believe rational, but there are limits, and it is too clear for extended argument that color cannot be made the basis of a statutory classification affecting the right set up in this case."

THE DECISION:
Judgment of the District Court of Texas for the Western District reversed

Powell v. Alabama

POWELL et al., HAYWOOD PATTERSON,
and CHARLEY WEEMS, Petitioners

v.

STATE OF ALABAMA, Respondent

287 U.S. 45   Decided November 7, 1932

**Mr. Justice Sutherland
delivered the opinion of the Court.**

Attorney Walter H. Pollak, of New York City,
represented Powell et al.

Attorney Thomas E. Knight, Jr., of Montgomery,
Alabama, represented the State of Alabama.

THE ISSUE:

Due Process of Law re right of accused to counsel

SUMMARY OF THE FACTS:

"The petitioners, . . . are negroes (*sic*) charged with the crime of rape, committed upon the persons of two white girls. The crime is said to have been committed on March 25, 1931. The indictment was returned in a state court of first instance on March 31, and the record recites that on the same day the defendants were arraigned and entered pleas of not guilty. There is a further recital to the effect that upon the arraignment they were represented by counsel. But no counsel had been employed . . . and the record does not disclose when, or under what circumstances an appointment of counsel was made, or who was appointed. . . . Each of the three trials was completed within a single day. . . . The juries found defendants guilty and imposed the death penalty upon all. The trial court overruled motions for new trials and sentenced the defendants in accordance with the verdicts. The judgment was affirmed by the state supreme court. Chief Justice Anderson thought the defendants had not been accorded a fair trial and strongly dissented."

The case came to the Supreme Court of Alabama on writ of certiorari.

THE QUESTION:

". . . whether the defendants were in substance denied the right of counsel, and if so, whether such denial infringes the due process clause of the Fourteenth Amendment."

THE FINDINGS:

"In this court the judgments are assailed upon the grounds that the defendants, and each of them, were denied due process of law and the equal protection of the laws, in contravention of the Fourteenth Amendment, specifically as follows: (1) They were not given a fair, impartial, and deliberate trial; (2) they were denied the right of counsel, with the accustomed incidents of consultation and opportunity of preparation for trial; and (3) they were tried before juries from which qualified members of their own race were systematically excluded. . . .

"The only one of the assignments which we shall consider is the second, in respect of the denial of counsel; . . . It thus will be seen that until the very morning of the trial no lawyer had been named or definitely designated to represent the defendants. Prior to that time, the trial judge had 'appointed all the members of the bar' for the limited 'purpose of arraigning the defendants.' Whether they would represent the defendants thereafter, if no counsel appeared in their behalf, was a matter of speculation only, or, as the judge indicated, of mere anticipation on the part of the court. Such a designation, even if made for all purposes, would, in our opinion, have fallen far short of meeting, in any proper sense, a requirement for the appointment of counsel. . . ."

THE DECISION:

"The United States by statute and every state in the Union by express provision of law, or by the determination of its courts, make it the duty of the trial judge, where the accused is unable to employ counsel, to appoint counsel for him. In most states the rule applies broadly to all criminal prosecutions, in others it is limited to the more serious crimes, and in a very limited number, to capital cases. A rule adopted with such unanimous accord reflects, if it does not establish the inherent right to have counsel appointed at least in cases like the present, and lends convincing support to the conclusion we have reached as to the fundamental nature of that right.

"The judgments must be reversed and the cause remanded for further proceedings not inconsistent with this opinion.

"Judgments reversed."

Norris v. Alabama

CLARENCE NORRIS, Petitioner

v.

STATE OF ALABAMA

294 U.S. 587–599   Decided April 1, 1935

Chief Justice Hughes
delivered the opinion of the Court.

Attorney Samuel S. Liebowitz, of New York City,
represented the petitioner.

Thomas E. Knight, Jr., Attorney General of Alabama,
represented the respondent.

THE ISSUE:

Equal protection—exclusion of Negroes from grand juries and petit juries

SUMMARY OF THE FACTS:

Clarence Norris was one of nine Negroes indicted in March 1931, in Jackson County, Alabama, for rape. On being brought to trial in that county, eight were convicted. The Supreme Court of Alabama reversed the conviction of one and affirmed that of seven, including Norris. The U. S. Supreme Court reversed the judgments on the ground that the defendants had been denied due process in that the trial court had failed in the light of circumstances disclosed, and of the inability of the defendants at that time to obtain counsel.

After the remand, a motion for change of venue was granted and the cases were transferred to Morgan County. Norris was brought to trial in November 1933. A motion was made to quash the indictment on the ground of exclusion of negroes (*sic*) from juries in Jackson County where the indictment was found. A motion was also made to quash the trial venire in Morgan County on the ground of exclusion of negroes (*sic*) from juries in that county. The State joined issue on this charge and after hearing the evidence, the trial judge denied both motions. The trial then proceeded resulting in the conviction of Norris who was sentenced to death. On appeal, the Supreme Court of the State decided the federal question raised by Norris and affirmed the judgment. The U. S. Supreme Court granted a writ of certiorari.

THE QUESTION:

Does exclusion of Negroes from jury service deny defendants of that race equal protection of the law contrary to the Fourteenth Amendment?

THE FINDINGS:

"We think that this evidence failed to rebut the strong prima facie case which the defendant had made. That showing as to the long-continued exclusion of negroes (sic) from jury service, and as to the many negroes (sic) qualified for that service, could not be met by mere generalities. If, in the presence of such testimony as defendant adduced, the mere general assertions by officials of their performance of duty were to be accepted as an adequate justification for the complete exclusion of negroes (sic) from jury service, the constitutional provision—adopted with special reference to their protection—would be but a vain and illusory requirement. The general attitude of the jury commissioner is shown by the following extract from his testimony: 'I do not know of any negro (sic) in Morgan County over twenty-one and under sixty-five who is generally reputed to be honest and intelligent and who is esteemed in the community for his integrity, good character and sound judgment, who is not an habitual drunkard, who isn't afflicted with a permanent disease or physical weakness which would render him unfit to discharge the duties of a juror, and who can read English, and who has never been convicted of a crime involving moral turpitude.' In the light of the testimony given by defendant's witnesses, we find it impossible to accept such a sweeping characterization of the lack of qualifications of negroes (sic) in Morgan County. It is so sweeping, and so contrary to the evidence as to the many qualified negroes (sic), that it destroys the intended effect of the commissioner's testimony.

"In Neal v. Delaware. . . . decided over fifty years ago, this Court observed that it was a 'violent presumption,' . . . that the uniform exclusion of negroes (sic) from juries, during a period of many years, was solely because, in the judgment of the officers charged with the selection of grand and petit jurors, . . . 'the black race in Delaware were utterly disqualified by want of intelligence, experience, or moral integrity, to sit on juries.' Such a presumption at the present time would be no less violent with respect to the exclusion of the negroes (sic) of Morgan County. And, upon the proof contained in the record now before us, a conclusion that their continuous and total exclusion from juries was because there were none possessing the requisite qualifications, cannot be sustained."

THE DECISION:

"We are concerned only with the federal question which we have discussed, and in view of the denial of the federal right suitably asserted, the judgment must be reversed and the cause remanded for further proceedings not inconsistent with this opinion.

Reversed."

Brown v. Mississippi

ED BROWN, Henry Shields,
and Yank Ellington, Petitioners

v.

STATE OF MISSISSIPPI, Respondent

297 U.S. 278   Decided February 17, 1936

**Chief Justice Hughes
delivered the opinion of the Court.**

Attorney Earl Brewer of Jackson, Mississippi,
represented Brown, Shields and Ellington.

Attorneys William Dow Conn, Jr., and
William H. Maynard, both of Jackson, Mississippi,
represented the State of Mississippi.

THE ISSUE:
Due Process in General

SUMMARY OF THE FACTS:

Three Negro farm laborers, Ed Brown, Henry Shields and Yank Ellington, were indicted for murder of one Raymond Stewart on April 4, 1934. His death occurred on March 30, 1934. The three men were arraigned and pleaded their innocence. Counsel was appointed by the Court to defend them. They were found guilty and sentenced to death.

The only evidence against them was confessions obtained by force and physical torture. When they were arrested, a deputy sheriff and others seized Ellington; when he denied the crime, the deputy hanged him by a rope to a tree; when let down, he was tied to the tree and severely beaten. He was permitted to return home when he still refused to "confess." A day or two thereafter, a deputy returned to his home, arrested him and departed with the prisoner towards the jail in an adjoining county. On the way, after a severe beating, Ellington confessed. Confessions were obtained from Brown and Shields under similar circumstances. This confession was used at the trial. The marks of the rope around Ellington's neck were plainly visible at the time of the trial.

At the trial, "This deputy was put on the stand by the state . . . and admitted the whippings. . . . Two others who had participated in these whippings were introduced and admitted it—not a single witness was introduced who denied it. The facts are not only undisputed, they are admitted, and admitted to have been done by officers of the state, in conjunction with other participants, and all this was definitely well known to everybody connected with the trial, and during the trial, including the state's prosecuting attorney and the trial judge presiding."*

The conviction was affirmed by the Supreme Court of Mississippi. The case came to the Court on Writ of Certiorari.

THE QUESTION:

"The question in this case is whether convictions, which rest solely upon confessions shown to have been extorted by officers of the State by brutality and violence, are consistent with the due process of law required by the Fourteenth Amendment of the Constitution of the United States."

THE FINDINGS:

"The rack and the torture chamber may not be substituted for the witness stand. The State may not permit an accused to be hurried to conviction under mob domination—where the whole proceeding is but a mask. . . .

"In the instant case, the trial court was fully advised by the undisputed evidence of the way in which the confessions had been procured. The trial court knew that there was no other evidence upon which conviction and sentence could be based. Yet it proceeded to permit conviction and to pronounce sentence. The conviction and sentence were void for want of the essential elements of due process, and the proceeding thus vitiated could be challenged in any appropriate manner. . . . It was challenged before the Supreme Court of the State by the express invocation of the Fourteenth Amendment. That court entertained the challenge, considered the federal question thus presented, but declined to enforce petitioners' constitutional right. The court thus denied a federal right fully established and specially set up and claimed. . . ."

THE DECISION:

". . . judgment [of the Mississippi Supreme Court] must be reversed."

* [Quoted by Mr. Justice Holmes from the dissenting opinion of Mississippi Supreme Court Judge Griffith.]

Hale v. Kentucky

JOE HALE, Petitioner

v.

COMMONWEALTH OF KENTUCKY, Respondent

303 U.S. 613   Decided April 11, 1938

Per Curiam Decision.

Attorneys Charles H. Houston and Leon A. Ransom,
both of Washington, D.C., represented Hale.

Attorney A. E. Funk, of Frankfort, Kentucky,
represented the Commonwealth of Kentucky.

THE ISSUE:

Systematic exclusion of Negroes from jury service

SUMMARY OF THE FACTS:

Joe Hale was indicted in 1936 for murder in Mc-Cracken County, Kentucky. He moved to set aside the indictment on the ground that the jury commissioners had excluded Negroes from the jury lists. He showed that there were 8,000 Negroes in the total population of 48,000 for McCracken County and that there were 700 Negroes of a total 6,700 persons qualified for jury service. He also offered evidence that there has never been a Negro on the juries of that county from 1906 to 1936. He alleged that this demonstrated "a long, continued, unvarying and wholesale exclusion of negroes (*sic*) from jury service in this County on account of their race and color." This practice was alleged to have been "systematic and arbitrary."

Hale was convicted and sentenced to die. His conviction was affirmed by the Court of Appeals of Kentucky.

"On petition for rehearing, the motion (to set aside the indictment) which had been omitted from the record was brought to the attention of the Court of Appeals. Rehearing was denied. On petition to this Court for certiorari the parties stipulated that the motion to set aside the indictment as filed by petitioner in the trial court might be read and considered as a proper part of the record. Certiorari was granted, . . ."

THE QUESTION:

Is the equal protection of the laws denied to defendants, whenever by an action of a State, all persons of a particular race are excluded from jury service solely because of their race or color?

THE FINDINGS:

"On argument at this bar, the Attorney General of the State expressly disclaimed reliance upon the omission from the original record on appeal of the motion to set aside the indictment, as the fact of the motion had been brought to the attention of the Court of Appeals upon the application for rehearing, and conceded that, if the facts set forth in the affidavits submitted upon that motion were sufficient to show a denial of constitutional right, the judgment should be reversed.

"We are of the opinion that the affidavits, which by the stipulation of the State were to be taken as proof, and were uncontroverted, sufficed to show a systematic and arbitrary exclusion of negroes (sic) from the jury lists solely because of their race or color, constituting a denial of the equal protection of the laws guaranteed to petitioner by the Fourteenth Amendment. . . ."

THE DECISION:

"The judgment [of the Court of Appeals of the Commonwealth of Kentucky] is reversed, and the cause is remanded for further proceedings not inconsistent with this opinion. It is so ordered.

"Reversed and remanded."

Gaines v. Canada

STATE OF MISSOURI ex rel. GAINES

v.

CANADA et al.

305 U.S. 337   Decided December 12, 1938

**Chief Justice Hughes
delivered the opinion of the Court.**

Attorneys Charles H. Houston and S. R. Redmond
represented the State of Missouri
at the relation of Lloyd Gaines.

Attorneys William S. Hogsett and Fred L. Williams
represented S. W. Canada et al.

THE ISSUE:

Admission of Negro to state-endowed educational facility

SUMMARY OF THE FACTS:

In August of 1935, Lloyd Gaines, a Negro citizen of Missouri, graduated with a B.A. from Lincoln University, an institution which, although maintained by the state for the higher education of Negroes, nonetheless had no law school. Gaines then filed application for admission to the law school of the University of Missouri. He was advised by the registrar of that institution to communicate with the president of Lincoln University for the purpose of receiving state aid to pursue his law studies at any of a number of appropriate schools outside the state of Missouri.

Gaines was subsequently advised to apply to the State Superintendent of Schools for aid under the Missouri statute governing such aid. It was admitted at the time that his "work and credits at the Lincoln University would qualify him for admission to the School of Law of the University of Missouri if he were found otherwise eligible." He was refused admission upon the grounds that it was "contrary to the constitution, laws and public policy of the State to admit a negro (*sic*) as a student in the University of Missouri." At the time of this refusal, it was brought out that there were schools of law in connection with state universities in four adjacent states, Kansas, Nebraska, Iowa and Illinois, where non-resident Negroes were admitted.

Gaines nonetheless asserted that refusal of the law school of the University of Missouri to admit him constituted a denial by the state of the equal protection of the laws and a violation of the Fourteenth Amendment of the Constitution. He brought action for mandamus to compel the curators of the University to admit him, but his suit was denied both by the Circuit Court and the Supreme Court of the State of Missouri.

The case was then referred to the Supreme Court on writ of certiorari.

THE QUESTION:

Is the exclusion of a Negro from a state-endowed educational facility solely on the grounds of race a denial of his rights to equal protection guaranteed in the Fourteenth Amendment of the Constitution and hence void?

THE FINDINGS:

". . . **the fact remains that instruction in law for negroes (sic) is not now afforded by the State, either at Lincoln University or elsewhere within the State, and that the State excludes negroes (sic) from the advantages of the law school it has established at the University of Missouri.**

"**It is manifest that this discrimination, if not relieved by the provisions we shall presently discuss, would constitute a denial of equal protection. . . .**

"**The basic consideration is not as to what sort of opportunities, other States provide, or whether they are as good as those in Missouri, but as to what opportunities Missouri itself furnishes to white students and denies to negroes (sic) solely upon the ground of color. The admissibility of laws separating the races in the enjoyment of privileges afforded by the State rests wholly upon the equality of the privileges which the laws give to the separated groups within the State. The question here is not of a duty of the State to supply legal training, or of the quality of the training which it does supply, but of its duty when it provides such training to furnish it to the residents of the State upon the basis of an equality of right. By the operation of the laws of Missouri a privilege has been created for white law students which is denied to negroes (sic) by reason of their race. . . .**

". . . **petitioner's right was a personal one. It was as an individual that he was entitled to the equal protection of the laws, and the State was bound to furnish him within its borders facilities for legal education substantially equal to those which the State there afforded for persons of the white race, whether or not other negroes (sic) sought the same opportunity.**"

THE DECISION:

"The judgment of the Supreme Court of Missouri is reversed and the cause is remanded for further proceedings not inconsistent with this opinion."

Lane v. Wilson

I. W. LANE, Plaintiff

v.

WILSON et al.

307 U.S. 268   Decided May 22, 1939

Mr. Justice Frankfurter
delivered the opinion of the Court.
Attorneys Charles A. Chandler and
James M. Nabrit, Jr., represented I. W. Lane.
Attorneys Joseph C. Stone and Charles G. Watts,
represented Jess Wilson et al.

THE ISSUE:
Registering to vote

SUMMARY OF THE FACTS:
Pursuant to the invalidation of the *"Grandfather Clause"* in 1915, a special session of the Oklahoma legislature enacted a new scheme for registration as a prerequisite to voting. New registration requirements affected all eligible citizens who had not voted in the general election of 1914. Such persons had to apply for registration between April 30, 1916 and May 11, 1916, unless some legitimate cause (illness or absence from the country) could be shown to exempt them from this obligation.

On October 17, 1934, I. W. Lane, a Negro citizen of Oklahoma, attempted to register for a general election, but was turned away by county election officials on the basis of the 1916 state statute. He had been qualified for registration in 1916 but did not then get on the registration list. The evidence presented at the trial did not conclusively indicate whether he had in fact tried to register in 1916 and what, if any, circumstances prevented him from doing so.

Inasmuch as Lane failed to be registered in 1916, he thereby permanently lost the right to register and hence the right to vote. He then contended that the Oklahoma statute governing this right was unconstitutional and brought suit before both the Circuit Court of Appeals for the Tenth Circuit and the United States District Court for the Eastern District of Oklahoma. In both cases, the Oklahoma Court ruled in favor of the defendant.

The case was then referred to the Supreme Court on a writ of certiorari.

THE QUESTION:
Is the Oklahoma statute disqualifying Negro voter registrants constitutional?

THE FINDINGS:
"We . . . cannot avoid passing in the merits of plaintiff's constitutional claims. The reach of the Fifteenth Amendment against contrivances by a state to thwart equality in the enjoyment of the right to vote by citizens of the United States regardless of race or color, has been amply expounded by prior decisions. . . .

"The Amendment nullifies sophisticated as well as simple-minded modes of discrimination. It hits onerous procedural requirements which effectively handicap exercise of the franchise by the colored race although the abstract right to vote may remain unrestricted as to race. When in Guinn v. United States, supra, the Oklahoma "Grandfather Clause" was found violative of the Fifteenth Amendment, Oklahoma was confronted with the serious task of devising a new registration system consonant with her own political ideas but also consistent with the Federal Constitution. We are compelled to conclude, however reluctantly, that the legislation of 1916 partakes too much of the infirmity of the "Grandfather Clause" to be able to survive.

". . . the narrow basis of the supplemental registration, the very brief normal period of relief for the persons and purposes in question, the practical difficulties, of which the record in this case gives glimpses, inevitable in the administration of such strict registration provisions, leave no escape from the conclusion that the means chosen as substitutes . . . were themselves invalid under the Fifteenth Amendment. They operated unfairly against the very class on whose behalf the protection of the Constitution was here successfully invoked."

THE DECISION:
"The judgment of the Circuit Court of Appeals must, therefore be reversed and the cause remanded to the District Court for further proceedings in accordance with this opinion."

Chambers v. Florida

CHAMBERS et al., Petitioners

v.

STATE OF FLORIDA, Respondent

309 U. S. 227   Decided February 12, 1940

Mr. Justice Black delivered the opinion of the Court.

Attorneys Leon A. Ransom and S. D. McGill
represented the petitioners.

Attorney Tyrus A. Norwood represented the respondent.

THE ISSUE:

Due process in obtaining a confession

SUMMARY OF THE FACTS:

About nine o'clock on Saturday, May 13, 1933, Robert Darcy, an elderly white man, was robbed and murdered in Pompano, Florida. Between half an hour and one hour later Charlie Davis, a petitioner, was arrested, and within 24 hours, 25 to 40 Negroes living in the community, were arrested without warrants and confined to jail in Fort Lauderdale.

About 11 p.m. on Monday, May 15, the prisoners were taken to the Dade County jail in Miami because, as the sheriff testified, he felt the possibility of mob violence and "wanted to give protection to every prisoner . . ."

Prisoners were subjected to questioning and cross questioning from Sunday, May 14, to Saturday, May 20 (with the exception that several suspects were in the Dade County jail for more than one night).

From the afternoon of Saturday, May 20, to sunrise on the 21st, the petitioners underwent persistent and repeated questioning. The Supreme Court of Florida stated that questioning "was in progress several days and all night before confessions were secured."

Sometime early on Sunday morning May 21, Woodward, one of the petitioners, "broke." The State's Attorney was called, but dissatisfied with the confession, he left the jail requesting that he be called when the sheriff got "something worthwhile." After one week's denial of all guilt, the petitioners "broke." The State's Attorney was again called in, and his questions and the petitioners' answers were recorded stenographically.

From the time of arrest to the time of sentencing, petitioners were never, either in jail or in court, wholly removed from the custody and control of those whose persistent pressure brought about the confessions.

The case to court on writ of certiorari.

THE QUESTION:

Are convictions which rest solely upon confessions shown to have been extorted by officers of the state by violence and duress consistent with the due process of law required by the Fourteenth Amendment of the United States Constitution?

THE FINDINGS:

"We are not impressed by the argument that law enforcement methods such as those under review are necessary to uphold our laws. The Constitution proscribes such lawless means irrespective of the end. And this argument flouts the basic principle that all people must stand on an equality before the bar of justice in every American court. . . .

"Due process of law, preserved for all by our Constitution, commands that no such practice as that disclosed by this record shall send any accused to his death. No higher duty, no more solemn responsibility, rests upon this Court, than that of translating into living law and maintaining this constitutional shield deliberately planned and inscribed for the benefit of every human being subject to our Constitution—of whatever race, creed or persuasion."

THE DECISION:

"The Supreme Court of Florida was in error, and its judgment is

"Reversed."

Smith v. Allwright

LONNIE E. SMITH, Petitioner

v.

S. E. ALLWRIGHT, Election Judge, et al., Respondents

321 U.S. 649   Decided April 3, 1944

Mr. Justice Reed delivered the opinion of the Court.

Attorneys Thurgood Marshall and William H. Hastie
represented the petitioner.

No appearance for respondents.

THE ISSUE:
The right to vote in primary elections

SUMMARY OF THE FACTS:
Suit was first filed by Lonnie E. Smith in the District Court of the United States for the Southern District of Texas against the election judges, Allwright et al. The District Court denied the relief sought by Smith, and the Circuit Court affirmed the action of the District Court. The Supreme Court then granted permission for writ of certiorari.

"This writ of certiorari brings here for review a claim for damages in the sum of $5,000 on the part of petitioner, a Negro citizen of the 48th precinct of Harris County, Texas, for the refusal of respondents, election and associate election judges respectively of that precinct, to give petitioner a ballot or to permit him to cast a ballot in the primary election of July 27, 1940, for the nomination of Democratic candidates for the United States Senate and House of Representatives, and Governor and other state officers. The refusal is alleged to have been solely because of the race and color of the proposed voter."

THE QUESTION:
Does the Texas statute forbidding a Negro citizen to vote in a primary election conflict with the Fifteenth Amendment to the U.S. Constitution?

THE FINDINGS:
"It may now be taken as a postulate that the right to vote in such a primary for the nomination of candidates without discrimination by the State, like the right to vote in a general election, is a right secured by the Constitution. . . .

"The United States is a constitutional democracy. Its organic law grants to all citizens a right to participate in the choice of elected officials without restriction by any state because of race. This grant to the people of the opportunity for choice is not to be nullified by a state through casting its electoral process in a form which permits a private organization to practice racial discrimination in the election. Constitutional rights would be of little value if they could thus be indirectly denied. . . .

"Here we are applying, . . . the well established principle of the Fifteenth Amendment, forbidding the abridgement by a state of a citizen's right to vote."

THE DECISION:
Judgment of the United States Circuit Court of Appeals for the Fifth Circuit is reversed.

Morgan v. Virginia

IRENE MORGAN, Appellant

v.

COMMONWEALTH OF VIRGINIA, Appellee

328 U.S. 373   Decided June 3, 1946

Mr. Justice Reed delivered the opinion of the Court.

Attorneys Thurgood Marshall of New York City
and William H. Hastie of Washington, D.C.
represented Irene Morgan.

Abram P. Staples, Attorney General of Virginia,
represented the Commonwealth.

THE ISSUE:

Segregation of the races on public vehicles in interstate travel

SUMMARY OF THE FACTS:

The appellant, Irene Morgan, a Negro, was traveling on a Greyhound bus from Gloucester County, Virginia, through the District of Columbia, to Baltimore, Maryland, the destination of the bus. There were other passengers, both white and colored. On her refusal to accede to a request of the driver to move to a back seat, which was partly occupied by other colored passengers, so as to permit her vacated seat to be used by white passengers, a warrant was obtained and appellant was arrested, tried and convicted of a violation of the Virginia Code.

The Virginia Supreme Court of Appeals upheld the conviction.

THE QUESTION:

Does the Virginia statute compelling racial segregation of interstate passengers in vehicles traveling interstate conflict with the provisions of the interstate commerce clause of the Constitution?

THE FINDINGS:

"**The interferences to interstate commerce which arise from state regulation of racial association on interstate vehicles has long been recognized. Such regulation hampers freedom of choice in selecting accommodations. . . .**

"**As no state law can reach beyond its own border nor bar transportation of passengers across its boundaries, diverse seating requirements for the races in interstate journeys result. As there is no federal act dealing with the separation of races in interstate transportation, we must decide the validity of this Virginia statute on the challenge that it interferes with commerce, as a matter of balance between the exercise of the local police power and the need for national uniformity in the regulations for interstate travel. It seems clear to us that seating arrangements for the different races in interstate motor travel require a single, uniform rule to promote and protect national travel. Consequently, we hold the Virginia Statute in controversy invalid.**"

THE DECISION:

Judgment of the Supreme Court of Appeals of Virginia is reversed.

Patton v. Mississippi

EDDIE (BUSTER) PATTON, Petitioner

v.

STATE OF MISSISSIPPI, Respondent

332 U.S. 463–469   Decided December 8, 1947

Mr. Justice Black delivered the opinion of the Court.

Attorney Thurgood Marshall, of New York City, represented Patton.

Attorney George H. Ethridge, of Jackson, Mississippi, represented the State of Mississippi.

THE ISSUE:

Systematic exclusion from jury service on account of race

SUMMARY OF THE FACTS:

Eddie (Buster) Patton, a Negro, was indicted, tried and convicted for murder of a white man in the Circuit Court of Lauderdale County, Mississippi. At his trial, and on appeal, he alleged that all qualified Negroes were systematically excluded from jury service in that County solely because of race. The exclusion of Negroes from jury service in Lauderdale County was accomplished pursuant to the statutes of Mississippi which limited jury service to qualified voters. The state maintained that there were few qualified Negro voters in the County, accounting for the absence of Negroes from service on juries, and that such procedure was valid under prior decisions of the Supreme Court.

THE QUESTION:

Is the equal protection of the laws denied to defendants, and are they deprived of due process of law contrary to the Fourteenth Amendment to the United States Constitution, whenever by an action of a State, all persons of a particular race are excluded from jury service solely because of their race or color?

THE FINDINGS:

"Sixty-seven years ago this Court held that state exclusion of Negroes from grand and petit juries solely because of their race denied Negro defendants in criminal cases the equal protection of the laws required by the Fourteenth Amendment. A long and unbroken line of our decisions since then has re-iterated that principle, regardless of whether the discrimination was embodied in statute or was apparent from the administrative practices of state jury selection officials, and regardless of whether the system for depriving defendants of their rights was 'ingenious or ingenuous.' . . .

"We hold that the State wholly failed to meet the very strong evidence of purposeful racial discrimination made out by the petitioner upon the uncontradicted showing that for thirty years or more no Negro had served as a juror in the criminal courts of Lauderdale County. When a jury selection plan, whatever it is, operates in such way as always to result in the complete and long-continued exclusion of any representative at all from a large group of Negroes, or any other racial group, indictments and verdicts returned against them by juries thus selected cannot stand. . . ."

THE DECISION:

"The judgment of the Mississippi Supreme Court is reversed and the case is remanded for proceedings not inconsistent with this opinion."

Sipuel v. University of Oklahoma

ADA LOIS SIPUEL, Petitioner,

v.

BOARD OF REGENTS OF THE UNIVERSITY OF OKLAHOMA et al., Respondents

332 U.S. 631   Decided January 12, 1948

Per Curiam Decision.

Attorneys Thurgood Marshall, of New York City, and Amos Hall, of Tulsa, Oklahoma, represented Ada Sipuel.

Attorneys Fred Hansen, of Oklahoma City, Oklahoma, and Maurice H. Merrill, of Norman, Oklahoma, represented the University of Oklahoma.

THE ISSUE:
Equal Education

SUMMARY OF THE FACTS:
"On January 14, 1946 the petitioner [Ada Lois Sipuel], a Negro, concededly qualified to receive the professional legal education offered by the State, applied for admission to the School of Law of the University of Oklahoma, the only institution for legal education supported and maintained by the taxpayers of the State of Oklahoma. Petitioner's application for admission was denied, solely because of her color.

"Petitioner then made application for a writ of mandamus in the District Court of Cleveland County, Oklahoma. The writ of mandamus was refused, and the Supreme Court of the State of Oklahoma affirmed the judgment of the District Court."

The case was on writ of certiorari.

THE QUESTION:
Does the equal protection clause of the Fourteenth Amendment require that the state provide legal education for Negroes as soon as it does for applicants of any other group?

THE FINDINGS:
"The petitioner is entitled to secure legal education afforded by a state institution. To this time it has been denied her although during the same period many white applicants have been afforded legal education by the State. The State must provide it for her in conformity with the equal protection clause of the Fourteenth Amendment and provide it as soon as it does for applicants of any other group. . . ."

THE DECISION:
"The judgment of the Supreme Court of Oklahoma is reversed and the cause is remanded to that court for proceedings not inconsistent with this opinion.

"The mandate shall issue forthwith."

Bob-Lo v. *Michigan*

BOB-LO EXCURSION COMPANY, Appellant,

v.

PEOPLE OF THE STATE OF MICHIGAN, Appellee.

333 U.S. 28–45   Decided February 2, 1948

Mr. Justice Rutledge
delivered the opinion of the Court.

Attorney Wilson W. Mills, of Detroit, Michigan,
represented Bob-Lo Excursion Company.

Attorney Edmund E. Shepherd, of Lansing, Michigan,
represented the People of the State of Michigan.

THE ISSUE:
Accommodation to persons aboard carriers engaged in foreign commerce

SUMMARY OF THE FACTS:
The operator of vessels used to transport patrons between Detroit, Michigan, and an amusement park owned by it on Bois Blanc ("Bob-Lo"), an island located in Canadian waters, was convicted in a state court of violating the Michigan Civil Rights Act by refusing passage to Sarah Elizabeth Ray, a Negro. In June of 1945, she and some 40 other white girls, all members of a class conducted at the Commerce High School, had planned an excursion to Bois Blanc for June 21. Upon her arrival aboard ship, Miss Ray was told that she could not go along on account of her color. She was asked to leave the ship and did so.

THE QUESTIONS:
(1) Is the Michigan Civil Rights Act with respect to "full and equal accommodations" aboard vessels engaged in interstate commerce valid?
(2) Does the commerce clause forbid the application of the Michigan statute?

THE FINDINGS:
Accepting the State Court's compulsion that the vessel was a "public conveyance" within the statutory requirement of "full and equal accommodations, advantages, facilities and privileges of . . . public conveyances on land and water" six members of the court, concurring in an opinion clause did not forbid the application of the Michigan Statute in the present instance. Mr. Justice Douglas, with the concurrence of Mr. Justice Black, who also joined in the opinion of the court, thought the case was controlled by the principle that a state may lawfully require a carrier in interstate and foreign commerce to render equal service to all. Mr. Justice Jackson and Mr. Justice Vinson dissented on the ground that the matter was properly one for Federal regulation and so was outside the sphere of state action.

THE DECISION:
To question 1, the answer is "Yes;" to question 2, "No." Judgment [of the Michigan Supreme Court] is affirmed in favor of the State of Michigan.

Lee v. Mississippi

ALBERT LEE, Petitioner

v.

STATE OF MISSISSIPPI, Respondent

332 U.S. 742   Decided January 19, 1948

**Mr. Justice Murphy
delivered the opinion of the Court.**

Attorney Forrest B. Jackson,
of Jackson, Mississippi, represented Lee.

Attorney Richard Olney Arrington, of Jackson,
Mississippi, represented the State of Mississippi.

THE ISSUE:

Procedure under the due process clause of the Fourteenth Amendment

SUMMARY OF THE FACTS:

Petitioner, a 17-year-old Negro, was convicted by a grand jury in Mississippi on a charge of assault "with intent to ravish a female," and sentenced to 18 years imprisonment. As prime evidence, the state offered the testimony as to an alleged oral confession obtained from Lee. Objection was made by Lee's lawyers that the confession had been secured as the result of physical threats and violence toward the petitioner, several hours prior to the confession.

A judgment against Lee was subsequently returned, and upon appeal to the Mississippi Supreme Court, the conviction was reaffirmed.

THE QUESTION:

Is a confession obtained under duress or by coercion valid?

THE FINDINGS:

"The sole concern now is with the validity of the conviction based upon the use of the oral confession.

"The due process clause of the Fourteenth Amendment invalidates a state court conviction grounded in whole or in part upon a confession which is the product of other than reasoned and voluntary choice."

THE DECISION:

Judgment reversed and remanded to the Mississippi Supreme Court.

Hurd v. Hodge

JAMES M. HURD and Mary I. Hurd, Petitioners,

v.

FREDERIC E. HODGE, Lena A. Murray Hodge,
Pasquale DeRita, et al. (No. 290)

334 U.S. 24–36   Decided May 3, 1948

Chief Justice Vinson
delivered the opinion of the Court.

Attorneys Charles H. Houston and Phineas Indritz
represented the petitioners.

Attorneys Henry Gilligan and James A. Crooks
represented the respondents.

THE ISSUE:

Restrictive covenants regarding sale of lots to Negroes

SUMMARY OF THE FACTS:

A white real estate dealer sold three restricted properties to Negro petitioners who subsequently occupied them. Suits to enforce terms of the restrictive agreement were instituted in the Federal District Court by whites owning other property on the block subject to the terms of the covenants.

The case came to court on writ of certiorari.

THE QUESTION:

Is the court enforcement of the restrictive covenant valid under the due process clause of the Fifth Amendment?

THE FINDINGS:

". . . the explicit language employed by Congress to effectuate its purposes, leaves no doubt that judicial enforcement of the restrictive covenants by the courts of the District of Columbia is prohibited by the Civil Rights Act. That statute, by its terms, requires that all citizens of the United States shall have the same right 'as is enjoyed by white citizens *** to inherit, purchase, lease, sell, hold, and convey real and personal property.' That the Negro petitioners have been denied that right by virtue of the action of the federal courts of the District is clear. . . . White sellers, one of whom is a petitioner here, have been enjoined from selling the properties to any Negro or colored person. Under such circumstances, to suggest that the Negro petitioners have been accorded the same rights as white citizens to purchase, hold, and convey real property is to reject the plain meaning of language. We hold that the action of the District Court directed against the Negro purchasers and the white sellers denies rights intended by Congress to be protected by the Civil Rights Act and that, consequently, the action cannot stand. . . .

". . . enforcement of restrictive covenants in these cases is judicial action contrary to the public policy of the United States, and as such should be corrected by this Court in the exercise of its supervisory powers over the Courts of the District of Columbia."

THE DECISION:

"We cannot presume that the public policy of the United States manifests a lesser concern for the protection of such basic rights against discriminatory action of federal courts than against such action taken by the courts of the States."

Judgment reversed.

Shelley v. Kraemer

J. D. SHELLEY, Ethel Lee Shelley, His Wife,
Petitioners

v.

LOUIS KRAEMER and Fern W. Kraemer, His Wife,
Respondents

334 U.S. 1–23   Decided May 3, 1948

**Chief Justice Vinson
delivered the opinion of the Court.**

Attorneys George L. Vaughn and Herman Willer
both of St. Louis, Missouri,
represented J. D. and Ethel Shelley.

Attorney Gerald L. Seegers of St. Louis, Missouri,
represented Louis and Fern Kraemer.

THE ISSUE:
Restrictive covenants

SUMMARY OF THE FACTS:
On February 16, 1911, 30 out of a total of 39 owners of property in the city of St. Louis, Missouri signed an agreement, which was subsequently recorded, providing in part:

" '. . . the said property . . . shall [not] be . . . occupied by any person not of the Caucasian race, it being intended hereby to restrict the use of said property for said period of time [50 years] against the occupancy as owners or tenants of any portion of said property for resident or other purpose by people of the Negro or Mongolian race.' "

At the time this action was brought, four of the premises were occupied by Negroes, and had been so occupied for periods ranging from 23 to 63 years. A fifth parcel had been occupied by Negroes until a year before this suit was instituted.

On August 11, 1945, pursuant to a contract of sale, petitioners Shelley, who are Negroes, received a warranty deed to the parcel in question. [The] petitioners had no actual knowledge of the restrictive agreement at the time of purchase. On October 9, 1945, the owners brought suit in the Circuit Court of St. Louis seeking to divest petitioners Shelley of title to the land. The trial court denied the request, but the Supreme Court of Missouri reversed the decision and directed the trial court to divest petitioners Shelley of title to the land they were already occupying.

Case to the Court on writ of certiorari.

THE QUESTION:
The validity of court enforcement of private agreements, generally described as restrictive covenants, which have as their purpose the exclusion of persons of designated race or color from the ownership or occupancy of real property.

THE FINDINGS:
"It cannot be doubted that among the civil rights intended to be protected from discriminatory state action by the Fourteenth Amendment are the rights to acquire, enjoy, own and dispose of property. Equality in the enjoyment of property rights was regarded by the framers of that Amendment as an essential pre-condition to the realization of other basic civil rights and liberties which the Amendment was intended to guarantee . . .

"Here the particular patterns of discrimination and the areas in which the restrictions are to operate, are determined, in the first instance, by the terms of agreements among private individuals. Participation of the State consists in the enforcement of the restrictions. . . . The crucial issue with which we are here confronted is whether this distinction removes these cases from the operation of the prohibitory provisions of the Fourteenth Amendment. . . .

"That the action of state courts and of judicial officers in their official capacities is to be regarded as action of the State within the meaning of the Fourteenth Amendment, is a proposition which has long been established by decisions of this Court. . . .

[Previous cases demonstrate] ". . . the early recognition by this Court that state action in violation of the Amendment's provisions is equally repugnant to the constitutional commands whether directed by state statute or taken by a judicial officer in the absence of statute. . . .

"The short of the matter is that from the time of the adoption of the Fourteenth Amendment until the present, it has been the consistent ruling of this Court that the action of the States to which the Amendment has reference, includes action of state courts and state judicial officials. . . .

"We hold that in granting judicial enforcement of the restrictive agreements in these cases, the States have denied petitioners the equal protection of the laws and that, therefore, the action of the state courts cannot stand."

THE DECISION:
"For the reasons stated, the judgment of the Supreme Court of Missouri . . . must be reversed."

Cassell v. Texas

LEE CASSELL, Petitioner

v.

STATE OF TEXAS, Respondent

339 U.S. 282   Decided January 5, 1950

Mr. Justice Reed delivered the opinion of the Court.

Attorney Chris Dixie, of Houston, Texas,
represented Cassell.

Attorney Joe R. Greenhill, of Houston, Texas,
represented the State of Texas.

THE ISSUE:

Racial discrimination in the selection of juries

SUMMARY OF THE FACTS:

In a motion to quash the indictment which resulted in his conviction for murder in the Criminal District Court No. 2, Dallas County, Texas, Lee Cassell asserted that he "suffered unconstitutional discrimination through the selection of white men only for the grand jury that indicted him;" and that "the Dallas County grand-jury commissioners for 21 consecutive lists had consistently limited Negroes selected for grand-jury service to not more than one on each grand-jury. . . ."

In explaining the fact that no Negroes appeared on this grand-jury list, the commissioners said that they knew none available who qualified; at the same time they said they chose jurymen only from those people with whom they were personally acquainted.

The Texas Criminal Court of Appeals denied the motion to quash the indictment and upheld Cassell's conviction of murder.

THE QUESTION:

"Review was sought in this case to determine whether there had been a violation by Texas of petitioner's federal constitutional right to a fair and impartial grand jury."

THE FINDINGS:

"We have recently written why proportional representation of races on a jury is not a constitutional requisite. . . . Succinctly stated, our reason was that the Constitution requires only a fair jury selected without regard to race. . . .

"It may be assumed that in ordinary activities in Dallas County, acquaintanceship between the races is not on a sufficiently familiar basis to give . . . jury commissioners an opportunity to know the qualifications for grand jury service of many members of another race. An individual's qualifications for grand-jury service, however, are not hard to ascertain, and with no evidence to the contrary, we must assume that a large proportion of the Negroes of Dallas County met the statutory requirements for jury service. When the commissioners were appointed as judicial administrative officials, it was their duty to familiarize themselves fairly with the qualifications of the eligible jurors of the county without regard to race and color. They did not do so here, and the result has been racial discrimination. . . .

"Discrimination may be proved in other ways than by evidence of long continued unexplained absence of Negroes from many panels. The statements of the jury commissioners that they chose only whom they knew, and that they knew no eligible Negroes in an area where Negroes made up so large a proportion of the population, prove the intentional exclusion that is discrimination in violation of petitioner's constitutional rights."

THE DECISION:

"The judgment of the Court of Criminal Appeals of Texas is reversed."

McLaurin v. Oklahoma State Regents

G. W. McLAURIN, Appellant,

v.

OKLAHOMA STATE REGENTS FOR HIGHER EDUCATION,
BOARD OF REGENTS
OF UNIVERSITY OF OKLAHOMA, et al., Appellees

339 U.S. 637–642   Decided June 5, 1950

**Chief Justice Vinson
delivered the opinion of the Court.**

Attorneys Amos T. Hall, of Tulsa, Oklahoma, and
Robert L. Carter, of New York City,
represented McLaurin.

Attorney Fred Hansen, of Oklahoma City, Oklahoma,
represented Oklahoma State Regents et al.

THE ISSUE:
Equal Education

SUMMARY OF THE FACTS:
G. W. McLaurin, a Negro citizen of Oklahoma, after having been admitted to graduate instruction in the state University of Oklahoma, was given different treatment from other students, by requiring him to occupy a seat in a row in the classroom specified for colored students, at a designated table in the library, and at a special table in the cafeteria.

Motion by the appellant to remove these conditions was denied by the District Court which held that such treatment did not violate the provisions of the Fourteenth Amendment.

THE QUESTION:
". . . whether a state may, after admitting a student to graduate instruction in its state university, afford him different treatment from other students solely because of his race."

THE FINDINGS:
"We conclude that the conditions under which this appellant is required to receive his education deprive him of his personal and present right to the equal protection of the laws. . . . We hold that under these circumstances, the Fourteenth Amendment precludes differences in treatment by the state based upon race."

THE DECISION:
"Appellant, having been admitted to a state-supported graduate school, must receive the same treatment at the hands of the state as students of other races.

"The judgment is reversed."

Sweatt v. Painter

HEMAN MARION SWEATT, Petitioner,

v.

THEOPHILUS SHICKEL PAINTER, et al., respondents.

339 U.S. 629   Decided June 5, 1950

**Chief Justice Vinson
delivered the opinion of the Court.**

Attorneys W. J. Durham and Thurgood Marshall
represented Heman Marion Sweatt.

Price Daniel, Attorney General of Texas, and
Attorney Joe R. Greenhill represented Painter et al.

THE ISSUE:

Admission of Negro to state-endowed educational facilities

SUMMARY OF THE FACTS:

Petitioner Sweatt, a Negro, filed an application for admission to the University of Texas Law School for the February, 1946 term. His application was rejected. Sweatt thereupon brought suit against the appropriate school officials to compel his admission. At that time, there was no law school in Texas which admitted Negroes.

The State Court recognized that the action of the State in denying Sweatt equal opportunity deprived him of protection afforded by the Fourteenth Amendment. The court, however, continued the case for six months until such time as substantially equal facilities were erected for Negroes. In December of 1946, the court then denied the request on the grounds that the authorized university officials had adopted an order calling for the opening of a law school for Negroes the following February.

Sweatt, however, refused to register in the new school. The Texas Court of Civil Appeals ordered the case returned for further proceedings in the trial court. A hearing was then held on the issue of the equality of facilities at the newly established school as compared with the University of Texas Law School. The hearing resulted in the decision that the facilities were "substantially equivalent" to those granted white students at the first Texas School.

The Texas Supreme Court subsequently denied the Sweatt petition, but the U.S. Supreme Court opened a new trial to decide on the "manifest importance" of the constitutional issues.

THE QUESTION:

". . . does the Equal Protection Clause of the Fourteenth Amendment limit the power of a state to distinguish between students of different races in professional and graduate education in a state university?"

THE FINDINGS:

"In terms of number of the faculty, variety of courses and opportunity for specialization, size of the student body, scope of the library, availability of law review and similar activities, the University of Texas Law School is superior. What is more important, the University of Texas Law School possesses to a far greater degree those qualities which are incapable of objective measurement but which make for greatness in a law school. Such qualities, to name but a few, include reputation of the faculty, experience of the administration, position and influence of the alumni, standing in the community, traditions and prestige. It is difficult to believe that one who had a free choice between these law schools would consider the question close. . . .

". . . petitioner may claim his full constitutional right: legal education equivalent to that offered by the State to students of other races. Such education is not available to him in a separate law school as offered by the State."

THE DECISION:

"We hold that the Equal Protection Clause of the Fourteenth Amendment requires that petitioner be admitted to the University of Texas Law School."

Judgment of the Supreme Court of Texas is reversed.

Henderson v. United States

ELMER W. HENDERSON, Appellant,

v.

UNITED STATES OF AMERICA, Interstate Commerce
Commission, and Southern Railway Company, Appellee.

339 U.S. 816–826   Decided June 5, 1950

Mr. Justice Burton delivered the opinion of the Court.

Attorneys Belford V. Lawson, Jr., of
Washington, D.C., and Jawn Sandifer,
of New York City, represented Henderson.

Attorney General McGrath, Solicitor General Perlman,
and Attorneys Allen Crenshaw and Charles Clark,
all of Washington, D.C.,
represented the United States of America.

THE ISSUE:

Discrimination by the Southern Railway Company
against Negro passengers

SUMMARY OF THE FACTS:

On May 17, 1942, appellant Elmer W. Henderson,
a Negro passenger on an interstate train traveling
from Washington, D.C., en route to Birmingham,
Alabama, was denied dining service, although at least
one seat at the tables reserved for Negroes was unoccupied, the other seats at the tables being taken by
white passengers.

In October 1942, Henderson filed a complaint
with the Interstate Commerce Commission alleging
that the foregoing conduct violated #3 (1) of the
Interstate Commerce Act, whereupon, the United
States District Court of Maryland held that the railroad's general practice was discriminatory. Accordingly, the company modified its rules, which now
provided for the reservation of 10 tables, exclusively
and unconditionally, for white passengers, and one
table in the same way for Negroes, and called for a
curtain or partition between that table and the others.

The new regulations met with the Court's approval, and judgment was made in favor of the
Southern Railway Company.

THE QUESTION:

". . . whether the rules and practices of the Southern Railway Company, . . . violate #3 (1) of the
Interstate Commerce Act."

THE FINDINGS:

"**The right to be free from unreasonable discriminations belongs . . . to each particular person. Where
a dining car is available to passengers holding tickets
entitling them to use it, each such passenger is
equally entitled to its facilities in accordance with
reasonable regulations. The denial of dining service
to any such passenger by the rules before us subjects
him to a prohibited disadvantage. Under the rules,
only four Negro passengers may be served at one
time and then only at the table reserved for Negroes.
Other Negroes who present themselves are compelled
to await a vacancy at that table, although there may
be vacancies elsewhere in the diner. The railroad
thus refuses to extend to those passengers the use of
its existing and unoccupied facilities. The rules impose a like deprivation upon white passengers whenever more than 40 of them seek to be served at the
same time and the table for Negroes is vacant. . . .**

"**As was pointed out in Mitchell v. United States
. . . the comparative volume of traffic cannot justify the denial of a fundamental right of equality of
treatment, a right specifically safeguarded by the
provisions of the Interstate Commerce Act.**"

THE DECISION:

"The judgment of the District Court [of Maryland] is
reversed and the cause is remanded to that court
with directions to set aside the order of the Interstate
Commission which dismissed the original complaint
and to remand the case to that Commission for further proceedings in conformity with this opinion."

Brown

v.

Board of Education

OLIVER BROWN et al., Appellants,

v.

BOARD OF EDUCATION OF TOPEKA,
Shawnee County, Kansas, et al.*

347 U.S. 483   Decided May 17, 1954

**Chief Justice Warren
delivered the opinion of the Court.**

Attorneys Robert L. Carter, Thurgood Marshall,
Spottswood W. Robinson III, Louis L. Redding and
Jack Greenberg; Attorney General of Delaware,
H. Albert Young, and Assistant Attorney General J. Lee Rankin
argued the cases for the appellants.

Assistant Attorney General of Kansas, Paul E. Wilson;
Attorneys John W. Davis and T. Justin Moore, and
Attorney General of Virginia, J. Lindsay Almond, Jr.
argued the cases for the respondents.

*This ruling embraced three other cases:
Briggs v. Elliott; Davis v. School Board,
Prince Edward County, and Gebhart v. Belton.

THE ISSUE:
Equal Education

SUMMARY OF THE FACTS:

"In each of the cases, minors of the Negro race, through their legal representatives, seek the aid of the courts in obtaining admission to the public schools of their community on a nonsegregated basis. In each instance, they had been denied admission to schools attended by white children under [state] laws requiring or permitting segregation according to race. This segregation was alleged to deprive the plaintiffs of the equal protection of the laws under the Fourteenth Amendment. In each of the cases, other than the Delaware case, a three-judge federal district court denied relief to the plaintiffs on the so-called 'separate but equal' doctrine announced by this Court in *Plessy* v. *Ferguson*, . . .

"The plaintiffs contend that segregated public schools are not 'equal' and cannot be made 'equal,' and that hence they are deprived of the equal protection of the laws."

The case came to court on writ of certiorari.

THE QUESTION:

". . . does segregation of children in public schools solely on the basis of race, even though the physical facilities and other 'tangible' factors may be equal, deprive the children of the minority group of equal educational opportunities?"

THE FINDINGS:

"Here, unlike Sweatt v. Painter, there are findings . . . that the Negro and white schools involved have been equalized, or are being equalized, with respect to buildings, curricula, qualifications and salaries of teachers, and other 'tangible' factors. Our decision, therefore, cannot turn on merely a comparison of these tangible factors in the Negro and white schools involved in each of the cases. We must look instead to the effect of segregation itself on public education. . . .

"Segregation of white and colored children in public schools has a detrimental effect upon the colored children. The impact is greater when it has the sanction of law; for the policy of separating the races is usually interpreted as denoting the inferiority of the negro (sic) group. A sense of inferiority affects the motivation of a child to learn segregation with the sanction of law, therefore, has a tendency to [retard] (sic) the educational and mental development of Negro children and to deprive them of some of the benefits they would receive in a racial[ly] (sic) integrated school system. . . .

"We conclude that in the field of public education the doctrine of 'separate but equal' has no place. . . . Therefore, we hold that the plaintiffs and others similarly situated for whom the actions have been brought are, by reason of the segregation complained of, deprived of the equal protection of the laws guaranteed by the Fourteenth Amendment. This disposition makes unnecessary any discussion whether such segregation also violates the Due Process Clause of the Fourteenth Amendment."

THE DECISION:

"Because these are class actions, because of the wide applicability of this decision . . . the cases will be restored to the docket . . . [for] further arguments [by the parties]. . . . The Attorneys General of the states requiring or permitting segregation in public education will also be permitted to appear as amici curiae upon request to do so by September 15, 1954, and submission of briefs by October 1, 1954.

"It is so ordered."

Amos Reece v. Georgia

AMOS REECE, Petitioner,

v.

STATE OF GEORGIA

350 U.S. 85   Decided December 5, 1955

Mr. Justice Clark delivered the opinion of the Court.

Attorney Daniel Duke of Atlanta, Georgia,
represented Amos Reece.

Attorneys Eugene Cook, Robert Hall and
E. Freeman Leverett of Atlanta, Georgia,
represented the State of Georgia.

THE ISSUE:

Due process of law re effective assistance of counsel

SUMMARY OF THE FACTS:

Amos Reece, a Negro, was convicted of the rape of a white woman in Cobb County, Georgia. He had been arrested on October 20, 1953, and held in the county jail until his indictment three days later. On October 24, the day after his indictment, two local attorneys were appointed to defend him. On October 30, before his arraignment, Reece moved to quash the indictment on the ground that Negroes had been systematically excluded from service on the grand jury. The motion was overruled after a hearing. On the same day, he was tried, convicted and sentenced to be electrocuted. The Supreme Court of Georgia held that the motion to quash was properly denied because, by Georgia practice, objections to a grand jury must be made before the indictment is returned. The case was dismissed on another ground, not pertinent here, and remanded for a new trial.

Before his second trial Reece filed a special plea which alleged systematic exclusion of Negroes from the jury commission, the grand jury which indicted him and the petit jury about to be put upon him. The plea also stated that Reece had neither knowledge of the grand jury nor the benefit of counsel before his indictment. The state's demurrer to this plea was sustained, and Reece was tried again and sentenced to be electrocuted.

THE QUESTION:

Does the petitioner's motion support his claim of a denial of due process?

THE FINDINGS:

"We need not decide whether, with the assistance of counsel, he [Reece] would have had an opportunity to raise his objection during the two days he was in jail before indictment. But it is utterly unrealistic to say that he had such opportunity when counsel was not provided for him until the day after he was indicted. In Powell v. State of Alabama . . . this Court held that the assignment of counsel in a state prosecution at such time and under such circumstances as to preclude the giving of effective aid in the preparation and trial of a capital case is a denial of due process of law. The effective assistance of counsel in such a case is a constitutional requirement of due process which no member of the Union may disregard. Georgia should have considered Reece's motion to quash on its merits.

"In view of this disposition, it is not necessary that we consider other issues first raised by Reece in his plea in abatement at the second trial."

THE DECISION:

"The judgment is reversed and the cause is remanded for further proceedings not inconsistent with this opinion."

Fikes v. Alabama

WILLIAM EARL FIKES, Petitioner,

v.

STATE OF ALABAMA

353 U.S. 191   Decided January 14, 1957

**Chief Justice Warren
delivered the opinion of the Court.**

Attorney Jack Greenberg represented Fikes.

Attorney Robert Straub
represented the State of Alabama.

THE ISSUE:
Due process relative to óbtaining a confession under pressure

SUMMARY OF THE FACTS:
William Fikes, an illiterate Negro and citizen of Selma, Alabama, was convicted of burglary with intent to commit rape. After repeated sessions of questioning, lasting a week, Fikes confessed. During that time his father and a lawyer were prevented from seeing him. During the second week of incarceration, another confession was made. Fikes' conviction and death sentence were affirmed by the Supreme Court of Alabama.

THE QUESTION:
Do confessions obtained during extended incarceration constitute a denial of due process?

THE FINDINGS:
"There is no evidence of physical brutality, and particular elements that were present in other cases in which this Court ruled that a confession was coerced do not appear here. On the other hand, some of the elements in this case were not present in all of the prior cases. . . . The totality of the circumstances that preceded the confessions in this case goes beyond the allowable limits. The use of the confessions secured in this setting was a denial of due process.

". . . We hold that the circumstances of pressure applied against the power of resistance of this petitioner, who cannot be deemed other than weak of will or mind, deprived him of due process of law. So viewed, the judgment of conviction in this case cannot stand.

THE DECISION:
"The judgment is reversed, and the cause is remanded for proceedings not inconsistent with this opinion."

Heart of Atlanta v. United States

HEART OF ATLANTA MOTEL, INC., Appellant
v.
UNITED STATES et al.
379 U.S. 803   Decided December 14, 1964
Mr. Justice Clark delivered the opinion of the Court.
Archibald Cox, Solicitor General,
represented the appellant.
Attorney Robert McDavid Smith
represented the appellees.

THE ISSUE:
The constitutionality of the Civil Rights Act of 1964, Title II

SUMMARY OF THE FACTS:
The Heart of Atlanta Motel, located on Courtland Street, two blocks from downtown Peachtree Street, Atlanta, Georgia, has 216 rooms available to transient guests. It is readily accessible to Interstate Highways 75 and 85 and State Highways 23 and 411.

The motel owner solicits patronage from outside the state of Georgia through various national advertising media, including national magazines; maintains over 50 billboard and highway signs throughout the state; and accepts convention trade from outside Georgia. Approximately 75% of its registered guests are from out of state.

Prior to passage of the Civil Rights Act of 1964, the motel had followed a practice of refusing to rent rooms to Negroes, and it alleged that it intended to do so. In an effort to perpetuate the policy, the motel filed suit, contending that Congress in passing the Act exceeded its power to regulate commerce under the U.S. Constitution and that the said Act violated both the 5th and 13th Amendments.

The United States countered that the unavailability to Negroes of adequate accommodations interfered significantly with interstate travel; that Congress under the commerce clause had power to remove such obstructions and restraints; and that neither the 5th nor the 13th Amendments were violated by such Congressional regulation.

The U.S. District Court for the Northern District of Georgia sustained the constitutionality of the pertinent sections of the Act. The case was then referred to the Supreme Court.

THE QUESTIONS:
(1) Does Congress have a rational basis for finding that racial discrimination by motels affected interstate commerce?
(2) If it has such a basis, were the means selected to eliminate that evil appropriate?
(3) Is Title II of the 1964 Civil Rights Act, also known as the public accommodations clause, constitutional?

THE FINDINGS:
"The Senate Commerce Committee made it quite clear that the fundamental object of Title II was to vindicate 'the deprivation of personal dignity that surely accompanies denials to equal access to public establishment.' At the same time, however, it noted that such an objective has been and could be readily achieved 'by Congressional action based on the commerce power of the Constitution. . . .'

"Our study of the legislative record, made in the light of prior cases, has brought us to the conclusion that Congress possessed ample power in this regard, . . . It is the power to regulate; that is, to prescribe the rule by which commerce is to be governed. This power like all others vested in Congress, is complete in itself, may be exercised to its utmost extent, and acknowledges no limitations, other than are prescribed in the Constitution. . . .

"That Congress was legislating against moral wrongs in many of these areas rendered its enactments no less valid. In framing Title II of this act Congress was also dealing with what it considered a moral problem. But that fact does not detract from the overwhelming evidence of the disruptive effect that racial discrimination has had on commercial intercourse. It was this burden which empowered Congress to enact appropriate legislation, and, given this basis for the exercise of its power, Congress was not restricted by the fact that the particular obstruction to interstate commerce with which it was dealing was also deemed a moral and social wrong. . . .

"The power of Congress over interstate commerce is not confined to the regulation of commerce among the states. It extends to those activities intra-state which so affect interstate commerce or the exercise of the power of Congress over it as to make regulation of them appropriate means to the attainment of a legitimate end."

THE DECISION:
Judgment of the U.S. District Court, Northern District of Georgia, affirmed

Katzenbach v. McClung

NICHOLAS DeB. KATZENBACH, Acting Attorney General, et al., Appellants

v.

OLLIE McCLUNG, SR. AND OLLIE McCLUNG, JR.

379 U.S. 802   Decided December 14, 1964

Mr. Justice Clark delivered the opinion of the Court.

Archibald Cox, Solicitor General, represented the appellants.

Attorney Robert McDavid Smith represented the appellees.

THE ISSUE:

The constitutionality of the Civil Rights Act of 1964, Title II

SUMMARY OF THE FACTS:

"Ollie's Barbecue is a family-owned restaurant in Birmingham, Alabama, specializing in barbecued meats and homemade pies, with a seating capacity of 220 customers. It is located on a state highway, 11 blocks from an interstate one, and a somewhat greater distance from railroad and bus stations.

"The restaurant caters to a family and white-collar trade with a takeout service for Negroes. It employs 36 persons, two-thirds of whom are Negroes.

"In the 12 months preceding the passage of the Act, the restaurant purchased locally approximately $150,000 worth of food, $69,783 or 46% of which was meat that it bought from a local supplier who had procured it from outside the state.

"The District Attorney expressly found that a substantial portion of the food served in the restaurant had moved in interstate commerce. The restaurant has refused to serve Negroes in its dining accommodations since its original opening in 1927, and since July 2, 1964, it has been operating in violation of the Act. The court below concluded that if it were required to serve Negroes it would lose a substantial amount of business."

The U.S. District Court, Northern District of Alabama, held that the Act could not be applied under the 14th Amendment, and stated further that "there was no demonstrable connection" between food purchased in interstate commerce and sold in a restaurant and the conclusion in Congress that discrimination in the restaurant would affect that commerce.

The case was then referred to the Supreme Court for rehearing.

THE QUESTIONS:

(1) Does Congress have a rational basis for finding that racial discrimination by restaurants affected interstate commerce?

(2) If it has such a basis, were the means selected to eliminate that evil appropriate?

(3) Is Title II of the 1964 Civil Rights Act, also known as the public accommodations clause, constitutional?

THE FINDINGS:

"The basic holding in Heart of Atlanta Motel, supra, answers many of the contentions made by the appellees. There we outlined the over-all purpose and operational plan of Title II and found it a valid exercise of the power to regulate interstate commerce insofar as it requires hotels and motels to serve transients without regard to their race or color. In this case we consider its application to restaurants which serve food a substantial portion of which has moved in commerce.

"Section 201(A) of Title II commands that all persons shall be entitled to the full and equal enjoyment of the goods and services of any place of public accommodation without discrimination or segregation on the ground of race, color, religion, or national origin; and Section 201(B) defines establishments as places of public accommodation if their operations affect commerce or segregation by them is supported by state action. Sections 201(B) (2) and (C) place any 'restaurant . . . principally engaged in selling food for consumption on the premises' under the Act 'if . . . it serves or offers to serve interstate travelers or a substantial portion of the food which it serves . . . has moved in commerce . . .'

"The power of Congress in this field is broad and sweeping; where it keeps within its sphere and violates no express constitutional limitation it has been the rule of this Court, going back almost to the founding days of the Republic, not to interfere.

"The Civil Rights Act of 1964, as here applied, we find to be plainly appropriate in the resolution of what the Congress found to be a national commercial problem of the first magnitude. We find it in no violation of any express limitations of the Constitution and we therefore declare it valid."

THE DECISION:

Judgment of U.S. District Court, Northern District of Alabama, reversed

Glossary of Court Terms

AFFIDAVIT

A statement of facts in writing sworn to before an authorized magistrate or officer, for instance a notary.

AFFIRM

To ratify, confirm, reassert. The instance where a higher court upholds the ruling of a lower court.

AMICUS (AMICI) CURIAE

(Latin: Friend [friends] of the court)

A person or group, not actually a party to a case, who in the interest of justice, makes an argument or files printed statements before the court on behalf of parties affected.

APPEAL

A complaint asking a higher court to correct or reverse a decision made by a lower court. *Appellant:* The person making the appeal. *Appellee:* The person against whom the appeal is made.

ARRAIGN or ARRAIGNMENT

Notification of the accused before a court of the charges against him before placing him in custody to await trial.

BAR, At the

Refers to the court sitting in session. A trial "at the bar" is one held before a full court.

CERTIORARI, Writ of

(Latin: To be informed of)

A method whereby a higher court orders a decision made by a lower court brought before it for review.

COUNSEL

The attorney or lawyer who represents a client in court. Used also for plural. Example: Messrs. Carter, Marshall and Redding, counsel for the plaintiff.

DEFENDANT

The person against whom charges are made in a court.

DISSENT

Disagreement with a majority opinion; the written statement setting forth that disagreement.

DOCKET

A list of legal cases to be tried or acted upon.

DUE PROCESS OF LAW

The exercise of governmental powers while preserving constitutional safeguards of individual rights.

DURESS

To obtain an action through force or harrassment, such as use of threats or physical violence.

ENJOIN

A court order commanding a person or body to hold off on the performance of a certain act.

ERROR, Writ of

Action whereby a higher court requires a lower court to submit its record of a decision in which certain errors are alleged to have been made.

ESTOPPEL

A legal action preventing the assertion or denial of certain facts until a final decision has been made in court.

ET AL

Abbreviation for "et alii"; Latin for "and others."

EX PARTE

(Latin: On one side only; in behalf of)

In the heading of a case signifies that the

name following is of the party for whom the court action has been started.

EX REL

(Abbreviation for the Latin "ex relatione," meaning: upon relation or information) Proceedings instituted in the name of the state, but at the request of an individual with a private interest in the matter.

FINDING

The result of deliberations of a jury or court.

GRAND JURY

A jury, usually of from 12 to 23 members, called to investigate an accusation against a person charged with a criminal offense and instructed, if necessary, to ask for an indictment.

HABEAS CORPUS, Writ of
(Latin: You have the body)
An order to bring a party before a court or judge. The writ to inquire into the cause of arrest in order to obtain release.

INDICTMENT

A written accusation made by a prosecutor charging a person with an offense.

INJUNCTION

An order issued by a court forbidding a defendant or his associates from performing some act.

ISSUE

A single, certain and material point arising from arguments of opposing parties.

JURISDICTION

The authority by which courts and judicial officers decide cases.

MANDAMUS, Writ of (Latin: We command)
An order issued by a court forcing the performance of a particular act.

PETITIONER

One who presents an application to a court

to obtain satisfaction for an alleged wrong.

PETIT JURY

A jury of 12 persons who decide upon the issues of a trial.

PER CURIAM (Latin: By the court)

A brief, usually unanimous, opinion of a court made without lengthy discussion.

PRIMA FACIE
(Latin: At first sight, on the face of it)
Something presumed to be true unless disproved by contrary evidence.

QUASH

To overthrow, annul or make void.

QUESTION

The essential problem or the matter to be inquired into.

REDRESS

Satisfaction for an offense committed against a person.

RESPONDENT

The person against whom court action is brought. The person opposing a petition.

STATUTE

A law enacted by a municipal, state or federal legislature.

SUPRA (Latin: Above)
Mentioned before.

VENIRE (Latin: To come)
To appear in court.

VENUE

Removal of a case from one county or district to another for trial.

WARRANT

An order issued by a judge or other competent person directing the performance of an act.

WRIT

An order used by a court to force the performance of a lawful duty.

Notes

SECTION ONE: THE HOUSE OF BONDAGE

Philip Corven of Virginia Petitions for Freedom
A century before the American Revolution, Negro slaves appealed to state and local governments for freedom and respect for human rights. In some instances these petitions were granted. The records do not indicate the disposition in Corven's case.

Bracketed material supplied by the editor.

☐ PALMER, WILLIAM P. (ed.). *Calendar of Virginia State Papers*. Vol. I. Richmond: 1875, pp. 9–10.

The Germantown Quakers' Anti-Slavery Resolution
This document has been called the earliest known protest against slavery in the American Colonies. It is certainly one of the earliest expressions by an American organization questioning the morality of the traffic in men-body.

☐ MODE, PETER GEORGE (ed.). *Source Book and Bibliographical Guide for American Church History*. Menasha, Wisc.: George Banta, 1921.

"Felix" of Massachusetts Protests Enslavement
Feelings of a Northern slave in the years immediately preceding the American Revolution included yearnings for "liberty and life," comparable to the advocacy of "liberty or death" by the Colonists.

☐ The Appendix: or Some Observations on the Expediency of the Petition of the Africans Living in Boston. . . . By a Lover of Constitutional Liberty. Boston: E. Russell, pp. 9–11. Copy in the Boston Athenaeum.

Jefferson's Early Draft of the Declaration of Independence
The censures against the king for permitting and encouraging slavery were stricken to appease Southern states.

☐ GUERNSEY, ALFRED H. and HENRY M. ALDEN (eds.). *Harper's Pictorial History of the Great Rebellion*. Chicago: McDonnell Brothers, 1866, Vol. I, pp. 6–7.

Jefferson's Dilemma: The Immorality of Slavery —The Inferiority of Negroes
François Barbé-Marbois, Secretary to the French Legation at Philadelphia, toward the end of 1780 sent a questionnaire to members of the Continental Congress seeking information about the American states. Joseph Jones of the Virginia delegation forwarded the questionnaire on Virginia to Thomas Jefferson who was then Governor of Virginia. Jefferson's reply constitutes a small book entitled, *Notes on the State of Virginia*. The discussion of Negro differences and possible inferiority is contained in a section of the "Notes" entitled "Administration of Justice." The immorality of slavery is considered in a section entitled, "The Particular Customs and Manners That May Happen To Be Received in That State."

☐ WASHINGTON, H. A. (ed.). *The Writings of Thomas Jefferson*. New York: H. W. Derby, 1859, Vol. VIII, p. 372 ff and 403 ff.

The Quock Walker Case
This is the first case involving the rights of slave-master and slave to be decided by the Supreme Judicial Court of the Commonwealth of Massachusetts. Although the case was not reported, Chief Justice Cushing's notebook contained the decision. This extract was quoted from the Cushing papers by Chief Justice Horace Gray in 1874.

☐ HART, ALBERT BUSNELL (ed.). *Commonwealth History of Massachusetts*, New York: The States History Company, 1927–1930, Vols. I–V.

Falconbridge Relates the Horrors Aboard Slave Ships
Alexander Falconbridge, an English surgeon whose need of funds made it necessary for him to accept employment aboard ships engaged in the slave trade, authored a pamphlet in two parts: describing the experiences of white seamen aboard the slave ship [part one]; and the experiences of the slaves themselves [part two]. This entry consists of the second part.

Falconbridge later left the sea and worked diligently in antislavery causes. For a brief time he acted as governor of a West African coastal colony whose population was made up of free Negroes and runaway slaves. Today this colony is the independent nation known as Sierra Leone.

☐ FALCONBRIDGE, ALEXANDER. *An Account of the Slave Trade on the Coast of Africa*. London: 1788. (Copy available in the Schomburg Collection of Negro Literature and History of the New York Public Library.)

George Washington's Plan for Manumission
It is generally conceded that the will was written on July 7, 1799, but because of infirmity, Washington did not add the terminal "nine." ". . . I have set my hand and seal this ninth day of July, in the year one-thousand-seven-hundred and ninety and of the independence of the United States the twenty-fourth."

☐ Original Document preserved in Fairfax County Court House, Virginia.

Benjamin Banneker's Letter to Thomas Jefferson
Benjamin Banneker was a free Negro from Maryland whose reputation as a gifted mathematician and astronomer won him a place on the three-man com-

mission which surveyed and planned the site of the nation's capital.

☐ Tyson, Martha E. *Banneker, The Afric-American Astronomer*. Philadelphia: The Friends Book Association, 1844, p. 39 ff.

Jefferson's Reply to Banneker

Cordial and apparently admiring, Jefferson's letter may not reflect his truest feelings. In other correspondence, he expressed doubt that the almanac was entirely Banneker's work.

☐ Woodson, Carter G. (ed.). *The Mind of the Negro as Reflected in Letters Written During the Crisis 1800–1860*. Washington: Association for the Study of Negro Life and History, Inc., 1926, pp. xxvii–xxviii.

Richard Allen and Absalom Jones
Denounce Philadelphia Ingratitude

The publication of Matthew Carey's "A Short Account of the Malignant Fever, Lately Prevalent in Philadelphia . . . ," in which Negroes were accused of taking advantage of their position as nurses to steal and otherwise impose upon white victims of cholera, produced an answering pamphlet from Absalom Jones and Richard Allen. This work was entitled, *A Narrative of the Proceedings of the Black People, during the Late Awful Calamity in Philadelphia, in the Year 1793*. Jones and Allen, pioneers in the Negro church, were among the "Elders of the African Church" referred to in Carey's "account."

☐ Jones, Absalom and Richard Allen. *A Narrative of the Proceedings of the Black People, during the Late Awful Calamity in Philadelphia in the Year 1793*. Philadelphia: Printed for the authors by William W. Woodward at Franklin's Head, 41 Chestnut Street, 1794.

Richard Allen and Absalom Jones
Speak Out Against Slavery

The obvious parallels of the condition of the Negro in the United States with the biblical account of the Children of Israel in Egypt have been a recurring theme since the early days of slavery. In the winter of 1960, the editor heard the Reverend Ralph D. Abernathy, of the Southern Christian Leadership Conference, state in a speech in Brooklyn that he was returning to Egypt—referring to his departure the following day for Alabama.

This statement was appended to the specific rebuttal of Carey's anti-Negro "account of the malignant fever . . ."

☐ Jones, Absalom and Richard Allen. *A Narrative of the Proceedings of the Black People, during the Late Awful Calamity in Philadelphia in the Year 1793*. Philadelphia: Printed for the authors by William W. Woodward at Franklin's Head, 41 Chestnut Street, 1794.

The Importation of Slaves Prohibited

Under the Provisions of Article I, Section 9, of the Constitution, Congress was forbidden to take action to prohibit the migration or importation of slaves although it had the right to impose a "tax or duty on such importations not exceeding ten dollars for each person." On March 2, 1807, Congress passed "An Act to Prohibit the Importation of Slaves Into Any Port or Place Within the Jurisdiction of the United States From and After the First Day of January, and the Year of Our Lord, One Thousand Eight Hundred and Eight."

☐ *U.S. Statutes at Large*, Vol. II, p. 426 ff.

SECTION TWO: LET MY PEOPLE GO

William Hamilton Refutes Alleged Negro Inferiority

William Hamilton, a New York Negro actor, was one of the founders and major influences of the later "Convention For the Improvement of the Free People of Colour."

☐ *An Address to the New York African Society for Mutual Relief, Delivered in the Universalist Church, January 2, 1809*. (Copy available in the Boston Athenaeum.)

James Forten of Philadelphia
Protests Negro "Registration"

James Forten, member of a distinguished and prosperous free Negro family of Philadelphia, authored *A Series of Letters by a Man of Color*, and was active in the Abolitionist Movement.

☐ Woodson, Carter G. *Negro Orators and Their Orations*. Washington: Associated Publishers, 1925, pp. 42–51.

Resolutions Against Proposed Colonization in Africa

The American Colonization Society was formed in December, 1816. Its membership included many prominent white citizens as well as several slave owners. The purpose of the Society was to deport free Negroes to Africa, thereby removing a possible threat to the sanctity of the institution of slavery. These statements from Negroes in Philadelphia and in Richmond indicate Negro rejection of the plan.

☐ Garrison, William Lloyd. *Thoughts on African Colonization or An Imperial Exhibition of the Doctrines, Principles & Purposes of the American Colonization Society. Together with the Resolutions, Addresses & Remonstrances of the Free People of Color*. Boston: Garrison and Knapp, 1832, Part II, pp. 62–63.

The Missouri Compromise

When the territory of Missouri, acquired via the Louisiana Purchase, applied for statehood in 1818, a debate over extension of slavery began that extended for a period of almost three years. Under the terms of the Louisiana Purchase, inhabitants of the new territory were guaranteed rights of liberty, property and religion. When Missouri applied for statehood, there were a few thousand slaves in the territory, and the question of whether or not they were "property" under the terms of the Louisiana Purchase was debated in Congress for several months. The Tallmadge Amendment of 1819 which sought to eliminate slavery in the territory was passed in the House of Representatives but was put down in the Senate. The Taylor Amendment of 1820 in the House of Representatives and the Tallmadge Amendment of 1820 in the Senate were both more accommodating to existing slave interests, but intended to restrain the growth of slavery.

Under the terms of the Missouri Enabling Act and the Constitution of Missouri, as submitted to the Congress of the United States, and Congress' own resolution for the admission of Missouri, slavery was extended into the new state. A factor which softened the anti-slavery bloc's resistance was Maine's admission to the Union as a "free" (non-slave) state during this same period.

☐ The Tallmadge Amendment: *Journal of the House of Representatives,* 15th Congress, Second Session, p. 272.

☐ The Taylor Amendment: *Annals of the Congress of the United States,* 16th Congress, First Session, Vol. I, p. 947.

☐ The Thomas Amendment: *Annals of the Congress of the United States,* 16th Congress, First Session, Vol. I, p. 427.

☐ Missouri Enabling Act: *U.S. Statutes at Large,* Vol. III, p. 545 ff.

☐ The Constitution of Missouri: POORE (ed.). *Federal and State Constitutions,* Vol. II, pp. 1107–8.

☐ Resolutions for the Admission of Missouri: *U.S. Statutes at Large,* Vol. III, p. 645.

Reverend Nathaniel Paul, Albany (N.Y.)
Baptist Preacher, Hails Emancipation in New York
Reverend Paul, Pastor of the First African Baptist Society of Albany, used the emancipation celebration in New York to predict the end of slavery throughout the world and to exhort the Negroes of New York to use their newfound freedom to discredit the notion of Negro inferiority.

☐ PAUL, NATHANIEL. *An Address Delivered on the Celebration of the Abolition of Slavery in the State of New York, July 5, 1827* (pamphlet). Albany: Trustees, First African Baptist Society, 1827, p. 15 ff. (Copy available in the Schomburg Collection of Negro Literature and History of the New York Public Library.)

Freedom's Journal, First Negro Newspaper, Appears March 16, 1827
Freedom's Journal was a joint endeavor of the Reverend Samuel E. Cornish, pastor of the African

Presbyterian Church in New York, and John Russwurm, a graduate of Bowdoin College and the first Negro college graduate in the United States.

Although Russwurm later went to Liberia, Cornish continued the publication with the title *Rights of All* until 1830.

☐ Microfilm copies of *Freedom's Journal* are available in the Schomburg Collection of Negro Literature and History of the New York Public Library.

Freedom's Journal Reports a Lynching
This item, believed to be the earliest American newspaper account of the lynching of a Negro, appeared in the pages of *Freedom's Journal* August 3, 1827, some 44 days after the account was written on June 20 with the dateline Tuscaloosa, Alabama.

☐ Microfilm in the Schomburg Collection of Negro Literature and History of the New York Public Library.

Minutes of the First Negro Convention
This founding convention, held in Philadelphia in September of 1830, set the stage for the many succeeding Negro conventions. Although the names of the "giants" of the period dominate the published records of the meeting, it has been argued that the idea of calling this convention originated with young Hezekiah Grice of Maryland.

☐ *Constitution of the American Society of Free Persons of Colour, for Improving Their Condition in the United States; for Purchasing Land; and for the Establishment of a Settlement in Upper Canada, Also the Proceedings of the Convention, with Their Address to the Free Persons of Colour in the United States.* Philadelphia: 1831.

The Liberator, First Edition
After the *Genius of Universal Emancipation* which he edited with Benjamin Lundy discontinued publication, Garrison went to Boston where, with Isaac Knapp, he established *The Liberator,* perhaps the most important single factor in shifting abolitionist emphasis away from gradual emancipation. Langston Hughes quotes Garrison's description of his mission: "I have a system to destroy, and I have no time to waste."

The Liberator was a weekly newspaper, and publication lasted from 1831 to 1865. It enjoyed its widest circulation in the Negro community; Garrison himself admitted that of the 450 subscribers during its first year of publication, 400 were Negroes. At a later point when the subscription figures rose to 2,300, 1,700 were said to be Negro.

☐ GARRISON, WENDELL PHILLIPS and FRANCIS JACKSON GARRISON. *William Lloyd Garrison: The Story of His Life Told by His Children.* Boston: Houghton Mifflin and Company, 1889, Vol. I, p. 224 ff.

Philadelphia Negroes
Petition the Pennsylvania Legislature

Accompanying this memorial was a "statement of facts" regarding Negroes in Pennsylvania, and asserting that: (1) Of 549 public assistance cases in 1832, only 22 were Negro, about 4% of the total as contrasted with the population ratio of 8¼%; (2) Tax paper receipts indicated that more than $2,000 annually was paid by Negroes and yet the expenditures from public funds for Negro poor came only to about $2,000 a year. Annual rents paid by Negroes exceeded $100,000 annually; (3) Many Negroes were owners of their own property. No less than 11 meeting houses (six Methodist, two Presbyterian, two Baptist, one Episcopalian) and one public hall were owned exclusively by Negroes. These holdings had an aggregate value which was estimated to exceed $100,000. To these were added two Sunday Schools, two tract societies, two Bible societies, two temperance societies, and one female literary institution; (4) Negroes had established more than 50 benevolent societies, which had annual expenditures in excess of $7,000; (5) Despite the "difficulty of getting places for our sons as apprentices to learn mechanical trades, owing to the prejudices with which we have to contend," there were between four and five hundred people in Philadelphia who were employed as mechanics; (6) While grateful for public and private benevolencies aiding education, those Negroes who could afford to, paid for their children's education.

☐ *The Liberator,* April 14, 1832.

Reverend Nathaniel Paul
Protests Mistreatment of Lady Educator

In 1831, Samuel Cornish had formulated a plan for opening a school for Negro young people in New Haven. The plan was never put into action because of opposition from the city fathers of New Haven. Shortly thereafter, Prudence Crandall, a Quaker from Canterbury, Connecticut, who operated a school for girls, admitted a Negro student. When white parents boycotted the school Miss Crandall accepted an all-Negro enrollment to the chagrin of the community. The community's outrage expressed itself in mob action, damaging the buildings of her school. Miss Crandall was arrested and after the trial was imprisoned. Reverend Nathaniel Paul's letter, dispatched from London, upbraids Judge Andrew T. Judson, the presiding magistrate.

☐ *The Liberator,* November 23, 1833.

Constitution of the American Anti-Slavery
Society and Its Declaration of Sentiments

In the wake of the British Parliament's enactment of the West Indian Emancipation Law, abolitionist fervor in the United States was intensified and the Anti-Slavery Society was organized.

One of the guiding spirits in the formation of the Anti-Slavery Society was William Lloyd Garrison who successfully put down opposition expressed against the formation of the society. Garrison was the author of the Declaration of Sentiments.

☐ Platform of the American Anti-Slavery Society and Its Auxiliaries. New York, 1860, pp. 3, 4.

☐ GARRISON, WENDELL PHILLIPS and FRANCIS JACKSON GARRISON. *William Lloyd Garrison: The Story of His Life Told by His Children.* Boston: Houghton Mifflin and Company, 1889, Vol. I, p. 408 ff.

David Ruggles, New York Bookseller,
Refutes an Anti-Abolitionist

Dr. David M. Reese issued a pamphlet in 1834 called "A Brief Review of the First Annual Report of the American Anti-Slavery Society." In the pamphlet Dr. Reese alleged that the abolitionists constituted an un-American threat to law and order and that emancipation was neither expedient nor possible. It was his feeling that his pamphlet ended once and for all the abolitionists' ferment.

David Ruggles, a Negro abolitionist, answered Dr. Reese with a privately published pamphlet entitled *The "Extinguisher" Extinguished: or David M. Reese, M.D. "Used Up."*

☐ New York: 1834. (Copy available in the Schomburg Collection of Negro Literature and History of the New York Public Library.)

South Carolina
Resolutions on Abolitionist Propaganda

Because abolitionist propaganda might produce slave uprisings and was patently hostile to the institution of slavery, many Southern states adopted stringent measures to regulate or prohibit circulation of abolitionist literature within their states. The South Carolina Resolutions set forth that state's determination to exercise its sovereignty to uphold slavery.

☐ *Acts and Resolutions of South Carolina,* 1835, p. 26 ff.

Resolutions of African
Methodist Episcopal Church Annual Conference

At the tenth annual conference of the Pittsburgh (or Western) District of the AME Church, with delegates from Pittsburgh, Cincinnati, Chillicothe, Zanesville, Richmond, Union Town, Hillsboro and Columbus, the Right Reverend Morris Brown, Senior Bishop, presiding, the doctrine of "good works" achieved an expanded interpretation to embrace social needs.

☐ *AME Church Magazine.* Brooklyn: Vol. I, No. 1, September 1841, pp. 7, 8.

Announcement of New York Teachers' Meeting

With education its primary function, the call made clear that improvement of the lot of Negroes in other areas required action.

☐ *The Liberator,* November 26, 1841.

Charles Lenox Remond Addresses
Massachusetts Legislative Committee
Against Segregation in Travel

Remond, a Massachusetts abolitionist and American Anti-Slavery Society Lecturing Agent, made this statement before the Legislative Committee of the Massachusetts House of Representatives.

The reference to R. M. Johnson is to the Kentucky Colonel, Richard M. Johnson, Vice President of the United States during the Van Buren Administration. Prior to becoming Vice President, Johnson, with no attempt at concealment, lived with a Negro woman, Julia Chinn. They had two daughters, both of whom married white men. Julia Chinn died in 1833.

☐ *The Liberator,* February 25, 1842.

Prigg vs. The Commonwealth of Pennsylvania

According to Henry Steele Commager, while this case established the exclusive power of Congress governing the disposition of fugitive slaves, it also interpreted the police powers of the states in such a manner as to call forth from the states "a series of Personal Liberty Laws which largely nullified the Fugitive Slave Laws."

☐ 16 Peters, 539.

Henry Highland Garnet Urges Slave "Resistance"

Garnet was one of many young men at the National Negro Convention held in Buffalo, August 21–24, 1843. A former newspaper editor and then a Presbyterian pastor in Troy, New York, Garnet's speech, "An Address to the Slaves of the United States" won him a national reputation at age 27. The address came within one vote of being accepted as the sentiment of the Convention.

☐ *A Memorial Discourse; by Rev. Henry Highland Garnet, Delivered In The Hall of the House of Representatives, Washington City, D.C. on Sabbath, February 12, 1865. With an Introduction by James McCune Smith, M.D.* Philadelphia: Joseph M. Wilson, 1865, p. 44 ff.

Editorial in the Inaugural Edition of The North Star

Against the advice of some other abolitionists, Douglass brought to fruition plans for the publication of his own anti-slavery journal with the assistance of Martin R. Delany, co-editor. In another editorial in the opening edition, which he addressed to abolitionists, especially white abolitionists, he asserted that *The North Star* would do "a most important and indispensable work, which it would be wholly impossible for our white friends to do for us." He further explained "that the man who has suffered the wrong is the man to demand redress—that the man struck is the man to cry out—and that he who has endured the cruel pangs of slavery is the man to advocate liberty."

☐ *The North Star* (Issues on microfilm are available in the Schomburg Collection of Negro Literature and History of the New York Public Library.)

Clay's Resolutions on Slavery in the
Territories and the District of Columbia

The new territories acquired as the result of the Mexican War rekindled the old disputes centering on the extension of slavery. Northerners wanted slavery banned in the territories of California and New Mexico, and Southerners were equally insistent that slavery be permitted there. The debate reached a climax when California applied for statehood after drafting a constitution forbidding slavery. Clay's resolution sought to chart a course acceptable to both northern and southern interests. The debate continued, however, until September, 1850, when five bills which bore the collective title, Compromise of 1850, were passed incorporating most of Clay's proposals, including a strengthened Fugitive Slave Act.

☐ *U.S. Senate Journal,* 31st Congress, 1st Session, p. 118 ff.

The Georgia Platform
on the Extension of Slavery Question

A convention was held at Milledgeville, Georgia to consider the Compromise of 1850. The platform was comprised of the resolutions passed at that convention. Moderate and essentially pro-Union in its tone, the platform was drafted by Charles J. Jenkins.

☐ STEPHENS, A. H., *The War Between the States.* Vol. II, Appendix B.

Resolutions of the Nashville Convention
Opposing Congressional Control of Slavery

Representatives from nine slave states, in a convention at Nashville, Tennessee, adopted these essentially moderate resolutions. The original sponsors of the convention were more radical Southern leaders. However, when the convention acted in June, the moderates were "in the driver's seat." A second convention was called by the radicals in November of 1850. It was attended by only a handful of delegates, and its resolutions denounced the Compromise of 1850 and asserted the right of secession.

☐ *Resolutions, Addresses and Journal of Proceedings of the Southern Convention,* p. 57 ff.

"What to the Slave is the Fourth of July"

Fourth of July orations are a quintessential part of the American celebration of independence. The designation as Fourth of July orator is usually reserved for a community's most distinguished resident. Mindful as he must have been of the honor intended, Douglass could not let pass the opportunity to remind his listeners of the irony of a Negro called upon to extol the virtues of *liberty* in America.

☐ DUNBAR, ALICE MOORE (ed.). *Masterpieces of Negro Eloquence.* New York: The Bookery Publishing Company, 1914, p. 42 ff.

Robert Purvis Protests Segregated Education

Robert Purvis, who had been active in the convention movement, and who was one of the founders of the Philadelphia Negro Library, in this letter addressed to the Philadelphia Tax Collector, revived an age-old American distaste for *taxation without representation*.

☐ *The Liberator*, December 16, 1853.

The Sentencing of Mrs. Douglas
for Teaching Negro Children to Read

In most Southern states it was unlawful under the slave codes to teach slaves to read or write. However, in Virginia, the ban included all Negroes. Although it was not unusual for the prohibitions to be disregarded, in some instances, as in the present case, they were enforced. Mrs. Douglas is believed to have served the full term of her sentence.

☐ LAWSON, JOHN D. (ed.). *American State Trials*. St. Louis: F. H. Thomas Law Book Co., 1914–1936, Vol. VII, p. 56 ff.

Appeal of the Independent Democrats
Against the Nebraska Slavery Bill

This Appeal, signed by six of the most prominent American abolitionists, was provoked by Stephen A. Douglas's effort to push through the Kansas-Nebraska Bill. The Appeal was widely circulated and in the view of some historians, it created a climate leading to the Republican Party's founding.

☐ SCHUCKERS, JACOB WILLIAMS. *Life and Public Services of S. P. Chase*. New York: D. Appleton, 1874.

The Kansas-Nebraska Act

With the passage of the Kansas-Nebraska Act, the Missouri Compromise of 1820 was repealed, and the doctrine of squatter sovereignty gained circulation. Neither Northern nor Southern interests were satisfied with the bill; Southerners resented the doctrine of squatter sovereignty, and Northerners were equally opposed to the abrogation of the Missouri Compromise. In July, 1854, the New Republican Party had come into existence.

☐ *U.S. Statutes at Large*, Vol. X, p. 277 ff.

Massachusetts Personal Liberty Act

This bill is felt to have been a reflection of public abhorrence of the treatment accorded Anthony Burns, a widely known fugitive slave. For all practical purposes it made the Fugitive Slave Act of 1850 unenforceable in the state of Massachusetts. The bill was passed over the veto of Governor Gardner.

☐ *Acts and Resolves Passed by the General Court of Massachusetts in the Year 1855*, p. 924 ff.

Dred Scott vs. Sandford

The Dred Scott case is one of the most famous in the history of the Supreme Court. The case came to the High Court almost 10 years after Dred Scott instituted suit in the Circuit Court of the County of St. Louis, Missouri, on July 1, 1847. Scott, who became the slave of Dr. John Emerson in 1835 in Missouri, was later removed to Illinois and from there to the Territory of Wisconsin. Slavery was forbidden in both Illinois and Wisconsin. Scott instituted suit on the basis of his having lived for a time on free soil. The Court considered three main questions: (1) Whether Scott was a citizen of the state of Missouri, which was important if the Federal Court was to have jurisdiction; (2) Whether residence in the free areas of Illinois and Wisconsin gave Scott his freedom, and (3) Whether the Missouri Compromise was constitutional. The Court answered all three questions: "No."

☐ 19 Howard, 393.

SECTION THREE:
THE WALLS CAME TUMBLIN' DOWN

John Brown's Speech
After Being Adjudged Guilty of Treason

John Brown, the fiery abolitionist, and a small band of his followers successfully captured the government armory at Harpers Ferry, Virginia on October 16, 1859. U.S. Marines, commanded by Colonel Robert E. Lee, stormed the armory and captured Brown and some of his aides. Brown was charged with treason and inciting slaves to murder. He was found guilty and sentenced to death by hanging.

One of the Negroes in Brown's party, Osborne Perry Anderson, later published his account of the incidents under the title *A Voice From Harpers Ferry*.

☐ LAWSON, JOHN D. (ed.). *American State Trials*. St. Louis: F. H. Thomas Law Book Co., 1914–1936, Vol. VI, p. 800 ff.

The Correspondence
of a Slave-owner and Her Former Slave

Mrs. Logue's letter was dated February 20, 1860 and the Reverend Loguen's answer, March 28.

☐ *The Liberator*, April 27, 1860.

Lincoln's Proposals for Compensated Emancipation

Lincoln made many attempts to have Congress and the South agree to plans for compensated emancipation. He was especially hopeful that the Border States would endorse the scheme, but despite his personal attempts at rallying support, his proposals insuring slavery's gradual abolishment were not acted upon.

☐ RICHARDSON, JAMES D. (ed.). *Compilation of the Messages and Papers of the Presidents*. Washington, D.C.: Bureau of National Literature and Art, 1904.

William Wells Brown Presses for
Negro Participation in the Civil War
The Negroes saw the Civil War as their fight too, and frequently appealed for the right to join the Union forces. Some wrote personal appeals to the Secretary of War and other state and federal officials. Attempt was made to arouse public opinion in behalf of Negro participation in the war. Speaking before the New York Anti-Slavery Society, William Wells Brown advanced the merit of the Negro's pleas for "a chance to rise by his own efforts."

☐ *The Liberator,* May 16, 1862.

Greeley and Lincoln Exchange Views on Slavery
While Horace Greeley, publisher of the New York *Tribune* was not an active member of abolitionist organizations, he was quite vocal in his condemnation of slavery. His *Prayer of Twenty Millions* was an "open letter" calling upon the President to stop equivocating about fighting "Slavery with Liberty."

Lincoln's reply indicates once more his feelings that if he could save the Union without emancipating the slaves he would do so.

☐ Moore, Frank (ed.). *The Rebellion Record.* New York: G. P. Putnam, 1864. Supplement, Vol. I, p. 480 ff.

The Emancipation Proclamation
On the advice of Secretary of State William Henry Seward, Lincoln delayed issuing a Preliminary Proclamation until the Union forces had won a significant battle. After the Battle of Antietam, Lincoln acted. On September 22, 1862 his Preliminary Proclamation was announced and was restated in final form on January 1, 1863.

It is important to note that the Emancipation Proclamation applied only to the states in "rebellion against the United States." All slaves were not yet free.

☐ *U.S. Statutes at Large,* Vol. XII, pp. 1268–9.

SECTION FOUR:
THE WILDERNESS OF EMANCIPATION

Resolution of the Illinois State Legislature in
Opposition to the Emancipation Proclamation
The Emancipation Proclamation, while hailed by the radical Republicans, was attacked by many Northern Democrats. The Democratic legislature of Illinois interpreted Mr. Lincoln's proclamation as a subversion of the announced purposes of the Civil War.

☐ *Illinois State Register,* January 7, 1863.

A Negro Eyewitness
Describes Anti-Negro Violence in Detroit
Anti-Negro violence flared up in many Northern communities immediately following the Emancipa-

tion Proclamation. The Detroit riots in March and the bloody "Draft Riots" in New York, July 13–17, probably stemmed from a variety of white resentments: Negroes were felt to be the cause of the War; they were a threat in the labor market and, not unlikely, their quest for freedom and for a measure of equality was even then seen as desiring "too much too soon."

This account was given by Thomas Buckner.

☐ *A Thrilling Narrative from the Lips of the Sufferers of the Late Detroit Riot.* Detroit: Published privately by the author, 1863.

Sgt. Carney (CMH) Tells About Himself
Nine Negroes won the Congressional Medal of Honor in the Civil War. One of them, Sgt. William H. Carney, a member of the all-Negro Fifty-fourth Massachusetts Volunteers, was cited for outstanding bravery exhibited in the charge on Fort Wagner in the Harbor at Charleston, South Carolina, July 18, 1863.

☐ *The Liberator,* November 6, 1863.

Sentiments of the Colored People of Memphis
on the First Anniversary
of the Emancipation Proclamation
New Year's Day has long been celebrated in the Negro community as Emancipation Day. Thanksgiving is the keynote of such celebrations, but it is also an occasion for reassessing the status of the Negro in the United States and launching plans for further advance.

☐ *The Liberator,* January 29, 1964.

Congress Establishes the Freedmen's Bureau
The Freedmen's Bureau was Congress' recognition of federal responsibility for the gigantic task of Reconstruction. When Congress passed a second bill enlarging the scope of the Bureau on February 19, 1866, President Andrew Johnson vetoed it, thereby setting the stage for the long power struggle between the President and the "radical" Congress. On July 16, Congress overrode Johnson's veto, and the life of the Bureau was extended with broader powers.

☐ *U.S. Statutes at Large,* Vol. XIII, p. 507 ff.

The "Black Code" of Mississippi
Many Southern states passed laws intended to cope with the problems posed by the freedmen. They were sometimes less stringent than the laws passed by Mississippi, but were always greatly restrictive. Military governors often suspended these laws, and Constitutional and Congressional relief were provided later by the Fourteenth Amendment (1868) and the Civil Rights Act (1875), respectively.

☐ *Laws of Mississippi,* 1865, p. 82 ff.

The Thirteenth Amendment
With the passage of the Thirteenth Amendment,

slavery was outlawed throughout the land. The language of the Emancipation Proclamation, "then, thenceforth and forever free" was thereby translated into the law of the land.

☐ RICHARDSON, JAMES D. (ed.). *Compilation of the Messages and Papers of the Presidents.* Washington, D.C.: Bureau of National Literature and Art, 1904.

The First Reconstruction Act
With the radical Republicans scoring a major electoral victory in the mid-term elections of 1866, Congress went to work on the radical plan for Reconstruction. Andrew Johnson vetoed the bill, but Congress passed it over his veto.

☐ *U.S. Statutes at Large,* 39th Congress, Vol. IV, p. 428 ff.

The Fourteenth Amendment
In giving Negroes citizenship with privileges and immunities, the Fourteenth Amendment effectively reversed the dicta of the Dred Scott decision.

☐ RICHARDSON, JAMES D. (ed.). *Compilation of the Messages and Papers of the Presidents.* Washington, D.C.: Bureau of National Literature and Art, 1904.

KKK Rules of Order
The Ku Klux Klan was a secret society formed by whites in the South (Pulaski, Tennessee) in either 1865 or 1866. The Constitution, formally called a "Prescript," was ratified in 1867, and "revised and amended" in 1868. Dedicated to the revival of white supremacy, the Klan did not hesitate to use unlawful means to achieve its purposes. The Negro was the primary target of Klan terror and violence.

Nowhere in the "Prescript" is the title, Ku Klux Klan, used. Rather, three asterisks are substituted for the name of the organization. The name is said to have been arrived at as several suggested names were being considered. "In this number was the name 'Kukloi' from the Greek word *kuklos* meaning a band or circle. At mention of this someone cried out: Call it 'Ku Klux.' 'Klan' at once suggested itself and was added to complete the alliteration."

The Klan disbanded in 1869 but has had sporadic reincarnations since that time.

☐ LESTER, J. C. and D. L. WILSON. *The Ku Klux Klan,* W. L. Fleming (ed.). New York: The Neale Publishing Co., 1884, p. 154 ff.

First Negro Senator
Makes His First Speech to the Senate
Hiram Revels took his seat in the United States Senate on February 25, 1870. He was not only the first Negro elected to the "upper" house of Congress, but he was replacing Jefferson Davis, who had been President of the Confederate States of America. In his "maiden" speech, Revels made it clear that he would champion the cause of all loyal citizens "irrespective of color or race."

☐ *Congressional Record,* 41st Congress, Second Session, March 16, 1870.

The Fifteenth Amendment
The Fifteenth Amendment abolished race, color or former slavery as conditions affecting eligibility to vote.

☐ RICHARDSON, JAMES D. (ed.). *Compilation of the Messages and Papers of the Presidents.* Washington, D.C.: Bureau of National Literature and Art, 1904.

"Ku Klux Klan" Act
This Act, which attempted to guarantee Negroes the benefits of the Thirteenth, Fourteenth and Fifteenth Amendments, was popularly called the "Ku Klux Klan" Act. It was eventually ruled unconstitutional by the Supreme Court.

☐ *U.S. Statutes at Large,* Vol. XVIII, p. 13 ff.

Heroism of Negro Troops
Ten years after the event, Congress hears General Butler's recollections of the gallantry and courage of Negro troops under fire.

☐ *Congressional Record,* 43rd Congress, January 6, 1874.

The Civil Rights Act
By this Act, Congress prohibited racial discrimination in public places. The Supreme Court held that the law was unconstitutional in 1883 in the Civil Rights Cases. The rationale stated that the rights protected were social, not civil, and that Congress did not have authority to regulate such matters. This ruling in effect ended federal attempts at implementing the Fourteenth Amendment.

☐ *U.S. Statutes at Large,* Vol. XVIII, p. 335 ff.

Grant's Proclamation to Deter Terrorism
The attempts of the Democratic Party to regain its former strength in South Carolina included intimidation of Negro voters by the sight of white members of "Rifle Clubs" attending Republican meetings "with a view to impress the blacks with a sense of danger of longer holding out against white rule." Grant's proclamation commanded the terrorists to desist and disperse.

☐ *Congressional Record,* 44th Congress, Appendix, 1877, p. 230.

Mrs. Selina Wallis
Tells the Senate How Her Husband Was Murdered
The unreconstructed South was determined to rise again and did not always worry about legal or humanitarian niceties. Negro members of the Republican Party gambled with their lives in tense periods

of political activity. Here, Mrs. Wallis tells how her husband died. Mr. Wallis had been a Republican.

☐ Senate *Report* No. 512, 48th Congress, 1st Session, p. 69 ff.

Booker T. Washington's Address
at the Opening of the Cotton States' Exposition

Booker T. Washington, whose career carried him from a slave cabin to the presidency of a great Negro college, has in recent years been criticized for his advocacy of industrial rather than political advancement and his belief that "friendly relations" were possible between Southern whites and Negroes.

☐ WASHINGTON, BOOKER T. *Booker T. Washington's Own Story of His Life and Work*. Naperville, Illinois: J. L. Nichols & Co., 1916, pp. 137–143.

Plessy vs. Ferguson

Under a Louisiana law of 1890, railway companies operating coaches in that state were required to segregate Negro passengers. The Supreme Court upheld the law as a valid exercise of state police power. The decision gave rise to the doctrine of "separate but equal" which persisted for 58 years.

☐ U.S. Supreme Court *Reports,* 1896, Vol. 163.

The Last Negro in Congress Says "Goodbye"

On March 4, 1901, Congressman George H. White's term in the House ended. For the first time since Reconstruction there was not a single Negro member of Congress. Prior to his departure, White prophesied that the Negro would return. The prophecy was not fulfilled until after the passage of 28 years.

☐ *Congressional Record,* January 29, 1901.

SECTION FIVE:
BOUND FOR THE PROMISED LAND

Dr. DuBois' Affirmation of Faith

Dr. DuBois' "credo," which first appeared in a New York periodical, became so popular that it was reprinted in the Negro press. Many Negroes framed reproductions of the "credo" to hang on their walls.

☐ *The Independent,* New York, Vol. LVII, No. 2914 (October 6, 1904), p. 787.

The Niagara Movement Sets Forth Its Principles

The Niagara Movement was organized by Dr. DuBois and a group of 28 other Negro professional and business men who shared Dr. DuBois' feeling that the Booker T. Washington program was certainly inadequate—if not a retreat from Negro advance. Dr. DuBois had written them:

> "The time seems more than ripe for organized, determined and aggressive action on the part of men who believe in Negro freedom and growth. Movements are on foot threatening individual freedom and our self respect. I write you to propose a Conference during the coming summer. . . ."

The organization took its name from Niagara Falls. The Falls were close by the site of the first meeting and symbolized the power the founders wanted the movement to develop.

☐ Reprint of the original ·brochure available in the Schomburg Collection of Negro Literature and History of the New York Public Library.

The Birth of the NAACP

The National Association for the Advancement of Colored People is the congenital heir of the Niagara Movement. Eight members of the original NAACP Board of Directors were members of the Niagara Movement. Mary White Ovington, later author of an NAACP pamphlet describing the founding, was a young white reporter on the New York *Evening Post* who covered the 1906 meeting (at Harpers Ferry, Virginia) of the Niagara group. The call was written by Oswald Garrison Villard.

☐ Pamphlet: *How the National Association for the Advancement of Colored People Began.* Mary White Ovington.

The Urban League Emerges

The National Urban League represented another approach to the problem of discrimination in America. Formed by prominent educators, philanthropists and social workers, it tried to improve job opportunities for Negroes by persuading employers to change discriminatory employment practices.

The story of the League's emergence is told here by its first national Executive Secretary, Eugene Kinckle Jones.

☐ Pamphlet: *The Urban League—Its Story.* (Typed copy in the Schomburg Collection of Negro Literature and History of the New York Public Library.)

Founders Launch Journal of Negro History

Recognizing the need "to treat the record of the race scientifically and to publish the findings to the world," Carter G. Woodson, who received his Ph.D. from Harvard in 1912, called the first meeting of the Association for the Study of Negro Life and History, publishers of the *Journal of Negro History* and the *Negro History Bulletin.* The Association sponsors Negro History Week annually.

☐ The record of the founding meeting is quoted by Dr. Charles H. Wesley in the introduction to the 10th edition of Dr. Woodson's well-known study, *The Negro in Our History,* published by Associated Publishers, Inc., Washington, D.C.

World War I

Negroes in World War I totaled approximately 367,000 servicemen and 1,400 commissioned officers. At least 100,000 were assigned to duty in Europe. The first Americans decorated for bravery in France were Harry Johnson and Needham Roberts of the New York 369th Infantry Regiment. Individual awards of the Croix de Guerre and the Legion of Honor were made to 171 members of the 369th. Awards of the Croix de Guerre were made to the entire 369th, 371st and 372nd Infantry Regiments.

Valor and gallantry did not dispel racial feeling during this war to "Make the World Safe for Democracy." Race riots and lynchings documented white resentment of the Negro; and his uniform did not shield the Negro soldier from insults and affronts. In Spartanburg, South Carolina, when interracial violence threatened, Negro troops were shipped overseas.

Some Negroes wondered why there wasn't a campaign to *"Make Democracy Safe in America."*

Marcus Garvey Outlines Program of U.N.I.A.
In 1914 the Universal Negro Improvement Association (U.N.I.A.) was founded by Marcus Manasseh Garvey in his native Jamaica, West Indies. He later came to the United States and in 1917 reorganized U.N.I.A. The growth of the organization was phenomenal, and in a short time Garvey was the best-known Negro leader in the world.

☐ Speech: *The Principles of the Universal Negro Improvement Association,* delivered at Liberty Hall, New York City, November 25, 1922.

Congressman DePriest on Equal Justice
Oscar DePriest, the son of Alabama ex-slave parents, was elected to Congress from Chicago's Third Ward in 1928. He remained in Congress until 1934 when he was defeated by a Negro Democrat, Arthur W. Mitchell.

☐ *Congressional Record*—House, 73rd Congress, First Session, May 3, 1933, p. 2822 ff.

The Lynching of Claude Neal
The first published compilation of lynching statistics was Ida B. Wells's pamphlet, *A Red Record,* which appeared in 1895. This national disgrace was discussed on the floor of the House of Representatives in 1900 by Congressman George White when he introduced the first federal anti-lynching legislation. When Oscar DePriest came to Congress in 1929, Negroes were still being lynched. This harrowing account was one of many means used by the NAACP to highlight the need for Congressional action to outlaw lynching.

☐ Pamphlet: *The Lynching of Claude Neal.* New York: NAACP, 1934. (Reprinted by permission of NAACP.)

Executive Order 8802
Fair Employment Practice in Defense Industry. The United States accelerated its defense production after World War II began in Europe. Defense industries were loaded down with government contracts, yet many contractors had discriminatory hiring practices. Routine protests from civil rights groups and individuals proved ineffective. Under the leadership of A. Philip Randolph, president of the Brotherhood of Sleeping Car Porters, a March-On-Washington was planned. President Roosevelt called a meeting of Negro leaders to forestall the "March." Lerone Bennett describes the meeting in *Before the Mayflower.*

Failing to dissuade the group, Roosevelt acceded to their demands for an Executive Order requiring fair employment practices in defense industries. The Order was issued seven days later. The March was called off.

Copies of this poster were hung in government offices and many industrial plants.

☐ Executive Order 8802—*Federal Register,* Vol. VI, No. 125, Friday, June 27, 1941, p. 3109 ff.

World War II
One of the first heroes of the Second World War was Dorie Miller, a Negro messman stationed aboard the battleship *Arizona* at Pearl Harbor. Miller is credited with bringing down four Japanese planes during the Japanese attack on Pearl Harbor, December 7, 1941.

Discrimination yielded somewhat during the war. The Navy and Marines accepted Negroes for general service. Negro ROTC training units were organized. Four Negro captains commanded integrated Merchant Marine "Liberty Ships." (Eighteen of these ships bore the names of famous Negroes.) Negro women served in the various services; and Colonel Benjamin O. Davis, Jr. commanded the 332nd Fighter Group, which flew more than 3,000 missions and is credited with downing 300 enemy aircraft. On July 1, 1945, Colonel Davis was named Commanding Officer of Godman Field, Kentucky.

One million Negroes, women and men, wore the uniforms of the United States' armed services during World War II. That America still denied them full measure of liberty, justice and human dignity rarely caused impairment of their effectiveness as animate weapons in the "arsenal of democracy."

President Truman
Ends Segregation in the Armed Forces
With the inauguration of the Selective Service program, Negroes again realized that their role in the nation's defense would be largely menial. Negro leaders began campaigning for use of Negro troops commensurate with their skills and experience rather than on the basis of race. (College graduates assigned to maintenance units were not uncommon during World War II.) Gestures—the promotion of Colonel Benjamin O. Davis to the rank of brigadier general; half measures—the acceptance of Negroes for *general* service by the Navy and Marine Corps; special projects—the Air Force pilot training school at Tuskegee, *all* failed to silence the call for equal treatment in the military.

After much discussion, extended Congressional hearings and voluminous special studies, integration became the order of the day by direction of the Commander in Chief, Harry S. Truman.

☐ Executive Order 9981—*Federal Register,* Wednesday, July 28, 1949, p. 4313.

Brown vs. Board of Education

After almost threescore years the Court reviewed the doctrine of "separate but equal" established in 1896 by the decision in Plessy vs. Ferguson. Reversing the dictum of the Plessy case, the Court avowed: "Separate educational facilities are inherently unequal."

A year later, on May 31, 1955, the Court ordered the implementation of the decision with "all deliberate speed."

☐ 347 U.S. 483.

Ninety-Six Southern Congressmen
Denounce the Supreme Court

The sanctity of the institution of judicial review was challenged by a coalition of Southerners in Congress. Calling the desegregation decision abusive and accusing the Court of usurping legislative powers, they pledged themselves to effecting a reversal of the decision and to the resistance of integration by any lawful means.

☐ *Congressional Record*—Senate, March 12, 1956, p. 4460 ff.

President Eisenhower's Little Rock Intervention

In an attempt to head off the integration of Little Rock's Central High School, Governor Orval Faubus called up the Arkansas National Guard to turn away Negro pupils who might attempt to enter.

In a surprising action, President Eisenhower—no champion of Negro rights (he had been lukewarm about integration of the Armed Forces)—federalized the National Guard and summoned the full power of the federal government to secure compliance with the U.S. District Court's ruling that integration must begin.

Governor Faubus retreated, and nine children of Little Rock, with military escorts, integrated Central High School.

☐ Executive Order 10730, *Federal Register,* Vol. XXII, No. 186 (Documents 57–7977), September 24, 1957, p. 7628 ff.

President Kennedy Authorizes Troops to End
Segregation at University of Mississippi

After exhausting other technical devices to prevent the enrollment of James Meredith, 29-year-old Air Force veteran, at the University of Mississippi, Governor Ross Barnett finally planted himself before the doors of the school, declaring that he would prefer death to permitting a Negro within the precincts of "Ole Miss." He was later joined by a mob of students and segregationists from various parts of the South.

Troops authorized by President Kennedy's Executive Order fired tear gas and eventually quieted the rioting, but not before casualties included two deaths and several injuries. As 22,000 soldiers stood guard, James Meredith was finally enrolled at the university. He later graduated on August 18, 1963.

☐ Executive Order 11053. *Federal Register,* Tuesday, October 2, 1962, p. 9693.

Governor Wallace Defies the Supreme Court

The New York *Times* headlined the capitulation: "Alabama Admits 2 Negroes to State University After Wallace Bows to U.S. Force."

In fulfillment of a campaign pledge to "stand in the schoolhouse door" to prevent further desegregation of the Alabama school system, Governor Wallace stood on the steps of the University of Alabama's Foster Auditorium and four times denied admission to Vivian Malone and James Hood. The Negro students, both 20 years old, planned to register at the Dixie school. A Birmingham realtor, now Commander of federalized troops from the 31st Division, Brigadier General Henry V. Graham, finally told the governor it was his "sad duty" to order him to stand aside. After another verbal volley, the governor left the Tuscaloosa campus and returned to Montgomery. Vivian Malone and James Hood were registered.

(The day before in Oxford, Mississippi, U.S. troops stationed near the campus of the University of Mississippi to protect James Meredith and Cleve McDowell were withdrawn.)

☐ New York *Times.* Wednesday, June 12, 1963.

President Kennedy
Calls for Action to End Segregation

Summoning the nation to face squarely a "moral crisis," President Kennedy asked "every American . . . to stop and examine his conscience." The speech was a landmark in the nation's history. No other President had publicly tied the national position on racial matters to the nation's morality. It was perhaps also a watershed in President Kennedy's growth as man and chief executive. In his bylined report of the address, Tom Wicker of the New York *Times* observed:

> "Mr. Kennedy's address was one of the most emotional speeches yet delivered by a President who has often been criticized as being too 'cool' and intellectual. Near the end of his talk, Mr. Kennedy appeared to be speaking without a text, and there was a fervor in his voice as he talked about the plight of some Americans."

☐ New York *Times,* Wednesday, June 12, 1963.

Birmingham Manifesto

The Reverend Fred Shuttlesworth has been called "the most courageous civil rights fighter in the South" by Dr. Martin Luther King, Jr. And the campaign against segregation in Birmingham dramatized the plight of the Southern Negro to the nation. Segregationists resisted with mass arrests, night sticks, fire hoses, police dogs and pistol butts as Negroes persisted with boycotts, voter registration drives, pray-ins, and freedom songs. Children became heroes in crowded jails, and the name "Bull" Connor was boldly inscribed in the book of infamy.

☐ S.C.L.C. *Newsletter,* Vol. I, Number 10, July, 1963, p. 2.

Episcopal Bishop's Message at Whitsuntide

The thrust of civil rights became the principal domestic concern in the America of 1963. Churches and churchmen, recognizing the spiritual implications of the Negro's call for "Freedom Now," reviewed the tenets of their faith and voiced their conviction that right—and righteousness—were on the Negro's side.

In his Whitsuntide epistle, Bishop Arthur Lichtenberger, Presiding Bishop of the Episcopal Church, exhorted Episcopalians to prayer and action.

☐ "The Presiding Bishop's 1963 Whitsuntide Message" (June 2, 1963) reprinted in a leaflet *This Is An Appeal To You!,* published by the National Council, Episcopal Church Center, New York.

The Cardinal's Message to New York Catholics

Speaking at the dedication of New York City's Drew Houses on July 11, 1963, Francis Cardinal Spellman told his listeners that the Negro must be made to feel at home in his American house. An extract from this address was circulated to all churches in the Archdiocese and was read in lieu of the sermon at all diocesan masses on Sunday, July 14.

☐ Extract from Statement by Francis Cardinal Spellman, July 11, 1963 . . . (Copy supplied by the New York Archdiocese).

Reform Judaism's Call to Racial Justice

The 47th Biennial General Assembly of the Union of American Hebrew Congregations, Reform Judaism's central body, adopted a "Commitment on Racial Justice" which said in part:

> "So long as synagogue and church, and their memberships, are not completely free of the taint of racism, the voice of America's religions cannot speak truly in behalf of equality and freedom."

The group's Commission on Social Action circulated a draft proposal of "A Call To Racial Justice" which has been adapted by many congregations throughout the nation with only minor concessions to local conditions.

☐ *A Call To Racial Justice* [draft proposal]. From the Commission On Social Action of Reform Judaism.

The March on Washington

MAMMOTH RALLY OF 200,000 JAMS MALL IN SOLEMN, ORDERLY PLEA FOR EQUALITY
*Largest Demonstration On Civil Rights
Urges Passage of Legislation*
(Headlines in the Washington *Post,*
Thursday, August 29, 1963)

They came from everywhere and from all walks of life. They were movie stars, famous personalities, congressmen, entertainers, clergymen, educators, civil rights leaders, sociologists and just plain folks. They were dressed in blue jeans and seersucker suits; mail order dresses and designer originals; they looked cool or they looked starchy. They were young and they were old. They were happy and they were troubled. They were there.

Mahalia Jackson sang and brought tears to their eyes—then she turned them into swaying hand-clapping revivalists. Martin Luther King described his dream of a better America. It was their dream too.

It was an experience beyond duplication. It was the biggest demonstration the nation's capital had ever seen.

It was a great day.

The Civil Rights Act

A century after the Emancipation Proclamation, on June 21, 1963, without fanfare, H.R. 7152, a civil rights bill, was introduced in the House of Representatives. One year later, on July 2, 1964, it emerged as the Civil Rights Act of 1964.

Its progress had been slow—and wordy.

1. Six Congressional Committees sat for 81 days and heard 269 witnesses.
2. In nine days of debate from January 31 to February 10, 1964 the House filled 477 pages of the Congressional Record.
3. As of June 20, 1964, the Senate debate had filled 2,890 pages of the Congressional Record during the 83-day period—736 hours and 10 minutes—from March 9 through June 20.
4. June 9–10, Senator Robert C. Byrd, Democrat of West Virginia, talked against the bill for 14 hours.

To Senator Byrd, the Act was contrary to nature's laws.

To Roy Wilkins, NAACP executive secretary, it was the "Magna Carta" of human rights.

To Fred L. Shuttlesworth, president of the Alabama Christian Movement for Human Rights, it was "the second Emancipation Proclamation."

To all law-abiding American citizens, it was the law of the land.

☐ Public Law 88—352, 78 Stat. 247.

Bibliography

GENERAL

AIKIN, CHARLES. *The Negro Votes.* San Francisco: Chandler Publishing Co., 1962.

APTHEKER, HERBERT. *American Slave Revolts.* New York: Columbia University Press, 1943.

———— *Documentary History of the Negro People in the United States.* New York: Citadel Press, 1951.

BARDOLPH, RICHARD. *The Negro Vanguard.* New York: Vintage Press, 1959.

BONTEMPS, ARNA. *The Story of the Negro.* 3rd edition. New York: Alfred Knopf, 1958.

———— *One Hundred Years of Negro Freedom.* New York: Dodd, Mead and Co., 1962.

BRAWLEY, BENJAMIN. *A Short History of the American Negro.* New York: Macmillan, 1919.

———— *A Social History of the American Negro.* New York: Macmillan, 1921.

———— *Negro Builders and Heroes.* Chapel Hill: University of North Carolina, 1937.

———— *The Negro Genius.* New York: Dodd, Mead and Co., 1937.

BROWN, WILLIAM WELLS. *Rising Son: The Antecedents and Advancement of the Colored Race.* Boston: A. G. Brown, 1874.

———— *The Black Man; His Antecedents, His Genius, and His Achievements.* Boston: J. Redpath, 1863.

BUCKMASTER, HENRIETTA. *Let My People Go.* New York: Harper and Bros., 1941.

BUNCHE, RALPH. *Political Status of the Negro.* (Part of the Carnegie-Myrdal study. Manuscript available in the Schomburg Collection of Negro Literature and History of the New York Public Library.) 1940.

CALDWELL, ARTHUR B. *History of the American Negro and His Institution.* Vols. 1–7. Atlanta: A. B. Caldwell, 1917.

CHAMBERS, LUCILLE AROLA. *America's Tenth Man.* New York: Twayne Publishers, 1957.

CROMWELL, JOHN W. *The Negro in American History.* Washington: The American Negro Academy, 1911.

CULP, D. W. *Twentieth Century Negro Literature or a Cyclopedia of Thought on Vital Topics Relating to the American Negro Life, 100 of America's Greatest Negroes.* Naperville: J. L. Nichols and Co., 1902.

DELANY, MARTIN R. *Condition, Elevation, Emigration and Destiny of the Colored People of the United States, Politically Considered.* Philadelphia: Martin R. Delany, 1852.

DETWEILER, FREDERICK G. *The Negro Press in the United States.* Chicago: University of Chicago Press, 1922.

DUNBAR, ALICE MOORE (Ed.). *Masterpieces of Negro Eloquence.* New York: The Bookery Publishing Co., 1914.

DU BOIS, W. E. B. *The Negro.* New York: Holt, Rinehart and Winston, 1915.

———— *Black Folks Then and Now: An Essay in the History and Sociology of the Negro Race.* New York: Holt, Rinehart and Winston, 1939.

———— *The Souls of Black Folk: Essays and Sketches.* New York: Blue Heron Press, 1953.

EMBREE, DODWIN R. *Brown America.* New York: Viking Press, 1944.

———— *Thirteen Against the Odds.* New York: Viking Press, 1944.

EPPSE, MERL R. *The Negro Too in American History.* Nashville: National Publication Co., 1949.

FLEXNER, ELEANOR. *Century of Struggle.* Cambridge: Belknap Press, 1959.

FLIPPER, HENRY O. *Negro Frontiersman.* El Paso: Western College Press, 1963.

FRANKLIN, JOHN HOPE. *From Slavery to Freedom* (revised edition). New York: Alfred A. Knopf, 1956.

———— *The Negro Church in America.* New York: Schocken Books, 1964.

———— *The Negro in the United States.* New York: Macmillan, 1957.

FULLER, THOMAS O. *Pictorial History of the American Negro.* Memphis: Pictorial History, Inc., 1933.

GIBSON, JOHN W. and WILLIAM CROGMAN. *Progress of a Race: Or the Remarkable Advancement of the American Negro from Bondage of Slavery, Ignorance and Poverty to the Freedom of Citizenship, Intelligence, Affluence, Honor and Trust.* Naperville: J. L. Nichols and Co., 1929.

HART, ALBERT BUSNELL (Ed.). *Commonwealth History of Massachusetts.* Vols. 1–5. New York: The States History Co., 1927–1930.

HASKIN, SARA E. *Handicapped Winners.* Nashville: Dallas Publishing House of ME Church South, 1922.

HILL, FREDERICK TREVOR. *Decisive Battles of the Law.* New York: Harper and Bros., 1907.

HUGHES, LANGSTON and MILTON MELTZER. *A Pictorial History of the Negro in America.* New York: Crown Publishers, 1963.

JOHNSON, EDWARD A. *A School History of the Negro Race in America from 1619 to 1890.* New

York: Isaac Goldman Co., Printers, 1891.

LAWSON, JOHN D. *American State Trials*. Vol. 7. St. Louis: F. H. Thomas Law Book Co., 1917.

LOCKE, ALAIN L. *The Negro in America*. Chicago: American Library Association, 1933.

LOGAN, RAYFORD. *Negro in American Culture*. Princeton: Van Nostrand, 1957.

——— *Negro in American Life and Thought*. New York: Dial, 1954.

——— *The Negro in the United States*. Princeton: Van Nostrand, 1957.

MECKLIN, JOHN M. *The Ku Klux Klan; A Study of the American Mind*. New York: Russell and Russell, 1963.

MEIER, AUGUST. *Negro Thought in America, 1880–1915*. Ann Arbor: University of Michigan, 1963.

MODE, PETER GEORGE (Ed.). *Source Book and Bibliographical Guide for American Church History*. Menasha, Wisc.: George Banta, 1921.

NOWLIN, WILLIAM F. *The Negro in American Politics*. Boston: Stratford Co., 1931.

OTTLEY, ROI. *Story of the Negro in America*. New York: Viking Press, 1927.

OVINGTON, MARY W. *Portraits in Color*. New York: Viking Press, 1927.

REDDING, JAY SAUNDERS. *They Came in Chains: Americans from Africa*. Philadelphia: J. B. Lippincott, 1950.

RICHARDSON, JAMES D. (Ed.). *Compilation of the Messages and Papers of the Presidents*. Washington: Bureau of National Literature and Art, 1904.

SHAW, JAMES BEVERLY F. *The Negro in the History of Methodism*. Nashville: Parthenon, 1954.

SIMONS, W. J. *Men of Mark*. Cleveland: G. M. Rewell and Co., 1887.

U.S. President's Commission on Higher Education. *Higher Education for American Democracy*. Vols. 1–6. Washington: U.S. Government Printing Office, 1947.

WASHINGTON, BOOKER T. *The Story of the Negro*. Vols. 1–2. New York: Doubleday, 1909.

WHITE, WALTER F. *A Man Called White*. New York: Viking Press, 1948.

——— *Rope and Faggot; Biography of Judge Lynch*. New York: Alfred A. Knopf, 1929.

WILLIAMS, GEORGE W. *History of the Negro Race in America from 1619–1880*. 2 vols. New York: G. P. Putnam, 1883.

WILSON, JAMES Q. *Negro Politics; the Search for Leadership*. Glencoe, Ill.: Free Press, 1960.

WOODSON, CARTER G. *History of the Negro Church*. 2nd edition. Washington: Associated Publishers, 1921.

——— *The Mind of the Negro as Reflected in Letters Written During the Crisis 1800–1860*. Washington: Associated Publishers, 1926.

——— *The Negro in Our History*. 10th edition. Washington: Associated Publishers, 1962.

——— *Negro Orators and Their Orations*. Washington: Associated Publishers, 1925.

SECTION I
The House of Bondage (Pages 22–67)

Appendix (The): *Or Some Observations on the Expediency of the Petition of the Africans Living in Boston, and lately presented to the General Assembly of this Province to which is annexed, the Petition referred to Likewise Thoughts on Slavery with a Useful Extract from the Massachusetts Spy, of January 28, 1773, by way of an Address to the Members of the Assembly. By a Lover of Constitutional Liberty.* Boston: Russell Printers, 1773.

APTHEKER, HERBERT. *The Negro in the American Revolution*. New York: International Publishers, 1938.

BAKER, HENRY E. "Benjamin Banneker, The Negro Mathematician and Astronomer." *Journal of Negro History*. Vol. 3. [April, 1918], pp. 99–118.

CATTERALL, HELEN T. (Ed.). *Judicial Cases Concerning American Slavery and the Negro*. Vols. 1–5. Washington: Carnegie Institution, 1926–1937.

DONNAN, ELIZABETH (Ed.). *Documents Illustrative of the Slave Trade to America*. Vols. 1–3. Washington: Carnegie Institution, 1930–1935.

DOUGLASS, WILLIAM. *Annals of the First African Church in the United States of America*. Philadelphia: King and Baird, 1862.

DUMOND, DWIGHT L. *Anti-Slavery, the Crusade for Freedom in America*. Ann Arbor: University of Michigan, 1961.

DRAKE, THOMAS E. *Quakers and Slavery in America*. New Haven: Yale University Press, 1950.

DU BOIS, W. E. B. *The Suppression of the African Slave Trade to the United States of America, 1638–1870*. New York: Harvard Historical Studies I, 1896.

FALCONBRIDGE, ALEXANDER. *An Account of the Slave Trade on the Coast of Africa*. London: J. Phillips, G. Yard, 1788. (Copy available in the Schomburg Collection of Negro Literature and History of the New York Public Library.)

GREENE, LORENZO J. *The Negro in Colonial New England, 1620–1776*. New York: Columbia University Press, 1942.

JONES, ABSALOM and RICHARD ALLEN. *A Narrative of the Proceedings of the Black People, during the Late Awful Calamity in Philadelphia in the Year 1793.* Philadelphia: Printed for the authors by William W. Woodward at Franklin's Head, 1794.

MAZYCK, W. H. *George Washington and the Negro.* Washington: Associated Publishers, 1932.

MOORE, GEORGE H. *Historical Notes on the Employment of Negroes in the American Army of the Revolution.* New York: E. T. Evans, 1862.

NELL, WILLIAM C. *The Colored Patriots of the American Revolution.* Boston: Robert F. Walcut, 1886.

PALMER, WILLIAM P. (Ed.). *Calendar of Virginia.* Vol. 1. Richmond: 1875.

PHILLIPS, ULRICH B. *American Negro Slavery.* New York and London: D. Appleton and Co., 1918.

QUARLES, BENJAMIN. *The Negro in the American Revolution.* Chapel Hill: University of North Carolina, 1961.

SPEARS, JOHN R. *The American Slave Trade.* New York: Charles Scribner, 1900.

TYSON, MARTHA E. *Banneker, the Afric-American Astronomer.* Philadelphia: The Friends Book Association, 1844.

WASHINGTON, H. A. (Ed.). *The Writings of Thomas Jefferson.* New York: H. W. Derby, 1859.

WESLEY, CHARLES H. "The Concept of Negro Inferiority in American Thought." *Journal of Negro History.* Vol. 25. [Oct., 1940], pp. 540–560.

——— *Richard Allen, Apostle of Freedom.* Washington: Associated Publishers, 1935.

SECTION II
Let My People Go (Pages 68–151)

ADAMS, ALICE. *The Neglected Period of Anti-Slavery Agitation in America, 1808–31.* Boston: Ginn and Co., 1908.

An Address to the New York African Society for Mutual Relief, Delivered in the Universalist Church. January 2, 1809. (Copy available in the Boston Athenaeum.)

BARNES, GILBERT HOBBS. *The Anti-slavery Impulse 1830–1844.* New York: Harcourt, Brace and World, Inc., 1964.

COBB, THOMAS R. *An Inquiry into the Law of Negro Slavery in the United States of America.* Philadelphia: Johnson and Williams, 1858.

Constitution of the American Society of Free Persons of Colour, for Improving their Condition in the United States; for Purchasing Land and for the Establishment of a Settlement of Upper Canada. Also the Proceedings of the Convention, with their Address to the Free Persons of Colour in the United States. Philadelphia: 1831.

CROMWELL, JOHN W. *The Early Negro Convention Movement.* Washington: The American Negro Academy, 1904.

DOUGLASS, FREDERICK. *The Life and Times of Frederick Douglass.* Hartford: Park Publishers, 1884.

FONER, PHILIP S. (Ed.). *Life and Writings of Frederick Douglass.* Vols. 1–4. New York: International Publishers, 1950–1955.

GARNET, HENRY HIGHLAND. *A Memorial Discourse; Delivered in the Hall of the House of Representatives, Washington City, D.C. on Sabbath, February 12, 1865.* Philadelphia: Joseph M. Wilson, 1865.

GARRISON, WILLIAM LLOYD. *Thoughts on African Colonization or An Impartial Exhibition of the Doctrines, Principles and Purposes of the American Colonization Society. Together with the Resolutions, Addresses and Remonstrances of the Free People of Color.* Boston: Garrison and Knapp, 1832.

GARRISON, WENDELL PHILLIPS and FRANCIS JACKSON GARRISON. *William Lloyd Garrison: 1805–1879. The Story of His Life Told By His Children.* Vols. 1–4. Boston: Houghton, Mifflin and Co., 1889.

PAUL, NATHANIEL. *An Address Delivered on the Celebration of the Abolition of Slavery in the State of New York, July 5, 1827.* Albany: Trustees, First African Baptist Society, 1827. (Copy available in the Schomburg Collection of Negro Literature and History of the New York Public Library.)

RUGGLES, DAVID. *"The Extinguisher" Extinguished: or David M. Reese, M.D. "Used Up"* (pamphlet). New York: 1834. (Copy available in the Schomburg Collection of Negro Literature and History of the New York Public Library.)

SCHUCKERS, JACOB WILLIAMS. *Life and Public Services of S. P. Chase.* New York: D. Appleton and Co., 1874.

SMALL, EDWIN W. and MIRIAN R. SMALL. "Prudence Crandall, Champion of Negro Education." *New England Quarterly, Orono,* 1944, Vol. 17, pp. 506–529.

TURNER, LORENZO D. *Anti-Slavery in American Literature Prior to 1865.* Washington: The Association for the Study of Negro Life and History, 1929.

WASHINGTON, BOOKER T. *Frederick Douglas.* Philadelphia: G. W. Jacobs, 1907.

WESLEY, CHARLES H. "The Participation of Negroes in Anti-Slavery Political Parties." *Journal of Negro History,* Vol. 29 [Jan., 1944] pp. 32–74.

SECTION III
The Walls Came Tumblin'Down (Pages 152–169)

ANDERSON, OSBORNE PERRY. *A Voice from Harper's Ferry*. Boston: J. D. Enned, 1961.

APTHEKER, HERBERT. *The Negro in the Civil War*. New York: International Publishers, 1938.

BROWN, WILLIAM WELLS. *The Negro in the American Rebellion: His Heroism and Fidelity*. Boston: Lee and Shephard, 1867.

CAREY, MATTHEW. *Letters on the Colonization Society; and of its Probable Results*. 4th edition. Philadelphia: L. Johnson, 1833.

FRANKLIN, JOHN HOPE. *Emancipation Proclamation*. Garden City: Doubleday, 1963.

FURNAS, J. C. *The Road to Harper's Ferry*. New York: William Sloane Associates, 1959.

GIBSON, JOHN W. and WILLIAM CROGMAN. *The Colored American from Slavery to Honorable Citizenship*. Atlanta: J. H. Nichols, 1902.

GUERNSEY, ALFRED H. and HENRY M. ALDEN (Eds.). *Harper's Pictorial History of the Great Rebellion*. Chicago: McDonnell Bros., 1866.

MOORE, FRANK (Ed.). *The Rebellion Record*. New York: G. P. Putnam, 1864.

STEPHENS, ALEXANDER H. (Ed.). *A Constitutional View of the Late War Between the States, Its Causes, Character, Conduct and Results*. 2 Vols. Philadelphia: National Publishing Co., 1868–1870.

VILLARD, OSWALD G. *John Brown, 1800–1859; A Biography Fifty Years After*. Boston: Houghton, Mifflin and Co., 1911.

SECTION IV
The Wilderness of Emancipation (Pages 170–215)

A Thrilling Narrative from the Lips of the Sufferers of the Late Detroit Riot. Detroit: Published privately by the author, 1863.

DONALD, HENDERSON H. *The Negro Freedman*. New York: H. Schuman, 1952.

DU BOIS, W. E. B. *Black Reconstruction*. Philadelphia: Saifer, 1952.

——— *Black Reconstruction in America*. New York: Russell and Russell, 1962.

FLEMING, W. L. *Documentary History of Reconstruction*. Vols. 1–2. Cleveland: A. H. Clark, 1906.

LANGSTON, JOHN MERCER. *From the Virginia Plantations to the National Capital—or The First and Only Negro Representative in Congress From the Old Dominion*. Hartford: American Publishing Co., 1894.

LESTER, J. C. and D. L. WILSON. *The Ku Klux Klan*. W. L. Fleming (Ed.). New York: The Neale Publishing Co., 1884.

MORTON, RICHARD L. *The Negro in Virginia Politics, 1865–1902*. Charlottesville, Va.: University of Virginia Press, 1919.

RICHINGS, G. F. *Evidences of Progress Among Colored People*. Philadelphia: George S. Ferguson, 1896.

SMITH, SAMUEL D. *The Negro in Congress, 1870–1901*. Chapel Hill: University of North Carolina, 1940.

WARMOTH, HENRY CLAY. *War, Politics and Reconstruction; Stormy Days in Louisiana*. New York: Macmillan, 1930.

WASHINGTON, BOOKER T. *Selected Speeches*. E. Davidson Washington (Ed.). Garden City: Doubleday, 1932.

WESLEY, CHARLES H. *The Collapse of the Confederacy*. Washington: Associated Publishers, 1937.

——— "The Employment of Negroes as Soldiers in the Confederate Army." *Journal of Negro History*, Vol. 4. [April, 1919], pp. 239–253.

WHARTON, VERNON L. *The Negro in Mississippi, 1865–1890*. Chapel Hill: University of North Carolina, 1947.

SECTION V
Bound for the Promised Land (Pages 216–325)

BATES, DAISY. *The Long Shadow of Little Rock*. New York: David McKay Co., Inc., 1962.

CRONON, EDMUND D. *Black Moses, the Story of Marcus Garvey and the Universal Negro Improvement Association*. Madison: University of Wisconsin Press, 1955.

DU BOIS, W. E. B. "Results of Ten Tuskegee Conferences." *Harper's Weekly*. June 22, 1901.

JACQUES-GARVEY, AMY (Ed.). *Philosophy and Opinions of Marcus Garvey*. New York: Universal Publishing House, 1923–1925.

LITTLE, ARTHUR W. *From Harlem to the Rhine; the Story of New York's Colored Volunteers*. New York: Covici Friede Publishers, 1936.

REDDICK, L. D. "The Negro Policy of the American Army Since World War II." *Journal of Negro History*, Vol. 38. [Jan., 1953], pp. 196–215.

SILVERA, JOHN D. *The Negro in World War II*. n.p.: Military Printing, 1946.

The Lynching of Claude Neal. (Anonymous pamphlet). New York: NAACP, 1934.

Urban League. *The Urban League—Its Story*. (pamphlet—Typed copy in the Schomburg Collection of Negro Literature and History of the New York Public Library.) New York: Urban League, 1940.

WHITE, WALTER F. *How Far the Promised Land?* New York: Viking Press, 1955.

Acknowledgments

My gratitude is boundless for the assistance, encouragement and advice I have received from numerous sources while this volume was in preparation. I am especially indebted to the editorial staff of Educational Heritage, Inc. who have extended themselves beyond the normal requirements of their assigned tasks. Without definition of their specific contributions I herewith acknowledge my appreciation to Walter Christmas, Harold Franklin, Roland Mitchell, Sheila Estick, Otto Lindenmeyer, Adolph Slaughter, Karl Folkes, Grace Ottley, Norton Taylor, Horace Varela, Bernard Shore and Irwin Feder. A special note of appreciation is due Clifford A. Bradshaw who has spent countless hours typing and retyping the manuscript in its various phases.

We have called upon the resources of many libraries and archives and without exception they have been understanding and cooperative. However, the exceptional courtesies shown our researchers by Mr. Wendell Wray, Acting Curator, and the staff of the Schomburg Collection cannot go unmentioned.

Despite my best wishes to compress within these pages a comprehensive study, I concede that there may be shortcomings and I must ask the reader to absolve all but myself for such failings. Granted extended mortality, perhaps I shall achieve a higher degree of perfection in subsequent editions.

A. E. C.

Index

Abernathy, Rev. Ralph D. — 363
Adams, John Quincy — 69, 141
Adams, Joseph — 93
Addams, Jane — 228
Africa, Return to
☐ Resolution against — 80–81, 363
☐ Marcus Garvey's proposals — 234–239
African Colonization Society — 93
African Methodist Episcopal Church Resolutions — 110, 365
Agutter, William — 18
Alabama
☐ Constitution of — 271
☐ University of — 272
☐ *Birmingham Manifesto* — 276–277
☐ Supreme Court — 336, 337
Allen, John — 93
Allen, Richard — 92–94, 363
☐ Recall of Negro valor during cholera epidemic — 60–63
☐ Views on Slavery — 64–65
Allwright, S. E. — 343
Almond, J. Lindsay, Jr. — 355
Ambris River — 44, 46, 53
American Anti-Slavery Society — 73, 107, 365, 366
☐ Constitution — 102–104, 365
☐ Declaration of Sentiments — 104–105, 365
American Colonization Society — 101, 363
American Revolutionary War — 18, 25, 55, 123, 153, 362
Anderson, Chief Justice [John C.] of Alabama Supreme Court — 336
Anderson, Osborne Perry — 367
Angola — 53
Anti-Slavery, Sentiments of
☐ Germantown Quakers — 28–29
☐ "Felix" of Massachusetts — 30–31
☐ Early Draft of Declaration of Independence — 32–35
☐ Thomas Jefferson — 39–40
☐ Supreme Court of Massachusetts — 41
☐ Benjamin Banneker — 56–58
☐ Absalom Jones — 64–65
☐ American Anti-Slavery Society — 102–105
☐ Henry Highland Garnet — 120–123
☐ Horace Greeley — 166–168
☐ Abraham Lincoln — 168–169
☐ Colored People of Memphis, Tennessee — 179
Appeal of the Independent Democrats — 140–142, 367
Arnold, Benedict — 101
Arnold, John — 93
Arrington, Richard Olney — 348
Articles of Confederation — 25
Ashmore, Margaret — 117
Association for the Study of Negro Life and History — 231, 370
Attucks, Crispus — 24
Augustus, Scipio C. — 93

Bacon, Lord — 215
Bailey, Joseph W. — 332
Baker, Judge [Richard H.] — 139
Baldwin, William H., Mr. and Mrs.:
Founding of the Urban League — 229–230
Banneker, Benjamin: Correspondence with Thomas Jefferson — 56–59, 362–363
Barbé-Marbois, François — 362
Barnett, Ida Wells — 228, 371
Barnett, Governor Ross — 372
Bates, Ruby — 242–243
Battle of Antietam — 368
Beale, J. J. — 332
Beazley, Annie — 27

Beckley, Pendleton	333
Bennett, Lerone	371
Berea College Case	227
Berkeley, William	27
Bigham, J. A.	231
Bight Negroes	47
Bill of Rights of 1689	15
Birmingham Manifesto	276–277, 373
"Black Code" of Mississippi	182–183
Black, Cyrus	92, 93
Black, Justice Hugo L.	*264*, 342, 345
Blaine, James G.	20
Blakey, Clayton B.	333
Blatch, Harriet Stanton	228
Bob-Lo v. *Michigan*	347
Bonny River	52, 53
Bonny, Slave Market at	42, 44, 46, 50, 52, 53
Booth, John Wilkes	154
Botkin, B. A.	72
Bowers, John	93
Bowler, William	81
Bowles, Samuel	228
Bradley, Justice [Joseph]	209
Bratton, U. S.	334
Breckinridge, Sophonisba P.	231
Brewer, Earl	338
Broun, Heywood	242
Brown, Ed	338
Brown, George L.	93
Brown, Justice [Henry B.]	173
Brown, John: Speech after being adjudged guilty of treason	156–157, 367
Brown, Rev. Morris	365
Brown, Oliver	355
Brown, Robert	93
Brown, W. G.	20
Brown v. *Board of Education*	262–264, 265, 355, 372
Brown v. *Mississippi*	338
Brown, William Wells: On Negro participation in Civil War	164–165, 368
Bruce, Blanche K.	20
Buchanan, Charles H.	333
Buchanan v. *Warley*	333
Buckner, Thomas	368
Bulkley, W. L.	228
Burns, Anthony	367
Burnside, General [Ambrose E.]	165
Burr, Aaron	69
Burton, Belfast	92, 93
Burton, Justice Harold H.	*264*, 354
Burton, Mayor of Marianna, Florida	249
Butler, General [Benjamin Franklin]	369
Byrd, Robert C.	373
Byrne, Sheriff Gus	246
Cadwalader, John L.	201
Cain, Richard Harvey	20
Calhoun, John C.	141
Calvert, George	15
Campbell, Anthony	93
Campbell, Justice [John A.]	151
Canada, S. W.	340
Cannidy, George	248, 250, 251
Cannidy, Lola	244, 245, 246, 248, 249, 250, 251, 252
Cardozo, Francis L.	20
Cardozo, T. W.	20
Carey, [Matthew]: Author of pamphlet maligning the role of Negroes in cholera epidemic	62–63, 363
Carney, Sgt. William H.	178, 368
Carter, Lester	242
Carter, Robert L.	352, 355
Cassell, Lee	351
Cassell v. *Texas*	351
Catholic Interracial Council	281
Catron, Justice [John]	151
Chambers v. *Florida*	342
Chambliss, Sheriff W. F.	244, 250
Chandler, Charles A.	341
Chase, Chief Justice [Salmon P.]	142
Cheatham, Henry Plummer	20
Chevalier, Stuart	333
Child Welfare	218
Chinn, Julia	366
Civil Rights Act of 1866	195
Civil Rights Act of 1875	199, 368
Civil Rights Act of 1964	286–323, 358, 359, 373
☐ Digest of Civil Rights Act of 1964	324–325
☐ Johnson, President Lyndon B.: Speech	326–328
Civil War	19, 171, 173, 198, 218, 219, 368
Claghorn, Kate	228
Clark, Charles	354
Clark, Justice Tom C.	*264*, 356, 358, 359
Clark, William C.	69
Clay, Henry	126–129, 142, 366
Clay, M. L.	253
Clement, E. H.	228
Cleveland, President Grover	218
Colonization in Africa: Resolution against	80–81
Colored Freeman of Long Island	111
Commager, Henry Steele	366
Committee for Improving the Industrial Conditions of Negroes in New York	229, 230
Community Relations Service	321–322, 325
Compensated Emancipation: Lincoln's Proposals	160–163, 367
Compromise of 1850	127, 141, 366
Condorcet	59
Confederate States of America	153
Confiscation Act	166, 167
Conn, William Dow, Jr.	338
Connor, "Bull"	373
Constitution of the United States	19, 21, 25, 41, 69, 76, 85, 102, 103, 105, 116, 117, 118, 119, 127, 131, 143, 147, 148, 149, 150, 151, 162, 163, 168, 169, 186, 187, 195, 197, 200, 209, 210, 211, 214, 226, 242, 243, 261, 265, 266, 267–268, 269–270, 271, 273, 340, 363
Continental Congress	18, 33, 362
Convention for the Improvement of the Free People of Color	363
Cook, Eugene	356
Cornish, James	92, 93
Cornish, Samuel	88, 364, 365
Corven, Phillip	26–27, 362
Costigan-Wagner Anti-Lynching Bill	244
Couliette, Sheriff J. P.	244
Court Cases	330–359
☐ Glossary	360–361
Cowley, Robert	92, 93
Cox, Archibald	358, 359
Crandall, Prudence	101, 365
Craw, Lentey	81
Crawford, William H.	141
Crenshaw, Allen	354
Crooks, James A.	349
Curry, John	252–253
Curtis, Justice [Benjamin]	151
Cushing, Chief Justice [William]	362
Daniel, Justice [Peter Vivian]	151
Daniel, Price	353
Darcy, Robert	342

Davidson, Basil 17
Davis, Colonel Benjamin O., Jr. 371
Davis, Charles 342
Davis, Jefferson 153, 165, 221, 369
Davis, Solicitor General John W. 332, 355
Day, Justice [William R.] 333
Dean, Ann 178
Deavour, James 93
Declaration of Independence 15, 16, 17, 18, 21, 93, 95, 102, 148–149, 178
  ☐ Thomas Jefferson's early draft 32–35, 362
Delany, Martin R. 366
DeLarge, Robert Carlos 20
Delaware
  ☐ Supreme Court 262
Dempsey, E. H. 334
DePriest, Congressman Oscar 240–243, 371
DeRita, Pasquale 349
Desegregation of Public Education 294, 324
Desegregation of Public Facilities 293–294, 324
Deslonde, P. G. 20
Detroit Anti-Negro violence 176–177
Dewey, John 228
DeWitt, Alexander 142
Discrimination in Places of Public
  Accommodation 289–290, 324
District of Columbia 103, 109, 126, 130, 210
  ☐ Act to suppress slave trade in 129
  ☐ *Washington Daily News* 242–243
Dixie, Chris 351
Dolby, Joseph 63
Douglas, Stephen A. 70, 154, 367
Douglas, Justice William O. 264
Douglass, Frederick: July 4th speech 133–136, *134*, 366
  ☐ Dedication of *The North Star* 124–125, 366
Douglass, Margaret 138–139, 367
Draft Riots of New York 368
Dred Scott v. *Sandford:* Supreme Court
  Decision 19, 146–151, 153, 367, 369
Dreier, Mary E. 228
DuBois, W. E. B. 221, 226, 228, 370
  ☐ "Credo" 222–223
Dubuclet, Antoine 20
Duke, Daniel 356
Dumond, Dwight Lowell 18, 19, 73
Duncan, William 93
Dunmore, Lord 18
Dunn, Oscar J. 20
Durham, W. J. 353

Eboe Tribe 47
Eisenhower, President Dwight D.:
  Executive Order 267–268, 372
Ellington, Yank 338
Elliott, Dr. John L. 228
Elliott, Robert Brown 20
Emancipation Proclamation 155, 169, 174–175, 179, 227, 368, 369, 373
Emerson, Dr. John 367
Equal Employment Opportunity 303–321, 325
Ethridge, George H. 345
Evans, Rev. J. J. 20

Fagan, H. H. 253
Falconbridge, Alexander 42–53, 362
Faubus, Governor Orval 372
"Felix" of Massachusetts 30–31, 362
FERA [Federal Emergency Relief Administration]
  Purification League 256
Fifteenth Amendment 20, 173, 194, 332, 335, 343, 369
Fifth Amendment 349, 358
Fifty-Fourth Massachusetts Volunteers 155, 178, 368

Fikes v. *Alabama* 357
Fikes, William E. 357
First African Baptist Church of Brooklyn 368
First African Baptist Society of Albany 364
First Negro Convention, Minutes of 92–94, 364
First Reconstruction Act 185–186, 369
Fisher, Edward 62
Florida
  ☐ Marianna *Daily Times Courier* 244, 245, 248, 251, 252, 253, 254
  ☐ *The Florida Times* 245
  ☐ Marianna Riot 248–249
  ☐ *Jackson County Floridan* 254
  ☐ Jackson County 254–255
  ☐ Supreme Court 342
Forten, James: Protests Negro Registration 76–79, 80, 363
  ☐ Protests Restricted Negro Emigration 96–99
Fosdick, Dr. Harry 243
Fourteenth Amendment 19, 173, 186–187, 209, 210, 242, 262, 264, 265, 333, 335, 336, 339, 340, 342, 345, 346, 348, 350, 353, 355, 356, 359, 368, 369
  ☐ Enforcement Legislated 195–197
  ☐ "Separate but Equal" Doctrine 208–211, 262–264
Fox, George 137
Frankfurter, Justice Felix *264*, 341
Franklin, John Hope 70, 71
Freedmen's Bureau 173, 180–181, 368
Freedmen's Savings Bank 173
Freedom's Journal 88–91, 364
  ☐ First Editorial 88–90
  ☐ Reports Lynching at Tuscaloosa, Ala. 91, 364
Fremont's [General John Charles] Proclamation 167
Fugitive Slave Acts 117, 127–129, 145, 366, 367
Fugitive Slave Bill 130
Fulton, Robert 70
Funk, A. E. 339

Gaines, Lloyd 340
Gaines v. *Canada* 340
Gardiner, Peter 93
Garfield, James A. 173
Garnet, Henry Highland:
  Buffalo Convention Speech 120–123, 366
Garrison, William Lloyd:
  First Editorial in *The Liberator* 95, 155, 228, 364, 365
Garvey, Marcus: Outline of
  Program of UNIA 234–239, 371
Georgia
  ☐ *Georgia Platform* 130, 366
  ☐ Supreme Court 356
Germantown Quakers: Anti-Slavery Resolution 28–29, 362
Giddings, [Joshua Reed] 142
Gilligan, Henry 349
Gilmore, R. T. 253
Glorious Revolution of 1688 15
Glossary of Court Cases 360–361
Godwin, Elbert 334
Gold Coast 44, 47
Graeff, Abram op de 29
Graeff, Derick op de 29
Graham, Brigadier General Henry V. 372
Grandfather Clause 220, 332, 341
Grant, Ulysses S. 154, 170, 171, 173
  ☐ Proclamation 200–201, 369
Gray, Chief Justice [Horace] 362
Gray, William 61, 63
Greeley, Horace: Prayer of Twenty Millions 166–168, 368
Green, John 244, 250
Greenberg, Jack 355, 357
Greene, Deputy Sheriff S. Paul 254
Greenhill, Joe R. 351, 353

Grice, Hezekiah 93, 364
Grier, Justice [Robert C.] 151
Griffith, Supreme Court Judge of Mississippi 338
Grimké, Francis J. 228
Grisham, G. N. 231
Guinea 47, 50, 52
Guinn, Frank 332
Guinn v. *United States* 332

Habeas Corpus Act, 1863 197
Hague Conferences of 1899 219
Hale, Joe 339
Hale v. *Kentucky* 339
Hall, Amos T. 346, 352
Hall, Don Carlos 93
Hall, [George Cleveland] 231
Hall, Robert 356
Hall, Thomas C. 228
Halleck's [General Henry W.] Order 167
Hamilton, Alexander 69
Hamilton, William 74–75, 363
Hammond, James H. 71–72
Hancock, John 15
Hansen, Fred 346, 352
Haralson, Jeremiah 20
Harlan, Justice [John Marshall] 211, 275
Harley, E. 253
Harrell, Sheriff John 245
Hartgrove, W. B. 231
Hastie, William H. 343, 344
Hayes, Rutherford B. 171, 173
Hayes-Tilden Compromise 21
Haymarket Riot of 1886 218
Heart of Atlanta v. *United States* 358
Henderich, Garret 29
Henderson, Elmer W. 354
Henderson v. *United States* 354
Henry, Patrick 15
Herndon, C. C. 335
Herskovits, Melville 17
Hicks, Ed 334
Hill, James 20
Hinton, Frederick A. 93
Hirsch, Rabbi Emil G. 228
Hodge, Frederic E. 349
Hodge, Lena A. Murray 349
Hogsett, William S. 340
Holmes, Rev. John Haynes 228
Holmes, Justice Oliver Wendell 334, 335, 338
Holt, Hamilton 228
Homestead Act of 1862 154
Homestead Strike of 1892 218
Hood, James 372
Houston, Charles H. 339, 340, 349
Howell, Richard 93
Howells, William Dean 228
Hughes, Chief Justice Charles E. 337, 338, 340
Hughes, Langston 21, 364
Hunter's [General David] Order 167
Hurd, James M. 349
Hurd, Mary I. 349
Hurd v. *Hodge* 349
Hutchinson, Thomas 30
Hyman, John Adams 20

Illinois
☐ State Legislature: Resolution Opposing
    Emancipation Proclamation 174–175, 368
Importation of Slaves Prohibited 66–67
Independent Democrats, Appeal of 140–142, 367
Indritz, Phineas 349

Inferiority of Negroes: Jefferson's Views on 36–39, 362
☐ William Hamilton's Refutation 74–75, 363
Injunctive Relief Against Discrimination
    in Places of Public Accommodation 289–292, 324
Intervention and Procedure in Civil Rights Cases 321, 325

Jackson, [Alexander L.] 231
Jackson, Forrest B. 348
Jackson, Mahalia 373
Jackson, Justice Robert H. 264
James II 15
Jay, Chief Justice John 69
Jefferson, Thomas 16, 17, 69
☐ Early Draft of Declaration of Independence 32–35, 362
☐ Inferiority of Negroes 36–39, 362
☐ Immorality of Slavery 39–40, 362
☐ Correspondence with Benjamin Banneker 56–59, 362–363
☐ Proviso of 1784 140
Jenkins, Charles J. 366
"Jim Crow" 113, 173, 214, 219, 225
Johnson, President Andrew 170, 173, 368, 369
Johnson, Harry 370
Johnson, President Lyndon Baines 21
☐ Address on Civil Rights Bill 326–328
☐ Address on Voting Rights 11–13
Johnson, Vice President [Richard M.] 115, 366
Jones, Absalom 60–65, 363
☐ Recall of Negro valor during cholera epidemic 60–63
☐ Views on Slavery 64–65
Jones, Augustin G. 21
Jones, Eugene Kinckle 370
Jones, Joseph 362
Journal of Negro History 231, 370
Judiciary Act of 1789 116
Judson, Judge Andrew T. 365

Kansas-Nebraska Act 143, 367
Katzenbach, Nicholas 359
Katzenbach v. *McClung* 359
Kelley, Florence 228
Kellor, Frances 229
Kennedy, President John F.: Executive Order 269–270, 281
☐ Call to end segregation 272–275, 372
Kentucky
☐ Court of Appeals 333, 339
Kimberly, Dennis 101
King, John 250
King, Dr. Martin Luther, Jr. 14, 373
Kitchin, [Claude] Congressman from North Carolina 214
Knapp, Isaac 364
Knight, [Thomas E., Jr.] Attorney General
    of Alabama 243, 336, 337
Knights of Labor 218
Knollenberg, Fred C. 335
Knox, Henry 69
Knox, J. E. 334
Kraemer, Fern W. 350
Kraemer, Louis 350
Ku Klux Klan 173, 240, 253–254
☐ "KKK Act" 195–197, 369
☐ Rules of Order 188–189, 369

Lane, I. W. 341
Lane v. *Wilson* 341
Langston, John Mercer 20
Lawson, Belford V., Jr. 354
League for the Protection of Colored Women 230
Lee, Albert 348
Lee, Clinton 334
Lee, Robert E. 154, 170, 367
Lee, Samuel J. 20
Lee v. *Mississippi* 348
Lee, William 55

Legal Glossary   360–361
Leibowitz, Samuel S.   337
Leveck, Charles H.   93
Leverett, E. Freeman   356
Lewis, Captain Meriwether   69
Lichtenberger, Bishop Arthur   278–279, 373
Lincoln, Abraham   154, 155, 160–163, 166–169,
                              170, 173, 227, 240, 274, 367, 368
☐ Letter to Horace Greeley   168
☐ Proclamation of Amnesty and Reconstruction   170
Liverpool   49, 50, 53
Locke, John   15–16
Logue, Mannasseth   158–159
Logue, Sarah (Mrs. Mannasseth)   158, 367
Loguen, The Rev. Mr. [J. W.]   158–159, 367
Long, Huey   256
Long, Jefferson Franklin   20
Lord Baltimore   15
Lord Dunmore   18
Louisiana Purchase   69, 363–364
Louisiana Territory   69
Lowell, Judge [John]   240
Lucas, Charles   27
Lundy, Benjamin   364
Lynch, Rev. Frederick   228
Lynch, John Roy   20
Lynching
☐ First Newspaper Account, Freedom's Journal   91
☐ Claude Neal   244–256

McClung, Ollie Sr. and Jr.   359
McCormick, Cyrus   70
McDowell, Cleve   372
McDowell, Mary E.   228
McGill, S. D.   342
McGrath, Attorney General J. Howard   354
McLaurin, G. N.   352
McLaurin v. Oklahoma State Regents   263, 352
McLean, Justice [John]   119, 151
Madison, James   69
Malone, Vivian   372
Manumission
☐ Appeal of Phillip Corven   26–27
☐ George Washington's plan   54–55, 362
☐ Roman   75
☐ Constitution of Missouri   84
☐ Lincoln's plan for Compensated
   Emancipation   160–163, 170
March on Washington   14, 284–285, 371, 373
Marot, Helen   228
Marshall, Thurgood   343, 344, 345, 346, 353, 355
Massachusetts
☐ Supreme Court, Commonwealth of   41, 362
☐ Constitution of Commonwealth   115
☐ Personal Liberty Act   144–145, 367
Mayflower Compact   15
Maynard, William H.   338
Meltzer, Milton   21
Meredith, James   269, 270, 372
Merrill, J. G.   228
Merrill, Maurice H.   346
Michigan
☐ Anti-Negro Violence in Detroit   176–177, 368
☐ Civil Rights Act   347
☐ Supreme Court   347
Milholland, John E.   228
Miller, Dorie   371
Miller, Thomas Ezekiel   20
Mills, Wilson W.   347
Minton, Justice Sherman   264
Mississippi
☐ "Black Code"   182–183, 368

☐ University of   269, 338, 345
☐ Supreme Court   338, 345, 348
Missouri
☐ Compromise of   83–85, 143, 153, 363–364, 367
☐ Enabling Act   83, 140, 364
☐ Constitution of   84, 140, 364
☐ Map   84
☐ Admission to Union   85, 140, 363–364
☐ Supreme Court   340, 350
Mitchell, Arthur W., Congressman from Illinois   371
Mitchell v. United States   354
Monroe, President James   141
Moore v. Dempsey   334
Moore, Frank   334
Moore, T. Justin   355
Moorland, Jesse E.   231
Morel, Junius C.   92, 93, 94
Morgan, Irene   344
Morgan, Margaret   116, 117
Morgan v. Virginia   344
Morse, Samuel   70
Moskowitz, Dr. Henry   228
Mud-Sill Speech   71–72
Murphy, Justice Frank   348
Murray, George Washington   20

NAACP Legal Defense and Educational Fund   331
Nabrit, James M., Jr.   341
Nash, Charles Edmund   20
Nashville Convention, Resolutions of   130–131, 366
National Association for the Advancement of Colored
   People   221, 227–228, 244, 245, 281, 331, 370, 371
National League on Urban Conditions Among Negroes 230
Neal, Claude   244–256, 371
Neal v. Delaware   337
Nebraska: Slavery Bill   140–142, 143
☐ Independent Democratic appeal against   140–142
Negro
☐ Emigration   76–79, 96–99
☐ Participation in Civil War   155, 198, 368
☐ In World War I   232–233, 370–371
☐ In World War II   258–259, 371
Nelson, Justice [Samuel]   151
New Calabar, Slave Market at   42, 45, 52
New Mexico Bill   141
New York
☐ Emancipation of Slaves   86–87
☐ Teachers' Meeting   111, 365
☐ Southern Aid Society of New York City   138
☐ Tribune   166–168, 368
☐ Anti-Slavery Society   368
☐ Draft Riots   368
Newman, James   93
Newspapers:
☐ Freedom's Journal: First Negro Newspaper   88–91, 364
☐ Liberator: Abolitionist Organ   95, 364
☐ The North Star: Negro Anti-Slavery
   Journal   124–125, 366
Niagara Movement   224–226, 370
Niger, Alfred   93
Nineteenth Amendment   218
Nixon, L. A.   335
Nixon v. Herndon   335
Nondiscrimination in Federally
   Assisted Programs   302–303, 324
Norris, Clarence   337
Norris, Isaac   16
Norris v. Alabama   337
Norwood, Tyrus A.   342
O'Hara, James Edward   20
O'Meara, Joseph   331
Oklahoma
☐ Constitution of   332

□ Supreme Court — 340
Old Calabar, Slave Market at — 42, 52
Ordinance of 1787 — 140
O'Reilly, Leonora — 228
Ormrod, John — 63
Ovington, Mary W. — 228, 370

Paine, Tom — 14
Painter, Theophilus Shickel — 353
Parkhurst, Rev. Dr. Charles H. — 228
Parrott, Russell — 80
Paschall, Benjamin Jr. — 92, 93
Pastorious, Francis Daniel — 29
Patterson, Haywood — 242, 336
Patton, Eddie (Buster) — 345
Patton v. *Mississippi* — 345
Paul, Rev. Nathaniel — 86–87, 100–101, 364, 365
Penn, William — 15
Pennsylvania
□ Negro Registration — 76–79
□ Statute of March 26, 1826 — 116–117
□ Judiciary Act of 1789 — 116
□ Supreme Court — 116
Perlman, Philip B. — 354
Personal Liberty Laws — 366
Peters, Rev. Dr. John P. — 228
Peters, Sampson — 93
Peterson, Daniel — 93
Petition of Philadelphia Negroes — 96–99
Phillips, Wendell — 113, 114
Pinchback, Pinckney B. S. — 20
Plessy v. *Ferguson* — 173, 208–211, 219, 262, 264, 265, 355, 370, 372
Pollak, Walter H. — 336
Pollard, Claude — 335
Pooser, W. — 256
Pope John XXIII — 280–281
Pope Paul VI — 281
Porras, Charles — 335
Post, Louis F. — 228
Powell, [Ozie] — 336
Powell v. *Alabama* — 336, 356
Preston, D. P. — 253
Price, Victoria — 242
Prigg v. *the Commonwealth of Pennsylvania* — 116–119, 366
Prosser, Gabriel — 73
Pullman Strike of 1894 — 218
Purvis, Robert — 99, 137, 367

Quarles, Benjamin — 16, 71

Rainey, Joseph Hayne — 20
Raleigh, Sir Walter — 215
Randall, John — 15
Randolph, A. Philip — 371
Randolph, Edmund — 69
Rankin, J. Lee — 355
Ransier, Alonzo Jacob — 20
Ransom, Leon A. — 339, 342
Rapier, James Thomas — 20
Ray, Sarah Elizabeth — 347
Reconstruction — 19, 21, 171, 173
□ Act of 1867 — 185–186, 369
Redding, Louis L. — 355
Redmond, S. R. — 340
Reece, Amos — 356
Reece v. *Georgia* — 356
Reed, Justice Stanley F. — 264, 343, 344, 351
Reese, Dr. David M. — 106, 107, 365
Reform Jews: Call to Racial Justice — 282–283, 373
Registration and Voting Statistics — 320–321, 325
Remond, Charles Lenox — 112–115, 366

Republican Party — 21, 193, 367, 370
Revels, Hiram — 20, 190–193, 369
Revenue and Currency Acts of 1764 — 23
Reynolds, Whitney — 177
Rifle Clubs — 200–201, 369
Robbins, Dr. Jane — 228
Roberts, Needham — 370
Roberts v. *City of Boston* — 265
Robinson, M. — 253
Robinson, Spottswood W., III — 355
Robinson, W. R. — 253
Rogers, William — 93
Rolfe, John — 23
Roosevelt, Franklin D.: Executive Order — 257, 371
Roosevelt, Theodore — 219, 221
Rousseau, Jean Jacques — 16
Ruggles, David — 106–107, 365
Rush, [Dr. Benjamin] — 62
Russell, Charles Edward — 228
Russwurm, John B. — 88, 364
Rutledge, Justice [Wiley] — 347

Salter, William M. — 228
Sandifer, Jawn — 354
School Tax: Robert Purvis Protest — 137
Scottsboro Case — 241–243
□ *Powell* v. *Alabama* — 336, 356
Seegers, Gerald L. — 350
Segregation
□ In Armed Services Ended — 260–261
□ In Travel — 112–115
"Separate but Equal" Doctrine
□ *Plessy* v. *Ferguson* — 208–211
□ *Brown* v. *Board of Education* — 262–264
Seward, William Henry — 368
Shad, Abraham D. — 93
Shanholster, Mike — 245, 246
Shelley, Ethel Lee — 350
Shelley, J. D. — 350
Shelley v. *Kraemer* — 350
Shepherd, Edmund E. — 347
Shepherd, Emmet G. — 253
Sherman Anti-Trust Act of 1890 — 218
Shields, Henry — 338
Sholtz, Governor [David] — 249
Shorts, Charles — 93
Shuttlesworth, Frederick L. — 277, 373
Sierra Leone — 362
Simmons, D. A. — 335
Simpson, Alex — 72
Simpson, Ben — 72–73
Sipuel, Ada Lois — 346
Sipuel v. *University of Oklahoma* — 346
Slaughter House cases — 210
Slave Trade — *48, 51*
□ Continental Congress, Resolution of — 18, 25
□ Unconstitutional — 41, 66–67
□ Women Slaves — 42–43, 48–49, 53
□ Black Traders — 42–45
□ Act to Suppress in District of Columbia — 129, 130
Smalls, Robert — 20, 155
Smith, Annie — 244, 250, 254
Smith, Gerrit — 142
Smith, Herbert — 250
Smith, John — 23
Smith, Joseph — 228
Smith, Lonnie E. — 343
Smith, Nelson H. — 277
Smith, Robert McDavid — 358, 359
Smith, Sallie — 244, 254
Smith v. *Allwright* — 343

Index □ 383